Conversations with Jim Harrison

Revised and Updated

Literary Conversations Series
Monika Gehlawat
General Editor

Conversations with Jim Harrison

Revised and Updated

Edited by Robert DeMott

University Press of Mississippi / *Jackson*

The University Press of Mississippi is the scholarly publishing agency of the Mississippi Institutions of Higher Learning: Alcorn State University, Delta State University, Jackson State University, Mississippi State University, Mississippi University for Women, Mississippi Valley State University, University of Mississippi, and University of Southern Mississippi.

www.upress.state.ms.us

The University Press of Mississippi is a member of the Association of University Presses.

First printing 2019
∞

Library of Congress Cataloging-in-Publication Data

Names: Harrison, Jim, 1937–2016, interviewee. | DeMott, Robert J., 1943–
    editor.
Title: Conversations with Jim Harrison / edited by Robert DeMott.
Description: Revised and updated | Jackson : University Press of Mississippi,
    [2019] | Series: Literary conversations series | Includes bibliographical
    references and index. | Originally published : Jackson : University Press
    of Mississippi, 2002. |
Identifiers: LCCN 2018037725 (print) | LCCN 2018041318 (ebook) | ISBN
    9781496819666 (epub single) | ISBN 9781496819673 (epub institutional) |
    ISBN 9781496819680 (pdf single) | ISBN 9781496819697 (pdf institutional)
    | ISBN 9781496819642 (hardcover : alk. paper) | ISBN 9781496819659 (pbk. :
    alk. paper)
Subjects: LCSH: Harrison, Jim, 1937–2016—Interviews. | Authors,
    American—20th century—Interviews. | LCGFT: Interviews.
Classification: LCC PS3558.A67 (ebook) | LCC PS3558.A67 Z46 2019 (print) |
    DDC 813/.54 [B] —dc23
LC record available at https://lccn.loc.gov/2018037725

British Library Cataloging-in-Publication Data available

Books by Jim Harrison

Plain Song. New York: W. W. Norton, 1965.

Walking. Cambridge, MA: Pym Randall Press, 1967.

Locations. New York: W. W. Norton, 1968.

Stony Brook Holographs. Stony Brook, NY: Stony Brook Poetics Foundation, 1968. (With Robert Duncan, Denise Levertov, Jerome Rothenberg, Louis Simpson, Jonathan Wieners, Charles Simic.)

Five Blind Men. Fremont, MI: Sumac Press, 1969. (With Dan Gerber, George Quasha, J. D. Reed, Charles Simic.)

Outlyer and Ghazals. New York: Simon and Schuster, 1971.

Wolf: A False Memoir. New York: Simon and Schuster, 1971.

A Good Day to Die: A Novel. New York: Simon and Schuster, 1973.

Letters to Yesenin. Freemont, MI: Sumac Press, 1973.

Farmer. New York: Viking Press, 1976.

Returning to Earth. Berkeley, CA: Ithaca House, 1977.

Letters to Yesenin and Returning to Earth. Los Angeles: Center Publications, 1979.

Legends of the Fall. New York: Delta/Seymour Lawrence, 1979.

Warlock. New York: Delta/Seymour Lawrence, 1981.

Natural World: A Bestiary. Barrytown, NY: Open Book, 1982.

Selected and New Poems, 1961–1981. New York: Delacorte Press/Seymour Lawrence, 1981.

Sundog: A Novel: The Story of an American Foreman. New York: E. P. Dutton/Seymour Lawrence, 1984.

The Theory and Practice of Rivers: Poems. Seattle, WA: Winn Books, 1986.

Dalva. New York: E. P. Dutton/Seymour Lawrence, 1988.

The Theory and Practice of Rivers and New Poems. Livingston, MT: Clark City Press, 1989.

The Woman Lit by Fireflies. Boston: Houghton Mifflin/Seymour Lawrence, 1990.

Book for Sensei. Pacifica, CA: Big Bridge Press, 1990. (With Michael Rothenberg, Michael McClure, Philip Whalen, Joanne Kyger, Andrei Codrescu.)

Just Before Dark: Collected Nonfiction. Livingston, MT: Clark City Press, 1991.

The Raw and the Cooked. New York: Dim Gray Bar Press, 1992.

Julip. Boston: Houghton Mifflin/Seymour Lawrence, 1994.

After Ikkyu and Other Poems. Boston: Shambhala, 1996.

The Sumac Reader. Edited by Joseph Bednarik. East Lansing: Michigan State University Press, 1997. (With Dan Gerber.)

The Road Home. New York: Atlantic Monthly Press, 1998.

The Shape of the Journey: New and Collected Poems. Port Townsend, WA: Copper Canyon Press, 1998.

The Beast God Forgot to Invent. New York: Atlantic Monthly Press, 2000.

The Boy Who Ran to the Woods. Illustrated by Tom Pohrt. New York: Atlantic Monthly Press, 2000.

Chatter and Feathers: Little Ornithophagic Correspondence: November 1999–April 2000. France: Manoir de Pron, 2000. (With Gérard Oberlé.)

The Raw and the Cooked: Adventures of a Roving Gourmand. New York: Atlantic Monthly Press, 2001.

A Conversation. West Chester, PA: Aralia Press, 2002. (With Ted Kooser.)

Conversations with Jim Harrison. Edited by Robert DeMott. Jackson: University Press of Mississippi, 2002.

Off to the Side: A Memoir. New York: Atlantic Monthly Press, 2002.

Braided Creek: A Conversation in Poetry. Port Townsend, WA: Copper Canyon Press, 2003. (With Ted Kooser.)

True North: A Novel. New York: Grove Press, 2004.

Livingston Suite. Illustration by Greg Keeler. Boise: Limberlost Press, 2005.

Republican Wives: A Novella. New York: Atlantic Monthly Press, 2005.

The Summer He Didn't Die. New York: Atlantic Monthly Press, 2005.

Saving Daylight. Port Townsend, WA: Copper Canyon Press, 2006.

Returning to Earth. New York: Grove Press, 2007.

Letters to Yesenin. Port Townsend, WA: Copper Canyon Press, 2007.

The English Major. New York: Grove Press, 2008.

The Farmer's Daughter. New York Grove Press, 2010.

The Etiquette of Freedom: Gary Snyder, Jim Harrison, and "The Practice of the Wild." Edited by Paul Ebenkamp. Berkeley: Counterpoint, 2010. (With Gary Snyder.)

In Search of Small Gods. Port Townsend, WA: Copper Canyon Press, 2010.

Songs of Unreason. Port Townsend, WA: Copper Canyon Press, 2011.

The Great Leader: A Faux Mystery. New York: Grove Press, 2011.

Brown Dog: Novellas. New York: Grove Press, 2013.

The River Swimmer: Novellas. New York: Grove Press, 2013.

The Big Seven: A Faux Mystery. New York: Grove Press, 2015.

Dead Man's Float. Port Townsend, WA: Copper Canyon Press, 2016.

The Ancient Minstrel: Novellas. New York: Grove Press, 2016.

A Really Big Lunch. Introduction by Mario Batali. New York : Grove Press, 2017.

Conversations with Jim Harrison, Revised and Updated. Edited by Robert DeMott. Jackson: University Press of Mississippi, 2019.

Contents

Introduction

After we die we hover for a while
at treetop level with the mourners
beneath us, but we are not separate
from them nor they from us.
They are singing but the words
Don't mean anything in our new language.
  —**Jim Harrison**, "Insight" (from *In Search of Small Gods*)

Late on the afternoon of March 26, 2016, in the middle of writing a poem, Jim Harrison keeled over at the desk of his winter residence in Patagonia, Arizona, and died of heart failure. He was seventy-eight years old and for much of the previous five years had been in declining health, limited by a series of body betrayals and episodes of chronic pain, and by the death, six months earlier, of Linda King Harrison, his beloved wife of fifty-six years. Harrison's oldest friend, novelist Thomas McGuane, predicted his death would "cut many adrift." For his friends, family, and legions of admirers, McGuane said, "the death of Jim Harrison leaves an extraordinary vacancy."[1]

In the days and weeks that followed, Gregg Orr, Harrison's resolute, hawk-eyed bibliographer, tallied more than a thousand individual tributes, memorials, condolences, appreciations, and reminiscences in both print and electronic media here and abroad by everyone from the ranks of the celebrated and famous to the legions of common readers and everyday people who made up a large part of Harrison's reading constituency. The outpouring of grief, astonishment, disbelief, even anger, from what his longtime friend Doug Peacock called the "Tribe of Jim," was worldwide. Harrison's death, Peacock said, left "a hole in the sky."[2] For a brief span following his death, Jim Harrison was "trending" on social media, a cyber event that he—who wrote his books in longhand with inexpensive pens on lined yellow pads, rarely wore a watch, never used a computer, and only latterly and grudgingly owned a cell phone—would never have sought in life and would have considered a dubious honor at best, though it is possible to believe he would have been gratified by the universal show of affection from his planet of followers. A few months after his death, organized tributes to and celebrations of his life and career were held in Paris and Lyon, Flagstaff and Livingston, as well as at informal wakes, spontaneous dinner parties, and cocktail hours at bars and taverns in a hundred other less exotic places. The following year, in 2017, organized tributes and ceremonial gatherings were held in Chicago, New York City, and Traverse City, Michigan, site of an especially elaborate and highly publicized memorial event.

One year after Harrison's death Grove Press published *A Really Big Lunch*, an anthology of his uncollected food writings with an introduction by Chef Mario Batali that met popular and critical acclaim and served to keep the long tradition of Harrison book publications alive into the posthumous era. When Harrison died, he was one of those rare literary artists whose major books of poetry, fiction, and nonfiction were all in print, and had been for a long time, a situation more than any other that fulfilled his definition of success. It is all a writer can ask, he said repeatedly, and was proof that he had kept unswervingly true to his writerly covenant, even at a high cost to himself. As with many other things in his purview, Harrison had the last word: "Death," he wrote in "Larson's Holstein Bull," in *In Search of Small Gods*, "steals everything but our stories."

In his case, in the fifty-one years from 1965 through 2017, that amounted to publishing forty-two acclaimed volumes of poetry, fiction, and nonfiction prose, plus a handful of smaller, limited-edition chapbook-style works, numerous individual single-sheet letterpress poetry broadsides, approximately twenty screenplays (not all of them produced), and hundreds of magazine and journal pieces. His was a remarkable achievement indicating that, if Harrison was unashamedly "quadra-schizoid" (his oft-repeated term) in his choice of writing in multiple genres, he was also unstinting, even old-fashioned, in his devotion to and possession by art as a singular path of being and a sustained calling. If you can't give your entire life to writing, he said over and over, why bother? Harrison was obsessed by many things, but he was addicted to writing and intoxicated with language.

For me, the expressions of grief and loss following Harrison's death were a summons to action, a way to fill at least part of the void left by his passing, beyond listening to the handful of his witty voicemails I had saved on my iPhone. In assembling this collection of interviews for a new generation of Harrison readers, I have brought forward a number of the interviews that first ran in the earlier version of *Conversations with Jim Harrison* (2002), including those by Harrison and McGuane, Elliott and Sommerness,

Bonetti, Fergus, Cross, Jousse and Ostria, Wachtel, Walker, DeMott and Smith, Preston and Michel, dropped a handful of others, and have added one earlier piece (Winegar), plus eight more recent pieces to cover the era from 2002 to 2016 (Bednarik, Birnbaum, Elam, Ahl, Walton, Dombrowski, Dennis, Nowogrodzki). Overall, I have favored traditional literary question-and-answer interviews, because they allow Harrison to develop his responses more elaborately than in many of the numerous but briefer newspaper and popular magazine profiles that strike me as being more like gossip because his comments were often reduced to snappy one-liners. In doing so I have sometimes sacrificed snapshot for panorama. The fact is, however, that in the past decade, since Harrison's fame ramped up to an unprecedented degree, personal encounters and profile-style appreciations have been more prevalent than ever before, and one of those shorter takes is included here as well to round out the record (Walton).

The preponderance of interviews with Harrison focus on his fiction, and that pattern is reflected here as well. But there are exceptions. Thierry Jousse and Vincent Ostria's interview in *Cahiers du Cinema* (held over from the earlier edition) pertains to Harrison's screenwriting career, a neglected area of concern, and it is representative of a host of foreign (especially French) interviews that, if gathered, would make up an additional, substantial volume in their own right. Karin Winegar's quick portrait of Harrison in Minneapolis in 1983 is instructive because it shows some of the Harrisonian mystique already emerging. Joseph Bednarik's and Angela Elam's talk sessions with Harrison foreground his poetry, the genre closest to his heart, though not so much that of most interviewers. Chris Dombrowski's colorful, earthy profile shows us Harrison as fly fisherman (his lifelong passion) practicing "Jim Yoga" on the Big Hole River near Melrose, Montana, one of Harrison's favorite hideaway "thickets," the basis for some scenes in his 2008 novel, *The English Major*, and the landscape of the poem sequence "River I" through "River VII" in his 2011 collection, *Songs of Unreason*. Christopher Walton and Jerry Dennis encounter in person and by telephone the elder Harrison at his winter home in southernmost Arizona. So does Peter Nowogrodzki, whose gritty and wrenchingly realistic interview was the last Harrison gave before he died, and as such, like Dombrowski's profile, has a special poignancy for its unvarnished view of the lion in winter. Sometimes the apple cannot be polished, the lily cannot be gilded, because ribald mythology needs its sobering counterpoint for full effect and disclosure.

In no way, however, should the amount of space allotted to fiction in these following conversations be taken to reflect Harrison's own preference.

He remained as committed to poetry (which he called "the true bones" of his life) as he was when he first began writing. Since 1998 when his *The Shape of the Journey: New and Collected Poems* appeared—at 460 pages itself equal to a life's work for many writers—Harrison published seven more volumes of poetry, the last one, *Dead Man's Float*, just months before he died. It's not for nothing he repeatedly considered himself a poet, emphasizing the artistic side of his writerly identity. Which is to say, for many, there will never again be another writer with switch-hit talents quite like Jim Harrison. Cold comfort, perhaps, but all who traveled in his orbit or followed his trajectory or now mourn his passing and feel something akin to the haunting Portuguese notion of *saudade*, or irretrievable loss, that Harrison himself so often commented on, can be thankful that he left behind those countless stories that will go on offering pleasure, wisdom, and delight. Despite everything, "he got his work done," as he was fond of saying in his best faux-Marine voice, to which it can only be added, "Amen."

✦ ✦ ✦

Jim Harrison had a reputation as an independent, private, and even reclusive writer, who chose to live in areas of the United States that are often a long drive from major airports and metro centers. He was a sophisticated citizen of the world who knew the cultures of Hollywood, Manhattan, and Paris first hand. Yet by his own admission he was also an "outlyer," fiercely attached to rural locales in northern Michigan and its Upper Peninsula, southernmost Arizona, north-central Nebraska, and southwestern Montana's Paradise Valley. Harrison knew those regions intimately and respectfully, and they provided the geographical landscape, flora and fauna, dramatic weather, spiritual current, and protagonists for much of his fiction from *Wolf : A False Memoir* (1971) to *The Road Home* (1998) to *True North* (2007) and *The English Major* (2008) to the collected *Brown Dog: Novellas* (2013), and beyond into his many books of poetry and nonfiction as well. Harrison was an avowed cultural geographer and a keen observer of geopieties, who considered experience of place as significant as that of character. "It starts with the sense of the landscape and the history of the landscape," he told Angela Elam in an interview included here, and flows out from there. Cliff, the road-tripping narrator of *The English Major*, says, "You have to log the journey" through the United States to get "the look and feel of it." In doing so, Harrison redefined the meaning of regionalism and road narratives.

Harrison's beloved flyover regions, far removed from America's left and right "dream coasts," harbored numerous personal "thickets," "panic holes," and hideouts, which enabled his writing by framing reality, promoting ritual, creating anonymity, providing solace and ruminative quiet, or furnishing restorative habitats. Besides Harrison's permanent residences in Michigan, Montana, and Arizona, his collection of secret places also provided him with the opportunity to blend into the foliage, to see but not be seen, insofar as that was possible. At his back-lot writing bungalow in Lake Leelanau, he told Patrick Smith and me, "Your only alternative as an artist is to create your own habitat for your soul. I figured out that my main obsession is freedom, and if I didn't have the freedom of close access to the natural world, I wasn't going to survive."

To survive, Harrison always preferred to keep his distance and remain "off to the side" (as he titled his memoir), but despite his preference for seclusion and longing for freedom, he was exceedingly generous with his time and energy, quite liberal and forthcoming with his opinions about his work, and increasingly—even disarmingly—cooperative about himself, as five decades of interviewers have found out.[3] Yet for such an animated and brilliant conversationalist Harrison can be guarded about personal revelations. His playful riff with McGuane, "A Chat with a Novelist," the earliest piece printed here, is a cautionary text for future conversations involving Jim Harrison himself, because something is always being kept back, though it isn't always clear what that something is. Talking becomes a form of self-protection, a hide-and-seek strategy that allows him to satisfy convention while also keeping his innermost material intact for his art.

Harrison's renown—not always deserved but then not always disputed either—as a rowdy, cantankerous, go-his-own-way bad boy of American letters started early and often preceded him and clashed with interviewers' perceptions, so that his unruly, outrageous reputation and exotic cult status have made him the subject of distorted myths (some of which he aided and abetted in fostering). Even as early as 1983 in an interview with Karin Winegar, included here, he spent a portion of his time—not entirely successfully—refuting or dismissing charges of his "macho" image, a label that stuck to him like pine pitch during the coming decades.[4] Expecting a brawler, a boor, a lout, a misogynist, a gangster, a ruffian, or a primitive wild man, interviewers were surprised to find him disarmingly thoughtful, sensitive, candid, and erudite. For all his emphasis on strenuous physicality and fleshly presence, it is nearly impossible to read a page of Harrison's prose without encountering his references or allusions to art, music, literature, cinema, or philosophy. It is a situation that sometimes caused confusion, resentment, and misrepresentation in his less accommodating followers.

In Harrison's lexicon, both nature and culture are necessary components of a fully realized, observant life. For every reference to organic processes, natural places, or animal denizens in his work there are equally frequent allusions to the aesthetic domain. The Huron Mountains of Michigan's Upper Peninsula and James Joyce's *Finnegan's Wake*, Nebraska's Sandhills and New York's Museum of Modern Art exist not as schizophrenic opposites or self-cancelling binaries, but in a mutually enriching, harmonious balance of affinities in Harrison's world view. And because Harrison had an entertaining and vivid story for nearly everything that happened in his uncloistered life, determining who the real Jim Harrison was can be complicated, even challenging.

Regarding the phenomenon of interviews, about which he was generally wary or suspicious, he admitted to Kay Bonetti in a 1984 interview reprinted here, that he had gotten "so weary or strange about interviews because I've been too trusting on a couple of occasions. The trouble is anything you read about yourself seems to be sort of inaccurate; well, maybe everything that everybody writes about everybody is inaccurate." Rather than indulge the illusions, ephemeralities, and artificialities associated with interviewers interested primarily in addressing his personality, Harrison clearly favored being in the condition of art, as he informed Brice Matthieussent.[5] Indeed, Harrison told his sister-in-law, the poet Rebecca Newth, "Miles Davis used to say, 'Everything you need to know about me is in my music,'" and while on one plane this is certainly true, nevertheless—as this collection testifies (and Harrison himself admitted to Newth)—plenty of people, "curious" about his life, have sought out his conversation anyway.[6] The subtitle of an early interview in this book—"A Good Day for Talking"—rings a signature chord.

Benefits can come from such encounters, too, for he told Patrick Smith and me that through interrogation he sometimes learns about his own work: "People ask particular questions about what's in your books that never occurred to you on any conscious level. Also your explanations are curiously quite often not as interesting as somebody else's, so you feel a little alien about it, like you're already flying to a different planet." Alien flight or not, Harrison's patience and generosity with interviewers was remarkable, at least up to the critical point where they did not impinge on his family obligations or writing schedule, or demand more of him than he was willing to give, a situation that threatened to become increasingly annoying in his later years. But trade-offs were possible: "Age focuses you," he told journalist

Christopher Walton a few years ago. "You are much better concentrated. There's more time when you travel less, don't do book tours, avoid interviews or public appearances. You walk the dogs, fish, hunt, cook, and write."

From the time sixteen-year-old Harrison transferred his religious fervor from born-again evangelism to writing poetry, until recently in his consistently productive later years, pursuing art was a central reason for being. His desire to be a writer was a combination of patently romantic convictions about the appeals of an unbridled, hedonistic artist's life (he was fond of noting that Byron got laid often) and a profound boredom with the middle-class way of life. A precocious teen from a hard-working, rural Michigan family, Harrison had grown up with a tradition of physical outdoor pursuits (farming, hunting, fishing, camping), and yet he also had a markedly philosophical and aesthetic side. Reading John Keats when he was fourteen set him on the path to be a poet. Encouraged by his parents and at least one memorable high-school teacher and librarian, Bernice Smith, Harrison read widely in all kinds of literature, from the typical boy's adventure fare by Zane Grey, Ernest Seton Thompson, to the most daunting modernist texts by Arthur Rimbaud, Rainer Maria Rilke, James Joyce, William Faulkner. He also traveled to New York, Boston, Colorado, and California during those generative years and began to form strong opinions about the relationship of art to life and the need for writers to be outsiders.

In July 1956 the eighteen-year-old Harrison wrote a letter to John Ciardi, poetry editor of *Saturday Review*, in which he complained harshly about the contemporary poet following a "vogue instead of the nature of his emotions." He also submitted to Ciardi a handwritten poem, the first he had ever sent out to be considered for publication. "The Existentialist" was, Harrison admitted, "influenced" by Jean-Paul Sartre and Soren Kierkegaard, not exactly popular authors for a rural teen. His free-verse poem contained some brooding night thoughts typical of an angst-filled teenager, but in identifying the locus of "a little life," not in "inspired rhymes of cinder stars / but the remnants of snow in April," it also pointed the way to his awareness of nature as a prime register of value and to the commonplace as a ground of being for art.[7] A decade later these aspects marked Harrison's first book of poems, *Plain Song* (1965), but they also reverberate through the whole of his career, right up through his last book of poems, *Dead Man's Float* (2016), published shortly before his death. Although "The Existentialist" was never published, it is an important glimpse into Harrison's formative imagination and the dimensions of his future passion in which writing required a complete commitment. The poem also adds resonance to his statement forty-four years later in 2000 to his Copper Canyon Press poetry editor, Joseph Bednarik, which is included in this edition: "Well, you do take vows just like a priest or a Zen student takes vows. What did Charles Olson say that was incredible? 'One must only traffic in one's own sign.' That excludes every other thing in your life. To me it's always been important to belong to nothing, other than my marriage. . . . But you belong to nothing except this." It was a statement about the arc and conviction of his own determined self-fashioning that he repeated countless times in various ways.

Restless and peripatetic, Harrison dropped out of Michigan State University several times during his undergraduate days to pursue his own course of instruction. After his father and sister Judith died in a car crash in the fall of 1962, a devastated Harrison left graduate school for several years, though he was eventually shepherded through the MA degree requirements by his mentor, Herbert Weisinger. It was a redemptive story he recounted often in the following interviews, and has become part of the permanent store of Harrisonian legend. So have equally colorful stories of his friendships with such eminences as Mario Batali, Jimmy Buffett, Russell Chatham, Will Hearst, Thomas McGuane, Jack Nicholson, and others, his hot and cold success as a screenwriter in Hollywood, his subsequent phase of profligate excess in the late seventies and early eighties (caused by "ordinary human greed," he confessed to Jim Fergus in 1986), his periodic bouts with crippling depression (which he acknowledged but rarely elaborated on outside of *Letters to Yesenin*), and, in his last five years—from 2011 to 2016 (his most celebrated in terms of widespread fame and international recognition)—his frequent physical setbacks and ailments that curbed his once vigorous outdoor life, only to be replaced by a late-life regimen of daily writing and enormous productivity. A month before Harrison died, he told Peter Nowogrodzki, "I don't know what else to do so I write. It's my way of seeing the world."

In an otherwise restless existence, commitment is all. "The way you eat bespeaks your entire attitude toward life," Harrison told Jim Fergus in his 1986 *Paris Review* interview that is included here. In an interview with Sedge Thompsen on National Public Radio, Harrison spoke of the "erotics of writing," which he defined as "an intoxication with the ordinary in life. I think writers get lost by being very brilliant about perimeters and being very brilliant about edges, and then they forget the core. Food and sex are at the core."[8] Harrison's collection of nonfiction, *The Raw and the Cooked: Adventures of a Roving Gourmand* (2001), is prefaced by a parable—Harrison called it a "metaphor"—entitled "The Man Who Ate Books." His take on the world, much like Walt Whitman's and Henry Miller's, was characterized by his self-confessedly "fatal" appetite for language and experience, his hunger to devour life in as many of its varied guises and forms as possible. He smoked like a chimney, drank like a sailor on shore leave, and ate like there was no tomorrow. Eating, devouring, ingesting, tasting became the central bodily metaphors and gustatory tropes that linked all his most compelling pursuits, including cooking, hunting, fishing, reading, and writing. He introduces *The Raw and the Cooked* this way: "Even the occasional glories of our sexual lives can be drawn into this picture. . . . All of our sensualities and passions merge because we are one person and it's best not to neglect any of those passions if we wish to fully live our lives." Not surprisingly, Harrison referred to himself as a "feral songbird."

Whether considered as justification or rationalization, Harrison's catchy gastronomical motto—"Eat or Die"—transcends his food journalism and reveals an orientation toward the world's body that has resulted in an unbroken skein of attention and inclusiveness, not only for himself but for his characters as well (many of whom transparently share their author's specific interests, habits, obsessions). Harrison's signature character creations, in pursuit of their place in the world, exhibit a single-minded energy and hunger that reflected Harrison's own resolutely anti-Calvinist mandate. His conception of fictional characters widened and ramified over the years. As Harrison increasingly abnegated his own ego (the result of long-standing Zen practice and his psychoanalysis with Lawrence Sullivan, his New York "mind doctor"), he entered more fully into Dogen's world of ten thousand things. This is not a matter of mechanical "discipline" (a word he always abhorred), but of soulful empathy and openness, and a willingness to listen to the demands of his own considerable dream life and dictates of his conscience. Indeed, he has gone so far as to argue persuasively for portraying the entire range of human emotion in his writing, even if it means risking sentimentality, long thought to be one of the cardinal sins of literary criticism. "The novelist who refuses sentiment refuses the full spectrum of human behavior. . . . I would rather give full vent to all human loves and disappointments, and take a chance on being corny, than die a smartass," he confessed to Wendy Smith.[9] If understanding just who Jim Harrison was gets complicated in the following pages, it will help to keep this clear-cut admission in mind.

Although this compilation is merely suggestive of the larger record of Jim Harrison's vast archive of oral, print, video, and electronic media interviews and appearances at home and abroad, it should prove useful in creating a historical context for many of his published works. While Harrison does not slavishly interpret his texts directly, he does situate them among their participatory and ambient circumstances. His comments provide a parallel conversation to the one carried on in his prose and poetry and reveal a highly literate and intellectual writer whose work and talent is best measured against a vast historical textual tradition. An omnivorous reader and compulsive researcher with a trap-door memory and recall, Harrison has never been reticent about quoting or praising influential writers, whose names and deeds appear often in these interviews. Consequently, they provide ample evidence of his affinity with a wide range of international literary forbears, ancestors, and precursors, from William Faulkner, James Joyce, Herman Melville, John Steinbeck, and Henry Miller to Halldor Laxness, Fyodor Dostoyevsky, Albert Camus, Rainer Maria Rilke, Sergei Yesenin, Rene Char, Antonio Machado, and Gabriel García Márquez, all of whom in varying degrees of efficacy provided needed "blood transfusions."

More importantly, these talks will supply a loosely related narrative of his progress as a major contemporary American writer who was equally and comfortably at home in poetry, fiction, and nonfiction. This collection should also aid in signifying the depth and range of Harrison's considerable intellectual and political preoccupations, his fierce social and ecological conscience (especially about America's deplorable "soul history" regarding Native Americans, and our rapacious treatment of the natural world), his aesthetic beliefs and stylistic orientations in poetry and prose, and his authorial obsessions, not the least of them his pioneering efforts to perfect the novella form, for which he is considered a contemporary master, and the frequency of adopting a trespass vision with which he defied polite narrative conventions and storied habits and created memorable, resolute female characters who take male prerogatives to themselves (Dalva, Clare, Julip Durham). In addition, these interviews show his pet peeves, candor, arrogance, humility, sense of humor and irony, and his unflagging patience, even when kept from his requisite daily "full dress nap," or posed with the same questions over and over, or when prompted to recount again and again his litany of key formative life experiences.

Like so many serious literary artists before him, Harrison remains an innovative, powerful, and savvy writer whose true subject is the capacious and tragic dimension of individual consciousness. When Casey Walker asked him in 1997 to describe "the core, the spirit" of his work, Harrison replied in an interview included here: "The consciousness, I would say. Otherness. Otherness to remind ourselves of the bedrock of life, and death, and love, and suffering." And yet despite the prevalence of this multifaceted theme and a challenging, even acrobatic, level of interrelatedness in his work, Harrison has not yet reached the critical academic audience in America he deserves (though this was not a noticeable cause of disappointment to him). This neglect is partly his own doing. After a brief stint as an administrative assistant and teacher at SUNY Stony Brook, Harrison left the university environment for good, because he believed it was important to remain resolutely on the outside. Except for occasional readings, public appearances, award conferrals, and the like, Harrison never returned to academia, though he satirized it unmercifully in characters such as Michael in *Dalva* and Shelley in his novellas "Brown Dog" and "The Seven-Ounce Man."

Jim Harrison was a straight shooter, deliberately profane, even offensive, and sometimes down right unapologetically crude in his opinions on nearly every topic of interest to him under the sun, especially the liabilities of university creative writing programs ("industrialization of writing"), and the deleterious effects of political correctness and group thinking regarding sexuality and masculine conduct (his novella "The Beige Dolorosa" is a prime example). The poet laureate of appetite in all its configurations and permutations is not a writer for all tastes or sensibilities, because his habitual excesses and obsessive quirks have not always been easy to embrace. So to get the best Harrison has to offer, readers need to make room for the less savory aspects as well, even the tiresomeness of hypermasculinity. That is exactly why Harrison is considered a "writer's writer," whose ferocious independence, technical abilities, versatility, serious, unremitting attention to craft, and creative priorities are cherished.

Harrison's generosity toward younger writers is legendary and bears honoring over and over. If the hundreds of dust jacket encomia and otherwise praiseful statements Harrison has penned in the last fifty years are any indication, then many of our most respected and accomplished contemporary writers, from Sherman Alexie, Rick Bass, and Chris Dombrowski to Jeffrey Lent and Colum McCann to Terry Tempest Williams and Callan Wink, have looked to him for affinities, influence, advice, encouragement, guidance, support, camaraderie, and friendship. What Gertrude Stein once said of Paris applies to Harrison—it isn't what he gave you, so much as what he didn't take away. To sense that liberatory gift is to begin to understand how and why Harrison has created a strongly committed—even fanatical— international following among general readers in two dozen or so different languages, but also among book specialists—reviewers, media critics, and independent booksellers (how he loved Lemuria, Horizon Books, Elliot Bay, Tattered Cover, and Square Books, to name just a few of the prominent indies!). He is one of those broadband cult writers who still reaches a wide and diverse audience that often cuts across national, racial, gender, regional, and cultural lines. Whether he will be found out to be otherwise in our fast-shifting landscape of allegiances remains to be seen.

The interview selections included here approximate the original conversations in varying ways, some more spontaneously, some less so, some more editorially polished, some less so, than others. Inevitably, there is also overlapping, repetition, echoing, and call and response. Anyone who ever interviewed Harrison probably found it was impossible to ignore (and probably not be delighted by) Harrison's discursive style, digressive manner, and rough-hewn raspy voice trailing cigarette smoke, not to mention his iconic head with its single good eye and weathered face. "An amazing face, an iconic face, and Harrison's goofy left eye was like the bump in Anna Akhmatova's nose; an essential, defining imperfection," Tom Bissell aptly noted in 2011. A face "still handsome," Terry McDonell claims "in the manner of a mahogany stump."[10]

Readers accustomed to the complex rhetorical structure and striated quality of Harrison's fiction and the surprising mind flights of his poetry will glimpse some of those same acrobatic patterns among several of the following pieces. Harrison often talks around a subject first, going this way, then that, before he finds the route he wants to follow. He habitually contextualizes his answers by providing a kind of intellectual or emotional surround. In short, Harrison often feels his way haltingly toward his answer (a process some interviewers have been more desirous of replicating than others). Asked by Eleanor Wachtel whether he has found a balance in his life, Harrison replied:

> But I don't know if that's true. I think balances are temporary and any time you think you could fix yourself in one place, that's absurd. Properly, life lived properly, is a river. Or that Yeatsian concept that life is best viewed as a dance. You know, an interminable dance. So, if I thought that I had reached some point, I would hit myself over the head because the path is the way. You have to keep reaching the point on the continuum, you know. It never stops, even for a moment. I would say there is a bit more consolation now, because what I had thought as a young writer was that I would never whine if my books stayed in print and so they have. So that's the only thing you hope for.

The river, the dance, the path: though Harrison wasn't so naive as to be unmindful that end results and tangible products issue from entitled self-interest and determined agency, these three metaphors emphasize process as a kind of reward in itself and summarize his fluid, mythic way of being in the world. Fishing, cooking, writing: you're a "dead duck," he said often, if you don't love the process and make the process your own.

The interviews are arranged in the order of when they were conducted, rather than the order of their publication. Interviews that were conducted over an extended period of time, or interviews that are composites of two or more sessions with Harrison (Wachtel; DeMott and Smith) are appropriately noted. In two instances I have compared the original audio version with the subsequent printed version and have noted that there are differences (Bonetti) or incorporated with permission original interview material deleted from the published account (Wachtel, Dennis, Nowogrodzki). Obvious typographical and factual errors by interviewers and/or editors have been silently corrected. I have not, however, corrected Harrison's occasional fibs, memory glitches, or misprisions. Harrison's sprightly memoir, *Off to the Side* (2002), constellated among other way points around his life's main obsessions—alcohol, strip clubs, hunting, fishing, dogs, private religion, France, the road, nature, and natives—provides an intimate template of his life's autobiography, his densely packed portfolio of enthusiasms and passions, which is also to be found piecemeal in nearly everything else he wrote since the mid-1960s, especially in *Just Before Dark, The Raw and the Cooked,* and *A Really Big Lunch,* and further elaborated on in the autobiographical pieces "Tracking" in *The Summer He Didn't Die* (2005) and "The Ancient Minstrel" in *The Ancient Minstrel* (2016). Astute readers will see frequent relationships between events in Harrison's life and in those of his fictive characters. Harrison was a complex, multifaceted person complicit in forwarding a certain view of his life, and embodying a bundle of contradictions and inconsistencies, so a healthy dose of Keats's negative capability—one of Harrison's favorite conceptual strategies—is necessary for smooth sailing in these pages. The vagaries of time and the imperfections of memory being what they are, no attempt has been made to reconcile conflicting versions of Harrison's responses in these interviews, though on a number of signal issues and formative events he was remarkably uniform.

Harrison's writings are not so much discrete, isolated points on a linear trajectory, as they are a web of related, overlapping texts. Characters emerge in one novel, disappear, then surface again in a later text, as does Dalva Northridge in *Dalva* and *The Road Home,* the Brown Dog series ("Brown Dog," "The Seven-Ounce Man," "Westward Ho," "The Summer He Didn't Die," "Brown Dog Redux," "He Dog"), David Burkett in *True North* and

Returning to Earth, and the Simon Sunderson texts, *The Great Leader*, *The Big Seven*, and "The Case of the Howling Buddhas" in *The Ancient Minstrel*. More than that, however, nearly everything Harrison wrote illuminates and is connected to everything else he wrote. Fiction, poetry, essays, memoir, journalism, interviews, often radiate from a central personal, autobiographical nexus, and sometimes, but not always, the voices too overlap and echo one another. The dialogue in Harrison's fiction and the talk in his life merge in a border area, where the narrative of voices and the voices of narrative mingle. "With me," he once told me, "it's all about presence." Harrison's writings are lapidary and, as with Faulkner's works rather than Hemingway's, reading through them is like peeling an onion or artichoke: as layer after layer is exposed, we travel deeper and deeper into the meaning of the whole. The words of Herbert Weisinger, Harrison's revered teacher and intellectual mentor, are appropriate here: "It is not until the inner-most core is reached," Weisinger states, "that the meaning of the whole is revealed, and, as one penetrates deeper and deeper . . . layer upon layer is seen . . . each with a character of its own but which can be fully understood only in relation to the others, until the centre is reached . . . which binds together and unifies the layers into a single comprehensive structure."[11] That is a literary archeology project Harrison's legions of readers should find encouraging; its prospects should provide incentive enough to keep reading, discussing, and sharing his work for a long time to come.

✦ ✦ ✦

By the third week of October 2016, the Absaroka Mountains to the east of Livingston, Montana, were tipped with snow, and the cottonwoods along the Yellowstone River had pretty well shed their leaves. The air had an ambient quality to it, the sky seemed to go on forever, and the autumn light, clear and sharp, had a way of penetrating every nook and cranny of the splendid Paradise Valley landscape. A crowd of seventy to seventy-five family members, colleagues, compatriots, and friends, invited from far and near across the United States, convened on the evening of the 22nd at Livingston's landmark Murray Hotel and the adjacent Second Street Bistro to attend Jim Harrison's memorial celebration and to partake of the spectacular multi-course dinner hosted in his and wife Linda's honor by daughters Jamie Potenberg and Anna Hjorstberg and orchestrated by Chef Brian Menges. There were copies of Jim's latest books for every attendee—fiction from Grove Press courtesy of publisher Morgan Entrekin, and *Dead Man's Float*, Jim's last book of poems,

Rae,
I wonder if you
will enjoy this?
I think its changing
my life/perspective
in a way.
His poems are good
too. Here's one.
xor Myr.

May 4.

courtesy of Joseph Bednarik and Copper Canyon Press, and a lovely folded letterpress poem, "To Jim at the River," by Dan Gerber published by Tangram Press. It was a time of good cheer, bounteous generosity, and well-met fellow feeling, but amid the splendors of the evening, with its free flow of great food, sublime wines and liquors, heartfelt speeches, earnest talk, hilarious reminiscences, introductions, and re-acquaintances, there was occasion for private recollections and somber memories.[12]

Mine went back to the beginning: I first encountered Jim Harrison when I read "A Sporting Life," an article on upland bird hunting that appeared in *Playboy* in 1976 and was eventually reprinted in *Just Before Dark* (1991). I was born and raised in New England, and like Harrison, had more or less misspent my youth by excessive trout fishing and grouse hunting in Connecticut and Vermont—willful personal indulgences which always made me feel slightly guilty and socially marginal, particularly in a college setting, at least until I read and absorbed Harrison on such subjects. Few have written as vibrantly about outdoor pursuits as Harrison has. For its refusal to traffic in stereotypes or to endorse misguided notions of sporting life, his candid essay is as sharp now as it was forty-plus years ago. Those qualities of common-sense realism, incisive insight, hyperattentiveness, and robust enthusiasm—evident throughout all of his work—are as sustaining now as they have ever been. However the deepest lesson had less to do with woods and waters per se than with the necessity to seek an "opposite field," a separate identity, an arena of physical activity apart from the work-a-day routine of spoken or written words.

Seeking a far field was a recipe for maintaining sanity, I told him when I approached him for the first time twenty years later, in January 1996, at a Key West Literary Seminar, a conference on "American Writers and the Natural World." He seemed less interested in the fact that I was assigning his fiction in graduate seminars, had supervised a couple of MA theses on his work, and was then in the process of directing a PhD dissertation about him than the news that I had recently started working a brilliant young English setter who was already making her mark as a brag dog. On that basis, over swapped tales about the ups and downs of training companion bird dogs, I established a fortuitous contact that led to a couple of lengthy interviews that doctoral student Patrick Smith and I conducted in Lake Leelanau, Michigan, in 1997 and 1998 (the transcript of those hours and hours of early visits came to more than 150 pages), and then to the idea for the first version of this book, which appeared in 2002, and more than anything else, to a crucial friendship that lasted two decades, eclipsed traditional polite academic dimensions, and provided me with a level of sustained generosity, hospital-ity, and brotherly comradeship that I did not think possible.

During that stretch I spent time with Jim, which meant cooking, eat-ing, talking, in Arizona, Florida, Michigan, Nebraska, North Carolina, Ohio, Pennsylvania, and especially Montana, where we fished together annually for a dozen years.[13] And we drank and caroused at some of his storied venues—the Bluebird Tavern in Leland, Dick's Pour House in Lake Leelanau, the Night Before Lounge in Lincoln, the Owl Lounge and Murray Hotel in Livingston, the Hitchin' Post in Melrose, and the Wagon Wheel in Patagonia. He contributed essays to two of my nonscholastic book proj-ects, *Afield: American Writers on Bird Dogs* (2010) and *Astream: American Writers on Fly Fishing* (2012), and he made both of those collections more memorable and lively than they might otherwise have been. I did not know Jim the way his lifelong compatriots, fellow travelers, various soul mates, publishers and editors, and family members knew him, with their long tradition of intricate and intimate shared histories, but I was honored and flattered and humbled, too, to have been considered a valued friend, a dedi-catee of one of his novella collections (*The Farmer's Daughter*), a brief men-tion in his memoir, and best of all, a member of his poetry group list serve, superintended by Joyce Harrington Bahle, which for many years brought a group of us via email Jim's latest poem, fresh from the oven as it were, sometimes two or three a day in the latter era when his productivity soared to improbable heights. Even as some of his later fiction ran in familiar paths, his poetry was fresh and startling in its power and immediacy. Either way, it was gratifying to know that he was alive as a creative force in the world, and that recognition made a profound, seismic difference to me.

So in a sense, a cherished part of my life since 1996 began and ended with Jim Harrison. Not a day goes by when I don't miss him or wonder what he would have thought about this or that fiddle faddle in the current daily shit storm of history, politics, and culture, the "stupefying banalities," as he called them in a letter to me. Late nights, when I am most susceptible to loss and grief, even despair, I think of Jim Harrison, yes, I think of Jim Harrison with his many foibles and excesses, his geniuses and glories, and I'm able to go on. Now, besides the memories of two decades, there are always the poems, fiction, and essays to rely on for his wisdom, his incomparable voice, his unswerving insights to what truly matters in these otherwise fractious and venal times. The man is gone but his art continues. In 2019 Copper Canyon Press plans to issue a retrospective anthology of his poetry, tentatively titled *The Essential Poems of Jim Harrison.* And who knows but that sometime in the future we might at last see publication of his five-decade correspondence with Tom McGuane. Until then, there is a full-length documentary on Harrison being developed by two Michigan journalist/filmmakers, Christopher Walton and Steven Byrne. Etienne Savin, Stephen Spencer, and Paul Hoy are responsible for the popular "Jim Harrison Author Page" on Facebook. In that vein, I like to think that this updated book of interviews is a way of not just hearing his voice again, but of saying thanks for those gifts he continues to gives us.

Whether they knew it or not, numerous people lent their part toward this updated *Conversations with Jim Harrison*: Nancy Richards and Annie Benefiel, past and present archivists for the Jim Harrison Collection in Special Collections & University Archives at Grand Valley State University, which houses the largest, richest Harrison archive in the world; editors Katie Keene, Mary Heath, and Valerie Jones at University Press of Mississippi who were willing to take a chance on this very first updated volume in the Press's Literary Conversations series; Morgan Entrekin, Judy Hottenson, and Amy Hundley of Grove Press who have honored Harrison's prose for many decades and have kept it in print and before the public with gusto; ditto Joseph Bednarik, Harrison's extraordinarily gifted poetry editor at Copper Canyon Press; family members Steve and Jamie Potenberg, Max and Anna Hjortsberg, brother David Harrison, and sister Mary Dumsch who have been supportive and generous presences; Attorney J. Stephen Sheppard, Harrison's lawyer and literary agent at Cowan, DeBaets, Abrahams, and Sheppard, LLP, for his continuing stewardship of Harrison's words and estate; my Ohio University colleague Dominique Duvert for French-English translations; Harrison cronies and soul mates—especially the fabulously generous Guy de la Valdène—but also Mario Batali, Russell Chatham, Jim Fergus, Dan Gerber, Ted Kooser, Tom McGuane, Hank Meijer, and Doug and Andrea Peacock, whose various kindnesses remain highly valued. And a shout out to Lilli Ross and Aaron Parrett, movers and shakers in the first go-round of the Jim Harrison Society, the wildest and woolliest, least strait-laced academic group ever formed in the American Literature Association. Also Marc Beaudin, John and Jenice Benton, Tom Carney, Bill Castanier, Todd Davis, Michael Delp, Jerry Dennis, Chris Dombrowski, Joanne Drilling, Ron Ellis, Tom Huggler, Christopher Johnson, Randy Lawrence, Dave Lint, Tracy McLain, Michael Pollack, Brian Railsback, Mike Ryan, and Doug Stanton, who kept the flames burning with ongoing interest, information, insights, curiosity, and dialogue. To my partner Kate Fox—deepest love and appreciation for her enormous beneficent presence in my life.

Profound thanks are due, once again, to Joyce Harrington Bahle, Jim's indispensable right-hand woman, estate executor, business manager, eagle-eyed typist, public communicator, hardboiled guardian, and overall aide-de-camp. Harrisonians everywhere owe her a debt of unending gratitude. Also kudos to trusted pal Gregg Orr, Harrison's tireless bibliographer and Harrison Society compatriot and all-around good friend; to Peter Lewis for his inspired conversation, for sharing his insights, and for filling in gaps in the chronology of Harrison's life since the first edition of this book was published; and to jack-of-all-trades Danny Lahren for decades of friendship, stories, advice, and good times, in and out of fishing.

Finally, of course, this book is dedicated to the memory of Jim and Linda Harrison. And also to the late Dr. Gregg "Beef" Torrey and my student, the late Dr. Patrick Smith, unparalleled Harrison aficionados and irrepressible pals and founding members and guiding spirits in the Jim Harrison Society. They all left the scene too soon.

RD

Athens, OH/Cameron, MT
July–August 2018

Notes

1. "Postscript: Jim Harrison, 1937–2016," *New Yorker*, March 28, 2016.
2. "Jim Harrison and the Art of Friendship," *Daily Beast*, April 2, 2016.
3. My chapter (updated with Gregg Orr), "Annotated Interviews with Jim Harrison," in Gregg Orr and Beef Torrey, eds., *Jim Harrison: A Comprehensive Bibliography, 1964–2008.* (Lincoln: University of Nebraska Press, 2009), 213–63, is incomplete but digests 126 interviews by Harrison through 2008. I can only guess that in the past nine years the number is probably equal that. Harrison's first two serious interviews, as far as can be determined, were by Dennis Knickerbocker in the *Grand Rapids Press* (December 26, 1971), and by Eric Siegel in the *Detroit Free Press* (April 16, 1972). The third known interview, by Ira Elliott and Marty Sommerness in 1976, is included here. I deposited all of my research materials pertaining to *Conversations with Jim Harrison*, including interviews, transcriptions, notes, documents, to-and-from correspondence with Harrison and others, to the Jim Harrison Archive at Grand Valley State University's Special Collections and Archives. At nine boxes and five linear feet of shelf space, it is only a portion of GVSU's enormous and richly detailed holdings (http://gvsu.lyrasistechnology.org/repositories/2/resources/469). For a personal view of the Harrison collection, see Joseph Bednarik's "A Pilgrimage to Jim Harrison's Archive," published in the online version of *Brick: A Literary Magazine*, June 28, 2018, accessible at https://brickmag.com/a-pilgrimage-to-jim-harrisons-archive/.

4. As Harrison's French translator, Brice Matthieussent, says in "La Strategie du Furet" ["The Strategy of the Ferret"], his preface to his alphabetized guide book to Harrison's life and art, *Jim Harrison de A à W* (Paris: Christian Bourgois Editions, 1995), 9, "les Francais manifestent souvent un net penchant pour le mythe." That is, the French show a distinct inclination toward mythologizing American writers. In fact, they lead the pack in this regard and are fond of presenting Harrison in such guises as "The Sorcerer of Michigan," "The Sentimental Ogre of Michigan," "The Bear That Loved Men," "America's Coyote," "Big Jim," "Poor Little Jimmy," "Mozart of the Plains," and so on. These colorful monikers all center around seemingly conflicted or irreconcilable aspects of Harrison's personality. Here is Matthieussent again (translated by Dominique Duvert): "J. H. lets himself be nicknamed Big Jim by his friends, but he often talks about himself as Poor Little Jimmy. Which image should we choose? The one about the giant or the one about vulnerability? Which nickname is the right one? Is there even one? How can we see clearly through all these smokescreens?" (11). American journalists have also done their share of mythologizing Harrison as a tough guy of American letters. The most egregious example is Jim Ricci's "One-on-One Iron Person Can Hold His Center," *Detroit Free Press*, August 1, 1991, 1F, a purportedly humorous account of the reporter's boxing match–style show down between himself and Harrison ("notorious macho and celebrated literary carnivore"), in which Ricci pulls a last minute, come-from-behind win over the novelist. Ricci's willful misrepresentation is best judged by his retraction in *Detroit Free Press* a week later in which he apologized for wrenching Harrison's words and actions out of context and ignoring the bulk of their talk, which had been serious conversation about art and writing. A number of hyperbolic fan blogs and off-the-cuff interviews in the cyber world continue to play up the image of Harrison as a bully-boy character rather than as a consummate artist. Recently, Joseph Rakowski asked Harrison, "If you could fist-fight one person, who would it be?" To which Harrison replied in part: "No, those feelings aren't here anymore." See "15 Reviews & Interview with Jim Harrison," in *Three Guys One Book* (December 31, 2013), accessible at http://threeguysonebook.com/15-reviews-interview-with-jim-harrison/.

5. Jim Harrison, *Jim Harrison: entre chien et loup*, produced and directed by Georges Luneau and Brice Matthieussent, 78 min., Paris: Planete Cable/Cine Cinemas Cable/Gedeon, 1993, videocassette. (English version titled *Jim Harrison: Half Dog and Half Wolf*.) Harrison's twenty-six-minute interview with Matthieussent follows the fifty-two-minute documentary film portion of the program. It is also available as a paperback volume (1994) in French and available from Amazon. The vain aspect of personality, which Harrison deplored in himself (because it is an illusory mask made up every day to face the world and conflicts), is not to be confused with his fascination—voiced several times in the following collection of interviews—for the "mystery of personality" he found in human beings at large. This he considered endlessly compelling. The title of the documentary film pays homage to Harrison's oft-stated preference for twilight, the hour between dog and wolf.

6. Rebecca Newth, "For Harrison, Writing a Matter of Shifting Gears," *Arkansas Democrat-Gazette*, May 15, 1994, 8J. See also Harrison's "From the Dalva Notebooks: 1985–1987," in *Our Private Lives: Journals, Diaries, Notebooks*, ed. Daniel Halpern. (New York: Vintage, 1990), 211: "Went . . . to edit interview. Can't get beyond first page by the second day because I'm not currently interested in anything I've ever said. . . ."

7. Harrison's poem and his exchange of letters with Ciardi are in the Michigan State University Library's Department of Special Collections and are quoted with permission.

8. Harrison appeared on NPR's nationally syndicated program *Fresh Air* on August 23, 1990. (My transcription.)

9. *Publishers Weekly* 237, no. 3 (August 1990): 59.

10. See Tom Bissell, "The Theory and Practice of Not Giving a Shit: On a Visit with Jim Harrison," in *Magic Hours: Essays on Creators and Creation* (San Francisco: Believer Books, 2012), 274. Bissell's essay appeared in 2011 as "The Last Lion," in *Outside Online*. Terry McDonell's comment is in his chapter "Little Jimmy" in *The Accidental Life: An Editor's Notes on Writing and Writers* (New York: Alfred A Knopf, 2016), 155. Benjamin Polley, who interviewed Harrison five months before his death, said his "wrinkled face looked like a broken-in baseball mitt." See "Jim Harrison: A Writer's Life," in the *Whitefish Review*, no. 19 (Summer 2016): 119. The issue also contains tributes to Harrison by Rick Bass, Tom Brokaw, Tom Crawford, Chris Dombrowski, David James Duncan, William Kittredge, Thomas McGuane, Teddy Macker, Doug Peacock, and Annick Smith. The issue also includes four graphic black-and-white photographs by Erik Petersen of Harrison in his Livingston, Montana, writing bungalow. See also Andy Anderson's striking late-life photographs of Harrison at www.andyandersonphoto.com/blog/?tag=jim-harrison. An internet search will turn up a number of on-camera, late-life Harrison appearances on YouTube and the like. See, for example, "A Day with Jim Harrison," a nine-minute, seventeen-second-long video by Grove Press Associate Publisher, Judy Hottenson, which was filmed in and around Harrison's Patagonia, Arizona, *casita* a few months before he died. Footage of Harrison speaking about and reading briefly from his novel *The Seven Deadly* (2015) is interspersed with his brief, humorous address to book sellers a year earlier.

11. *Tragedy and the Paradox of the Fortunate Fall* (East Lansing: Michigan State University Press, 1953), 8.

12. For another attendee's view of the Livingston memorial, see Chris Dombrowski's "Want to Honor Jim Harrison? Make His Memorial Dinner," in *Outside Online*, March 26, 2018, accessible at https:www.outsideonline.com/2291316/behind-scenes-jim-harrisons-farewell-dinner. His piece gives some menu details as well as catching the spirit of the evening.

13. See my introduction to Orr and Torrey, eds., *Jim Harrison: A Comprehensive Bibliography*, xv–xxxi; my chapter, "Fishing with Jim Harrison," in *Angling Days: A Fly Fisher's Journals* (New York: Skyhorse Publishing, 2016), 124–28; Joanne Drilling, "The River Kings," in *Cincinnati Magazine*, May 24, 2017, at http://www.cincinnatimagazine.com/forkopolisblog/the-river-kings/; and Callan Wink, "Fly-Fishing Confidential," *Men's Journal*, November 27, 2013, accessible at http://www.mensjournal.com/magazine/fly-fishing-confidential-20131127.

Chronology

1937	James Thomas Harrison born December 11 in northern Michigan town of Grayling, the second of five children of Winfield Sprague Harrison (government agriculture agent) and Norma Olivia (Wahlgren) Harrison. Both parents avid readers.
1940	Harrison family moves to Reed City, Michigan.
1945	Harrison accidentally blinded in his left eye by playmate with broken glass laboratory beaker. Intensifies his lifelong obsession with fishing.
1951	Though raised Congregationalist, Harrison experiences religious conversion at Baptist revival and becomes preacher at fundamentalist youth fellowships and president of Bible Club. Opens to the world of poetry after reading John Keats.
1952–56	Family moves to Haslett so Harrison children can be within commuting distance of Michigan State University. Father works for United States Soil Conservation Service. Harrison attends Haslett Rural High School where he plays offensive left guard and defensive middle linebacker on football team. English teacher and librarian Bernice Smith encourages Harrison's sophisticated reading interests with *Nation* and *Saturday Review*. In 1953 after a summer working as busboy at Stanley Hotel in Estes Park, Colorado, religious urge fades and he transfers his fervor to literary pursuits. During sophomore year, announces intention to become a writer; receives first typewriter for seventeenth birthday. In 1954, in the summer before his junior year, Harrison and a friend drive to Greenwich Village in New York for a few days to investigate bohemian life. Elected president of graduating class and of student council but resigns from latter. Graduates from Haslett and in September 1956, enrolls at Michigan State University.
1957–59	A period of restlessness, occasional travel, and temporary residence in New York City, San Francisco, and Boston. Drops out of Michigan State toward the end of his freshman year and

hitchhikes to New York's Greenwich Village (at different times lives on McDougal Street and Grove Street). Meets Jack Kerouac at Five Spot Café in Bowery. Returns to Michigan State in the fall of 1958, but drops out. Goes to Boston, then hitchhikes to California. Works at various odd jobs, including as crop picker. In 1959 returns to Michigan State. At Michigan State part-time jobs include working at library and horticulture farm. Marries Linda May King on October 10, 1959.

1960   Earns BA degree, Michigan State University. Daughter Jamie Louise Harrison born May 21. Fellow students at Michigan State include poet and novelist Dan Gerber, novelist and screenwriter Thomas McGuane, both of whom later become lifelong friends, and Robert Datilla, who later becomes Harrison's agent.

1962   Father and younger sister Judith killed by drunk driver in head-on automobile accident in November. Harrison leaves graduate program at Michigan State.

1963–64   Moves to Cambridge, Massachusetts, and lives with brother John, a Harvard librarian, and sister-in-law Rebecca, in apartment on Kirkland Street; frequents Grolier Bookshop and meets local poets; works for two years as book salesman at Campbell and Hall, a general wholesaling firm, and is joined by wife and daughter in apartment in Allston, Massachusetts. In December submits ten poems to *Poetry*.

1965   Publishes three poems in *Nation* on February 15 and April 5, and five poems in *Poetry* in August. On April 19 is one of four poets to appear at the Poetry Center (New York City) as part of "Discovery '65" series, a program designed for poets who have not been published in book form, but who have books ready for publication. On the strength of reading ten of Harrison's poems, Denise Levertov recommends his first book, *Plain Song*, for publication by W. W. Norton. Moves to Kingsley, Michigan. Has odd jobs as laborer, hod carrier, brick layer, and carpenter. Encouraged by mentor Herbert Weisinger to complete graduate work, Harrison writes essay about his poems which becomes Michigan State University master's thesis, "The Natural History of Some Poems."

1966   Harrison earns MA degree in comparative literature at Michigan State University. Cancels teaching position at Northern Michigan University to follow Weisinger to State University of New York,

Stony Brook, where he becomes Weisinger's assistant, then assistant professor of English.

1967   Receives National Endowment for the Arts grant. Publishes limited-edition chapbook, *Walking*. In September attends World Poetry Conference in Montreal. In October participates in Writers and Artists' March on the State Department, Washington, DC, to protest Viet Nam war.

1968   Publishes limited edition (126 copies) book of poems, *Locations*. With Weisinger and Louis Simpson organizes world poetry conference at Stony Brook June 21–23. Contributes "Dreams" to *Stony Brook Holographs* (Stony Brook, NY: Stony Brook Poetics Foundation), a collection of handwritten poems by various hands. Though listed in the 1968–69 Stony Brook catalogue as assistant professor, in June resigns and returns to Michigan. Purchases Lake Leelanau, Michigan, home at 701 South French Road. Spends summer in Paradise Valley near Livingston, Montana, initiating a lifelong attraction to the area. First issue of *Sumac* (poetry magazine) appears in the fall, edited by Harrison and Dan Gerber.

1969   Awarded Guggenheim fellowship. As part of Poets in the Schools program, gives poetry readings and residencies in the Southwest. Sumac Press publishes *Five Blind Men* including Dan Gerber, George Quasha, J. D. Reed, and Charles Simic. Begins to work sporadically on a novel, "Cities of the North." In October suffers severe back injury when he falls from bluff during grouse hunting trip along Manistee River and spends a month in traction at Munson Hospital in Traverse City.

1970   While recovering from back injury (complicated by penicillin poisoning) is urged by McGuane to complete a novel. Meets painter and writer Russell Chatham in Key West and they become lifelong friends. Publishes essay "The Real Fun of the Fair Was the Horse Pulling," in *Sports Illustrated*'s August 31 issue, beginning association with *SI* that lasts until 1976.

1971   Daughter Anna Severin Harrison born April 6. Publishes novel *Wolf: A False Memoir* and poems *Outlyer and Ghazals*. Sumac ceases publication after nine issues, but Sumac Press continues and eventually publishes twenty-one individual books. In October makes literary pilgrimage to Moscow and Leningrad with Dan Gerber.

1973   Publishes novel *A Good Day to Die* and poems *Letters to Yesenin*, which he considers an "anti-suicide note." In February travels to Africa with Dan Gerber and their wives.

1974   With Thomas McGuane and Richard Brautigan contributes to and acts in *Tarpon*, documentary movie on saltwater fly fishing filmed in Key West, Florida, directed by Christian Odasso and Guy de la Valdène, and featuring musical soundtrack by friend Jimmy Buffett. Loan from Brautigan buys him time to complete *Farmer*.

1975   Publishes novel *Farmer*. "A Gun for Big Fish," a story concerning Harrison by Richard Brautigan, appears in *Esquire* in March. Writes screenplay of *A Good Day to Die* for documentary filmmaker Frederick Wiseman, but film is never made. Meets actor Jack Nicholson on the Montana film set of *Missouri Breaks*.

1976   Contributes foreword, "The Singular Excitement of Water Sports," to *Sports Afloat* (New York: Time-Life Books).

1977   Publishes poetry collection *Returning to Earth*.

1978   In New York City on January 26 and 27 takes part in Roundtable Conversation interview at Academy of American Poets, and is featured author at Donnell Library Center's Storyteller's Art series. Visits Nicholson on Durango, Mexico, set of *Going South*; Nicholson loans Harrison $30,000 to pay off debts and finance writing for a year. Meets Seymour "Sam" Lawrence, who becomes his publisher at Delacorte, Dutton, and Houghton Mifflin. In winter visits Jolli Lodge in Lake Leelanau, where he writes novella "The Man Who Gave Up His Name," and in concentrated nine-day burst "Legends of the Fall," a novella based in part on journals kept by William Ludlow, his wife's great-grandfather, an immigrant Cornish mining engineer who accompanied General Custer on Black Hills expeditions.

1979   Publishes combined reprint volume *Letters to Yesenin and Returning to Earth* and breakthrough novella collection *Legends of the Fall* (includes "Legends of the Fall," "Revenge," and "The Man Who Gave Up His Name"). Beginning with *Legends*, all Harrison's major books feature dust jacket cover art by landscape painter Russell Chatham. Begins writing screenplays in Hollywood for Warner Bros. Work as contract screenwriter lasts until 1997. Employs Joyce Harrington (later Bahle) as full-time, permanent administrative assistant. Purchases nine-hundred-square-foot cabin with outbuildings on forty acres bordering the

Sucker River in Burt Township, just south of Grand Marais, in Michigan's Upper Peninsula.

1981 Publishes novel *Warlock* and poetry collection *Selected and New Poems, 1961–1981*. Publishes first of four food columns in *Smoke Signals*, a small-press, limited-circulation literary journal in Brooklyn, New York.

1982 *Selected and New Poems, 1961–1981* appears in paperback and is the last book of poems he publishes with a large commercial firm. Publishes limited-edition (350 copies) chapbook of poems, *Natural World: A Bestiary*, with black-and-white photographs of Diana Guest's sculptures.

1983 In March conducts writing workshops at Hamline University and the Loft in Minneapolis.

1984 Publishes novel *Sundog: A Novel: The Story of an American Foreman, Robert Corvus Strang, as told to Jim Harrison.*

1986 Publishes signed limited edition of poems, *The Theory and Practice of Rivers and Other Poems.*

1987 Fishes the Yellowstone River with Dan Lahren, who becomes regular fishing guide, confidante, and personal aide for the remainder of his life.

1988 Publishes major novel *Dalva*. Beginning with premiere issue, Harrison becomes contributing food editor of *Smart*, mass-circulation magazine.

1989 In January Russell Chatham's Clark City Press publishes *The Theory & Practice of Rivers and New Poems*. In the January/February issue of *Smart*, publishes first of ten "Sporting Food" columns which continue through October/November 1990. Film *Cold Feet*, co-written earlier with Thomas McGuane, directed by Robert Dornhelm and starring Tom Waits, Keith Carradine, and Sally Kirkland, is released on May 19. Later in May gives commencement address for daughter Anna's graduation from Leelanau School in Glen Arbor, Michigan.

1990 Publishes novella collection *The Woman Lit by Fireflies* (includes "Brown Dog," "Sunset Limited," and "The Woman Lit by Fireflies"). *Revenge*, feature film based on novella of same name, directed by Tony Scott and starring Kevin Costner, Anthony Quinn, and Madeleine Stowe, is released. Harrison receives screenwriting credit with Jeff Fiskin. Publishes preface to *Russell Chatham: One Hundred Paintings* (Livingston, MT: Clark City

Press). Contributes poem, "The Same Goose Moon," to limited-edition (126 copies) multiple-author chapbook *Book for Sensei*. Receives Mark Twain Award from the Center for the Study of Midwestern Literature and Culture for distinguished contributions to midwestern literature. Purchases a small adobe *casita* on Sonoita Creek in Patagonia, Arizona, and begins regular winter attendance, November through April.

1991   Publishes *Just Before Dark: Collected Nonfiction*. Publishes introduction, "The Chippewa-Ottawa," to George Weeks, *Mem-ka-weh: Dawning of the Grand Traverse Band of Ottawa and Chippewa Indians* (Grand Traverse, MI: Grand Traverse Band Tribal Council). In March publishes in *Esquire* the first of twenty-five monthly food columns, "The Raw and the Cooked," that continues through December 1993.

1992   Publishes *The Raw and the Cooked*, a limited-edition (126 copies) chapbook of three *Esquire* food columns, illustrated by Deborah Norden. Works on filmscript "The Last Posse," a western, for producer Douglas Wick and Harrison Ford, and a filmscript about photographer Edward S. Curtis for Columbia Pictures. Neither is produced.

1993   Contributes essay to Diana Guest's *Stonecarver*. Is subject of documentary film by George Luneau and Brice Matthieusent, *Jim Harrison: entre chien et loup* (*Jim Harrison: Half Dog & Half Wolf*). In October is honored by Institut Lumière in Lyon, France.

1994   Publishes novella collection *Julip* (includes "Julip," "The Seven-Ounce Man," and "The Beige Dolorosa"). *Wolf* (film) released (not based on *Wolf: A False Memoir*), directed by Mike Nichols and starring Jack Nicholson, Michelle Pfeiffer, and James Spader. Harrison is associate producer and shares screenwriting credit with Wesley Strick. Publisher and friend Seymour Lawrence dies.

1995   *Legends of the Fall* (film) directed by Edward Zwick and starring Anthony Hopkins and Brad Pitt is released. Wins Saturn Award for *Wolf* screenplay. Publishes introduction, "Hunting with a Friend," to Guy de la Valdène's *For a Handful of Feathers* (New York: Atlantic Monthly Press). Begins researching "Earth Diver," another novel about Dalva Northridge. French translator Brice Matthieussent publishes *Jim Harrison de A à W* (Paris: Christian Bourgois Editions). In December contributes the first of many short essays to *Kermit Lynch Wine Merchant Newsletter*.

1996   In January is a featured participant in fourteenth annual Key West Literary Seminar, "American Writers and the Natural World." Publishes *After Ikkyu and Other Poems* (Boston: Shambhala). *Carried Away*, feature film version of *Farmer*, directed by Bruno Beretta and starring Dennis Hopper and Amy Irving, is released. Critic Edward C. Reilly publishes monograph in Twayne's United States Authors Series, *Jim Harrison*, the first scholarly book in English to treat Harrison's career.

1997   Publishes introduction to *The Sumac Reader*, edited by Joseph Bednarik (East Lansing: Michigan State University Press). On March 5 is featured author for Portland Arts and Lectures program at Arlene Schnitzer Concert Hall. From May 17 to 19 is featured participant at eighth annual Etonnants Voyageurs (Astonishing Travelers) "Festival International du Livre" in Saint-Malo, France. Ends Hollywood screenwriting career. Publishes foreword, "High on the Hog," to Roger Welsch, *Diggin' In and Piggin' Out: The Truth about Food and Men* (New York: HarperCollins). On November 6 appears with Dan Gerber and Joseph Bednarik at Michigan State University event honoring *Sumac*.

1998   Publishes novel *The Road Home* in French in July, then in English in October. Signed copy of *The Road Home* left at Chef Mario Batali's Babbo Ristorante in Manhattan, initiating a close relationship. In September Copper Canyon Press becomes Harrison's poetry publisher and brings out *The Shape of the Journey: New and Collected Poems*. In mid-November attends International Festival of Authors in Toronto. Becomes contributing editor to *Men's Journal*, mass-circulation magazine, and consultant to Orvis sporting goods company.

1999   In Denver on April 8 is presented with seventh annual Evil Companions Literary Award (given annually by Center for Literary Publishing and *Colorado Review* to writer living in or writing about the American West). Wins Michigan State University College of Arts and Letters Distinguished Alumni Award. In May is honored at tenth annual Etonnants Voyageurs "Festival International du Livre" in Saint-Malo, France. *The Shape of the Journey* is finalist for Los Angeles Times Book Prize.

2000   Novella collection *The Beast God Forgot to Invent* (includes "The Beast God Forgot to Invent," "Westward Ho," and "I Forgot to Go to Spain") published in French in April, then in English in

October. *Chatter and Feathers: Little Ornithophagic Correspon-dence: November 1999–April 2000*, an exchange of letters with bibliophile and gourmand Gérard Oberlé, is printed in France in a limited run of 350 copies. Publishes autobiographical children's recovery story *The Boy Who Ran to the Woods*, illustrated by Tom Pohrt. Wins Spirit of the West literary achievement award from Mountains and Plains Booksellers Association. In October is awarded Michigan State University's Distinguished Alumni Award. On December 5 is included in *San Francisco Chronicle*'s "50 over 50" list of American writers in their prime. Ianthe Brau-tigan's *You Can't Catch Death: A Daughter's Memoir* (New York: St. Martin's Press) about novelist/poet Richard Brautigan appears with numerous references to Harrison.

2001   Begins writing book-length memoir. Serves as featured speaker at ceremony on May 4 marking Carnegie Mellon University's annual Pauline Adamson Awards for Excellence in Writing. In late May, inaugural meeting of Jim Harrison Society held at American Literature Association Conference, Cambridge, Massachusetts, which continues regularly until 2007, then irregularly. In Novem-ber publishes *The Raw and the Cooked*, collection of food col-umns, later named one of *Saveur Magazine*'s top food memoirs of all time. Also publishes *A Conversation*, limited-edition (two hundred copies) letterpress book of poems with Ted Kooser.

2002   Publishes *Off to the Side: A Memoir*, later chosen as a New York Times Notable Book of the Year. *Conversations with Jim Harri-son*, edited by Robert DeMott, published by University Press of Mississippi. *The True Bones of My Life: Essays on the Fiction of Jim Harrison*, by Patrick Smith, published by Michigan State Univer-sity Press. In February participates in interview and conversation with Peter Lewis at Lannan Foundation, Santa Fe, New Mexico. From May 8 to 10 serves as one of five featured writers at Ohio University's eighteenth annual Spring Literary Festival in Athens. From October 13 to November 20 goes on a ten-city book tour promoting *Off to the Side*. Besides appearances at independent bookstores, on October 30 is a visiting writer in Albany at New York State Writers Institute "Literary Conversations" series, on November 4 appears in a conversation with Will Hearst at Herbst Theater in San Francisco Public Library's "City Arts and Lectures" series, and on November 16 appears at Texas Book Fair in Austin.

Contributes introduction to *On the Trail to Wounded Knee: The Bigfoot Memorial Ride* by Guy Le Querrec (Guilford, CT: Lyons Press). Sells longtime residence in Lake Leelanau, Michigan, and moves to Livingston, Montana, to be close to daughters and grandchildren. Eventually purchases home with ten acres on Old Yellowstone Trail North in the Paradise Valley, a dozen miles south of city.

2003   Publishes *Braided Creek: A Conversation in Poetry*, an exchange in poetry with longtime friend, Ted Kooser, which wins poetry award from Society of Midland Authors. Begins contributing regular column, "Eat or Die," to *Brick*, a Toronto literary journal, and continues doing so for twenty-seven subsequent issues. In February is a featured author at international symposium, "New Writing in France and America," at Winthrop-King Institute for Contemporary French and Francophone Studies at Florida State University in Tallahassee. In November takes part with Guy de la Valdène and Peter Lewis in thirty-seven-course meal in France orchestrated by Gérard Oberlé and Chef Marc Meneau at the latter's L'Esperance. Parade of dishes drawn from seventeen cookbooks published between 1624 and 1823.

2004   Publishes novel *True North*. In February spends a week in Cancun and Merida, Mexico. On March 29, "Father Daughter," his first published short story, appears in the *New Yorker*. On March 30–31 serves as a featured writer at Western Carolina University's second annual Spring Literary Festival in Cullowhee. On May 9 is featured writer at Hailey, Idaho, Cultural Center. From May 14 to June 14 makes twelve-city *True North* book tour. Contributes introduction to new edition of Pablo Neruda's *Residence on Earth*, published by New Directions. Contributes food essay, "A Really Big Lunch," based on attendance at Chef Oberlé's sixtieth birthday celebration, to the *New Yorker*'s September 6 issue. On September 9 Deauville (France) Festival of American Cinema gives Harrison its annual Literary Prize for *True North*. Sells his beloved cabin in Grand Marais near Lake Superior in Michigan's Upper Peninsula. Contributes preface to Kermit Lynch's *Mes aventures sur les routes du vin* (Paris: Payot).

2005   Publishes novella collection *The Summer He Didn't Die* (includes "The Summer He Didn't Die," "Republican Wives," and an autobiographical essay, "Tracking"), which is a finalist for the Story

Prize. On March 24 gives tenth anniversary lecture at the Wallace Stegner Center at the University of Utah in Salt Lake City. In May travels to France for several weeks. "A Really Big Lunch" selected for *The Best American Travel Writing 2005*. Publishes *Livingston Suite*, a limited-edition (750 copies), fine-press chapbook illustrated by Montana writer/artist Greg Keeler. In September attends reception at Grand Valley State University in Allendale, Michigan, which announces acquisition of extensive Harrison archive and papers, purchased with funds from Meijer Foundation, to be housed at its rare book facility, Seidman House. In October travels with wife Linda for two weeks in northern Italy.

2006   Publishes poetry collection *Saving Daylight*. On January 18 performs a reading and conversation with US Poet Laureate Ted Kooser for the Lannan Foundation, Santa Fe, New Mexico. On January 25 reads with two other finalists at Story Prize event held at New School in New York City but does not win award. Poem "On the Way to the Doctor's" is included in *The Best American Poetry 2006*. Appears with novelist Russell Banks in ninety-minute revisionist documentary film, *Amerique, Notre Histoire*, directed by Jean-Michel Meurice. William Barillas's *The Midwestern Pastoral: Place and Landscape in the Literature of the American Heartland* (Athens: Ohio University Press) appears with chapter on Harrison. David Pichaske's *Rooted: Seven Midwest Writers of Place* (Iowa City: University of Iowa Press) appears with chapter on Harrison. In November begins first of several annual week-long visiting writer stints at Grand Valley State University. Conceives a literary pilgrimage project to visit graves of writers whose work was intensely interesting to him.

2007   Publishes novel *Returning to Earth*. In February Harrison Archive is officially opened to the public at Grand Valley State University's Special Collections library. In March is featured reader at Tattered Cover Book Store in Denver. On May 16 is inducted into Academy of Arts and Letters in New York. Academy's Citation reads in part: "His stories, novels, and novellas (a form he has brilliantly rescued almost single-handedly) make up as significant a body of work as that of any living U.S. fiction writer. Beyond that, his poetry alone places him in the first rank of U.S. poets. Not since Robert Penn Warren has an American so excelled in writing both fiction and poetry." On June 8–10 is keynote speaker at inaugural Sun

Valley Food and Wine Festival in Idaho. On October 10 gives public reading at Loosemore Auditorium of Grand Valley State University, which sponsors limited edition (five hundred copies) of
broadside poem "Old Bird Boy," printed by New Michigan Press.
On October 14 is featured author at Cleveland Public Library's
Sunday Afternoon Writers and Readers Series. With Peter Lewis
visits grave of Antonio Machado in Collioure, France, then grave
of Albert Camus in Lourmarin, and René Char's cemetery (but not
gravesite) in Isla-sur-la-Sorgue, then graves of Colette and Guil-
laume Apollinaire in Pere-Lachaise. On November 13 receives the
Medal of the City of Lyon, France. Copper Canyon Press reissues
Letters to Yesenin. In December Chef Mario Batali organizes a sev-
entieth birthday celebration for Harrison in Patagonia. Later that
month Harrison's French publisher, Christian Bourgois, dies.

2008   Wins Pacific Northwest Book Award for *Returning to Earth.* Publishes novel *The English Major,* which is later chosen by the *New
York Times* as a Notable Book and by *San Francisco Chronicle* as a
Best Book of the Year. Contributes introduction to James Welch's
reprinted novel *The Death of Jim Loney* for Penguin Books Clas-
sic Series. On July 10, appears in East Lansing with other Michigan
State University graduates Thomas McGuane and Richard Ford, at a
"Michigan Author Homecoming" sponsored by Michigan Humani-
ties Council. Provides foreword to Robert Bringhurst's *The Tree of
Meaning: Language, Mind and Ecology* (Berkeley, CA: Counterpoint).

2009   Contributes a foreword, "Nebraska Redux," to *Jim Harrison: A
Comprehensive Bibliography, 1964–2008* (Lincoln: University
of Nebraska Press) by Gregg Orr and Beef Torrey. Contributes
foreword to Wyatt McSpadden's *Texas BBQ* (Austin: University of Texas Press). In July, his interview with Jeffrey Brown is
aired nationally on television on *PBS Newshour.* On August 24 is
featured in an episode on Montana in Anthony Bourdain's television program, *No Reservations,* on the Travel Channel. Publishes poetry collection *In Search of Small Gods.* On October 5
gives public reading at Meijer Center for Writing and Michigan
Authors at Grand Valley State University. For fiftieth wedding
anniversary visits Calgary, Alberta, with Linda. October 19–21.

2010   Publishes novella collection *The Farmer's Daughter* (includes
"The Farmer's Daughter, "Brown Dog Redux," and "The Games
of Night"). Provides foreword to *The Charles Bowden Reader*

(Austin: University of Texas Press). In May, documentary film *The Practice of the Wild,* featuring conversation between Gary Snyder and Harrison and directed by John J. Healey, coproduced by Harrison and Will Hearst, and filmed at Hearst's San Simeon estate, debuts in limited circulation in San Francisco in May, then in New York, and in Lyon at Institut Lumière, and is accompanied by companion volume *The Etiquette of Freedom: Gary Snyder, Jim Harrison and "The Practice of the Wild"* (Berkeley: Counterpoint), edited by Paul Ebenkamp. With Peter Lewis travels in France. With celebrity chef Mario Batali conceives a book project on regional American culinary traditions, "On the Track of the Genuine" (never completed).

2011   Wins PEN Oakland/Josephine Miles Literary Award. In January contracts severe case of shingles. In May travels to France and Spain. Speaks at Banquet Litteraire in Paris on May 8. Makes his last visit to Lulu Peyraud's Provencal Domaine Tempier vineyard and restaurant. On September 7 reads at Elk River Books, Livingston, Montana, with Peter Matthiessen, Doug Peacock, and Lois Welch to raise funds for film version of James Welch's *Winter in the Blood.* Appears in François Busnel's documentary film series, *Les Carnets des Routes.* Publishes novel *The Great Leader: A Faux Mystery* and poetry collection *Songs of Unreason.* Journalist William McKeen's *Mile Marker Zero: The Moveable Feast of Key West* (New York: Crown Publishers) appears, including numerous references to Harrison.

2012   Awarded Officier des Arts et Lettres by France's Ministry of Culture for "significant contribution to the enrichment of the French cultural inheritance." William Hjortsberg's *Jubilee Hitchhiker: The Life and Times of Richard Brautigan* (Berkeley: Counterpoint) appears, with frequent references to Harrison. Tom Bissell's *Magic Hours: Essays on Creators and Creation* (San Francisco: Believer Books) appears with chapters on Harrison. John Knott's *Imagining the Forest: Narratives of Michigan and the Upper Midwest* (Ann Arbor: University of Michigan Press) appears with chapters on Harrison. Diagnosed with spondylolisthesis and spinal stenosis. On October 10 undergoes lengthy spinal surgery in Bozeman. Endures various physical setbacks and ailments following shingles, fusion surgery, and persistent postherpetic neuralgia. In November enters Mayo Clinic, Rochester, Minnesota, for pain abatement.

2013   Publishes collection of novellas *The River Swimmer* (includes "The Land of Unlikeness" and "The River Swimmer") which reaches number thirty-two on *New York Times* extended best seller list. Also publishes *Brown Dog*, a collection of all the Brown Dog novellas (includes "Brown Dog," "The Seven-Ounce Man," "Westward Ho," "The Summer He Didn't Die," "Brown Dog Redux," and "He Dog"). Contributes "A Note on Tom Hennen" to Hennen's *Darkness Sticks to Everything: Collected and New Poems* (Port Townsend: Copper Canyon Press). In June is visited in Livingston by staff of Paris *Le Monde*, which conducts interview and photo shoot.

2014   Publishes novel *The Big Seven: A Faux Mystery*, again featuring retired Michigan State Police detective Simon Sunderson. Wins Michigan Author Award given annually by Michigan Library Association for outstanding body of work.

2015   Elected Fellow of Boston's American Academy of Arts and Sciences. On March 15, serves on a panel with Luis Alberto Urrea and Clara Jeffrey for the Lawrence Clark Powell Lecture on "Charles Bowden's Southwest," at ninth annual Tucson Festival of Books, broadcast nationally on C-SPAN. In July filmed and interviewed in Livingston by François Busnel, "Encounter with Jim Harrison," for French television show *La Grande Librairie*. Wife, Linda King Harrison, seventy-four, dies October 2 in Billings, Montana, hospital. Later in October, Anthony Bourdain films short episode with Harrison for the seventh season of his *Parts Unknown* television show.

2016   Publishes poetry collection *Dead Man's Float* and fiction book *The Ancient Minstrel* (includes autobiographical "The Ancient Minstrel," "Eggs," and "The Case of the Howling Buddhas"), which debuts at number fifteen on *New York Times* hardcover fiction list. Dies March 26 of heart attack while writing a poem at his desk in Patagonia. On May 15, *Anthony Bourdain: Parts Unknown*, is broadcast on CNN. Terry McDonell's *The Accidental Life: An Editor's Notes on Writing and Writers* (New York: Knopf) appears with numerous references to Harrison. Organized celebratory tributes and memorials held in September at Pompadou Center in Paris, and in October at Orpheum Theater in Flagstaff, Arizona, Murray Hotel and Second Street Bistro in Livingston, Montana, and at Institut Lumière in Lyon, France.

2017   In March Grove Press publishes posthumous collection of food essays, *A Really Big Lunch*, with introduction by Mario Batali. In April American Academy of Arts and Letters in New York City sponsors a tribute featuring lifelong friend Thomas McGuane. On October 21 650-plus people attend "Jim Harrison: A Really Big Tribute: An Evening of Life, Art, and Stories" organized by Joyce Harrington Bahle, Joseph Bednarik, and Gary Wilson, and featuring Will Hearst, Judy Hottenson, Colum McCann, Michael Ondaatje, Stephen Sheppard, Gary Snyder, Doug Stanton, Douglas Wick, Robert DeMott, and others at Traverse City Opera House in northern Michigan.

2018   Independent, nonprofit publisher, Copper Canyon Press, in concert with Joyce Bahle, Brown Dog Productions, and the Harrison Family, initiates "The Heart's Work: Jim Harrison's Poetic Legacy," a fund-raising project to secure his poetry copyrights, keep his poetry in print, and underwrite future publications, including release of a paperback edition of *Dead Man's Float* (with the poem Harrison was writing when he died), and *The Essential Poems of Jim Harrison*, slated for 2019.

Conversations with Jim Harrison

Revised and Updated

A Chat with a Novelist

Jim Harrison and Thomas McGuane / 1971

From *Sumac* 4 (Fall 1971): 121–29. Reprinted in *Just Before Dark: Collected Nonfiction* (Livingston, MT: Clark City Press, 1991), 225–34. Reprinted with permission of Jim Harrison and Clark City Press.

When I turned up Deep Creek Road the sheep bordered the cattle guard and their "ba ba ba bahhs" seemed to reflect the question: why would anyone live here? But I drove on through the Engleman spruce and withered sedge for a few miles then turned when I saw BUSHWACK PALACE branded into a rail fence with McGuane, Prop., below it. I drove another mile through a pasture of sudan grass noticing the flattened rattlers with their clouds of flies on the road, a few conical piles of bear doodoo with even more flies and prairie falcons hovering in abstract gyres above the trail. Why not live here? I queried myself. When I drew up to the ranch which closely resembled the movie set from *Shane* Mr. McGuane's huge dog jumped bristling onto the car hood but her master's voice called and we walked through the darkened house to a yet darker study. I noticed Mr. McGuane looked a trifle old for his age which hasn't been determined though I would guess between the mid-twenties and mid-thirties. Like the redoubtable Pynchon he makes an unfortunate fetish out of privacy. *Pourquoi?* Who knows. Perhaps no one cares but that's not what we're talking about, is it? There was a two gallon swiveled decanter of cheapish gin and some ice on his bare desk. Mrs. McGuane, nee Portia Crockett, brought in a pewter platter of braised leeks and sweetbreads which we nibbled at with a chilled off-year Chateau Margaux. Mr. McGuane glowered as if this intrusion for the sake of contemporary letters was unwelcome. He put on a Linda Ronstadt and a Dolly Parton album and sang along rather loudly with them, not well I might add. My questions punctuated this noise with some difficulty.

Interviewer: Is it true what you said about Bob?
Tom McGuane: Nope.

Int: You seem to key off the Midwest in your work. You were born and raised there but you commute between Montana and Key West without a nod to Michigan and its rich literary milieu. Why?
McGuane: I have a genetic horror of the Midwest, a dark image of the past where Mortimer Snerd screwed three thousand times a day to build that heartland race.

Int: Oh.
McGuane: Yet I miss those piney woods, those beaver ponds and rivers, the feebs and dolts who run the bait shops and gas stations, the arc welders in the legislature, the ham with chicken gravy that poisoned me in Germfask when I fished the Driggs.

Int: You're not denying your roots?
McGuane: Cut that shit out.

Int: A.O.K. What do you think of the Drug Generation?
McGuane: The Driggs is a fine river for brook trout.

Int: Must I always be a wanderer between post and pillar, the virgin and the garrison, the noose and the cocktail lounge?
McGuane: That's your bizness.

Int: Who do you think is really good right now?
McGuane: Grass. Hawkes. Landolfi. Cela.

Int: Do you care to elaborate?
McGuane: Nope.

Int: Were it possible, how would you derive the novels you would like to write?
McGuane: Cervantes, De Rojas, Rabelais, Swift, Fielding, Machado de Assis, Melville, Gogol, Joyce, Flann O'Brien, Ilf and Petrov, Peacock, Dickens, Kafka, Chesterton, Byron of the letters.

Int: Do you think Nabokov excessively conumdramatic?
McGuane: Is that like hydramatic?

Int: You jest, mega-fop!

(A two day interruption was made here to attend a Crow Indian Pow Wow. The interviewer became very ill from semi-poisonous tequila which he mistook for white table wine. The Custer Battlefield of Thomas Berger fame was visited. How life imitates art!)

Int: Officially Montana is your residence, is it not?
McGuane: Yes, the bleak cordillera of the Absaroka consoles me.

Int: Why don't you live on one of America's marvel coasts?
McGuane: I'm glad you asked. I've been to those places. And the Left there to which I belong was developing an attitude toward the people of the interior and the unfashionably pigmented poor that is best described as racist. For example the Left implicitly considers any white born in the South to be congenitally evil.

Int: What about the whole "novel scene" now?
McGuane: Only that the serial preoccupations of fiction could be replaced by the looped, the circuited, and the *Johnny Carson Show*. Even something so ductile as an eclair has an inner dynamism not inferior to a hard-on or a terrified Norway rat.

Int: I think most of our readers are unfamiliar with your interest in pastry.
McGuane: It ends with eclairs and their analogue reality (or not).

Int: I wonder how many of our readers realized that your aunt was the celebrated Irish novelist Flann O'Brien?
McGuane: Very few.

Int: What other things come to mind that our readers probably don't realize?
McGuane: What is the name of your magazine?

Int: *Sumac*, which unfortunately some think is French for stomach.
McGuane: Well one of the things that *Stomach* readers doubtless fail to realize is that D. H. Lawrence was Norman Douglas's wife. It was the first society function hazarded by the widely resented "surfboard aristocracy" of Tasmania, also I might add their first transvestite wedding.

Int: Oh. One critic describes your fictions as being "laced with canals of meaning and symbolism."
McGuane: Yes, yes . . .

Int: Is that true?
McGuane: O yes, yes, yes . . . Why gee yes.

Int: What do you think of, I think it was either Granville Hicks's or George Steiner's contention, that fiction should be spelled "fickshun?"
McGuane: No.

Int: What of your fabled love of animals?
McGuane: I would handily commit three hundred acts of artistic capitulation to keep my dog in Purina.

Int: Why have you never mentioned the Budweiser Clydesdales in your work?
McGuane: O god, hasn't that been done to death?

Int: May I ask for the first sentence of your new novel?
McGuane: Of course. "Upstairs, Mona bayed for dong."

Int: MMMMmmm. How ironical. Yesterday in the local tackle shop I was told you had invented a new fly for trout.
McGuane: Yes, I call it the Republican Indispensable. You tie it up out of pig bristles and carp feathers.

Int: Have you ever caught Gila trout in New Mexico?
McGuane: No.

Int: Arizona?
McGuane: O, not at all.

Int: Are you offended by calling a large trout "Larry Lunker" as do many of our sporting writers?
McGuane: Au contraire. The term frequently hangs on my lower lip like a figment of dawn.

Int: Are you stoned?
McGuane: No, intermittently never.

Int: What constitutes a horse's ass in our literature?
McGuane: A difficult question! I'd say 1. parsimony 2. sure fire Babbitry 3. snorkeling 4. New York 5. San Francisco 6. Irving Berlin 7. this is your life not theirs 8. pick up sticks 9. Mary Jane and Sniffles 10. U.S.A. Meatland Parcels 11. a million baby kisses 12. a bad cold 13. corasable bond.

(Mr. McGuane ran out in the rain to install a new starter solenoid in his Porsche 911T. We then left immediately for the Black Foot Reservation in Browning, Montana, to see the birthplace of James Welch. We were there for three days. Mr. McGuane unfortunately mistook tequila for a widely known ginger ale, hence spent much time yodeling in the thundermug as the Irish would put it.)

Int: I'm interested in what you think of Barton Midwood's contention that the modern novelist has lost his audience. They've all gone to the beach.
McGuane: Hopelessly true. We're lucky if they've gone no farther than the beach. If they were at the beach a year ago when Midwood made the statement they are surely in Tibet by now.

Int: What is the last book you didn't write?
McGuane: *The Possums of Everest.*

Int: I understand you were working on a contemporary western but have abandoned it?
McGuane: Yes, the book was centered in Big Pie Country or Big Fly Country, whatever you will. The title was *Ghost Riff-Raff in the Sky.*

Int: Why did you give up the title *Wandell's Opprobrium*?
McGuane: It would have sent everybody to Tibetan beach.

Int: Don't you think the title should have been *Walkie Talkie*?
McGuane: Not at all.

Int: Your politics, rather the lack of them, is a point of interest to some critics. Do you have a comment.
McGuane: I suppose I am a bit of Left. America has become a dildo that has turned berserkly on its owner.

Int: Do you feel lionized?
McGuane: I feel vermiculized.

Int: Do you have any deeply felt interest in poetry?
McGuane: O, a great deal. So much in fact that I find myself overwhelmed. I would like to add this, for decades the Pruniers' restaurants have had the reputation of being the best seafood restaurants in the world.

Int: What of your college years?
McGuane: I graduated from Black Pumpkin in 1956. Since then, I might add, our Pumpkin group has dominated American letters.

Int: What about the underground?
McGuane: What about the underground?

Int: I mean what about the Underground.
McGuane: Oh. The Underground has become the Overground, in essence a parable of the Gay Caballero.

Int: Is that in the same genre as the Spanish Cavalier?
McGuane: No. Only that every hamster is a hostage to fortune.

Int: Have we touched on organic gardening?
McGuane: We had one of those things out at the end of the lawn. A lot of work. Then a certain horse named Rex got loose in the night and ate the whole plot to ground level. Sad to say but the most organic thing in the world is pus. I read it yesterday.

Int: Are any of your friends living in domes?
McGuane: Yes. I have a close friend who has built a $100,000 home that looks precisely like a Spalding Dot.

Int: The golf ball, I presume?
McGuane: Yes. From time to time he and his family can be seen scuttling in and out one of its pores. It's a noble way of life. Also, they have a duck inside with them.

Int: Where has everyone gone?
McGuane: Bolinas.

Int: All of them?
McGuane: All of them.

Int: For the striped bass?
McGuane: For the patchouli.

Int: Why did you call your dog Biff?
McGuane: Sprat.

Int: Dink?
McGuane: Frab. . . . [snit].

The interview terminated here. An inevitable tedium seized us. Mr. McGuane attempted to sing from Jarry's *Ubu Roi* accompanying a Merle Haggard record. Then he read to me from some aerosol cans he gathered in the bathroom: "Never spray toward face or open flame, avoid inhaling. If rash develops discontinue use. Contains riboflavin." etc. . . .

A Good Day for Talking: An Interview with the Author of *Wolf* and *Farmer*

Ira Elliot and Marty Sommerness / 1976

From *October Chronicle* 1, no. 1 (October 29, 1976): 16–23. Reprinted with permission.

Visitors travel northwest from Traverse City to reach his sixty-acre farm in Leelanau County. During the cold, crisp days of autumn the roadway is carpeted with decaying leaves—orange, red-orange, brown, all swirling in the cold, clear winds coming off Suttons Bay. Well off the main road one can see a two-story wooden house, a weather-beaten shed, and an old, tin barn. When guests pull alongside a yellow pick-up truck parked in a dirt driveway he steps out of his house wearing faded jeans, boots, and a blue flannel shirt. He shows the way into his home, one wall lined with books—from Hemingways to Dostoyevskys to Joyces—and into a small, modestly furnished living room, the sunlight slanting through a corner window. He serves up burgundy wine in giant goblets.

This is Jim Harrison in his environment, the rural northern Michigan he writes about. Born in Grayling in 1937, Harrison was one of five children born to a country agricultural agent and his wife. He spent his youth in Reed City and Haslett, then set off to college in nearby East Lansing. He was graduated from Michigan State University in 1960 with a bachelor of arts degree. After some years of confessed loafing and gallivanting about the country, he received his master's degree in comparative literature from Michigan State in 1965; his thesis was a paper explaining how he got his first poetry published. He will return to his alma mater this February for a poetry reading, though he finds East Lansing "frightful."

After completing his formal education he taught for a short time in New York, a job he says he could not do again. He married in 1959 and now has two daughters, with whom he has shared his farm since 1967. Harrison says his early reputation was founded on four volumes of poetry, *Plain Song*,

Locations, Outlyer, and *Letters to Yesenin.* But he now believes he is known primarily for his three novels. In addition to his books, he has written for *Sports Illustrated, Esquire,* and the *New York Times Book Review.*

His first novel, *Wolf,* concerns one man's quest for identity and freedom through the primal levels of nature and sex. *A Good Day to Die*—which still brings unkind words—is a statement about the decay of America's ecology and how a band of individuals try to turn back the tide of civilization by blowing up a dam. His most recent work, *Farmer,* published earlier this year, is the account of a middle-aged schoolteacher and his battle to choose between a nymphet student and a widowed coworker.

Compared to Hemingway, Henry Miller, James Dickey, even Rabelais, Jim Harrison remains an eclectic soul who generally avoids the literary crowd, preferring local farmers and country people. Yet he has travelled from coast to coast, in France, South America, and Africa. The only livable American city is San Francisco, he says, and when he visits there he and fellow author Richard Brautigan enjoy bar-hopping together. But such indulgences are permitted only two months a year; the other months are devoted to working, sometimes locking himself in a shed—during the summer—or upstairs in a bare room lined with John MacDonald novels, for up to nineteen hours a day.

He prefers Wakoski over Plath, Chandler over Hammett, Hunter Thompson over James Reston. He admires the stamina of Joseph's Nez Perce Indians, and borrowed Chief Joseph's quote "today is a good day to die" for the title for his second novel.

He here discusses his work (including his latest project, a comic novel about Traverse City), drugs, the Nobel Prize, hunting, sex, death, Michigan State, Detroit, movies, country music, literary critics, and on and on. Slowly a portrait of the man and the artist emerges. The picture starts here. . . .

Chronicle: What do you think of book reviewers and critics?
Jim Harrison: Well, I think there's a difference between book reviewers and critics. Book reviewers are largely what we call in the trade pork and beaners. It's such an ill-paying job that you find that anyone with a very distinguished intelligence is not interested. I mean the only people that pay well for reviews is the *New York Times.* I reviewed a few times a year for the *Times Book Review* and it pays decently. But your average newspaper reviewer doesn't pay well at all. No, I never pay any particular attention to them. I just got a big batch of reviews from Spain where *A Good Day to Die* came out, but I don't read Spanish so I have no idea what they say.

Chronicle: How long have you been writing?
Harrison: Oh, I started when I was sixteen. But you know how you start, it's largely a joke. It was another eleven years before I published anything. That was the first book of poems. I was living in Boston and sent some to a poet I'd heard about and she'd just become a consulting editor for Norton and she said "Do you have some more?" and I did and she took the book. Actually, when I signed my first book contract I'd never published anything in a magazine, which is sort of ass backwards. It was a stroke of luck.

Chronicle: Are you still writing poetry?
Harrison: Oh, yeah. That's the center, you know. I started out, actually, writing fiction—short stories—but I've never published a short story. I wrote about twenty but I couldn't even find them now. It's the most exacting form, to work within the short form, same thing with poetry. You start short.

Chronicle: Your work doesn't appear to be the work of an academician so why did you work to earn your master's?
Harrison: The worst thing about academic writers and people who teach writing or live within an academic atmosphere is that it shears them of a base. People think after they teach a while that academic life is a microcosm of the rest of the world, which it very clearly isn't. It's sort of . . . well, do you read Hesse at all? He wrote a book called *Magister Ludi* which is *The [Glass] Bead Game*, a very closed, extraordinarily provincialized atmosphere, which maybe it should be for its purpose, for teaching. But I think that's terribly unhealthy for the writer, unless it's a writer of a particular kind. Let's say if I just continued writing poetry I would have been cornered into having to take a teaching position. Literally no one can make a living as a literary novelist. Then I started writing longish type essays for the back of *Sports Illustrated* and they pay very well. So every time I'd write one of those I'd have three months to work on my own things.

Chronicle: Do you find the atmosphere more real here than in an academic community?
Harrison: I wouldn't say it's more real. God, there's nothing more unpleasantly real than an academic community. It's good to know every sort of person. In an academic atmosphere you're not going to know, say, the farmer down the road or the country bartenders.

Chronicle: How do you physically and mentally get set for writing?
Harrison: On a novel I crank up for a long time. I haven't written a

novel I haven't thought about writing for three years. When it gets ripe enough in my brain I just sit down and write it. I write the first draft in usually about six weeks. I work every day, all day. The kind of novels I've written, so far at least, you have to get it all down before you change your mind. The alternative is not bothering to write it at all. That's something you're fighting all the time, what (Thomas) McGuane calls the loss of cabin pressure. I've started another one the other day and this one I've been cranking up a long time. For the first time I've taken a lot of notes because it's more elaborately structured than any novel I've worked with before.

Chronicle: Can you tell us about this new work?
Harrison: No, or I'll lose interest. It has to be a little foggy in your head so you can have some surprises when you sit down. It'll be my first comic novel.

Chronicle: Do you know how it ends?
Harrison: Yeah, I think. But I might change my mind by the time I get there. But you've got to keep it a little bit juicy and fuzzy. It's like a woman. Sometimes if you know her too well you lose interest, but if you can keep them deliciously mysterious you can at least maintain the fantasy. So it's worth going on. I wrote a bunch of screenplays last year and it was helpful in the sense that I wrote one comedy. I'm working on an idea now for (Jack) Nicholson whom I got to know over the last year and I don't have any idea whether it will be made or not.

Chronicle: What literary form do you feel most comfortable working in?
Harrison: None more than the other. I think if you've messed around as much as I have you tend to feel fairly comfortable in all of them.

Chronicle: Is writing hard?
Harrison: Oh, God yes. It's very definitely work.

Chronicle: Do you enjoy the actual process of writing?
Harrison: Yeah, that's the big thing. That's the only real reward you ever get out of it, is the joy of making a novel, in creating it. The pleasure once you get a little older, not to sound like an old crank, but the pleasure you get out of a really good review is about a minute and seventeen seconds. Although a really bad review can cause you anguish for a couple of days. But the thing that keeps you going is the pleasure of actually doing it.

Chronicle: Do you ever look through your books after they're finished?

Harrison: No, that would be sort of unhealthy. Occasionally when I'm very drunk I'll just look to see what I said and you can get some surprises because you don't really remember writing parts of it and it does interest you if you've forgotten it.

Chronicle: In *Farmer* there is a part which says Joseph poured himself a whishkey. Was that a typographical error?

Harrison: Oh of course it was. That book is the most free of typographical errors. But publishers have proofreaders, then my wife does it, then my daughter does it, then I do it, and you still have some errors. There's a printer's superstition that there has to be one error in a book, too. That's odd.

Chronicle: Do you ever try to avoid what might be called literary circles?

Harrison: I think it's only dangerous if you spend too much time in them. I think there has been a certain disintegration in Vonnegut's talents since he's moved to New York City. You didn't see that in *Breakfast of Champions*, but I think you do in this new book *Slapstick*. I don't like it at all but maybe it's only a momentary lapse. But he was a latecomer and he wanted his little kick of being recognized. [Saul] Bellow said something beautiful once. He said loneliness to a writer—since it's basically a lonely trade—is like a giant whale trying to survive on a single piece of plankton.

Chronicle: Do you enjoy the recognition? Do you enjoy people coming into your home?

Harrison: No, I hardly ever let anybody into my home. I'm really awful that way. I generally run for the fucking closet. I'll admit if I'm in New York or something like that in a cafe it's nice to meet a lot of influential people that have actually read your work and want to see you and everything. But not on working days. I know a lot of people up here that actually read my novels but we don't talk about it; they don't bother me. A wonderful thing about living in a place like this is the privacy.

Chronicle: What do you think about contemporary novels and novelists?

Harrison: I think of my immediate generation, those people from thirty to forty, McGuane is the best. Ed Hoagland had a good essay and . . . it hasn't been a particularly juicy time for new novelists. I don't see all that many and I read addictively. I think it happened to the generation of the twenties.

You didn't have any great number of good writers but you had three or four fabulous ones, like Faulkner, Hemingway, Fitzgerald, Sherwood Anderson, Dos Passos, so on like that. Now the people a generation ahead of me, say those early forties or fifties, you have a great number of really good writers, but no fabulous writers. It's sort of a reverse of the twenties. You've got a lot of fascinating novelists but you can't say, no matter how much you like Norman Mailer or Philip Roth or Updike or any of those people, Updike, Hemingway or Updike, Faulkner. He's just not in that league.

Chronicle: Would you say Bellow, Faulkner?
Harrison: Yeah, I think almost. I really felt good about Bellow getting the prize because I don't know who else they could have given it to. Really an extraordinary mind. But I read most of what Mailer writes except his boxing stuff which is sort of projected nonsense. Every time Mailer used to get drunk, he wanted to arm wrestle somebody and you know anyone in any grain elevator throughout the Midwest would've knocked him silly in a second. Know what I mean? I read my friends, like Brautigan, McGuane. The best novel of the last decade was clearly [Gabriel García] Márquez's *One Hundred Years of Solitude*. It takes your breath away. Or Gunter Grass's *Tin Drum*. Fabulous book. I read everything Tom Berger writes, Peter Matthiessen I love too. There's a reverse snobbism, too. Someone like Ed Doctorow was a very literary novelist and nobody ever bought his books so he wrote *Ragtime*, which I thought was a lovely book, very entertaining. Then everybody comes down on his case for writing a mass appeal book like that. When I used to go around giving poetry readings and they hear you've written some screenplays, you're always getting lectured about integrity by full professors who make three times as much as you. They're on the take from the state, as it were. Oh, you've gone Hollywood, whatever that means. It's largely an assortment of pimps and coke dealers, that's what Hollywood is, you know? The pimps being the agentry. It's an amusing place once you get used to it. I really got a sense of non-arrival when I was sitting at the pool at the Sunset Marquis. I recognized the people on either side of me and I was trying to think . . . and on one side of me reading was Harry Reems of *Deep Throat* and on the other side was Kinky Freedman of Kinky Freedman and the Texas Jewboys. He's a wonderful character. Writers, I think, are sometimes productive to the extent that they remain sort of childlike about certain things. They stay operative for that reason. That's the other thing. How can you stay childlike when you're at a university?

Chronicle: Why do you write about ordinary people, outside the university community?

Harrison: Because the people in Morrill Hall [Michigan State University English Department] bore me. A farmer who lives with an allegiance to a two-hundred-thousand-year-old agricultural cycle is infinitely more interesting to talk to. They notice things, their head isn't so full that they can't see things. But that's coming down a bit too hard because I also like to talk to auto company executives on airplanes. That's really fascinating. They tend to bark when they talk. They always want to tell you how unhappy they are. You ever go into Beggar's Banquet? It's such a shock to get a good meal in this state in a restaurant. I went to Detroit once four years ago. That was unbelievable. I was supposed to do a story for *Sports Illustrated* on a bar pool so I took a local hustler and bartender from here and went down to Detroit. It was unbelievable. It's like the old West, everybody's armed to the teeth and shooting at each other. Totally grotesque.

Chronicle: Is that the only time you've been to Detroit?

Harrison: Yes. Except through the airport. I don't see any reason to go there at all. I met the executive editor of the *Free Press* and he asked me if I ever wanted to write anything for them and I said yes, I want to write about Detroit as a basement city. All the grief their teams have given me since I was a little boy. Following the Tigers and the Lions, and I followed them faithfully for twenty-five years. You get to be one of these old fools who sits around talking about Bobby Lane. You read Bellow?

Chronicle: Some.

Harrison: I don't know. I don't know what you're particularly interested in because I thought of the whole compulsion to write novels as one that you don't largely examine. This idea of the goose trying to watch himself lay the golden egg, he's not going to do it. I'm having fun trying to write a long comedy about Traverse City. Maybe I'll have to move away when it comes out.

Chronicle: Is there material?

Harrison: Oh, yes. It's just like every place else, all that sense of self-congratulation that small cities have. It's not any different than Babbittry in *Main Street*. Sinclair Lewis, forty years ago. Lot of extremely pleasant people, though.

Chronicle: What about Hemingway?

Harrison: I don't really think about him much. I started doing a column for *Esquire* which I ran out of patience with after five months just because I don't have anything left of my journalism boogie. So I wrote about five columns for *Esquire* under "Outdoors." They wanted me to do a column on Hemingway, and it was one of the most difficult things I ever tried because it was only six pages. It occurred to me that I never examined my feelings about him. In some senses he was just such a pompous, wretched human being, in that macho sense. On the other side he was an unquestionably brilliant writer. A lot to admire about what the man did.

Chronicle: What about the Hemingway comparisons?

Harrison: Oh, I don't like those at all. I don't see any similarities, but maybe that's unusual. You know he was a doctor's son and doctors' sons—this is another off-the-wall comment—are peculiarly arrogant for some reason. And I can like them very much. Growing up in northern Michigan in an agriculture family naturally I fished and hunted, then when you reach the age of majority and you start reading Hemingway and you write books yourself and then somebody tells you because you're fascinated with fishing and hunting you're like Hemingway. Well, that's nonsense, you know? Faulkner fished and hunted all the time but it wasn't so well publicized. But it's fun talking to people in Key West who are illiterate but used to know Hemingway. I once met an old Cuban fisherman down there and we asked him about Hemingway and all he said was he's a wonderful boxer and was like a hippie—he didn't wear shoes. And that's all he remembered about Ernest Hemingway, that he was a wonderful fighter and didn't wear shoes. I think Faulkner had it down pat when he said it doesn't matter if a good writer has a swimming pool because he's a good writer, and if a bad writer has a swimming pool doesn't matter because he's a bad writer. Something crazy like that. But that's a particularly Zen functional attitude that those people had. You know a marvelous writer like Henry Miller is a health-giving writer.

Chronicle: With whom you've also been compared.

Harrison: Yeah, I don't think about that too much. Anytime in my twenties when I got depressed, I could read someone like Henry Miller and get out of it. Such tremendous thrust from his own late liberation. He didn't print a book until he was forty-three, I think it was.

Chronicle: Who, then, do you think has influenced you?
Harrison: Oh, everybody influences you. You just usually resent it when you see it in a review.

Chronicle: One review said Rabelais. How about it?
Harrison: Oh, a little bit, yeah. I always enjoyed reading him. You learn technically how to put together a novel in an interesting way. McGuane said he learned more from Raymond Chandler about putting together a novel than anybody else, and I certainly feel that way. Chandler and John MacDonald. I love to read MacDonald. I've read all fifty of them. Other people you learn nothing from but enjoy equally. Like Joyce. After Joyce there's no follow-up to *Finnegan's Wake*. He took that particular form as far as it goes. What could someone conceivably write after that? But it was a very gradual process, taking thirty-five years of his life. Oddly enough, I like some of the late Hemingway. I loved *Islands in the Stream*. That was the first book where curiously enough he could write about his children. He'd softened to the extent that he was less concerned with his own heroics. It was sort of a twilighter, an autumnal book.

Chronicle: Have you seen Mary Hemingway's book?
Harrison: Oh, I read some reviews of it, yeah. I don't largely like that kind of book. Well, I'll read it probably but mostly it's a self-protective collection of gossip, probably. Though I guess she admits how bad he could be.

Chronicle: Would you like to talk about *Wolf*?
Harrison: If you'd like. *Wolf* is a strange book to me because what happens is you write a book and then you're all done with it and I still get kind of curious, off-the-wall mail from that book. I got a strange letter from a guy that parked cars in Indianapolis in these big car lots, and they have this little shed in the middle and somebody had a paperback of *Wolf* and he read it and this almost total illiterate immigrant wrote me this letter about it. You know you get that strange kind of response to some things you write. McGuane and I were fishing in Key West and he said, "You got a Guggenheim, why don't you write a novel?' What had happened was I had a terrible hunting accident. I'd fallen down a cliff and it really screwed up my back and I had to be in traction at Munson (Medical Center in Traverse City). I just sat there and said gee, why don't I write a novel. It's intensely autobiographical because I couldn't think of anything else to write about. It's probably 85, 90 percent autobiographical.

Chronicle: What's the connection in your work between hunting and nature and sex?
Harrison: I'm not sure where the nexus of that would be. I don't think I hunt acquisitively, and when I did I was never a good shot. I don't know if that could be construed as being more or less sexual or not. In hindsight I'd say *Wolf* was basically about freedom, the compulsion to be free and to work it out for one's self.

Chronicle: How did the idea for *Farmer* come to you?
Harrison: With the smell of a weed in the barnyard. I wanted to somehow pay some debt to a way of life that was almost totally vanished. That is, a small farm as a way of life. You know when you get done with a novel you're walking around in a daze, you've been so immersed in it it's just a delicious feeling to work for a long time on something that gives you a great pleasure. After you finish it, though, you tend to have a total postnatal depression. In seven, eight books now I've never found out how to avoid that. I wish I could. Most people never get totally wiped out except sexually, and that's really the only time you're freed of your ego. That's why people in the sixties loved acid as much as they did because it freed you, if only for eight hours. Then I think people got scared of it.

Chronicle: Joseph drinks quite a bit in *Farmer*, Swanson drinks and smokes marijuana in *Wolf*. What are your feelings about smoking dope and other sorts of drug using?
Harrison: I don't smoke very much dope. I don't know anything I can say very interesting about drugs that's worth quoting. Just about everybody smokes a little dope. I don't think it's mystical. But I think the only drug I've had real problems with in my life has been alcohol, which has to be considered a drug like any other drug.

Chronicle: Have you ever tripped?
Harrison: Oh yeah, yeah. Not any great deal. You know, it's a funny thing, at Michigan State in 1960, I heard from a friend that you could write away to get peyote, so we sent off and for fifteen dollars we got one hundred peyote buttons from Smith Cactus Ranch, which had some fame at the time in Albuquerque, New Mexico. Sure enough. In the mail they come in a big box. There's all these little green, rotty looking mushrooms, so we all sat there at night and just started chomping them down. We had absolutely no idea what we were doing, and you know, of course, about three days

later . . . bleah! It was one of those total overdose numbers. I did about fifteen buttons of peyote. That was an impulse that took me years to get over. Although it was a very positive thing, because I don't believe in tripping if you're going to control it all. I don't see the point in these people who take a half a tab of half-assed acid. What's the point in it? I think a lot of people who don't do it should have at one point, you know?

Chronicle: What are your feelings about women's liberation?
Harrison: Well, I've gotten into an awful lot of trouble with those people, and not through any meaning myself. It's just like Diane Wakoski on my last novel—she's a very brilliant woman and she had felt I was condescending to women in there. But that was a fictional prerogative. She knew from me myself that I wasn't particularly that way. But I've really gotten irrationally laced into by those people so often in reviews and so on that I always feel very beleaguered, that nothing I can say will be the right thing to say.

I've been married seventeen years—I'm absolutely for them getting every prerogative that they can get, that any male has. I think that it's delightful in the sense that women are getting predatory like men used to be. I think it's very nice for them. It seems to be a saner situation than it used to be. American males are so basically asinine about sex. I mean, look at things like *Oui* and *Penthouse* and *Playboy*. It's just really startling if you try to remove yourself and think about it. It seems like they would really go after those people. Maybe they do, I don't know. All this new, radical scientific information about female sexuality is really startling. This new Hite book [Shere Hite's *The Hite Report*] that just came out. She just proves even Masters and Johnson were sort of a Rube Goldberg operation.

Anything that eases pain and frees people, I'm for. I hate to be blamed, though, for all the generalized repression, and I've gotten that at certain poetry readings. I was going to bring suit against one anthology because they used one of my poems to demonstrate male chauvinism. But they also used Yeats's poem, the one that's about "No one could love you for yourself for not your beautiful hair" and all that kind of thing. And they used Jagger's "Honky Tonk Women."

Chronicle: A good collection.
Harrison: Yeah, Waylon Jennings actually sings that better than Jagger, because you know Jennings has at least had sufficient amount of experience in the area, where Jagger doesn't sing it with great conviction. It's a lovely song. But, since I've freed my own self, I don't want to be blamed for

anybody else's bondage. With women, it is a very individual case. They're really rapaciously throwing out dumb husbands now, which I think should have happened long ago. You notice how much more direct and aggressive women are compared to say, five, six years ago? And it's even gotten up here, totally. Women can go to bars alone now where they never used to. It's odd that it's all happened without people all noticing it.

Chronicle: In *Farmer*, Joseph's father, though dead, played a big part in his life.
Harrison: Well, I can't remember who this new lady is who is writing so much about death.

Chronicle: Elisabeth Kubler-Ross.
Harrison: Kubler-Ross, yeah. I talked to an analyst-poet friend of mine, who was at Michigan State for a while, about this situation. Death is about the most important thing that can happen to you mentally. I mean the death of someone you love very much. Because other than having the loved one taken away from you very abruptly, it also reminds you for the first time that you're going to die. I mean the utter reality of death. Well, [García] Lorca said, what's there to write about except love, and suffering and death? They're the most notable things that happen in your life. In terms of Melville, they're about incomprehension. You come to that final black well when somebody dies because you basically don't comprehend it. You can't. Your animal body can't comprehend it. You think you know about it, but until it happens, nobody comprehends it at all.

Chronicle: In *Farmer* when Joseph's mother dies, the euthanasia bit was pretty subtle yet powerful. What about that?
Harrison: This tripey Jesuit at Notre Dame really attacked me for that in some review. Why sure, that's the hope for the naturalness of the book, of course. They're going to let her die and help her along, because that form of pain—that's why I picked stomach cancer—is the most brutal pain conceivable. You're never free from it. There's no pain like that. The body is literally rotting from the inside. That's what Mailer called the wild orgy of lost cells. Christ, it's up to the person, in my mind. When there's no recourse, some choose to live and some choose . . . I like that new California bill that lets people make that choice. These life support systems of course are so extraordinarily subtle now that they keep you cooking until the last cell gives up the ghost.

Chronicle: What are your favorite motion pictures and who are your favorite directors?

Harrison: Directors, I like Bergman, Fellini, Truffaut. I like crappy movies. I have a great appetite for junk like Don Siegel does, like *Dirty Harry.* I loved it. I've watched it about four times. It was entertainment. You had a real villain. That guy had to be the nastiest human being in the history of American fiction. Siegel does it so unfairly, it's really an extraordinarily fascist, junkie movie. He sets it all up. Once the guy pulls the girl's tooth out, everybody wants him to be blown away, when big Clint Killgood comes up with his .44. But see, people want Nicholson's characters rough. He knows how to choose scripts. He's a brilliant man. Did you see *Cuckoo's Nest?* A wonderful movie, I thought.

Chronicle: What about Robert Altman?

Harrison: I like *McCabe. Nashville,* I thought, was horrid. I love country music. None of them were good, except Keith Carradine. That song was the only good song in there. The rest of them were sort of parodic rip-offs. Real country music doesn't have irony in it. When you let all of these flaky actors make up their own country songs, its abuse of freedom. I enjoyed it in the sense I enjoy all Altman movies just to look at, but as a movie it was too self-conscious.

Chronicle: You didn't mention Kubrick.

Harrison: I'm not too crazy about Kubrick. It's too self-conscious again. I liked *2001* and I liked that one he made out of the Anthony Burgess novel [*A Clockwork Orange*]. That was a delicious movie. I didn't see that new one [*Barry Lyndon*]. I understand it's very boring. I don't see how you can do anything with someone like Ryan O'Neal. I don't want to be reminded that we're seeing a work of art in progress. I want the raw meat thrown on the floor. I want the work of art there instead of it being self-actuating, like the least successful Truffaut movie to me is *Day for Night,* which is a movie about a movie. The only person who seems to get away with that is Fellini, because he has a marvelous sense of humor . . . The same thing in a novel—I get tired of novels about professionals. *Wolf* is a novel about a professional, as opposed to the other two novels which were about people. But I don't know, that's a fine line. One of the great novels of the twentieth century was Joyce's *Portrait of the Artist as a Young Man,* so maybe I'm a little bit supersensitive about that. The most inspirational literature I ever read was Dostoevsky or Camus. Then I believe his assertions when he says you only have one choice in your life: it's whether or not to commit suicide. If you don't commit suicide, you have to treat your life with a great deal of energy and assertiveness. As a novelist, you don't want to withhold the evidence. I think that's the error in some of Hemingway's fiction as opposed to Faulkner, who had more of a tendency to allow them to be whole human beings. Hemingway had a tendency to the ideology.

Chronicle: What response to your work is most gratifying?
Harrison: I don't know. I think the best thing I ever heard was something Kafka said, "A book should serve as an axe for the frozen sea within us." If a book doesn't sort of break up your mind a little bit and give you a new sense of people, however small, then it's not worth reading.

Chronicle: What about John Gardner, John Barth, and Thomas Pynchon?
Harrison: Gardner I've never been able to read. Barth I could read—the early Barth but not the late stuff. By the time he got to *Giles Goat-Boy*, he sort of lost me. *End of the Road* I loved. I think that's the best Barth novel. And Pynchon, I didn't like *Gravity's Rainbow*, but what's the previous novel? *V.*, yeah. I liked *V.* But you can't be nationalistic, you have to look far and wide for your reading interests. There's no sense of talking about thinking about Pynchon when you've got someone else who did the same thing so much better, like Gunter Grass in *Dog Years* or *Tin Drum*. Everybody can have reverence for Faulkner or reverence for Hemingway, but that kind of novel has stabilized. It's a static experience in the past, largely about heroics which no longer has a top. The world had a top for Faulkner and it did for Hemingway. There were those old eternal verities: duty, honor, love, pride, pity. But we don't quite live with that world anymore. It's much nastier in many respects and the lines have blurred much more than they were before. The literary brain now has a great deal less structure.

Chronicle: Have you heard they are making a movie of Hunter Thompson's *Fear and Loathing in Las Vegas*?
Harrison: I don't see how they can. I always used to believe his political articles because when he first heard about Watergate rather than rationalizing and making a big sententious paragraph about it he said, "What I really want to do is take a gunny sack full of dead rats down to the White House and throw it over the fence." As an image it's much more convincing than someone like James Reston going on pompously for pages and pages.

Chronicle: Why do you want to write a comic novel?

Harrison: I don't mean comic in terms of slapstick. I mean comic in the classical sense that everything is not tragic. In good comic novels people die. I just wanted to tilt my world. I never can bear to do the same thing in two books in a row.

Chronicle: Where do you want to be in ten years?

Harrison: I just want to write some more novels.

Author's "'Hot, Hopeless" Life Mixes with Success

Karin Winegar / 1983

From *Minneapolis Star and Tribune*, March 8, 1983, C14. Reprinted with permission.

Jim Harrison would be equally at home gutting a grouse, sampling a '63 Chateau Latour, or discussing James Joyce.

Afloat in his conversation are bits of literary flotsam, references to Truman Capote, J. P. Donleavy and Kurt Vonnegut, tales of friends Jack Nicholson, Gary Snyder, and Peter Matthiessen, anecdotes about Zen roshis chugging fifths of Bushmills, and remembrances of a recent winter in Costa Rica "where the most attractive girls conceivable were two for twenty-five dollars."

Despite what he calls his "hot and hopeless" life, his books are tightly constructed, spare tales of irreverent, adventuresome men on emotional quests. At forty-four, he has been hailed by many critics and writers as one of the greatest fiction writers of this century.

Harrison broke into view in *Esquire* magazine in 1978 with a selection from his novella "Legends of the Fall." It was followed by the publication of three novels—*Farmer, Wolf,* and *Warlock*—and five collections of poetry.

He recently ventured out of the seclusion of his home in Michigan to conduct writing workshops at Hamline University and the Loft and to submit to bouts of media interviews in the Twin Cities.

Harrison arrived at the Loft three days earlier in scuffed cowboy boots, work pants, and a down vest, looking as if he had just come in from tracking javelinas or hunting elk on horseback, and asked, "Where can I get a drink?"

Now he prowled his hotel room shoeless in gray work pants and a blue short-sleeved shirt. A Scotch bottle, vitamins, half a dozen plastic coffee cups and Mr. Donut bags cluttered a room lit by a soundless color television.

Flopping on his stomach on a frayed, tan terrycloth bathrobe snarled among a jumble of bedclothes, he smoked a cigarette and talked.

His gull-wing eyebrows, swept-back hair, and the weary creak in his voice strongly evoke his friend and business partner Jack Nicholson, but the gap in his front teeth and his off-kilter eye give him a *bandito* cast.

He finished off the Scotch from a leaking plastic cup and autographed a book for a fan, signing his name with a little one-eyed caricature of himself.

Harrison has made only three workshop forays in the past seven years.

"I have an intense curiosity about Minnesota," he said. "I was here for the National Endowment for the Arts about twelve years ago. I was cracking up then; it was the middle of the winter and I was alone in Minneapolis. So I wanted to come back here just to see if it looked different. This is a well-paying gig, too. And it's not a lot of fun in northern Michigan in February, either."

"Midwesterners are charming," he added. "I'd done this at Yale and Harvard, and that was different because they have that arrogance of a sophomore. But here in the Midwest they tend to be flat and utterly sincere. They actually want to know something, something disingenuous like, 'How do I get to be a writer?' And it's quite sweet. It's utterly without irony."

Harrison's friends seem to be a roistering, irreverent pack that included Jimmy Buffett, Nicholson (whom he met on the set of *Missouri Breaks*, written by another friend, Tom McGuane), and Hunter Thompson. Harrison plays and socializes as hard as he works. "The axis I used to travel on for about three years until I came to my senses was between Beverly Hills, New York, Key West, Palm Beach, or Aspen," he explained. "But you do that and you are excluding the nature of reality in the twentieth century."

He still visits Nicholson in Aspen, however, which he describes as full of "orthodontists' children with pickup trucks and golden retrievers, hard-core alcoholics and major-league drug dealers, guys that are limping 'cause they've got about thirty grand in their boots, and people who offer you a toot from one of those 35mm film containers. But I quit doing drugs because it breaks down the social fabric—it rends the social fabric," he said with a chuckle.

Harrison never took a writing course and is skeptical about academic training of would-be writers.

"Maybe it can be taught, but I don't think I can teach writing," he said. "If the Loft was at the university, I wouldn't have come. I feel a vertigo and nausea around universities 'cause I think I was so unhappy at Michigan State, which is the flip side of this place. And at big colleges I still feel like it's like cafeteria food—there's no range in the spectrum. It's tremendously homogenized and bland. The main reason I won't go to see a publisher in Sweden is because it's a country without garlic."

"My stuff does better in England and France than here—they picked up Faulkner first, too," he continued. "I guess it's because he was part of the Eastern Corridor. I've observed that within what we could think of as the Balkanization of American literature, all the so-called effective power resides in the East. But they hate you if you are making a lot of money. And when I start making money, I behave like Leon Spinks."

He began writing at sixteen and says he felt "very arrogant and wonderful because I had chosen to be an artist like John Keats in this little school in northern Michigan. And at the same time, I was a linebacker and all that, too."

He married early and has two children (now twenty-two and eleven years old) with whom he shares his secluded Michigan home.

"I got married so I wouldn't die," he said. "I had the sense to get married 'cause I realized if I continued behaving the way I was, that I would die, and I became very fearful. What was I doing? I would hitchhike to San Francisco, then hitchhike to Boston, and then back again. I once got a ride from Indiana to Los Angeles with a bigamist from Philadelphia—three days of riding together. One time when I left for New York, my dad took me out to the highway. And all I had was a cardboard box with rope around it with my typewriter in it and my favorite authors, which were Rimbaud, Dostoyevsky, and Faulkner. And off I went to New York to be a bohemian."

"Now I want first class all the way. At my age, I loathe any form of discomfort or inconvenience. If my mousse isn't just right, I'm almost in tears." Harrison requires years to construct his characters before committing them to paper. Then the work may burst out in a few months of intense writing.

"And then I can't write another one for a couple of years, so that's when I do some first drafts of screenplays to make enough money to write the kind of novel I write." (He has written and sold nine, none of which has been filmed).

"Three years ago, I totally burned out," he said. I'd done four screenplays in one year, 'cause I wanted to see what it would be like to make really a lot of money. And I really made a pile; I bought a charter boat, a lot of bad stocks. We redid our house and built an enormous kitchen which cost 140 grand, and I paid for it in cash 'cause I hate debt. And I bought a summer place and another 130 acres adjoining our property. So I burned out and took nine months off. I basically sat and looked at the river."

When not writing, brooding, cooking, or traveling. Harrison spends several weeks a year tarpon fishing in Florida (he releases the fish alive) or hunting.

"What's important to me? My family. Bird hunting. I don't hunt mammals. I'm a good tracker and I go out with friends and follow deer through swamps, and they shoot it and eat it. Six of us once ate a whole deer in one day. But we had two cases of great Bordeaux with it. I've got a great wine cellar and it's nice to drink a great wine with venison or woodcock or grouse."

Critics and feminists have accused him of writing with a sort of Hemingway macho.

"I never was that interested in Hemingway," he said. "My brain tends to be sort of hot and hopeless and his heroes were always cool and collected and knew what they were doing. I've never been able for long to behave on that presumption, although I can carry it off for a while when it's really necessary."

"I get terribly exhausted about this macho thing. Christ, here I am a nice person who's never hit a woman, never raped anybody, been relatively happily married, so I get hung with this. So I say no, you've got it wrong, it's 'nacho,' not 'macho.'"

Harrison is currently working on "my first monster. There's a danger because big things are much easier to write: it's just a matter of typing something. But I've decided it's time to do something utterly ambitious."

An Interview with Jim Harrison

Kay Bonetti / 1984

From the *Missouri Review* 8, no. 3 (1985): 65–86. Reprinted in *Conversations with American Novelists: The Best Interviews from "The Missouri Review" and the American Audio Prose Library*, ed. Kay Bonetti, Greg Michalson, Speer Morgan, Jo Sapp, and Sam Stowers (Columbia: University of Missouri Press, 1997), 39–55. Also available in a longer, unedited version with additional material on audio cassettes from the American Audio Prose Library archive at the State Historical Society of Missouri (1-573-882-1187; http://shsmo.org/manuscripts/Columbia/c3851). Reprinted by permission of Kay Bonetti and American Audio Prose Library.

Interviewer: Could you tell us about your publishing history? You published a whole book of poems without ever having a single poem published.
Jim Harrison: I'd heard Denise Levertov read and I never published anything in my life. So I sent her poems and she wrote back that she'd just become the consulting editor at Norton and if I had more poems like this she would publish a book. After I got the book contract, I sent some poems off and they came out about the same time as the book, but that was true. It was an accident.

Interviewer: What happened with *Wolf*? How come you moved from three volumes of poetry to the novel?
Harrison: I fell off a cliff. I was in the hospital for a month and went into a coma and almost died. I sort of woke up and I couldn't do anything. I had to wear a body corset because I'd torn the muscles away from my lower spine. So Tom McGuane called me up and says, "Now that you're laid up, why don't you write a novel?" I said, "Jeez, I don't want to think about writing a novel." "Write a sort of autobiographical novel," he said and I said, "Okay, goodbye." Then I started writing the novel. I wrote *Wolf* in six weeks or a month. I sent it off the day before the mail strike, years ago, and the only copy of it was lost for a full month. I didn't even think it was important, because I didn't think of myself as a novelist. I wasn't very attached to it.

I'd sent it to my brother to make a copy because we were real broke. So he finally went into the New Haven post office and dug it out of the pile of mail there. I don't know how he managed that, but he's authoritative. Then the publisher got it and took it.

Interviewer: You also wrote some novellas . . .

Harrison: I always loved the work of Isak Dinesen, and Knut Hamsun, who wrote three or four short novels, so I thought I would have a try at it. I called the first one "Revenge"—my Sicilian agent gave me a little motto that struck me: "Revenge is a dish better served cold." The second of the novellas is called "The Man Who Gave Up His Name." I wrote it in a time of extreme mental duress. I envisioned a man getting out of the life he had created with the same intricate carefulness that he'd got into it in the first place. I suppose I was pointing out that if you're ethical you can't just disappear.

Interviewer: You've described yourself as a sensual Calvinist.

Harrison: Maybe that's true. I wrote a poem in which I said John Calvin's down there under the floorboards telling me I don't get a glass of wine till four o'clock. Not 3:57, but 4:00. I was talking to Kurt Ludkey last night about how if you're a total workaholic and you also drink too much you tend to control it, but that doesn't make you less of an alcoholic. It's just that you never, never have more drinks than you can remember.

Interviewer: Can you really drink like that?

Harrison: I have done that for years. I had a little trouble in my early thirties with it and then I began tightly controlling it. I went down to a Mexican fat farm in January because I was so exhausted from my novel. And I felt grotesque, I felt about like I do right now. So I didn't drink anything. I expected it would be awful and nothing happened. I didn't feel anything. Reagan's immigration chief was at this fat farm, and I said to him, "Don't you realize that you guys are hassling the greatest writer in the world about getting in and out of the United States?" I was talking about Márquez, who's the only writer on earth that I admire without qualification. He said, "Oh I didn't know that, what's the guy's name, we'll see what we can do."

Interviewer: Have they been denying him a visa?

Harrison: Yeah, they've been giving him trouble because they know he stops and sees Castro. But you know what he and Castro do all the time?

Cook. They cook all night. He gets there and he has fresh stuff he's picked up in Caracas or Mexico City. They cook veal and chicken, everything like that. And drink of course.

Interviewer: Your books are full of great cooks.

Harrison: What I always like in Boswell is the idea that if you're obligated to eat two or three times a day, you may as well do a good job of it. I once stopped to see John MacDonald and Betty Friedan was there and she asked me why I was so obsessed with cooking. I said, "Why, I cook to avoid adultery." And she says, "My God, are you a mess! To say such a thing." But it's sort of true. When I started cooking frequently, at least three times a week, my wife enjoyed it because it's no fun cooking if you have to cook all the time. And I could avoid going to the bar when I finished my work day.

Interviewer: A lot of writers seem to have problems with alcohol. Do you think there's anything necessary about the life of the writer that leads to extreme pain?

Harrison: Well, no. I think it's partly the profession. You're alone most of the time. You're creating other worlds all the time. And it's what Walker Percy talks about in that last book of his—it's the reentry problem. You know how I say, or, I have my narrator say, "It's your return to earth like some kind of burned out satellite." Something like that. Alcohol is the sedative when you finish the day's work—it helps you to re-emerge into the world.

Interviewer: Would you say that your personal life has been something of a stabilizing force?

Harrison: Oh my, yeah. You know I've been married twenty-four and a half years. Not in the clingy sense, it's just the way I prefer to live. Every time I think I'm a mess, a total mess, I sort of look around and find out that I'm not quite a total mess. It's like McGuane said, that alcoholism is a writer's black lung disease. Which is sort of true. But even that I seem have under control. I suppose that's a moralistic urge. Just to control. To control it.

Interviewer: You have that passage in *Sundog* where Strang says something about having made up rules when he was a kid. The narrator, Harrison, says, "I love rules." Can you tell me some of the rules?

Harrison: Do I have any fresh rules? Yeah. I was on page like 197 of that novel manuscript before I realized I was writing about my alter ego, and it blew one writing day. It totally terrified me.

Interviewer: How so?

Harrison: Strang worked on eleven dams, and I'd written eleven books. I mean it got that bad. And I felt utterly crippled. Just like Strang's been crippled by his work. I said, "Oh my god! Can I go on?" Well the energy of the novel had taken over, so it didn't matter.

Interviewer: The book is, by no means like, but reminds me of, *The Secret Sharer*. You wonder at the end about the secret sharer. Whether or not it's one person or two.

Harrison: That's giving me goosebumps. James Hillman, who's a Jungian psychiatrist, said that thing I quoted, "The notion that there's a light at the end of the tunnel has mostly been a boon to pharmaceutical companies." I love that.

Interviewer: Would you explain that?

Harrison: Well, tranquilizers and everything like that. It's because people think they can't bear the nowness of now. They can't bear the present tense. In Zen terms they're either rehearsing something they've already done, to make it come out right. Or they're expecting something to occur in the future. Or trying to change the past. It's like somebody might say, I'm revising my memoirs. I mean something ludicrous like that. A person like Strang is free from dread because he's consented totally to the present. Whereas the narrator, which is another portion of me, can't, can't accept anything.

Interviewer: Where did you get the character Strang?

Harrison: My brain. I met a few people, in an outward way, that did what he did. And I tried to create the kind of person they would become. On frequent trips all over the world, I would meet these men sometimes in hotels, and I'd ask them what they do. I met one in Costa Rica that was a foreman on a huge construction project, and in charge of 32,000 workers on this dam in the Amazon Basin. He was self-educated, from Tennessee. I became more and more interested in these people and then the character took shape. I wanted to create a hero who was free from dread. Dread and irony have gotten to be literary addictions. And I noticed there are some people that live without it. So I created this character named Strang. When I was thirteen I read about King Strang over here on Beaver Island. He was a Mormon apostate, and he had fifty girlfriends or wives. When you're thirteen you're horny as a toad and you don't even have one girlfriend and here's a guy that's got fifty. So this is what I had in mind. A man free from dread.

Maybe that's what I wanted—to be free from dread. I mean besides wanting a drink, I also want to be free from dread.

Interviewer: It has been said that Strang is the metaphor for the artist. How much do you use yourself, in your work?
Harrison: Strang isn't me though.

Interviewer: What about the sub-title, "As Told to Jim Harrison."
Harrison: That was just to have fun. Like Nabokov, I did that to throw people off the track. It is a little bit myself, but I had to have a contrast to Strang. I had to have somebody coming from way outside, coming into this world. And I had to know both people. You could say they're almost extremities of the right and left lobes of the same head.

Interviewer: You wrote this novel as a para-journalistic escapade.
Harrison: I was just pissed off. Everything is a novelty. Somebody's most utter and terrible grief is a minute and a half of the evening news. That kind of thing. I was thinking of David Kennedy at twelve sitting in that hotel room watching his father die. He didn't ever get over it.

Interviewer: Strang says almost immediately, "Tell me something bad that you've never really gotten over."
Harrison: I forgot I said that. But that's it. Like his niece can't get over being raped, any better than Karl can get over it. Karl was a strange character. Some people wanted more of him but Karl's effective because there's not more of him. He's the kind of guy that's terribly sensitive but often verges on being the town bully, because he is so eccentric. Karl on a surface level is very attractive to some people for the same reason they like Clint Eastwood. He got back at them. Tom McGuane had a motto over his kitchen door saying "Getting even is the best revenge." And that's okay, but Steve McQueen was out there and he looked at the motto and he said, "Tom, even *I'm* not that bad. That's really going too far."

Interviewer: In many ways that book is as much the narrator's book as it is Strang's.
Harrison: Well, it's unpleasant because everything the narrator could say is true to my experience. But you need a contrast. Strang isn't Strang if the whole book is Strang. The narrator comes to Strang. It's almost like that notion of monkey brain. You can't often evaluate yourself because it's your

own brain that's evaluating your own brain. Supposedly what removes us from animals is that we can stand back and look. But it's sometimes confusing. My cabin is the cabin that Strang is living in. So I go up there and I say, "Oh, my god, now I'm living in this novel, and I'm not sure which one I am."

Interviewer: And you took a swim like Strang, to test that swim.
Harrison: Last summer I did. I swam down the river.

Interviewer: Are you that strong a swimmer? Can you swim like Strang swims?
Harrison: Yeah, I used to swim. I remember when I was ten I swam twelve miles. When I was seven, there was a loon on our lake, and I never could get close to it, so I thought, "I'll trick the loon, go out at night and try to catch her." So I snuck out of the cabin, off I went in the dark. When I was getting ready to finally write that novel, I did something similar for that last scene. It's two o'clock in the morning, I've had a few drinks. I locked my dog in the cabin, went down the steps to the river, took off my clothes and swam with the current way down the river, and over two log jams in the middle of the night so I could get that feeling. It's very strange to swim down a river at night alone, naked. But that enabled me to imagine that last scene, say Julian and his son were down there, you'd see those lights off the trees, just the car lights way down.

Interviewer: The narrator and Strang are two sides of one being, together, it seems like. And the telling of the tale is the revelation of the wedding.
Harrison: What the narrator was finding in Strang is maybe what I found in the left side of my brain. And the tape device amplifies it, which is fun, because you have the more formal narrator, then you have the narrator off-the-wall. And some of the inserts have the narrator wondering what he's going to eat, wondering how he's going to get laid. Textural concretia, the "thinginess" of life. That's an old rule I have on the wall. Make it vivid.

Interviewer: Did you feel like you were taking a chance by letting in the possibility that Strang and the narrator really are brothers?
Harrison: No, I was flirting with that. No one will ever know. The only one that knew died.

Interviewer: The narrator is flirting with it. He wants to play with it and he doesn't.
Harrison: It was just an interesting possibility. But of course it's true.

Interviewer: They are brothers?

Harrison: It doesn't matter if they're blood brothers or what kind of brothers. That was all sort of unconscious. You write and you don't even know what you're writing when you're writing it. It just emerges.

Interviewer: At what point did you start realizing that you had a subject out of writing from what you know?

Harrison: Well, death did it to me. You can see it in my first book *Plain Song*. If people die then you better get down to business.

Interviewer: This was your father and sister? They died in a car accident.

Harrison: That was part of it. That was when I was twenty-two and I'd been writing since I was sixteen. I wanted to write poems like John Keats.

Interviewer: You started out wanting to be a poet?

Harrison: It was all the same to me. I'd read those romantic novels about artists like Vincent van Gogh and I was thinking that's what I want to be. I wanted to be a wild artist and have lots of love affairs and live in strange places. I have.

Interviewer: But I take it you've found out it's a lot more of a discipline than you thought?

Harrison: Oh, that's all it is. It's what Stevens said: technique is the proof of your seriousness.

Interviewer: Are you happy with *Sundog*?

Harrison: I don't know. It wouldn't occur to me to be happy with something I wrote. It's not healthy to even think about it.

Interviewer: After you've done it?

Harrison: Nope. It's all gone. I mean you're making me think about it now and it's not unpleasant. It's sort of interesting to get somebody else's point of view.

Interviewer: So you don't worry about judging or assessing your work?

Harrison: I don't think I'm very competitive about it. I don't see it as a horserace, the way some novelists are always rating each other. You know how in New York every day they take each other's temperature to see who's hot. I don't think that way too much.

Interviewer: You don't look back on a book and say I learned this problem in this novel?

Harrison: Oh, yeah. You do that to some extent. You write sometimes to find out what you know.

Interviewer: Do you think that the skills you learned in writing poetry transferred into your novels?

Harrison: Very much. Trying to bear down on the singularity of images. Movement. Those suites were good training for moving from image to mood to mood. It's like Mailer says, "Boy, if you're worried about getting people in and out of rooms, you've already blown it." The reader can get anybody they want in and out of rooms. They don't need your help.

Interviewer: You often use animals in your work.

Harrison: It's the same idea that the Indians had. One is naturally drawn to certain animals more than other animals. Now I like crows and coyotes and pigs for some reason.

Interviewer: Have you ever thought that out?

Harrison: I could pretend that I don't know what the associations are, but I do. The coyote is a sorcerer amongst animals. He's the trickster, he's the humpbacked flute player. He's an animal of immaculate, precise, and varied means. Intense curiosity, but cagey. I think I like that idea. And a crow is a garrulous semi-predator, semi-scavenger. Sort of foolish, but smarter than other birds. He just likes to fool around. Squawk all the time.

Interviewer: You mentioned pigs. . . .

Harrison: Yeah, I had a pet pig when I was a kid. But you know they're all going to get killed in November. It's a bit of a disappointment. Was it Hugo that said, "All of us are condemned to death with an indefinite reprieve"? A sort of catchy idea. He says that the ultimate that a human leaves is his skull.

Interviewer: You use the animal point of view without it being a pathetic fallacy. To use one of those school terms.

Harrison: As Strang says, "What's the sense in drawing conclusions about human behavior from animals when you can draw conclusions about human behavior from humans?" There's a danger of extrapolating, but they're our fellow creatures and always have been. What's the sense of ignoring them? I'm writing now about the drama of an English department. Lots of writers are going to start writing about government intervention in the arts. It's quieted literary magazines a great deal, you know.

Interviewer: You want to talk about that?

Harrison: I've just noticed it. Just like all the writers' schools have created less variety—there's a sameness. I said once that the Iowa Writers School on a yearly basis outproduces the English Romantic movement. It's all a delusion. What are you going to do with four thousand MFA's? It's ludicrous.

Interviewer: You did pay your dues though. You went through and got a master's yourself, didn't you?

Harrison: In comparative literature. I never took a writing course of any sort. In my life.

Interviewer: Do you advise against that across the board?

Harrison: No. Sometimes they're good. Look at Wallace Stegner's thing out there [Stanford University]. I mean, my god, look at the people he got out. Kesey, Robert Stone, McGuane. But you know what he did. They sat around and talked a little and he just sent them off to write.

Interviewer: You have a lot of friends who are writers. And then there are writers who avoid that sort of thing.

Harrison: Well, I don't see them that much and I think a lot of other writers partly like me because I'm not competitive. I simply don't care. Frankly, I mean I don't ever think about being number one or number seven or number three. Self-publicity or valuation isn't a productive thing for writers. Mailer's *A View from Here* was marvelous because it just totally pissed everybody off. And it was also so on the money. I love novels like his *Barbary Shore* and *Deerpark*. But the critics were totally unpleasant; those novels weren't part of the nativist tradition. That's why a lot of people hated *A Good Day to Die.* Kazin told me these are simply the nastiest people, they don't exist. I says, "Alfred, they're all over. It's just that people don't write about them." *Sundog* came out of my conviction that the American literary novel as opposed to a more commercial kind of novel tends to ignore about seven-eighths of the people. The literary novel often concentrates itself on people in New York, Los Angeles, academic and scientific communities. People don't write about the Strangs of the world because they don't know any of them. You're not going to meet any in Cambridge or New Haven. People like Strang don't loiter around universities and they don't feed at the public trough.

Interviewer: So you think that the academy has had a negative effect.

Harrison: I think I would agree with Faulkner when he said, "A writer can't be ruined by having a swimming pool if he's a good writer. If he's a bad writer, it doesn't matter if he has a swimming pool." So I don't think it matters, but it's had a tremendous leveling effect.

Interviewer: On the kinds of books written?

Harrison: Yeah, they're not as idiosyncratic. They've lost a charm and a self-taught aspect. These people keep track of their credits and that's how they get jobs. They say, "I have been published in *Shenandoah, Sewanee, Lust, Spook,* etc., etc." Where I pointedly have no notion of where I published anything, or little memory of it. I've never kept track.

Interviewer: So you'd approve of someone like Wallace Stevens, who sold insurance and wrote.

Harrison: It's important to know something. Knowing literature is different. Hollywood's always making movies about making movies. Or the movie business. Well, that doesn't play in Kansas. Who gives a shit? It's like making movies about dope. They think everybody does dope. Well, very few people do dope. Why do people in Topeka want to go see a movie about cocaine? They don't know shit from cocaine. Why should they? It's a sense of fungoid self-congratulation that you see in academic communities.

Interviewer: You think it leads to a more narrow vision in literature?

Harrison: Well, that's true. It's just like academic types who say to me, "Oh Jesse Jackson, yuck, oh he's fascist." "Oh stop," I say, "He got jobs for 200,000 blacks in Chicago, what have you ever done? He's a great orator. So he's a little spooky in some areas. But why are you talking about this man this way?"

Interviewer: Henry James said experience is never limited. It's the atmosphere of the mind.

Harrison: Well, that's true. You make your own environment wherever you go. I don't like to be exclusionary. I don't like art which, I think Williams says, cuts off the horse's legs to get him in the box.

Interviewer: You taught once, didn't you?

Harrison: [indelicate sound]

Interviewer: You felt like the town clown, is that what you said?

Harrison: No, it's just that teaching is overrated. It's just not very interesting. You're never done with the job, time's never your own.

Interviewer: As somebody who's worked as a journeyman writer for films in order to survive, what do you think about books being made from films, or movies being made from books?

Harrison: I don't have any feeling about it; they're different mediums and you're a fool if you don't realize that. Even when I write an adaptation of my own work, I like to feel free to change it as much as possible to adapt it to another medium. My ambition is to write a good movie; I want desperately to write a good movie.

Interviewer: Does it bother you that none of your books have become films?

Harrison: I only have one regret. John Huston and Jack Nicholson were going to do *Revenge* and Warners backed out because they didn't want John Huston to direct it. I felt badly then because I thought he would do a good job.

Interviewer: They pay you a lot of money, don't they?

Harrison: For some things they do. One time Sean Connery had read "Revenge" in *Esquire* and wanted me to write something for him. He found I was under contract to Warners and Warners got excited and says, "You gotta come out here." I says, "No, I'm not coming back out there, ever!" They sent a plane all the way from Burbank to Traverse City Airport and I got on it with a bottle of whiskey and a six-pack of beer and some deli sandwiches they'd got me and flew out there on condition they would fly me back the next day at noon. They'll do anything for you. It's curious isn't it, all those years when people were saying, "Poor Faulkner, he had to go to Hollywood." He wasn't nearly as unhappy as he pretended to be, because he had that dancing girl out there all that time. Though Blotner refused to acknowledge it in his biography. Where she said, "Billy liked to take baths together and sometimes we'd buy toys like rubber ducks" and you think, this is William Faulkner. I loved it. Faulkner for a while was getting three thousand dollars a week during the Depression to write screenplays. That's good money now, that was great money then.

Interviewer: Is the writing you do for the movies your substitute for teaching? I mean in the sense of surviving.
Harrison: Yeah. It is about the same thing and sometimes worse and sometimes better. It's better because it pays better.

Interviewer: Does that mean you can do it less often? Or less frequently?
Harrison: Maybe, but you get greedy. Somebody gives you $150,000 for a screenplay, you think, well why not write two. Get more. And then you say, well why not write three, and get even more. And by then, you're retired.

Interviewer: Does writing for the movies drain you?
Harrison: No. In the last twelve months I wrote three screenplays and that novel, and I don't think the three screenplays detracted from the novel. Just makes you tired generally. And I'm the most tired I've ever been in my whole life, right now.

Interviewer: You say that when a book comes out you get depressed.
Harrison: Uh huh, I don't like judgment. I can't stand criticism.

Interviewer: Not even good criticism?
Harrison: When Bernard Levin of the London *Times* decided I was immortal, I says, "Does that mean I have to take out my laundry in three hundred years?" No, it's okay. If you work very hard, what's wrong with getting admired.

Interviewer: But there's something in you that doesn't think that's right?
Harrison: Well, it's because people you love died, and they didn't get admired. That's part of it. It's stupid. I mean, you ought to be able to be valedictorian once in a while. It's like pursuing a beautiful model and seducing her and then feeling real bad after you'd literally been thinking about doing it for seven or eight years. Why bother? Why should I kill myself writing a book if I don't want to at least accept one pat on the back for what I'm doing?

Interviewer: What about the sense of place for you? It seems to me that you're a writer that has to be grounded in place.
Harrison: I think everybody does. I wrote *Locations* partly from that sensibility. But I'm no more a rural writer than Judy Rossner is a New York writer.

Interviewer: And yet, northern Michigan is pervasive in your work.

Harrison: Yeah, that's because that's where I was born and raised. When I get away from there, I don't think the writing is necessarily weaker as long as I know the other place.

Interviewer: Do you think there's a basic superiority in that "heart of the country" notion?

Harrison: I think what I believe most is actually, as Rilke said, "It's only in the rat race of the arena that the heart learns to beat." I think you have to do that. It's hard to find more small-minded people than you can find in some areas of Montana, in the most gorgeous part of the United States.

Interviewer: But they're also in New York City.

Harrison: Well, sure they are, but I mean the country in and of itself isn't going to do anybody any good.

Interviewer: It's what you bring to it.

Harrison: I was being evasive. I was thinking about an uncapped city water well that I almost fell into in Reed City. Memories are evoked by a location, and I was thinking of San Francisco, the bridge. Six hundred and ninety-three people have jumped off that goddamned bridge. There's something sort of haunted in the air there. Nobody would do that in Missouri, and they don't do it in northern Michigan. But in New Orleans, and San Francisco, these apparently perfect places where everybody's so happy, well that's why there are 400,000 homosexuals there. I mean, what the hell's going on? It's a spooky place, but very beautiful. Maybe it attracts them from the Midwest. None of those people ever even want to come to the Midwest, ever.

Interviewer: In *Farmer* the doctor tells Joseph that, yes, Robert's a homosexual and not to worry about it. He'll go to the city and find other people like him.

Harrison: Homosexuals will gather in one place, for the same reason that the rich all want to be in Palm Beach or Beverly Hills, or Grosse Point, or farmers all go to the Grange. I mean it's natural. And it's not all bad. Think of jazz clubs. If you have three hundred Sonny Rollins nuts and half are black and half are white, then there's no barrier left. It's the same with literature. I'm not a nationalist. I don't want to hear about American literature. It's world literature. And all this sniping about who's good in America is nonsense when you've got Gunter Grass, and Gabriel Marquez. Who is good is who is good wherever they are.

Interviewer: You're a wonderful reader. How much do you write for the ear?
Harrison: I don't consciously, but as a poet you do. Yeats would think of the entire rhythm of the poem before he would fill in the words. You know he says, "'I am of Ireland and the Holy land of Ireland and time runs on,' cried she." You say Jesus Christ, I don't know if it makes any sense, but it's beautiful. I think it comes from my early addiction to Stravinsky or Sonny Rollins or Miles Davis or Thelonious Monk. And that's finally the music you hear in your head and you hear word music in that way. I think I was seventeen when I read Joyce's *Finnegan's Wake* four or five times. I used to carry it around with me. It was my main sexual reading, I still think it's the sexiest book I've ever read. So *Hustler* magazine doesn't work with me at all. *Vogue* is better than *Hustler*.

Interviewer: Do you think your reputation as a macho writer is the source of the negative criticism your work has gotten?
Harrison: It's just faddism. When Prescott owned *Newsweek* rather than talking about my book he used me as an object lesson in what's wrong with contemporary writing because, he said, I had none of the new feminine sensibility. He's talking about a public movement, a woman's movement, that I don't think has anything to do with the novel. I mean you write novels. I'm not trying to get out the vote when I write a novel. A novel's a novel. Everybody can't be everything. I don't like to be attacked for reasons anterior to my work.

Interviewer: Do you think it's because you so often seem to use the stuff of yourself in your work?
Harrison: You are what you are. I'm not going to pretend that I'm a Manhattan restauranteur when I'm not. But it's the illusion, too. I've worked very hard to create the illusion. Wouldn't I be something if I was all the people that people think I am in all these books. God, what a mess.

Interviewer: Does the misunderstanding bother you?
Harrison: I don't actually care. I pretend to be more upset. *Esquire* offered me a case of whiskey if I would write two paragraphs answering a review. I wrote that it's a misuse of the word. Actually what macho is in Spanish is someone who would fuck a virgin with a swan or throw a rattlesnake into a

baby's carriage. Screw his mother. You know, cut his sister. So that's macho. I don't know what it has to do with me. I don't care about being misunderstood. I'm not pretending that I'm right and there's not a lot of my stuff that might be terribly cheap and wrong. That's neither here nor there if that's what they're dealing with. I don't want to be attacked for my failures as a supporter of the woman's movement. Because I'm a novelist.

Interviewer: Where do you find your characters? Do you use people whom you really know?

Harrison: Just modifications of them. There's such a crazed variety of people that you can take an eighth of this and a third of that and make a human being. In *Legends of the Fall* I found the character William Ludlow in journals; he's actually my wife's great-grandfather. But I've changed all the details of his life except the initial ones. He did lead an expedition into the Black Hills with Custer as his adjutant; he also did loathe Custer. And in real life he ended up owning some copper mines in northern Michigan, but I'd read his journals and was fascinated by the kind of man he was.

Interviewer: You've complained someplace about the fact that there's so little useful information in novels, nowadays.

Harrison: I mean useful to, as Robert Duncan would say, your soul. Life information without which we cannot live. Like Pound says, "Poetry is news that stays news."

Interviewer: Larry Woiwode says he's read that most writers are manic-depressive. Have you ever thought that you might be a manic-depressive?

Harrison: Oh, absolutely, but not to the point where I would need lithium and not so much in recent years. About ten years ago I went through a self-taught Zen training. I had severe colitis from a parasite I got in Leningrad and I thought I was going to go insane with the mood swings combined with physical problems. I got rid of the colitis by sitting. Usually I would go sit on a stump and then on a rock for three or four hours. For some reason that eased all that out, I'm still not sure why. Psychosomatic maybe. For instance I've had a chest cold off and on for a month and a half. I know I have it because I have a novel coming out. No one in the history of my family, including my father, was successful, and I have a lot of questions about whether it's proper to be successful. It's like the craving for anonymity—I've already blown the anonymity shot, but I'm still looking for it. I'm like the kid hiding under the bush or behind the barn. I've gotten so weary or strange about interviews because I've been too trusting on a couple of occasions. The trouble is anything you read about yourself seems to be sort of inaccurate; well, maybe everything that everybody writes about everybody is inaccurate. I've never been really keelhauled, but I read once an article about McGuane in *Village Voice* where they really did a job on him.

Interviewer: That can lead to the "gunfighter syndrome." Whenever a celebrity goes to a party you know that somebody there is going to become an asshole and you never know who it's going to be. I've seen people literally get up in Norman Mailer's face and stand on his feet.
Harrison: They never do that to McGuane who's 6'4" and weighs 220. It's because Mailer's shorter.

Interviewer: You said someplace that to be an artist you have to be able to hold a thousand different contradictory notions in your head all at once.
Harrison: I was thinking about that when you brought up that question on *Sundog*. Hillman said, "What have we done with this other who is given us at birth?" Well that's like that Secret Sharer idea or Rimbaud talking about my "other" and so on. The unrevealed heart of your personality.

Interviewer: Does that relate to the idea that the essence of all art is the ability to recognize paradox, irony?
Harrison: Or to be able to accept that good art does not specialize in cheap solutions.

Interviewer: Do you think, at least in the sense that Pound used the words, that all art is didactic?
Harrison: It's didactic, but boy you better hide it. I can't stand art that's preachy. I think Pound's best poems are free of obvious didacticism. The test is the aesthetic test. If somebody tells me he has things he wants to say, I say, "Well, I don't care, everybody has things they want to say." It's like Philip Roth puts it, anybody on the subway usually has a better story than an artist does. Because they're intensely occupied with life. Whereas we can't see a cow without saying cow. It's never going to happen in my life. My particular burden is to make sentences. My wife and I saw a man commit suicide in San Francisco last week. We were down under the Golden Gate Bridge and this asshole jumps off. I had a driver that day, sort of an elegant, faggy character, much better dressed than I was. He and my wife and I were standing down under the fort looking over this area, nothing was there. I

was watching a man fish. Then I heard a gargle, we looked back and a man had just jumped off the bridge, missed the water by twelve feet and his head was even gone. You know the impact of three hundred feet onto cement, your head vaporizes. My wife and the driver were contorted with horror, and trembling, and I immediately started making sentences. That's my only defense against this world: to build a sentence out of it.

The Art of Fiction: Jim Harrison

Jim Fergus / 1986

From *Paris Review* 30, no. 107 (1988): 52–97. Reprinted with permission of Jim Fergus, George Plimpton, and *Paris Review*.

This interview was conducted over a five-day period in mid-October of 1986 at Jim Harrison's farm in Leelanau County, Michigan. It was the middle of the bird-hunting season, and his friends, painter Russell Chatham and writer Guy de la Valdène, were staying with the Harrisons, as they have every fall for the past thirteen years. Harrison chose this particular time for the interview because it was essentially his only free time of the year, and because, as he put it, it is a time when he "tends to be intensely voluble and cheerful." Both Harrison and his wife of twenty-seven years, Linda, are accomplished cooks, as are Chatham and de la Valdène, and this is also, it must be said, a fattening time. An enormous portion of each day is devoted to planning, shopping for, preparing, discussing, and finally eating one breathtaking meal after another, at the end of which preliminary discussions and preparations for the next meal begin almost immediately.

A threatening sign outside, DO NOT ENTER THIS DRIVEWAY UNLESS YOU HAVE CALLED FIRST. THIS MEANS YOU, is belied by the inside of the farmhouse, a hospitable home with bookcases lining the walls, dogs and cats comfortably reclined on the furniture. I arrived in the evening, just in time to participate in a dinner party for twelve, so there was even more activity in the kitchen—the soul of the house—than usual; a lot of tasting from saucepans by guests and chefs alike, a certain amount of pilferage off the butcher block countertops by the pets, and much good-natured squabbling, giving of orders, and unsolicited cooking advice, mostly ignored. There is a brief uproar when Harrison discovers that someone has tampered with his game sauce; he demands to know who and why. For dinner we are being served an appetizer of woodcock, with grouse as an entree, as well as sundry side dishes, including marvelous garlic mashed potatoes, for which Linda has poached thirty cloves of garlic in butter.

Jim Harrison is a dark-skinned, robust man, with a Pancho Villa–style moustache—oddly Latin in appearance, although he is of Scandinavian heritage. He's been described as looking like a block layer (which he indeed was), a beer salesman, and a sumo wrestler; he bears himself with a most unique kind of physical grace, indescribable except to say that it has something to do with a style of movement which is not precisely linear. His eye—blinded in a childhood accident—is sighted off on a different plane, increasing the feeling that Harrison is a man with his own unique sense of balance.

Harrison is the author of seven books of fiction, including the novels *Dalva* (1988), *Sundog* (1984), and *Wolf* (1971), and the collection of novellas *Legends of the Fall* (1979); but he began writing as a poet, and has published six collections of poetry, most recently *The Theory and Practice of Rivers and Other Poems* (1986).

Because he prefers to be on the move, out of a total of almost fifteen hours of taped conversation only about two hours' worth was conducted in any kind of formal interview fashion—seated in Harrison's office, a converted granary near the house, or at my room in a nearby lodge on Lake Michigan, a room in which he had written much of *Legends of the Fall*. The rest was conducted informally, in conversation with the tape recorder running while touring the northern Michigan countryside in his car, or walking through the woods and fields with his bird dogs. Sometimes he carried a shotgun, although considerably more talking was done than hunting.

Conversing with the poet-novelist is somehow akin to watching his dogs work the cover for birds. They race off on tangents, describing broad loops and arcs, or tight circles, always returning in a controlled, if circuitous, pattern that is at once instinct, training, ritual, and play.

Harrison is a man of prodigious memory and free-wheeling brilliance and erudition, as well as great spirit and generosity, lightness and humor; so the reader should imagine wild giggles and laughter throughout, and supply them even when they seem inappropriate—especially when they seem inappropriate. Imagine, too, the sounds and the textures in the background of the tapes: the easy talk of friends and hunting cronies, the light, cold drizzle of the wettest fall in Michigan history, sodden leaves and branches underfoot, and always the ringing of the dogs' bells, sometimes nearby, sometimes barely discernible, fading into the woods.

A final editing of this interview was accomplished over a two-day period at his publisher's house in Key West, Florida, where Harrison with his family, was taking a much-needed ten-day break from work on his novel *Dalva.*

Jim Harrison: I wrote this in my notebook: "My favorite moment in life is when I give my dog a fresh bone." That comes from being the blinded seven-year-old hiding out in the shrubbery with his dog, whom he recognized as his true friend.

Interviewer: Do you think your childhood accident when you lost your sight in one eye gave you a different way of looking at things?
Harrison: Probably. I understand they believe that in other cultures, especially when it's the left eye.

Interviewer: You seem to have a remarkable memory for the events of your childhood, which you use a lot in your work.
Harrison: It's nondiscriminate and that's why you have to work hard at it. In terms of classic Freudianism, if you have a knot in your past that stops the flow of your life, it's a psychic impediment. Your memories enlarge in ways proportionally to how willing you are to allow them to enlarge.

Interviewer: Do you believe that a good memory is an essential attribute for a writer because it gives one a deeper well to draw from?
Harrison: Sometimes I wish I could forget more things. I have to make a conscious effort to free my mind, open it again because memory can be tremendously rapacious. Was it to you that I said jokingly that I had to go out and collect some new memories, I'm going dry? That's why I like movement.

Interviewer: This idea of movement and the metaphor of the river seem to be central to your work.
Harrison: It's the origin of the thinking behind *The Theory and Practice of Rivers.* In a life properly lived, you're a river. You touch things lightly or deeply; you move along because life herself moves, and you can't stop it; you can't figure out a banal game plan applicable to all situations; you just have to do with the "beingness" of life, as Rilke would have it. In *Sundog,* Strang says a dam doesn't stop a river, it just controls the flow. Technically speaking, you can't stop one at all.

Interviewer: But you have to work at it, make a conscious effort so that your life flows like a river?

Harrison: *Antaeus* magazine wanted me to write a piece for their issue about nature. I told them I couldn't write about nature but that I'd write them a little piece about getting lost and all the profoundly good aspects of being lost—the immense fresh feeling of really being lost. I said there that my definition of magic in the human personality, in fiction and in poetry, is the ultimate level of attentiveness. Nearly everyone goes through life with the same potential perceptions and baggage, whether it's marriage, children, education, or unhappy childhoods, whatever; and when I say attentiveness I don't mean just to reality, but to what's exponentially possible in reality. I don't think, for instance, that Márquez is pushing it in *One Hundred Years of Solitude*—that was simply his sense of reality. The critics call this "magic realism," but they don't understand the Latin world at all. Just take a trip to Brazil. Go into the jungle and take a look around. This old Chippewa I know—he's about seventy-five years old—said to me, "Did you know that there are people who don't know that every tree is different from every other tree?" This amazed him. Or don't know that a nation has a soul as well as a history, or that the ground has ghosts that stay in one area. All this is true, but why are people incapable of ascribing to the natural world the kind of mystery which they think they are somehow deserving of but have never reached? This attentiveness is your main tool in life, and in fiction, or else you're going to be boring. As Rimbaud said, which I believed very much when I was nineteen and which now I've come back to, for our purposes as artists, everything we are taught is false—everything.

Interviewer: How did you think at age fourteen that you might want to be a poet?

Harrison: Those years, fourteen, fifteen, sixteen, are a vital time in anybody's life, also a tormenting time. I wanted to be a preacher for a while, but then it seemed to me that whatever intelligence I had wouldn't allow it. That again would be a question of leaving out the evidence. So I think all my religious passions adapted themselves to art as a religion.

Interviewer: Did you always read a lot?

Harrison: Yes. My father was a prodigious reader and passed on the habit. He was an agriculturist but he also read all of Hemingway and Faulkner and Erskine Caldwell. He read indiscriminately. Both of my parents did.

Interviewer: That had to have been valuable training for you.
Harrison: A large part of writing is a recognition factor, to have read enough to know what good writing is. Finally, what Wallace Stevens said, which I love and which is hard to explain to younger writers, is that technique is the proof of your seriousness.

Interviewer: Did your rural background in any way prepare you to become a poet?
Harrison: My background used to embarrass me. I'd think, I want to be like Lord Byron, or Vincent van Gogh. And then I'd realize, how can a boy from a little farm town do that?

Interviewer: Didn't that give you more incentive to break out?
Harrison: And I think more power. I think the years I spent at manual labor as a block layer, a carpenter, a digger of well pits, have given me more physical endurance for later in my life. And in an utterly corny Sherwood Anderson way, it makes you think those long thoughts. If you're unloading fertilizer trucks for a dollar an hour all day long, and dreaming about New York City, it really means something. I remember a month before my first book of poems came out, I was working on a house foundation and the lumber truck couldn't get close enough to the excavation, so I had to wheelbarrow 1200 cement blocks for about seventy yards, load them and unload them. It was a cold, icy, early November day and it took me about nine hours to do it. That day I manually handled thirty-five tons worth of cement blocks, and that was for two and a half dollars an hour. When I got home I was hungry and tired, and what I had to show for it was right around twenty-five dollars. But you got a lot of thinking done.

Interviewer: Do you think that the physical endurance you developed in those years somehow translates onto the written page?
Harrison: I've never thought about that. What it does do for you is, if you can hoe corn for fifty cents an hour, day after day, you can learn how to write a novel. You have absorbed the spirit of repetition. When you look at my wife's garden you understand that; the beauty of the garden—the flowers and the vegetables—that's how an artist is in his work. And I think the background that at first nonplussed me—that rural, almost white-trash element—stood me in good stead as an artist, in the great variety of life it forced me into, the hunger to do things. Joseph in *Farmer* wanting to see the ocean—that's a reflection of my background. I can't tell you the thrill

I had when I hitchhiked to California to look at the Pacific. And then the same way with New York City. Our family had no money—there were five children—and I accumulated ninety dollars and my dad gave me a ride out to the highway. I had my favorite books and the typewriter he'd given me for my seventeenth birthday—one of those twenty-buck used typewriters—and my clothes, all in a cardboard box tied with a rope, and I was going off to live in "Greenwitch" Village. I was going to be a bohemian! I think I'd seen pictures of bohemians in *Life* magazine, and that's what I wanted to be. Also the girls looked really pretty. They had straight black hair and they wore turtlenecks. And my dad thought it was all fine. He wasn't insistent about me finishing college at the time. He knew that Hemingway and Faulkner didn't go to college.

Interviewer: What were the books you took with you?
Harrison: Rimbaud's *Illuminations*, in that Louise Varese translation, Faulkner's *The Sound and the Fury*, the King James Bible, Dostoyevsky's *Notes from Underground*, Joyce's *Finnegan's Wake*.

Interviewer: Having begun your career as a poet, how did you make the transition to fiction?
Harrison: I fell off a cliff while bird hunting and hurt myself, and I had to be in traction for a month. I had a long convalescence. Fortunately, I had the Guggenheim that year, or we would have been bankrupt. Tom McGuane suggested I write a novel while I was convalescing, and that's how I wrote *Wolf*. I sent it off and for a month it was lost in the mail strike. It was the only copy. When they accepted it for publication I was somewhat surprised. I thought, oh good, here's something else I can do, because the dominant forces in my life had always been novelists, along with a few poets.

Interviewer: In its form, *Wolf* is quite unconventional. It has a very personal, almost confessional quality. Does that reflect your background as a poet?
Harrison: At the time I hadn't written any fiction other than juvenilia, so naturally *Wolf* was a poet's book. I even have grave doubts whether it's a novel at all. That's why I called it a false memoir. I certainly came to the novel backwards, because poets practice an overall scrutiny habitually, and what's good later for their novels is that they practice it pointillistically. You read some reasonably good novelists who tell a story well enough in terms of a flat narrative, but they never notice anything interesting, whereas a poet

has folded and unfolded his soul somewhat like an old-fashioned laundry girl with the linen. His self is his vocation. As. W. C. Williams said, "no ideas but in things."

Interviewer: *Wolf* is a very angry book.
Harrison: *Wolf* reminds me somewhat of a heartbroken boy up on the barn roof, just sort of yelling. I've certainly become a nicer person over the years.

Interviewer: Do you think you've become nicer, or less angry, as a result of age?
Harrison: I don't think it's a result of age because, if anything, people get angrier as they go along. I think it's the result of a particularly long effort to make myself sane, at least on my own terms. As Ortega y Gasset said, "With no standard nothing has merit and man is capable of using even sublimity to degrade himself." An artist has to evolve some standards, because nobody's asking you to do this, and what you think of as your muse is really a couple dozen violent bacchantes.

Interviewer: Along these lines, Faulkner once said that nothing could ruin a first-rate talent, to which Normal Mailer replied that Faulkner made more asinine remarks than any other major American novelist.
Harrison: Except for Mailer. I think Faulkner was always defensive and he gave Chinese answers. And that question of the formation and disintegration of personality is such an enormous subject, an imponderable thing. Of course alcohol and drugs, marriage, jobs, everything can ruin talent if allowed to. But these are inscrutables, and finally Mailer is right and Faulkner is right, and the fact remains that Faulkner really ruined his talent later in his life with whiskey. I certainly know when I'm doing so. For instance, the whole first section of this new book I'm working on, *Dalva*, is written from the voice of a woman, and I can't get into her voice if I've had too much to drink the night before; I can't slip into her persona because it requires a conscious effort every day. The best thing I've ever read on the subject of alcohol and the writer was by Walker Percy, who defined it as a "re-entry" problem. The writer works in this totally solitary universe, and to re-enter the world he has to have a couple of belts, then a couple of belts on top of a couple of belts. And most people drink for no other reason than that they started drinking. It's essentially a sedative, and if you're a manic depressive in the first place, which is basically my configuration, you sometimes need a lot of sedation. But this is not a profitable question in the long

run, because what Faulkner called the raw meat on the floor is whether you do the job or not, and eventually everyone knows if you did the job or not. The fact is, I can only think of one American in our time who's lived up to the full promise of his talent, and that's Saul Bellow. He's the only person who brought his talent to the fruition that seemed promised way back with his first work.

Interviewer: After *Wolf,* your next novel, *A Good Day to Die,* took a more traditional form as a narrative. Was that a natural progression from poetry into fiction?

Harrison: No, I think it was the influence of Raymond Chandler and John D. MacDonald. I wanted to tell one of those simple tales that has a great deal of narrative urgency, propelled by characters who, once you've met them, you know it's going to be a godawful mess. These are people that nobody wants in their living room . . . except maybe Sylvia, in her white cotton underpants.

Interviewer: I can see where some people might find these characters objectionable. That's a disturbing book.

Harrison: The book came out of the feeling of the late sixties. In a sense it was the first Vietnam book. A critic in New York told me that such people don't exist, and I said, well, I'm afraid they do, in enormous quantity, as we were to see later.

Interviewer: Do you think the fact that you often write about people who are not exactly "mainstream" type characters has hurt you in terms of critical acceptance?

Harrison: It's occurred to me that some of the awkwardness I have in reception—not that I can't write badly—is because the kind of people I write about are utterly alien to almost everyone in the reviewing media.

Interviewer: Has it been a problem for you being labeled a "Michigan" or a "midwestern" writer?

Harrison: What I hate about this notion of regionalism in literature is that there's no such thing as regional literature. There might be literature with a pronounced regional flavor, but it's either literature on aesthetic grounds or it's not literature. In the view of those on the eastern seaboard, everything which is not amorphous, anything that has any peculiarities of geography, is considered regional fiction, whereas if it's from New York, it's evidently supposed to be mainstream. I told my agent, Bob Dattila, years ago that it struck me that the Upper East Side of New York was constitutionally the most provincial place I'd ever been. As far as interests go, it's as circumscribed as say, Fergus Falls, Minnesota, which is a Catholic farm community—it's that specific.

Interviewer: Do you think that it's still more difficult for a writer working in a different part of the country, with the possible exception of the South, to be recognized in New York?

Harrison: It's only a question of contiguity, population density, and literary friendships. Think of all the column inches the Mets got when they weren't very good. The media loathed the World Series between St. Louis and Kansas City. It's the same way with novelists.

Interviewer: You make forays into New York, but you've managed to maintain a certain isolation here at your farm and at your cabin in the Upper Peninsula.

Harrison: I'm lucky to be rurally oriented because I save myself a lot of problems by being where I am, by being that remote. I'm not overburdened by the regional concerns of New York. I think of Mailer or Vonnegut, and these are brilliant, brilliant people, and somebody's always pushing a microphone in their faces. Writers aren't trained that way. In terms of wisdom, we're usually not much smarter than the modern living page of the daily newspaper, and we can't always come up with something on the spot; so we're often made to sound stupid when forced to react spontaneously in a media situation.

Interviewer: Did you participate in the recent international PEN conference?

Harrison: No. My feeling about that is that there's nothing I can say about those issues that someone like Doctorow can't say better. Politically I'm clumsy and full of rages. Mailer, who tends to be a very genuine creature, arranged literally the best conference ever. He even got Donald Trump to pick up the room rates so these threadbare writers were living better than usual, and then they all jumped on him. What I particularly don't understand is that ignorance—when they had Shultz come in and speak and a lot of them booed him. If the purpose of PEN is to get imprisoned foreign writers out of jail, you'd think the first thing they'd do is tend to be a little polite to those in a position to help. Instead they booed him. They did that because most of us are terribly compromised people and we pick these little items to try to maintain our integrity. They get in a snit over George Shultz, who's a pushover, right? I would want to subdue my notion of integrity and get some writers out of jail.

Interviewer: I know you taught for a year at Stony Brook, and that you disliked it. You've remarked in the past about "academic" writers. Anything more to say about this?

Harrison: That's probably an old horse that doesn't need to be beaten any more. It wasn't very profitable in the first place. Certainly there are some very good writers who perforce teach, and they're not academic writers. There's the old notion I loathe of the writer as some kind of hysterical Ichabod Crane—the oddball on campus. That's a very comfortable existence, but I don't know if it's good for you finally. Certain professors will say, "I'm glad to see you're still writing poems," as if you've left the essential integrity of the teaching profession to defile yourself. I said a nasty thing in an interview once: "I'm always being lectured on integrity by professors who've spent a lifetime slobbering at the public trough."

Interviewer: Early in your career as a poet you received a National Endowment for the Arts grant, and then a Guggenheim. In terms of encouragement, how important was that to you?

Harrison: It was fine as long as it lasted but then it was absolutely grueling for years and years. I had a bit of a drinking problem which didn't make it any better. Those kinds of problems emphasize your basic manic-depressive tendencies. You had a boom-or-bust mentality. You'd make a little money, then you'd run down and buy a bottle of whiskey and some steaks, and everybody would be happy. It's how most blacks and Indians have to live.

Interviewer: As humiliating as it is to have to live that way, is there finally anything strengthening about it?

Harrison: How are they going to kill you if you've been through all that? You tend to take everything that passes afterwards with a grain of salt. The idea of getting bad reviews is not nearly as bad as getting no reviews, frankly. And it never stopped me from writing poems and novels, it didn't slow me down a bit. That comes from too deep a source. It's something you have to do. And at any given time during those fourteen or fifteen hard, impossible years I could have taken a well-paid teaching job, because I had that cachet as a poet and a novelist, but I refused to do it.

Interviewer: Did you ever get to the point where you thought you were just never going to make it?

Harrison: Yes, I did. *Wolf* actually did quite well for a first novel, and *A Good Day to Die* did all right, but the heartbreaker for me was the absolute failure of *Farmer*. That was something I couldn't handle because it just slipped beneath the waters. I think Viking took out one one-inch ad for it. That was a difficult period and I couldn't maintain my sanity. I had a series of crack-ups. I was at the point where I couldn't pay my taxes, which were a feeble amount. My oldest daughter won a full scholarship but I couldn't fill out the forms because I had no IRS returns to show what I made. That was the period out of which I wrote *Letters to Yesenin*, which is the book I've gotten the most mail on.

Interviewer: *Letters to Yesenin* deals with the consideration of suicide. At the end you come out against it as a valid option in your own life. Did you know right then that it was totally out of the question?

Harrison: I knew I'd been thinking about it during that bad period in the back of my mind, but I finally couldn't entertain the thought because I'd seen it in my circumstances as an utterly selfish and stupid thing to do, and then I evolved this theory that even the next meal is worth waiting for. Also, I wrote, "My three-year-old daughter's red robe hangs from the doorknob shouting stop."

Interviewer: Do you think that so many artists, perhaps poets in particular, commit suicide because they've painted themselves into a corner?

Harrison: Sure, and they don't have any resources left to get out. A metaphor isn't a free lunch, and you get the kind of metaphor that keeps you alive not that often. Sometimes you have to stay alive merely because you are alive. Of course, people commit suicide in a state of derangement where they don't realize that this is the last chance—they're not quite aware of it at the time. It seems a temporary measure.

Interviewer: After you'd made that decision, "decided to stay," as you put it at the end of *Letters to Yesenin*, what happened then?

Harrison: Curiously, things kept going downhill. I would get cheated on the most minor little screenplay. I'd write one for money and then they wouldn't pay me. These things kept happening. My older daughter is still angry about what we went through, and I must admit I am occasionally. But there's nothing unique about it, and all it does is make you enormously cynical. At the end of that ghastly time I met Jack Nicholson on the set of McGuane's movie, *The Missouri Breaks*. We got talking and he asked me if I had one of my novels with me, and I had one, I think it was *Wolf*. He read it and enjoyed it. He told me that if I ever got an idea for him, to call him up. Well, I never have any of those ideas. I wasn't even sure what he meant. I think he said later that I was the only one he ever told that to who never called. A year afterwards, I was out in LA and he called up and asked me to go to a movie. It was really pleasant, and I was impressed with his interest in every art form. It was right after *Cuckoo's Nest* and all these people tried to swarm all over him after the movie. Anyway, later he heard I was broke and he thought it was unseemly. So he rigged up a deal so that I could finish the book I had started, which was *Legends of the Fall*.

Interviewer: After your initial financial success, didn't you blow a tremendous amount of money and get yourself back in trouble?
Harrison: The first seventeen years of our marriage we averaged less than ten grand a year; so I was a babe in the woods, and the money junkies—the lawyers, brokers, accountants—can see you coming a mile away. For two years I was simply the Leon Spinks of the literary world. One morning, during the first year of success, I was reading the *Detroit Free Press* and I sort of got the shakes because it suddenly occurred to me that I'd gone from making ten grand to making as much money that year as the president of General Motors. Well, how are you supposed to be sane? Now that it's calmed down it's nice. I'm not making a third as much money, but at least I have a nice life. And that's what we all want, isn't it? Who wants to be crazy? I don't.

Interviewer: In the last few years you've done a good deal of screenplay writing. Does it worry you that you're spending too much time at it, to the detriment of your fiction?
Harrison: Naturally, I worry about that. But it's the only way I can make a living. I don't have any other way of getting any money. I have no other gifts except what I can pull out of my hat, my imagination. I made a very conscious choice between teaching and the film business. If I hadn't made a mess of my life, I could make a reasonably good living off my novels. I'm close to it.

Interviewer: Do you enjoy writing screenplays?
Harrison: Yes, I always have, but just lately, going from one to another, I'm

getting tired of it. But nobody made me do it. McGuane and I had a talk about this. The reason that writers get submerged in the film business is simply a result of ordinary human greed. There's nothing literary about it—it's just greed. Why should I blame Warner Bros. for my own greed? Faulkner always presented himself as this martyr to Hollywood. Well, bullshit. His family evolved such a high nut that he had to keep doing it, because he was supporting seventeen people—his brother's children, retainers, aunts, uncles, an alcoholic wife—and whether old Billy wanted to go to LA or not they stuck that sucker on the train and shot him out there to make some more money.

Interviewer: Wasn't there at one point a deal where John Huston was going to direct the screenplay you'd written of your novella "Revenge," and Jack Nicholson was going to star in it?

Harrison: My major disappointment in Hollywood was when that deal fell apart. But now, as I get older, that sort of thing doesn't bother me so much.

Interviewer: Do you still keep in touch with Nicholson?

Harrison: Sure, we're friends. He's an extraordinary person, really literate and intensely perceptive. I don't know any novelists who are more perceptive than he is, which after all is central to his profession too—to be perceptive about character. He's always aware of how people around him are changing, just as he's changing. He never tries to locate people or make them stay in one place.

Interviewer: This is perhaps another old horse that doesn't need to be beaten any more, but you've been accused of being a "macho" writer. Anything more to say about that one?

Harrison: All I have to say about that macho thing goes back to the idea that my characters aren't from urban dream-coasts. A man is not a foreman on a dam project because he wants to be macho. That's his job, a job he's evolved into. A man isn't a pilot for that reason either—he's fascinated by airplanes. A farmer wants to farm. But you know what it's like here and up in the Upper Peninsula. This is where I grew up. How is it macho that I like to hunt and fish? I've been doing it since I was four. I have always thought of the word "macho" in terms of what it means in Mexico—a particularly ugly peacockery, a conspicuous cruelty to women and animals and children, a gratuitous viciousness. You don't write—an artist doesn't create, or very rarely creates—good art in support of different causes. And critics have an enormous difficulty separating the attitudes of your characters from your attitudes as a writer. You have to explain to them: I am not all the men in my novels. How could I be? I'm little Jimmy back here on the farm with my wife and two daughters, and, at one time, three female horses, three female cats, and three female dogs, and I'm quite a nice person. So how can I be all these lunatics?

Interviewer: Nevertheless, there is clearly a lot of you in many of your protagonists, and though they are very different people in many ways, with different backgrounds and professions, you can almost see them growing from one to the next. More recently, you seem to be coming off that a bit.
Harrison: I think so. That's what I've become exhausted with. The reason I revere Faulkner is that he was such a pure storyteller, in the Conradian sense. He created a whole world, a whole reality, and any time you don't aim to do that, you're somehow involved in contemporary gossip. I don't to want to piss myself away on that kind of nonsense. And it's always this hyper gossip that turns out to be the most popular in any given age. Frankly, I can't imagine a nastier or more exhausting profession because in the long run you spend your life pulling everything out of your ass. Remember Coleridge's great quote: "What webs of deceit the spider spins out of his big hanging ass." That's in Coleridge's notebooks. I love that.

Interviewer: Has there been a conscious progression from the intensely personal material of your first novel to what you're trying to do now?
Harrison: Hopefully. This time, in *Dalva*, the first third and last third of the book are written from the voice of a woman. Why that's been brutally hard is that you don't get to use any of your easy accumulation of male resonances.

Interviewer: How do you give yourself the voice of a woman?
Harrison: It's taken about three years of hard work and, as such, is a trade secret.

Interviewer: As long as we're on the subject, who are some of the women novelists you admire?
Harrison: I don't think of women novelists but writers. Who do I read when they have something coming out? Denise Levertov, Joan Didion, Joyce Carol Oates, Diane Wakoski, Renata Adler, Alison Lurie, Toni Morrison, Leslie Marmon Silko, Ellen Gilchrist, Anne Tyler, Adrienne Rich, Rebecca Newth,

Rosellen Brown, Gretel Ehrlich, Annie Dillard, Susan Sontag. Those come immediately to mind. Also, Margaret Atwood.

Interviewer: You have said that you can't be a good artist unless you have a very well-developed feminine side.

Harrison: That's largely unaccepted but absolutely true. It comes from an idea in the area of psychology. The work of a man named James Hillman, an unbelievably brilliant man, has helped me to understand certain things. He asks, what have we done with our twin sister who we abandoned at birth? A man usually gives up the feminine because of our culture.

Interviewer: When you're writing about something that you can't know personally, is there ever any question of cheating?

Harrison: No, because you live through it in your imagination and you have to trust the truth of your heart's affections and the imagination.

Interviewer: You've always written your novels very quickly. Are you changing your work habits on this one?

Harrison: Writing out of this woman's voice has been so enormously difficult. I've never had more than a three-page day with her. It makes you feel like an ineffective bulldog, you keep worrying it and worrying it and nothing has come fast at all. And you have to wait until the bread comes fresh from the oven. I don't know if she's going to talk to me today or not. It's been sort of spooky.

Interviewer: Does the speed with which you usually write your novels have something to do with the poetry process?

Harrison: Yes, because you've already thought and brooded about it a lot. I think I wrote "Legends of the Fall," the title story, in about ten days. "Revenge" in about ten days. "The Man Who Gave Up His Name" was a little slower, that was probably two weeks. It just came that fast, it all came at once, and I couldn't "not" write it down that fast. Of course, those were some real long days—some eighteen-hour days. And I've never done that before or since.

Interviewer: Do you keep to a specific schedule when you're working?

Harrison: With this woman, I've had good luck starting very early in the morning which I've never been able to do before. My optimum hours are between two and four in the afternoon. I don't know why and it aggravates me. It's a circadian rhythm I can't avoid. And then between eleven and one at night. I always work a split shift.

Interviewer: Does it require a discipline to maintain that schedule?
Harrison: After you've been it this long there's no such thing as discipline. You write it when it's ready to be written. And I've tried several times to start novels when they weren't there and that's tremendously discouraging and anguishing. It's dogpaddling, and fraught with the stupidest kinds of anxieties.

Interviewer: What do you do when you can't write?
Harrison: I wonder, when a writer's blocked and doesn't have any resources to pull himself out of it, why doesn't he jump in his car and drive around the USA? I went last winter for seven thousand miles and it was lovely. Inexpensive too. A lot of places—even good motels—are only twenty-five dollars in the winter, and food isn't much because there aren't any good restaurants. You pack along a bunch of stomach remedies and a bottle of whiskey.

Interviewer: Is the gestation period a conscious process?
Harrison: Much of it, although the best things seem to arrive unconsciously, somewhat in the manner that your dreams invent people you don't know.

Interviewer: You said earlier that one's dream life is the foundation of art.
Harrison: It is for everyone whether they like it or not. Or that sleeping/waking period early in the morning. Your brain has spent the night evolving a sequence of metaphors that allows you to survive the day, and sometimes it comes out in such poignant, distinctive terms.

Interviewer: Hemingway spoke about stopping work when it was going well and then not thinking about it until the next day. Can you actually shut down the process at the end of the workday?
Harrison: Not altogether successfully. You wanted to give it as much chance to occur as possible, but not too much. It's similar to that Faulknerian notion that if you grovel before the muse, she'll only kick you in the teeth. You have to court her, do little dances, all these things you do to keep right with her.

Interviewer: Don't you also do very little rewriting?
Harrison: That's just an artificiality. The people who do a lot of rewriting haven't thought about it for three years. Some writers work it out on paper and I work it out mentally beforehand. It's only a habit.

Interviewer: I know that you allow very little, if any, editing of your work once it goes to the publisher. Why is that?

Harrison: Because I know what I want to say. If they want to publish the novel, fine, if not, not. I've been over it four or five times, so why should I let them fool with it? They're not writers.

Interviewer: I don't know many writers who don't feel they couldn't benefit at some point from sound editorial assistance.

Harrison: A woman at Viking, Pat Irving, did an extraordinary thing. On *Farmer* she suggested that chapter five should be chapter three and chapter three should be chapter five. So I switched it around and she was totally right. That's wonderful.

Interviewer: Does your publisher, Seymour Lawrence, ever ask you to accept editorial advice?

Harrison: No, he doesn't. But I might need some editing on this novel because I'm in a whole different area, and my editor who works with Sam Lawrence, Leslie Wells, is improbably alert and I would certainly listen to anything she had to say. But where this comes from, too, is the poem. Editors don't change poems.

Interviewer: You've always seemed interested in form, and in experimenting with form.

Harrison: I diagrammed the form of *Wolf* before I wrote it—just a picture of the form, no words. In *Farmer*, for example, I tell the reader how the book is going to end in the first two pages, then attempt to make the reader forget. It's similar to a Greek tale that people listen to two hundred times and still enjoy. The idea is that you make little suggestions, little parts to suggest a whole.

Interviewer: Did you ever have any formal training in music?

Harrison: No, but it was always very much of an interest. When I was in college, many of my friends were in music. That was pleasant because they taught me how to read scores, so when I was working as a farm laborer I could play Stravinsky's "Petrushka" in my head. Stravinsky was a hero of mine. Now I'm planning to write an opera with the composer Nicholas Thorne.

Interviewer: Dancing frequently seems to have a place in your work.

Harrison: When I was nineteen in New York I went to see dancing all the time. Up at Lewisohn Stadium, you could go for sixty cents and see Eric Bruhn or Eglevsky and the New York Ballet Company. I've always been fascinated by physical limitations. And I like it in the sense that kids dance before they're taught to. That's how the mind works. Part of it's from Yeats, who believed that the primary thing is to see life in terms of dance. To me, along with the river, the best metaphor is the dance. As Nordstrom said in "The Man Who Gave Up His Name," maybe swimming is dancing in the water. It's also a tantric motion, all those tantric Gods who are always dancing, they're always caught in a movement, no matter how ornate. They have a belt of snakes and a head of fire and seven eyes, and they're dancing. Those old myths keep coming up.

Interviewer: One reviewer called *Sundog* "a novel teeming with ideas." How has your interest in philosophy influenced your work?

Harrison: I think ideas are as real as trees. *Sundog* is actually a philosophical novel. I live around that structure although those ideas tend to emerge in my work as sort of irrational and metaphoric. What Bergson called *elan vital* interested me very early. You can see me as a fifteen-year-old reading Kant's *Critique of Pure Reason*, wondering why I didn't understand every bit of it. Then I went from Kant to Kierkegaard, to Bergson, to Nietzsche. Those questions started very early in my life, once I gave up temporarily on the Bible, though I still seem to write totally within a Christian framework in an odd way.

Interviewer: In what way?

Harrison: Well, I realized a couple of years ago that never has it occurred to me not to believe in God and Jesus, and all that. I never questioned it particularly. I was quite a Bible student, pored over and over it, both the Old and New Testament in the King James Version.

Interviewer: Do you feel that your style has evolved or changed in any particular direction?

Harrison: Well, I'm no longer interested in anyone getting fancy for the wrong reasons. I'm not interested in showing off anymore. I think what's important in style, which of course is someone's voice finally, is that you have a firm sense of the appropriate. There's a temptation to enter into rhetorical sections because they're fun to write. That's probably a problem William Styron has, particularly as he'd so good at it. It was very difficult for me in "Legends of the Fall," the title story, to subdue that impulse, because

I think I'm pretty good at it too when I cut loose, and I had to consciously subdue my more grandiose impulses.

Interviewer: So sometimes you have to consciously hold a style in?
Harrison: Absolutely, because you want the style, in that book especially, to burst at the seams. One editor told me that if "Legends" was four hundred and fifty pages rather than one hundred pages, I could make a fortune. But the whole reason it works is that it's only a hundred pages. Tristan isn't Tristan if he's babbling. And the grandeur is in people's minds.

Interviewer: Will this new book be longer than your others?
Harrison: This will be the first time I've written a novel that's five hundred pages.

Interviewer: Was it your intention from the beginning to try a longer work?
Harrison: No, but this was a larger idea and I couldn't do it in less. And what I did again is I over-researched it. That seems to be a nervous habit I've been involved in recently.

Interviewer: Do you dislike didacticism in literature?
Harrison: I hate it. I can't use most of what I know but I think it should be there as a resonating board. You should read enough to know what's going on throughout the world. Poets should know the history of the United States and South America. Congressmen certainly don't know any of it. That's why we're down in Central America when we have no business there. They don't even know that those countries down there think of themselves as separate entities. They keep referring to "Central America." Well, try passing that off on the Panamanians, the Costa Ricans, the El Salvadorans. It's amazing to me, for instance, how few people know anything about nineteenth-century American history. They don't know what happened to the hundred civilizations represented by the American Indian. That's shocking. I'm dealing with that in this book. To me, the Indians are our curse on the House of Atreus. They're our doom. The way we killed them is also what's killing us now. Greed. Greed. It's totally an Old Testament notion but absolutely true. Greed is killing the soul-life of the nation. You can see it all around you. It's destroying what's left of our physical beauty, it's polluting the country, it's making us more Germanic and warlike and stupid.

Interviewer: Does it ever discourage you that the artist can do so little to prevent this?

Harrison: No, he's doing all he can by writing well.

Interviewer: You have said that you thought it was dangerous for an artist to embrace causes.

Harrison: I think it's terribly dangerous. I think Mailer's "The Steps of the Pentagon" was terrific, but I don't know if it was worth what he put into it. I liked better that little novella he wrote, *Why Are We in Vietnam?* which was exactly why we were in Vietnam. For my purposes, I believe what Kierkegaard said, that you have to work out your own salvation with fear and trembling before you can get on with anyone else's program.

Interviewer: And yet the artistic sensibilities of many of the South American writers, for instance, are very much seasoned by the political climate.

Harrison: There's a danger in our lush society that the artist won't be taken seriously. For people as a whole it's been a fabulous system, but it's shit on certain people and continues to do so. I asked a group recently—and they got very angry when I brought this up—to try to explain to me the difference between apartheid and the Indian reservation system as it's been maintained by the Bureau of Indian Affairs. As far as I'm concerned, there isn't any. I went around to a half-dozen reservations last year and if you think these Indians are any better off than the blacks in Soweto you're full of shit. Some people think we got their land fair and square because of the Dawes Act. Well sure, but none of those Indians had MBAs. Red Cloud had never been in a bank. Read Mari Sandoz's book on Crazy Horse. I visited the actual murder site and it was closed because of budget restrictions! I was the only one there. All the tourists were over in the cavalry horse barns, which I wanted to get a bunch of Sioux to invade and torch. Can't you see them—a thousand mounted Sioux—riding out of the hills to destroy Fort Robinson? I think that's a magnificent idea. I'd be glad to join up as a nickel-plated Indian for that one. That area of our history is just ugly, ugly. I know this lawyer who worked for nine years as a volunteer at Pine Ridge. One night about three A.M.—we were drinking—he took me downstairs. Way back in the corner was a safe, and in the safe was a little pouch that belonged to this old woman. In the pouch was a stone that Crazy Horse had given to her mother, and this guy showed it to me, and he let me touch it. It was such a strange thing. You know, when the Sioux were being driven hither and yon by the Army until Crazy Horse's daughter died of pneumonia, he lay next to her on a burial platform for three days and three nights. Am I supposed to think that Ronald Reagan is as interesting as Crazy Horse, when he's not? What does it serve us to take these people seriously and not listen to what Black Elk said? And of course there's a grandeur in that area so hopelessly lost. Think of being a Sioux and knowing that. I can't imagine anything more painful than being an American Indian, and I'm dealing with some of those issues in this book. It's a mystery to me how we could be so generous in defeat to the Japs and the Germans, and yet so neglect and disregard the Indians. When so many are starving to death, the BIA was spending an average of six thousand dollars a year per Indian. Why don't we simply give them six thousand dollars a year in monthly allowance and then they wouldn't starve? They don't raise their voice in their own defense anymore because they have for over one hundred years and nobody payed any attention. Why should they continue trying to talk? A Sioux told me that reason they get drunk, other than that they're alcoholics, is because it's the only insulting thing they have left to do to us. Our doom as a nation will be unveiled in the way we have treated the blacks and Indians, the entire Third World. Washington is a flunked passion play.

Interviewer: You've never been afraid of poking fun at yourself in fiction, have you?

Harrison: Who wants to read about another nifty guy at loose ends? There's not a lot of self-knowledge in those novels which are published by the hundreds.

Interviewer: Are there any of your own novels that you like better than others?

Harrison: I actually never think about it. I'm always interested when reviewers compare my current work unfavorably to work that they never reviewed at all, like *Farmer*.

Interviewer: Do literary prizes mean anything to you—say, winning a Pulitzer Prize?

Harrison: No, not really. Any kind of prize is pleasant—especially to your mom, your wife, and kids—but I never got one. After you've written novels or books of poetry for a long time, your concerns become very different. That's just what you do, you've given your entire life over to it, and luckily it's panned out to the extent that they're printing your books. So as far as reputation goes, I'm not interested in any reputation that has to be sought. If there's anything more gruesome than Republican politics, it's literary politics.

Interviewer: So you don't feel any pressure at this stage in your career to write the "Big Book"?

Harrison: I feel absolutely no pressure of any kind. People don't realize how irrational and decadent an act of literature is in the first place, and to feel pressure in a literary sense is hopeless. I always think of an artist in terms of his best work, which I think is what he deserves. If he can do this, if he's taken the trouble, then this is what I think of him. The before and after is always there, but so what? He wrote well and nobody should wish to take it away from him. That's what people forget about James Jones, who wrote far and away the best war novel I can imagine. Why did they flog him sense-less for the rest of his life? I always felt, strangely, a real kinship with Jones, whom I never met, being from the Midwest.

Interviewer: They also did it to Steinbeck, particularly posthumously.

Harrison: I think *The Grapes of Wrath* is a monstrously underrated novel, and Steinbeck has been neglected. But that's okay, because he's Steinbeck and they're not. Where's their *Grapes of Wrath*? They didn't even write *The Grapes of Goofy*.

Interviewer: Do you feel any sense of competition with other writers?

Harrison: I don't know what that would be for I can't see the art processes as being a sack race. I've thought that over as part of the idea that when peo-ple whom you love very much die, why would you get in a sack race over the novel? And I think sometimes that bitterness of competition leads people to write the wrong kind of novel, the kind of novel they wouldn't otherwise write. I think Keats is still right in that the most valuable thing for a writer to have is a negative capability.

Interviewer: In what sense?

Harrison: Just to be able to hold at bay hundreds of conflicting emotions and ideas. That's what makes good literature, whereas opinions don't, and the urge to be right is hopeless. Think of the kind of material Rilke dealt with all his life. It's stupefying. Did you read Stephen Mitchell's new translation of *The Sonnets to Orpheus*? You see that the depth of his art is so dissociated from what we think of a literary existence. Your best weapon is your vertigo.

Interviewer: Is that a characteristic that might be somehow easier for a poet to cultivate than a novelist?

Harrison: Why? Look at Knut Hamsun's novels, or the best of Isak Dinesen. The best of Faulkner. It had nothing to do with that fractionated, dry, cold cliquishness of any given period. As Thomas Wolfe pointed out writing about Greenwich Village in the thirties, at any given time the most highly regarded artist in New York is very likely to be a puppeteer. That's always been true. In my formative years, when I was eighteen or nineteen, my religion was Joyce's *Finnegan's Wake.* I wore out two copies. I was insane for that book. Now it seems to me that so much of the postmodernist movement is intensely worn out, looking to European models for emotion that Americans never get to have. For instance, I was looking at Kundera, who's not my kind of novelist but he's certainly a very good writer, and he's earned his feelings; he's been through the complete bifurcation, the destruction of his country. For someone at the Iowa Writer's Workshop to use him as a model is absurd. That's how wrung out they are when they're hoping to use a European model that has nothing whatsoever to do with any feeling they could possibly have for their own country. I remember something Yeats said, and I was going to use it as an epigraph for my novel: "What portion of the world can the artist have who has awakened from the common dream, nothing but dissipation and despair."

Interviewer: You admire Márquez a great deal, don't you?

Harrison: He's simply done things that no American novelist has shown himself capable of. Look at *Chronicle of a Death Foretold*—it's such a strong juicy death, a death in primary colors. It's not a pastel death with a film of snot over it—chichi snot at that. It's right there. That's an aspect of Lorca's poetry I've always admired. I was in a snit the other day over the infantile mechanics of minimalism, the extreme posture of fatigue. Minimalism is that old cow, Naturalism, rendered into the smallest of print.

Interviewer: Can you name some of the younger novelists you admire?

Harrison: David Martin, who wrote *The Crying Heart Tattoo.* That's a fabulous book and so is Russell Banks's *Continental Drift.* James Welch, John Calvin Batchelor, and Charles Baxter are also very good. I wish Barry Lopez would write novels.

Interviewer: Anybody else?

Harrison: That's all I can think of right now. There's no sense in plugging one's friends because most of them don't need it anymore, frankly. What, am I supposed to give McGuane a plug? Of course you read your friends. In terms of sheer verbal wit and brilliance, I don't see anybody in our generation of his size.

Interviewer: Do you have any advice for younger writers?
Harrison: Just start at page one and write like a son of bitch. Be totally familiar with the entirety of the western literary tradition, and if you have any extra time, throw in the eastern. Because how can you write well unless you know what passes for the best in the last three of four hundred years? And don't neglect music. I suspect that music can contribute to it as much as anything else. Tend to keep distant from religious, political, and social obligations. And I would think that you shouldn't give up until it's plainly and totally impossible. Like the Dostoyevskian image—when you see the wall you're supposed to put your hands at your sides and run your head into it over and over again. And finally I would warn them that democracy doesn't apply to the arts. Such a small percentage of people get everything and all the rest get virtually nothing.

Interviewer: Hemingway said something to the effect that the further along you go in writing, the more alone you become. Has that been your experience?
Harrison: He was a marvelous writer but a bully, and bullies tend to become lonely souls. You're only as lonely as you want to be. Scott Fitzgerald said this very whiney thing, that in your forties friendship can't save you any more than love could in your thirties. That's preposterously stupid and self-serving. Many times, because of certain arguments, McGuane and I could have broken off our relationship, but we never did. We always overcame it one way or another, and have been corresponding weekly for twenty years.

Interviewer: Many of your protagonists seem to be seeking escape from their lives. Joseph in *Farmer* laying his farm to rest. Nordstrom in "The Man Who Gave Up His Name" very deliberately disassembling his life. Lundgren in *Warlock* trying in his fatuous way to fill the vacuum. Is there some metaphor at work here through which the artist can then move on to something else himself?
Harrison: I think part of that is a literary device. You don't want to catch the man on the job, you want to catch him quitting the job, because when he's on the job all he gets to do is work. You have to think of him as escaping into life rather than from it. Somebody gives you the most banal and demeaning life in the way of making a livelihood, and if you abandon that, you're

escaping—well, you'd have to be a nut case not to abandon it. It's that whole notion that Strang has of meaningful work. If you're an intelligent human being and you don't have meaningful work, then you'd better find it because your death, in those spooky terms, is stalking you every day. What those characters have in common, I suspect, is that they all want more abundance—mental heat, experience, jubilance. As a young man, Henry Miller saved my neck by offering these qualities.

Interviewer: And does that quest for abundance satisfy a similar need in the artist?

Harrison: The closest I've come to a perception of it keys off that prime metaphor of Neruda's—the interminable artichoke, the unfolding, a process which never stops. What people forget is that this is not a goal-oriented operation. The Buddhists say the path itself is the way. It's a matter of not stopping your perceptions and of the courage involved in following them. It's why you have to think of Rilke as the most courageous poet, and certainly Rimbaud, potentially, in terms of the sheer daring of his consciousness. But that's an interesting question, to tell you the truth, I've never thought about it. What you've done is created these people who fascinate you, created them perhaps because they'll try to answer some questions that you deeply need to be answered. Frankly, a writer should be a hero of consciousness.

Interviewer: Is there any sense of resolution for the writer at the end of a novel?

Harrison: I don't think you get a resolution so much as you've expanded your universe. At any point as an artist, like the universe itself, if you're not expanding you're contracting. It's an integral part of the life process. There's no stability involved, nothing ever stops, so the biggest problem as an artist—and it's been a problem all my life—is that of vertigo; and that's probably the source of the drinking, because, being a sedative, alcohol stabilizes. Though only on a temporary and somewhat destructive basis.

Interviewer: Do you have any problems with depression when you complete a book?

Harrison: No, just exhaustion. The last time, I had to go to that clinic in Mexico because I was exhausted. I'm trying to avoid it this time by approaching it more rationally, but I don't think I'll be able to. I'll probably have to go back to the clinic, or if I can't afford it, to my cabin.

Interviewer: Have you noticed your stamina decreasing as you get older?

Harrison: Actually, it's increased over what it was ten years ago. I usually dance a half-hour a day to Mexican reggae music with fifteen-pound dumbbells. I guess it's aerobic, and the weights keep your chest and arms in shape. You know that group Los Lobos? They go from ordinary rock music into this crazy border music which I love.

Interviewer: Will it be difficult for you writing this new book through the winter months, a time when you've habitually had mental problems?

Harrison: I think it will help me beat the rap. *Sundog* did it for me that one year because I wrote through that period, which was a conscious attempt to fight it. Then three weeks after I finished *Sundog* I went to Brazil. I defy anyone to be depressed on their first trip to Brazil. It's such a gorgeously strange place, and the music element is overwhelming. They were having an anti-nuclear march when I was there, holding up their signs while they marched to samba music. It was extraordinary. I stood there on the street corner with my hair standing on end. They said to me, "Okay you fucking American, why are you going to blow us all up? You going to blow us up before Carnival?" I said, "I'm sorry. I'm not doing it. I'm not even a senator." I was thinking that all the rest of the world is a victim of us and Russia.

Interviewer: Let me ask a question about where your passion for food and cooking enters into your life as an artist.

Harrison: I think it's all one piece. When you bear down that hard on one thing—on your fiction or your poetry—then you have to have something like cooking, bird hunting, or fishing that offers a commensurate and restorative joy. It comes from that notion that the way you eat bespeaks your entire attitude toward life. Consequently it can become obsessive, especially this time of year when Guy and Russell are here, because they're both such good cooks. And sometimes you can temporarily exhaust it, just as you can exhaust yourself with writing because you work so hard. For instance, in the last few years I've really tried to lighten up on this whole cooking thing when I'm at my cabin.

Interviewer: Does the metaphor of dance translate to play?

Harrison: I used to have second thoughts about my sporting life until my wife pointed out to me that where I really get into trouble is when I lose my sense of play. In one of Rilke's poems, he talks about this overdeveloped sense of heaviness that an artist acquires. It's what I put under the heading of "lugubrious masochism." You walk around and you feel like you're literally so heavy that you might fall through the crust of the earth. For this reason I've always been a fan of Peter Matthiessen's, in a peculiar, spiritual sense. He and Gary Snyder are writers who seem to live outside the whole framework of literary reputation and ambition. When I've run into them they seemed to have an air of being content with what they were doing that other writers don't have. Reputation is volatile and a writer will despair if he thinks he is, at any given time, a consensus of what the media thinks he is, because if the media's not thinking about him at all then he disappears. Surely you need some encouragement as the years go by, but if you look too far outside yourself you're going to forget what the original dream was when you were nineteen.

Interviewer: Can you really preserve that dream?
Harrison: Just of being an artist—in the old sense of the word. More a painterly notion of an artist, or a poet, than what we think of as a novelist. My first passion was to be a painter, but I was without talent.

Interviewer: A question of maintaining a sense of purity?
Harrison: Yes, the integrity of the total mission. It's a "calling" in religious terms. You feel called to be an artist, and the worst thing is the refusal of the call.

Interviewer: It would seem that that almost childlike integrity is constantly assaulted in an artist's life, especially in this age. How can you maintain it?
Harrison: That's why you keep yourself apart. The reason I have my cabin is that it's easier to suffocate now in this culture than it's ever been, in terms of sheer, continuous bombardment, and you're not supposed to suffocate if you're an artist.

Interviewer: Isn't there a danger of being too separate, too isolated?
Harrison: Absolutely. What is it that Rilke said, and it's the truest thing I remember about being an artist? I think he said, "It's only in the rat race of the arena that the heart learns to beat."

Interviewer: So it's necessary to enter into that world and then be able to get out of it unscathed?
Harrison: Intact. It's the Zen metaphor of the ox, the ten stages of the ox, to finally have no fences and to be able to return to the city. The whole point is

not to need any strictures and to still maintain balance and grace, and if you can't the danger is a life-and-death thing.

Interviewer: Metaphorically as an artist, or literally?
Harrison: Both. There are lots of ways of being killed. One of the main ways a person is killed as an artist is when he becomes mechanistic and repeats himself. Then he's dead. It's killed him as a human being and as an artist.

Interviewer: Isn't that something that all artists must eventually face, as there is a limit to one's experiences and capabilities?
Harrison: There's a limit to one's resourcefulness, but how do you know the limit? You have to push out and not do anything you've ever done before. It comes to that. The notion of change in fiction is that a train has to stay on its tracks, and animals, even more than we, are creatures of specific habits, which is why, once you learn their habits, they are quite easy to hunt. But a man can stop his car, get out; he can dive in a lake and swim across, and then climb a tree. So don't tell me you can't change your fiction. Habit is what destroys art. I've always been struck by those Cheyenne who did everything backwards when they were bored. There's a longing, a craving to know more than we get to know, sort of a Faustian notion that you want a lot of interesting things to occur before you die; and it strikes you that rather than wait around for them to occur, you're going to have to arrange most of them.

Interviewer: And your new novel pursues that longing?
Harrison: I think you design something, whether it turns out that way or not, that's very nearly impossible in terms of your own talent and then you try to do it. Here's something I wrote this summer. I was characterizing my new novel, what I wanted the mood, the feeling of it to be: "A novel written from the cushioned silence, out of the water, the first light, twilight, the night sky, the farthest point in the forest, from the bottom of a lake, the bottom of a river, Northern Lights, from clouds, the loam, also the city at midnight, Los Angeles at dawn when the ocean seems less tired having slept in private, from the undisturbed prairie, from attics and root cellars, the girl in the thicket, the boy looking the wrong direction for the moon . . ." That's all.

Interviewer: Do you think that this *Sports Illustrated* swimsuit calendar that you have above your desk is sexist?

Harrison: Yes and no. However, as a tree hung with apples bespeaks God's plenty, so does that model. It's an old Protestant trick.

Interviewer: What is this strange mobile hanging over the desk?
Harrison: That's a crow's wing I found. This is a toy pig my daughter gave me because I like pigs. Then someone read *Letters to Yesenin* for the first time this year, thirteen years later, and sent me this anti-suicide button. Here's a grizzly turd Douglas Peacock sent—that was a hard one to figure out how to hang. That's a pine cone from the forest where Lorca was executed. A Haitian baby shoe—that was found on the beach after the Haitian boat lift. A beaver pelt . . .

Interviewer: Those are talismans?
Harrison: Yeah, they are, aren't they?

Interviewer: And you have these little signs up on your bulletin board "Mortality." "The Glass Coffin." "Reality."
Harrison: Those are just little reminders. My wife put that "reality" sign up there when I was entering a depression. I never mentioned it, but it's her handwriting. And the glass coffin—I was dreaming that all these people were in glass coffins in a procession down the street and this brown person who looked like me but turned out to be my daughter went out and broke my glass coffin with a club and I popped out. She was bringing me awake to her difficulties and my own.

Interviewer: You have a ritualistic way of going about things, don't you?
Harrison: It's a bit embarrassing, isn't it? One night in my cabin I saw a flash of light and thought somebody was entering my driveway. I was so angry that I jumped out of bed and hit my head on the iron chandelier. I heard this horrible howling and yowling and I smashed through the back door to look for the car, but it was just a lightning storm. I was covered with sweat and my nose was distended, and I had long teeth and there was hair all over me. Obviously a little attack of lycanthropy, see? My dog wouldn't speak to me for two days. Perhaps it was all the anger finally coming out of me because I'd heard a wolf down in the delta, and three days later I saw the wolf right on my two-track. Two days later, I dreamed I found the wolf on the road and her back was broken, and I hugged her and she went all the way into me, and I remember thinking humorously in the dream—God, I've been trying

to lose weight all summer and now I have to carry this she-wolf around in my body. How can I ever hope to lose weight? But she didn't seem too heavy.

Interviewer: In *Wolf,* Swanson was trying to see a wolf, and in *Farmer,* Joseph was trying to see a coyote. And in your own life you finally did see a wolf after many years of looking for one. What's the importance of that?
Harrison: It's a shamanistic thing, a process that occurs in your dream life. It's very primitive because our brains are primitive in a Jungian sense. From the time I was a little boy I admired bears and wolves, and it became important for me to see one in the process of my life rather than going off and seeing one as a tourist. I know what we'll do. Grab your recorder and let's walk out here and see how many of the aspen hybrids I planted have survived . . . I'm going to get about five thousand of them and make a little woodcock covert right here, so I can have a singing woodcock in my backyard. Then I got this other idea, which is to fill up this whole pasture with planted and transplanted wildflowers, just keep planting them every year until this whole thing is a jungle of wildflowers and bushes. It's hard to think about but by the time I die, if I make it another twenty years, wouldn't it be wonderful to stand out here hidden from view in this big jungle of bushes and wildflowers? That's my idea of a nice thing.

Publishers Weekly Interviews: Jim Harrison

Wendy Smith / 1990

From *Publishers Weekly* 273, no. 3 (August 3, 1990): 59–60. Reprinted with permission of *Publishers Weekly*.

Though he spent brief periods in New York and Boston during his restless youth and though his riotous visits to Key West, Florida, and Hollywood with his friend Tom McGuane have been the subject of numerous journalistic accounts, Jim Harrison's home has always been in northern Michigan. He and his wife, Linda, live on a farm about fifty miles as the crow flies from Grayling, where he grew up. It's only a short drive from their house to Lake Michigan, across which lies the Upper Peninsula, even more rural and remote, where Harrison has a cabin he retreats to in the warmer weather— "Summer," wisecracks a character in his new book, *The Woman Lit by Fireflies*, out this month from Houghton Mifflin/Seymour Lawrence (Fiction Forecasts, June 1), "being known locally as three months of bad sledding."

The initial reason Harrison decided to return to the Midwest was financial. "After my first book was published [the poetry collection *Plain Song*, in 1965] we had nearly fifteen years where I averaged only ten grand a year," he says candidly. "I needed a place with a low overhead."

But there was more to it than that; when *Legends of the Fall*, a trio of novellas released in 1979, added a measure of economic security to his already established critical reputation, he chose to remain in Michigan. "Ever since I was seven and had my eye put out, I'd turn for solace to rivers, rain, trees, birds, lakes, animals," he explains. "If things are terrible beyond conception and I walk for twenty-five miles in the forest, they tend to go away for a while. Whereas if I lived in Manhattan I couldn't escape them."

He steers clear of urban literary life for the same reason he has steadfastly turned down academic jobs. "I had this whole heroic notion of being a novelist," he says. "I wanted to be a writer in the old sense of staying on the outside. I can live for about a year on the proceeds from the first draft of a screenplay, which sometimes takes only six weeks, and I think that's more fun than hanging around some fucking college town for ten months waiting for summer vacation."

Like his characters, the author is blunt and outspoken, with an earthy sense of humor and a boundless supply of charm that take the sting out of his sallies. When he's said something especially outrageous, he glances slyly at *PW*, inviting us to share his enjoyment of how wicked he is. Yet he also sprinkles his conversation with quotes from Yeats, Camus, Santayana, and Wittgenstein—Harrison is a complex man, by no means the macho figure some critics have taken him for.

This complexity can be seen in his work, both in the poetry collected in such volumes and *Returning to Earth* and, most recently, *The Theory and Practice of Rivers*, and in the series of novels and novellas for which he is best known, including *A Good Day to Die*, *Warlock*, *Sundog*, the remarkable *Dalva*—in which he definitely refuted the claim that he couldn't create believable women—and his latest. Though Harrison writes of such contemporary subjects as the rape of the natural landscape and the search for a meaning beyond materialism, none of his books can be reduced to a simple, one-sentence thesis. There is a mystery at the heart of each, a sense that beneath his beautiful, deceptively simple language lie deeper truths that can only be hinted at with words.

All of his ideas, he says, come to him in the form of images. The heroine of the title story in *The Woman Lit by Fireflies* first appeared as "a lady of about forty-nine climbing a fence behind a Welcome Center in tennis shoes. I had been thinking about Clare for years, worrying about her—you make somebody up and then you worry if she's going to be okay. I usually think about a novella or a novel for three or four years; all these images collect—Wallace Stevens said that images tend to collect in pools in your brain—and then when it's no longer bearable not to write it down, I start writing."

"The images emerge from dreams, or the period at 5:30 in the morning between sleeping and waking when you have that single durable image, like 'Nordstrom had taken to dancing alone' [the opening line of "The Man Who Gave Up His Name" in *Legends of the Fall*], which totally concentrates the character. I think you try *not* to figure out what they mean at that point, because what you're trying to do in fiction is reinvent the form; I want every fictional experience I have to be new. Once it gets didactic, then I say, Well, why not just write an essay? You don't create something so that people can draw conclusions, but to enlarge them, just as you have been enlarged by the experience of making it up. Art should be a process of discovery, or it's boring."

Harrison's own life has been a process of discovery. At age sixteen, in 1954, he decided he wanted to be a writer and headed for New York City, where he stumbled on "what I at the time called Green-wich Village," he says, pronouncing it like the color and laughing. "That's when I knew I wanted to be a bohemian; I wanted to meet a girl with black hair and a black turtleneck—and I did! Then I lived in Boston when I was nineteen; I went up there because I'd heard Boston was America's St. Petersburg, and my biggest enthusiasm in my teens was for Russian literature." He managed to squeeze in an education around his voyages, graduating from Michigan State in 1960, a year after he got married.

"I started out as a prose writer," he says, "Prose, poetry, I never separated them. But in your first notebook stage you tend toward poetry, because it's easier at that age. I tried to write prose, but I was never any good at the short story." In his mid-twenties, while living in Cambridge, Massachusetts, with his wife and baby daughter, "I discovered the Grolier Bookstore, where I used to hang out with other poets. I'd written some poems and sent them to Denise Levertov, who was the only poet I'd ever met. My friends at Grolier had mixed feelings when I arrived one Saturday with my first contract for a book of poems—that wasn't supposed to happen for a long time!"

But the proceeds from poetry weren't sufficient to keep Harrison in the East after a year at Stony Brook convinced him he wasn't cut out to be a teacher. By 1968 he and his family were settled in Michigan. It was nearly two years before he made another try at prose, prompted by his friend and fellow Michigan State grad, novelist Tom McGuane. "I fell off a cliff bird hunting and hurt my back. Tom said—he barely remembers this—'Well, you're not doing anything else, so why not write a novel?' I thought, Yeah, that's the ticket, and so I wrote *Wolf*; I had a Guggenheim, which made it easier. I sent my only copy to my brother, who was the science librarian at Yale, because I didn't want to pay to have it copied, but I sent it away two days before the mail strike, and it was lost. He went down to the main post office and finally dug it up. I had a book of poems [*Outlyer and Ghazals*, 1971] coming out with Simon & Schuster at the time, and they took the novel too, so I started out with a bang."

Alix Nelson at S & S was the first in a long line of nurturing women editors for Harrison. He speaks warmly of Pat Irving at Viking, who published his third novel, *Farmer*, and Pat Ryan, "who saved my neck, because she would give me assignments to write outdoor pieces for *Sports Illustrated*, and they paid well enough for us to live up here for several months."

The period after *Farmer* was published in 1976 was a difficult one, however. "It sold only a couple thousand copies—it sold ten times as many copies last year as when it came out—and it was a terrible disappointment. I thought, If this is the best I can do, and it's utterly and totally rejected, then I don't know where I'm even supposed to be. There didn't seem to be any room for what I wanted to do; what I valued most, no one in the literary community valued. I went into a long clinical depression, but I gradually recovered."

Professional salvation came in the form of Seymour Lawrence, then affiliated with Delacorte, who made *Legends of the Fall* Harrison's first commercially successful book. "I had written these three novellas, and my agent at the time said, 'No one's going to publish these; they're not short stories and they're not novels.' I thought, Sam Lawrence has a good record for taking literary writers and giving them a shot, so I sent them to him. Then Clay Felker did the whole of 'Legends of the Fall' and three-quarters of 'Revenge' [the third novella] in *Esquire*."

If *Legends* didn't exactly make Harrison rich, it did make him much more widely known; the sale of film rights to all three novellas enabled him to buy land in Michigan and launched the screenwriting career that now allows him to attend to his real writing with a minimum of distractions. Since that book, Harrison has followed Lawrence from house to house. "Sam's mostly a publisher and a very acute reader," he says. "The kind of author he wants is someone who knows his stuff."

For the line work every novel needs, the author has relied on his eldest daughter, who reads his manuscripts before anyone else, and two editors associated with Lawrence. "Leslie Wells edited *Dalva* at Dutton, and she is so pointed. I tend to organize something dramatic and then back away from it, and she can always see it. The first sexual scene between Duane and Dalva was too emotional for me to write, and both Leslie and my daughter said, 'Hey, let's let 'em really do it!' Now there's a wonderful girl who works for Sam, Camille Hykes, who's a good editor too." His financial negotiations are handled by "my Sicilian agent, Bob Dattila, which obviously means 'from Attila'—so he has always been my main protector!"

In recent years, Harrison's ride on what he describes as "this shuddering elevator that is the writer's life" has been relatively smooth. Though he considers poetry and fiction his primary work, he doesn't disdain the movies. "I'll keep writing screenplays even if I don't need the money, because I want to write one really good one. You can't write novels all the time, and I'm intrigued by the screenplay form." He is polite about the recent film made from "Revenge," starring Kevin Costner. "John Huston wanted to direct it twelve years ago, with Jack Nicholson, and Warner Bros. turned him down. It was disappointing to me at the time, but when they finally made it, it was almost a real good movie—almost. It did well in California, the South, and the Midwest, but not in New York. I doubt your average yuppie would think much of somebody dying for love—it would be out of the question."

There's a certain combativeness in Harrison's attitude toward the New York literary establishment but, he says, "It would be pompous of me to feel ignored when all nine of my books are in print. It's just that the nature of my books isn't by and large the kind of thing that interests Upper East Side New Yorkers.

"I like grit, I like love and death, I'm tired of irony. As we know from the Russians, a lot of good fiction is sentimental. I had this argument in Hollywood; I said, 'You guys out here in Glitzville don't realize that life is Dickensian.' Everywhere you look people are deeply totemistic without knowing it: they have their lucky objects and secret feelings from childhood. The trouble in New York is, urban novelists don't want to give people the dimensions they deserve.

"The novelist who refuses sentiment refuses the full spectrum of human behavior, and then he just dries up. Irony is always scratching your tired ass, whatever way you look at it, I would rather give full vent to all human loves and disappointments, and take a chance on being corny, than die a smartass."

Siren Song: Will Success Lure Poet/Novelist Jim Harrison out of His Midwestern Lair?

Robert Cross / 1992

From *Chicago Tribune Magazine*, August 30, 1992, 14–18, 24. © 1992, Chicago New Magazine. All rights reserved. Distributed by Tribune Content Agency, LLC. Reprinted with permission.

The poet and the movie star dine at Gibsons Steakhouse in Chicago while a cordon of waiters flicks away autograph loonies as if they were so many black flies. The movie star, Jack Nicholson, naturally draws most of the attention. His close friend, the poet Jim Harrison, is sometimes mistaken for Nicholson's bodyguard, but in a certain metaphorical sense, just the opposite might be true.

In New York, screenwriter Jim Harrison offers hospitality to a Columbia Pictures producer by dabbing a pound of beluga caviar over their shirred room-service eggs at the Hotel Carlyle. "Hell, let's have some vodka too," the producer suggests. And they do.

Novelist Jim Harrison, late at night, leaves his cabin in the Michigan woods, strips off his clothes, and jumps in the river. He plans to make one of his characters do likewise, and Harrison wants to know how it feels (brutally cold and deliciously scary).

Tracking all the movements of Jim Harrison would take the vigilance and sensitivity of a timber wolf. He lives on a farm in Lake Leelanau, Michigan, about fifteen miles north of Traverse City, and retreats often to an isolated cabin near Grand Marais, on the Lake Superior shore of the Upper Peninsula, almost as if he needs to remind himself and everyone else that too much celebrity could poison the well of imagination. Show business frequently calls him to the "dream coasts," where he still insists that the

81

hyphenated career described in photo captions—"novelist-screenwriter-poet"—is appallingly incomplete.

Harrison tends to juggle the lineup so that "screenwriter" falls somewhere near the bottom of the batting order (although studios do buy most of the caviar), and he certainly could add several other occupations, past and present: journalist, columnist, essayist, book critic, lecturer, farmer, carpenter, salesman, teacher, hunter, fisherman, and, as he put it one time, "professional pig, gourmand, and trencherman."

A steadily growing public knows Jim Harrison best for his powerful novella "Legends of the Fall"; the poignant *Dalva*, written in a woman's voice; and "Revenge," a tragic love story set in Mexico and adapted for the screen with Kevin Costner and Anthony Quinn heading the cast.

"Legends," too, may become a motion picture (Ed Zwick, director of *Glory* and creator of *thirtysomething* bought the rights to it), and this summer Harrison completed the sixth and final draft of an original screenplay, *Wolf*, in which Jack Nicholson is set to star under the direction of Mike Nichols.

Harrison's works invoke concise images of woods, water, plains, desert, mountains, and the serio/comic twists of the human psyche. Some speak of solitude and the sort of life he has treasured since his boyhood on a Michigan farm—grouse hunting, trout fishing, tramping through thickets, watching birds, and tracking wildlife.

He labored at writing and odd jobs in relative obscurity for most of his life, but now, in his fifty-fourth year, the old anonymity is beginning to elude him. Scholars find intellectual meat in his work, they press upon him invitations to do readings and they plead for literary-journal interviews.

Filmmakers admire Harrison's ability to spin yarns, so a lot of his product gets into play as potential material for the screen, making him, at last, quite rich. His novels and novellas have been published in nine languages. The French, in particular, adore Jim Harrison, and his books sell better there than they do here.

His output appeals to a highly eclectic audience, or several audiences, and as a result, nearly everything Harrison has ever done remains in print: *Wolf* (no relation to the movie script), *Farmer, A Good Day to Die, Warlock, Sundog, The Woman Lit by Fireflies*, seven volumes of poetry and a collection of essays, poetry, and journalism called *Just Before Dark* that appeared in paperback (Houghton Mifflin/Seymour Lawrence) just before July.

Harrison's column, "The Raw and the Cooked," runs in *Esquire*. Sometimes it deals with food. Mostly it serves up whatever happens to be stewing in his brain: "Once I prepared quail for an actress of some note who doubled as a vegetarian. She was appalled after dinner to discover she had eaten a living thing. 'Not after it was shot and plucked and roasted at 400 degrees for 23 minutes,' I offered, suspecting Quaaludes."

Harrison swings with no apparent effort from poetry to puckishness. In his introduction to *Just Before Dark*, for instance, he explains, movingly, his affinity to dusk, which during summer in the northern latitudes last almost till 10 P.M.:

"Walking at twilight owns the same eeriness of dawn. The world belongs again to its former prime tenants, the creatures, and within the dimming light and crisp shadows, you return to your own creature life that is so easily and ordinarily discarded. I have always loved best this time just before dark when the antennae stretch far and caressingly from the body."

"Brown Dog," a novella in *The Woman Lit by Fireflies* collection, begins: "Just before dark at the bottom of the sea, I found the Indian. It was the inland sea called Lake Superior."

Thus, as an American lit student might observe, Harrison's favorite time of day shades a long, pensive walk or splashes hilariously on the opening sentence of a tale involving a confused salvage diver who finds a well-preserved Native American corpse in the freezer compartment of the Great Lakes.

Harrison's books ring with something indefinable that often leaves reader sensing that his words will resonate through literary history. Maybe they will, and maybe they won't. But another Digby Diehl proclaims, "Somewhere in that big literary acreage staked out by Thoreau, Hemingway, and Hunter Thompson is a chunk of space for Jim Harrison." And Bernard Levin in the Sunday *Times* of London submits, "Jim Harrison is a writer with immortality in him."

At one point this summer, just before dark, in his Grand Marais log cabin, one could be certain of this: Harrison had in him a pound and a half of Lake Superior whitefish and about six ounces of red wine. A fisherman in town had given him the entrée that morning, and Harrison broiled it with a sauté of tarragon butter on the grill out back. That project consumed a good part of late afternoon, seasoned all the way with conversations about dear friends and literary giants.

Harrison's voice creaks and snaps like an old harness strap at a volume sufficient to make himself heard over the noise in Elaine's of Manhattan or the Dunes Saloon of Grand Marais (both of which he frequents). The writer does much of his talking in places like those or with packs of boisterous pals. He discusses the authors he likes with the enthusiasm a Michigan lumberjack might use talking about the great Detroit Tigers baseball teams of years past.

That day, like most days, Harrison's forty-eight-inch chest often shook with laughter against the faded blue cotton of a collarless shirt, and his teeth gapped merrily beneath a scraggly black mustache. His left eye, which is made of glass, tends to stray. It can lull people with its aspect of bored inattention, while the right eye, small and brown, fixes on everything with the unshakable scrutiny of a marsh hawk.

Although Harrison's ancestors lived in Sweden, they apparently came from a dark-skinned line, not the light blond usually associated with "that dour land without sunshine and garlic." As a result, some Western bartenders have refused him service on the grounds that they don't pour for Indians.

Will Jim Harrison some day walk among the literary legends himself? "Only black holes have real immortality," he scoffed, relighting an American Spirit cigarette that he had stubbed out only minutes before. "I think it's a young man's game to worry about it all the time.

"Years ago, when I was just still a poet, I thought I would be better off if ignored. My publisher, Seymour Lawrence, told me, 'You're the only one of my novelists who doesn't think he should be more famous than he is.' I'm actually more educated than most novelists in terms of literary history, and I've learned that what's good this week smells next week—or next year.

"Last year, a publisher asked me to write a blurb for a reissue of the Sherwood Anderson books. I said, 'Don't you have this ass-backwards? You mean Sherwood Anderson has to be plugged by an upstart?'"

Yet Harrison does concede occasionally that he just might be remembered. He recently published his Michigan State University master's thesis, "A Natural History of Some Poems," although with obvious reluctance. "I view this as juvenilia, of interest only to assistant professors, should my work prove durable," he remarked.

On one of the ten-thousand-plus-mile drives he occasionally takes to cure "bad brain," Harrison almost lost control near the edge of Arivaca Canyon in Arizona. "As the car slid toward the precipice on the frost-slick dirt," he later wrote, "I undid my seat belt and opened the door, under the assumption that a car is easier to replace than a novelist."

Such subtle intimations aside, Harrison generally regards the future as the collection of mysteries that life trots out every day. His character Brown Dog, the one who found the Indian sitting on the bottom of Lake Superior, simply notes:

I have my own theories about what people think of as the future. Imagine yourself lying in bed sleeping and dreaming of things people dream of—say, fish, death, being attacked, diving to the bottom of the ocean. . . . It makes the world seem blurred and huge. Then you wake up, and you're just B.D. in a ten-dollar war-surplus sleeping bag in a cold cabin. The first step is to pee and make coffee, which I can deal with, and after that, what happens is not in firm hands.

Harrison is one of the few literary personages in the United States who has managed not to get stuck in one stifling category. He seems to relish the glamor that brushes his life—dinners with Nicholson, meetings with the late John Belushi, fishing with novelist and old classmate Tom McGuane and actor Michael Keaton, hunting grouse with painter Russell Chatham and the Count Guy de la Valdène, schmoozing with Bill Murray, Orson Welles, John Houston, Jeanne Moreau, Federico Fellini, Kevin Costner, and Harrison Ford. Yet he flees all that for his farm or his cabin and seems equally taken with the sight of a bear rolling in the river mud as he is with the menu at Lutèce.

At his cabin this summer, Harrison was shaking off the aftereffects of a professional ordeal. He had just finished adding the final touches to, and attending the last (he hopes) meetings about, *Wolf*, the motion picture. "The main thing I've been trying to get ever since I fell apart in New York a month ago is what I think of as the time disease," he said, "the overwhelming sense that one slices one's life too thinly in too many directions. And I've been doing that for four years.

"Up here, I've always adapted quite well to so-called Indian time, measuring it by moons. I've learned from a Sioux friend how you can do everything backwards to feel better, to reverse your boredom. You get up and cook a big meal, eat it, have two shots of whiskey, take a nap, have a little lunch, eat breakfast and go to bed at nine. Or you go for walks where you've never been before, which is easy up here."

Harrison often turns to Native Americans for wisdom and solace, just as he has dabbled in Zen, alcohol, and cocaine over the years, although he has long since abandoned the last of those measures as largely useless. "My interest in Native Americans comes from the idea that I think I've seen the best that the white culture offers, and now I'd like to look into other stuff," he explained.

The *Wolf* script paid handsomely but evidently took slices of time that Harrison would rather have spent on some novellas he has in the works. "There was a sort of argument back and forth between me and Mike Nichols, the director," he said, "but now it's all healed up and I'm up here.

"It's about a guy who in a period of thirty days becomes a wolf. It starts in New York City and ends in Labrador. It's not a genre movie, not a werewolf picture, although that's where part of the disagreement came. It's more from an Inuit, and Eskimo, belief that if you're very ill physically or mentally—which they look at as the same—the only way you can have a chance of getting better is to go into the body of an animal. And you either come out the other side or you don't. Both are good things to them. They don't differentiate—'bad' animal, 'good' person. You do drop your rosary along the way, I suppose."

Jim Harrison in his solitude seldom needs to live his days backwards. During a steady rain one afternoon, he showed me a little of his territory: winding dirt roads and two-tracks through deep timber, pristine little lakes and the spectacular dunes lining the one big lake, Superior, that looms over some of his themes like a cold, wet sky. He expertly steered a massive Chevrolet van with four-wheel drive, a loaner he had agreed to test for *Automobile* magazine.

Harrison parked, got out, scanned the misty horizon, and croaked expertly at some ravens. They glanced his way out of curiosity and flapped a retreat toward distant trees. On one such excursion, Harrison said, a wolf crossed his path, almost as if to validate all the hours he spends in the wild looking for creatures, rare plants, and himself.

"I first heard the wolf four years ago, then I saw him three days later out on a two-track," he recalled. "Rangers theorize that they come over from Batchawana Peninsula in Canada and cross the ice at Paradise Point, north of the Soo [Sault St. Marie]. When you hear them cry out, it's overwhelming. My old Labrador would go up in the loft and hide under the bed. You feel blessed if you ever get to see one, because they're so hyperalert."

Harrison himself habitually sniffs the air for intruders. A sign near his barn yard in Lake Leelanau says, "Do not enter this driveway unless you have called first. This means you." At his cabin, a gentler sign cautions: "Please do not arrive unannounced. I may be working."

"Of course, nobody can announce, because I don't have a phone," Harrison said, obviously relishing the joke. Work: He may be putting words on paper with his pen, or he may be hiking thirteen miles into the wilderness. He may be casting flies or following his English Setter bird dog, Tess. He may be preparing elaborate meals for sportsman buddies from all over the world. Any of it could be classified as honest toil; the interesting parts of his life eventually find their way into poems or novellas, novels, columns, screenplays, or bar talk at the Dunes Saloon.

If a UP local suggests, in a particularly nasty way, that Harrison has been sleeping late, he might say, "OK, if you think I'm so lazy, let's compare tax returns." If a grizzled UP fishing guide or deerstalker implies that Harrison has tender feet, equally grizzled friends jump to Harrison's defense.

"He's an original character," says Mike Ballard, owner of the Dunes Saloon and a friend of Harrison's for the past decade. "When it comes to hunting and fishing, he knows what he's doing. There's no bull---- about it. One day we were looking for brook trout, and we had to cross seventeen beaver dams. It took us seven hours to get where we were going. That didn't bother Jim."

Harrison's Los Angeles–based agent, Bob Datilla, also attests to Harrison's tough nature. A Michigan State classmate, Datilla remembers Harrison and novelist McGuane as kids who devoured literature the way most young people immerse themselves in movies or pop music.

"I was from kind of a blue-collar family, and he and some of the other writers that were there just made reading books so attractive that they made me a lifelong reader," Datilla told me.

"I think the great thing about Jim and Hollywood and writing in general is that he's done what very few other writers—classic American writers, or anybody for that matter—has been able to do. He's not been ruined by Hollywood. In fact, he's using Hollywood as a kind of cross-training regimen. He still keeps writing his novels. He has a novel out every couple of years. He still keeps writing his poetry books, and he still keeps writing screenplays."

It sounds rather easy now, but much of Harrison's life in letters was darkened by clouds of poverty. He and Linda King, his wife of thirty-two years and college sweetheart, often struggled to clothe and feed themselves and the first of their two daughters, Jamie Louise. Harrison published volumes of poetry during his two years of teaching at the State University of New York at Stony Brook, a job he loathed. He quit and fled back to Michigan with his family in 1968 and soon after wrote his first novel, *Wolf: A False Memoir*. That one and *A Good Day to Die* (1973) were mildly successful, but *Farmer* (1975) was a financial flop.

His work did receive some nibbles and modest option payments by movie producers, thanks to Datilla's persistence, and grants from the National Endowment for the Arts and the Guggenheim Foundation helped, but Harrison in the mid-seventies despaired of ever fulfilling his dream of supporting himself and his family entirely with his writing. He and Linda had produced a second daughter, Anna Severin, and Jamie was ready for college, which Harrison couldn't afford.

Often, when authors find themselves in such straits, they fall back on teaching, try their hand at writing dog-food ads or make a desperate grab for movie cash. Some illustrious novelists have followed the cinematic route, including William Faulkner and F. Scott Fitzgerald, although the literati would tend to look upon those episodes as pacts with the devil. Harrison often says he regards film work as a legitimate outlet for a serious author and supporting one's family as a crucial responsibility.

From the time he was twelve, Harrison had fantasized leading a writer's life, hoping it would serve as an antidote to "middle-class boredom." He was born in Grayling, Michigan, a small town some fifty miles east of Traverse City, on December 11, 1937. His father, Winfield Sprague Harrison, was a farmer and a county agricultural agent. His mother, Norma Walgren Harrison, was the sort of strong, composed woman who appears from time to time in Harrison's fiction.

Harrison's recollections of the past tend to collect in pools of images rather than hard data. Many of those pools are dark and troubled. In a remarkable essay written last year for *Psychoanalytic Review* and reprinted in *Just Before Dark*, Harrison charts the depths.

At the age of seven, a playmate poked out his left eye when he tried to play "doctor" with her. ("I sometimes tell people I lost it in the Tet Offensive, but that's a lie.") When he was twelve, the seven Harrisons moved away from wide fields and pure rivers to East Lansing, so the children could attend college. That led to Harrison's first bout with acute melancholy, not only because he would miss the flora and fauna: A new set of classmates would have to get used to his artificial eye. For a long time, he has said, his left side carried a number of bruises, because he was always running into things.

At nineteen, Harrison ran off to New York, pursuing a "bohemian life." "I admired Hart Crane and Arthur Rimbaud," he told me, mentioning two of literature's more notorious rakehells. "I met Jack Kerouac at a party—a truly nice man—and one day I followed Aldous Huxley down the street for blocks."

He returned to Michigan and completed his schooling, still periodically engaged in bouts of depression. "My instability was further compounded by the deaths of my father and nineteen-year-old sister in an accident when I was twenty-one," he writes in the *Psychoanalytical Review* essay.

"These were the two people closest to me, and in the legal entanglements of the aftermath, I was witless enough to look at the accident photos left on an absent lawyer's desk. Those were the main events along with a number of other violent deaths of friends and relatives including seven suicides."

His response was to lash out with a fairly large body of work, a difficult task for any writer unwilling to compromise high literary standards. In 1975 a chance meeting with Jack Nicholson on a *Missouri Breaks* movie location eventually helped Harrison overcome his chronic shorts. His friends Tom McGuane had written the *Missouri Breaks* script and invited Harrison to visit Montana and watch the filming. Nicholson read and enjoyed Harrison's books, so the two of them had a great deal to discuss.

"Jack really liked his work," Datilla said, "but he didn't see anything he could do [as a film] and asked Jim, 'What are you doing next? Jim said he had some novellas in mind, and Jack said 'When can I see them?' being an anxious guy. Jim told him, 'Well, in a couple of years.'

"Jack said, 'A couple of years is an eternity.' And Jim told him, 'Hey, I gotta make a living. I have to do poetry readings and things like that.'"

"Jack gave him a check for $30,000 and said: 'Consider this an informal option so you don't have to do all these little things, so you can do it faster.' Jim agreed that if he didn't have to lecture or do all his columns and articles, he probably could get the novellas out in a year. And he did."

"I paid him back," Harrison said, "but he wasn't counting on it, let's say. But now he doesn't have to worry too much, what with those gross figures from Batman."

The novellas, helped along by the Nicholson grant—"Legends of the Fall," "The Man Who Gave Up His Name," and "Revenge"—sold briskly and stirred up Hollywood interest not only in those stories but in previous ones as well. Harrison's life as an obscure, tattered poet changed radically.

"I averaged twelve grand a year for ten years, and then I got a little more, up to thirty-five grand," Harrison said. "Then *Legends of the Fall* came out, and I was looking in the paper one day and I realized I was making more that year, out of the movie sales and everything, than the CEO of General Motors—about six hundred grand.

"I became a lunatic. That only lasted a couple years, year and a half, and then I settled down. I learned that with cocaine, you feel like you can ---- the world, but you can't at all. I was always a complete failure at marijuana because I'd feel horny for about twenty minutes, and then I'd want to go to sleep."

Harrison sipped some red table wine as he stirred fried potatoes in his tiny kitchen. "This is the time of day when normally I used to have my belts," he said, "but I found that belts don't work anymore at my age. After dinner, I lie down an hour. Then I go to the bar at 9:30, quarter to ten, and make my phone calls. Then I get to have a couple of highballs. I don't know how many nondrinking experiments you've made, but the No. 1 thing is you don't get to sleep if you don't have anything."

The log cabin, built in 1935 and superbly maintained ever since, is a weapon against indulgence and the demands of success overload. His wife, Linda, and aide-de-camp, Joyce Bahle, picked it out thirteen years ago, and Harrison signed the check for it without even stepping inside. The surroundings sold him, he said. The five-hour drive between the cabin and his home in Lake Leelanau prevents a case of cultural bends, and no one is likely to visit Grand Marais on the way to somewhere else, which forestalls plagues of transients.

"I like the drive," Harrison said, "because it cools me down on the way up, and on the way home, I gradually get to adjust to the mudbath that is my life. My favorite walking area is about thirteen miles from any human being. It's just nondescript wilderness, but I love it. In thirteen years of walking out there, I've yet to run into another human being, which makes it pleasant, right? That seems to be the whole point."

According to friends, the leap in financial fortune did not change him all that much, outwardly, even in his lunatic period. "If you've never had any money and suddenly you make a lot, strange things happen," said Dan Gerber, a poet, Leelanau County neighbor and another Michigan State classmate. "Jim got into a little trouble with the IRS. His telephone was ringing off the wall. He rented a house in Palm Beach, against my advice. He probably loaned a lot of money to people who never gave it back. It's that old thing about the bitch-goddess Success. Fame is the stupidest thing to desire, and Jim knows that. That's why he has the place in Grand Marais."

Seymour Lawrence publishes under his own imprint at Houghton Mifflin, and Harrison has entrusted his books to him almost exclusively since they first worked together in the seventies. "He's loyal. He's a sweetheart. I love to publish his works," Lawrence said. "His audience is growing with each book. We were able to get *Dalva* up to over 20,000 copies. *The Woman Lit by Fireflies* sold 25,000, and the next book should reach 30,000 to 35,000."

Rather inadvertently, perhaps, Harrison may have widened his readership by writing with a female perspective in *Dalva* and "Fireflies." The first is a wrenching saga concerning a mother searching for her lost son. In "Fireflies," a wife deserts her investment-analyst husband at a highway rest stop and flees into a cornfield. "He has settled once and for all the question of whether a great male writer can write in a woman's voice," says *Chicago Tribune* paperback critic Clarence Petersen. Some women in the literary world, of course, maintain that a male cannot possibly inhabit their lives.

"Why do I have to be limited to a man's point of view?" Harrison murmured over dinner in his cabin. "Why do I have to leave out half the world, both socio- and economical? People are always trying to put territorial limits on you."

Later that night at the Dunes Saloon, lumberjacks, fishermen, and farmers filled the place. An ornate mirror framed by stuffed fish, birds, and furry mammals reflected the customers' nodding tractor caps and glinting beer bottles.

A marquee-style sign on the wall said, "DUNE$ $ALOON WELCOME$ ALL THE SUMMER FUN PEOPLE," which I admired as a pragmatic demand for tourist bucks, subtle enough that a tourist might mistakenly interpret the message as a friendly gesture. But waitress Nancy Abbott quickly let the air out of that theory. "We just ran out of plastic S's, and so we had to use the dollar signs," she said.

Harrison went through his phone calls in the Dunes kitchen—wife and daughter back home downstate, a call back for a Columbia Pictures VP, a long conversation with a neighbor having marital problems.

Then he returned to his spot near the back door ("Where I can make a quick getaway if I see somebody I don't like"), sipped a Canadian whiskey, and chatted with people until his personal and strict midnight witching hour. "It's important to a writer to have nonwriter friends," he had mentioned earlier in the day. And clearly it was important to live like them too, when he could.

Harrison evidently worked hard to regain equilibrium after the initial shock of wealth. Spending most of it right away didn't work. Buying the cabin proved to be a partial solution. And extensive psychological counseling, he swears, did wonders for him.

"I've been seeing my guy fourteen years, when I get to New York four or five times a year," Harrison said over the noise of the jukebox and a crowded pool table. "And we have a thousand-letter correspondence. Those guys are great if you can get the good one. It's like going to see the medicine man. Some people warned me against it, said that sort of thing might untie my psychic knots and take away my imagination. But I don't think a person's knots are part of his energy.

"There are some profoundly ill but functional writers who have given us a lot of beauty, but I don't want to ---- die in the process. I want to live. It's better. We don't write out of sickness, we write out of health."

An Interview with Jim Harrison

Thierry Jousse and Vincent Ostria / 1993

From *Cahiers du Cinema*, no. 470 (July–August 1993): 24–30. Copyright *Cahiers du Cinema*. Translated into English by Dominique Duvert. Reprinted by permission of *Cahiers du Cinema*.

The writer Jim Harrison is a sturdily built man in his fifties, the writer of a handful of novellas and novels rooted in the great American tradition, among them *Legends of the Fall, Dalva,* and *The Woman Lit by Fireflies.* A wild man who is not unaccustomed to the sophistication of European culture. A heavy drinker, a big eater, also a gourmet, he evokes some of his passions in his latest book, *Just Before Dark,* a collection of articles published in various American magazines. But Jim Harrison's greatest affair remains nature in its purest form, the nature of the unspoiled territories of the American continent. A trout fisherman and game hunter, he spends a great part of his time deep in the state of Michigan in his cabin and in the forest. If he celebrates a virile universe, Jim Harrison is not a macho man à la Hemingway as some have described him. He is more of a sensualist, an epicurean at heart. But he is also the great champion of Indians and a former professor of literature who flirted with the beatnik and hippy spirit of the sixties and seventies. He is great friends with writer Tom McGuane and Jack Nicholson, and is also a regular in Hollywood, where he hangs out just long enough to bail himself out financially. At the time when the Institut Lumière in Lyon was paying homage to him, he talked to us about this difficult relationship between an authentic man and the jungle of the entertainment world that fascinates us (and him) so much. It was also an opportunity to take stock of the tumultuous relationship between the film industry and American writers among whom Faulkner, John Fante, Fitzgerald, and Rudy Wurlitzer stand in the frontline.

Interviewer: Could you enlighten us about some of the choices you made for your Carte Blanche at the Institut Lumière in Lyon? Why *Wild Strawberries* by Bergman or *8 ½* by Fellini, for example?

Jim Harrison: At first, I thought they had asked me to choose films mostly from a sentimental point of view. My family is half Swedish, so the people in Bergman's films remind me of crazy relatives who would not utter a word for days on end. They just sat. But my favorite film by Bergman is not *Wild Strawberries*, it's *Persona*. As for Fellini, I had dinner with him a few times in New York and that's a good memory. They put *8 ½* in the program but I prefer *La Strada*. I think that's his best film, before he added all this bric-a-brac. As he went on, his films became increasingly rococo. Did I also put Orson Welles's *Othello* on the list? I adore that film, but nobody likes it. It's like the films by Renoir that Jack Nicholson loves—for example, *Rules of the Game*. When I see them, I tear up. Technically *Chinatown* is better than *Five Easy Pieces*, but I feel closer to *Five Easy Pieces*.

Int: In your works, you mention a lot of Hollywood movie actors. How did you discover films?

JH: I lived in a small town where there was a movie theater. At the time, I seem to remember that the ticket was only a dime. Almost everybody went to the movie. So, as I was growing up, I saw hundreds and hundreds of films. Films are part of my reference system. Everybody knows Gary Cooper. He is one of the embodiments of American mythology. Although he is not responsible for it, his character became a cliché. The same goes for Robert Mitchum and Jack Palance, for those who saw all the films between 1945 and 1960.

Int: In *Wolf* you write: "Thousands of films poisoned my mind."

JH: When I talk about poison when referring to movies, it's because you can never get rid of them. All these different versions of reality—I'm writing a long novella about this right now—come floating in your mind. It happens just the same with novels as it does with films. I remember some scenes in novels just like some scenes in a film. Take *The Possessed* by Dostoevsky. The lights go off. Stavrogin and Kirilov are in the room. Kirilov gets up and bites Stavrogin's ear. It's utter terror, one of the most terrifying scenes that I know. The type of scene you can never get rid of. It becomes part of your imaginary heritage. A poet, Wallace Stevens, said: "There are image reservoirs in our minds." It's as though images were thousands of fish in the water.

Int: You also say in *Wolf* that you are hostile to television.

JH: Television is like an art book: it reduces images. In an art book, a work becomes very small. It's completely absurd. Television is a formidable thing. It reduces images that were not intended for the small screen. But I'm lucky, my secretary's husband has a movie theatre in the small town where I live. So I can get any film and see it in ideal conditions. You cannot compress the history of the West, pioneer films like those of John Ford, in a small Japanese box. It's impossible.

Int: You are talking about John Ford. Do you feel particularly close to western films?

JH: I'm trying to write one now. Westerns are part of my personal mythology. We all grew up with John Ford and westerns. He is the best. Nobody, by far, can hold a candle to him. And I went to Monument Valley. I took a long hike, at night, right before dawn. It was very cold, it was during winter. And I waited for daybreak. But could you show what I saw on a two-hundred-dollar Sony television?

Int: What kind of a western are you writing?

JH: It's a western that takes place during the twenties, at the time when the spirit of the West was fading away. In America, the twenties look like the eighties: people were rapacious. The country was almost destroyed because of greed. The film is called *The Last Posse*. A group of people gets together to go in pursuit of very bad outlaws. A number of the people who are part of the escapade come from the East and never rode a horse, but they believe in the myth of the West. But most of the people in this group die from exhaustion. It's the explosion of the myth. I wrote the script for Harrison Ford because he needs to do stronger things. They continue to make big-budget films, but his last truly good film was *Witness*. He is an excellent actor, but he makes films that are too big.

Int: Did you see Clint Eastwood's *Unforgiven*?

JH: No. I will not see it until I'm done with *The Last Posse*. It's the same with novels, I cannot read any when I'm writing, otherwise it turns into mush. But Eastwood is extraordinary.

Int: Don't you think that the great film about Indians still has to be made?

JH: Yes, but the director would have to be an Indian. There have been a few attempts in this direction. But we are very paternalistic with them. We always tell them what they have to do. It's a very difficult problem because they have a culture which is completely different from ours. In fact, it's a complicated question. Indians are not ambitious enough to become movie directors. It would also be necessary to make a movie on Indians before the Europeans arrived in America.

Int: You worked on a script about the life of the photographer Edward Curtis, who took many photographs of Indians at the turn of the century.
JH: It was a nightmare. I had written the script for Taylor Hackford, but we did not get along at all. Hackford wanted Curtis to kill someone, or something like that, to make the story more interesting. He can go to hell! (Laughter) When you are telling a director that you feel like killing him with your own hands, you know the project is over. When you want to tear his heart out, it's bad. It means you are too upset to work. I doubt the film will ever be made, but it's possible. We did not abandon the project. I talked to Nicholson about it and he thinks he'll be able to play Curtis until he is sixty-five and the producer Douglas Wick is still interested. He bought Curtis's originals for $100,000. The collection fills up a very large room. I did a great deal of research and I was very interested. Moreover, I'm going to return to it and try to write a script. What's troubling is that after he spent thirty-five years with Indians, Curtis became an Indian to an extent nobody ever reached. He was committed to an insane asylum—to pretend that you are crazy is sometimes a way to settle your problems. He was seen for the last time in 1932 in a Cheyenne reservation during a specific ceremony, quite a Dadaist ceremony. Only absolutely extreme things happen in it. At the beginning, somebody comes toward you, from afar, about a thousand yards away; he is painted half and half in back and in bright yellow. The ceremony goes on for a week. It's never been celebrated since. It's an incredible story. Curtis also danced with the Hopis with rattlesnakes in his mouth.

Int: In what context did you see European films for the first time?
JH: At eighteen or nineteen, when I was in college. At that time, for several years, I saw only foreign films. Later, I met Jeanne Moreau many times in New York, but we only had dinner together. We saw each other in restaurants and we talked about great films like *Jules and Jim, Shoot the Pianist, La Strada*, and Antonioni's first films, which were fascinating because they had a completely different way of looking at reality.

Int: Your novel *A Good Day to Die* stages a woman and two men. Were you influenced by *Jules and Jim*, a film you even quote in the novel?

JH: Maybe. At the time it was a very shocking film. In our culture, we don't often see two men openly sharing a woman. But one prefers to share a woman than to lose her, so of course, one gets used to it. It's the same thing in *A Good Day to Die*. By the way, would you know who the people are who have an option on my novel? They are French people who have had it for three years.

Int: No, but what do you think of American filmmakers of the sixties or seventies like Bob Rafelson, Arthur Penn, or Sidney Pollack, who made films when you were beginning to write?

JH: The best film by Sidney Pollack remains, by far, *They Shoot Horses, Don't They?* I had written a script for him because I wanted him to go back to the simplicity of this film, and to stop making syrup. One believes that more is more, but more is often less. We dump loads of nonsense. Rafelson was a very good director during a time, and then he and his wife got separated and he lost it.

Int: Pollack was supposed to film another one of your long novellas, titled "The Man Who Gave Up His Name."

JH: Yes. Another failure. Jack Nicholson was supposed to play Nordstrom, but at the last minute, they gave him the green light to direct *Two Jakes* and the project fell through. This kind of thing happens all the time. As soon as you have found the perfect people for a project, somebody comes to tell you (deep voice): "John Huston will never work for Warner Bros." But who are these damn Warner Bros.? It drives you nuts. It's the same for nineteenth-century authors: we don't care who Apollinaire's publisher was.

Int: You met Jack Nicholson on the set of *Missouri Breaks* by Arthur Penn.

JH: Toby Rafelson (Bob Rafelson's wife) gave him my first novel, *Wolf.* After that, he wanted to talk to me. It was a very strange meeting. We talked a little and he told me to call him if I had a topic for him. But I never called him. I saw him again a year later and he asked me why I had never called him. I told him I had not found anything for him. I'm not a very good businessman.

Int: And now, you follow his career, you see his films?

JH: Oh, yes, we've been friends since then. When I'm in Los Angeles, I stay at his place. I think he is by far our best actor. He has an extraordinary range. He does not always choose the best projects, but he is the American actor with the broadest range. He can play anything.

Int: In your last book, *Just Before Dark*, you talk about the dinners you had with Orson Welles. What kind of relationship did you have with him? Did you only talk about gastronomy?

JH: No, he talked about everything. Warner did not want John Huston to direct *Revenge* (an adaptation of the novella "Revenge," filmed in the end by Tony Scott with Kevin Costner). So Jack Nicholson, under torture, said that if they did not want Huston, he only wanted Orson Welles to do it. We then had extraordinary meetings with him. He loved to eat sumptuously and we put our meals on the expense account of Warner Bros. Our meetings were meals. But we practically did not talk about the project for the film. He said he was going to film the book directly. You know that Welles was in Brazil when he saw a picture of Rita Hayworth in *Life* magazine and, ten days later, he married her. He took the first plane and brmmmmm (he imitates the sound of an engine). Astonishing.

Int: What happened finally with *Revenge*?

JH: Everybody disappeared. It broke my heart. I had seen John Huston and Jack Nicholson in London at the time he was doing *The Shining*. Huston said (Harrison imitates the director's voice to perfection), "Let's make the movie." It was marvelous. And then, they go back to LA and Warner says: "No John Huston!" It was sad, mostly because at the time Warner said no to David Lean who wanted to adapt my novella "Legends of the Fall." That's the studio people for you!

Int: You did not participate in the last stages of the script?

JH: No, because the Screenwriters Guild was on strike and legally I did not even have the right to call production. Jack Nicholson made fun of them. He told Ray Stark (the producer of *Revenge*) that I had found a new brilliant ending for *Revenge*, but that I wanted $50,000 cash for it. He is an adept at this kind of joke. But Stark was ready to pay because Hollywood producers are always happy when they find a solution so a heroine does not die. Huston's point of view, on the contrary, was that the girl had to die (as in the novel). There were dozens of different endings for that story. But I could not contact them because the Screenwriters Guild inflicted severe fines if you contacted the producers (during the strike). In that case, you have to hide and call them from public phones. But I'm not that kind. And in any case, at that time, I was fed up with these people.

Int: Have you seen the film *Revenge*?
JH: Yes. They added some stupidities. The director (Tony Scott) makes fashion images: to have an Englishman film that was the worst idea. He did not know what to do. Kevin Costner was so furious that he did his own editing of the film for his private collection. I have not seen this editing but I was told that it's much better.

Int: About Kevin Costner, have you seen *Dances with Wolves*?
JH: Yes. I liked this movie because all my life, I studied the Indians and I find that they have never been treated in such an honest way in an American film. It is very true. There is a sentimental dimension that is a bit conventional, but it was an interesting film.

Int: Is Mike Nichols's film *Wolf* completely different from your novel by the same name?
JH: Yes, but the idea did not come from the book. During this bad period in Hollywood, at the same time when they refused to allow John Huston to direct *Revenge*, I was at my cabin and I suffered a true lycanthropy attack, which is terrifying. In the middle of the night, I thought that someone was coming to the cabin, but it was like a flash. I jumped out of bed and I hit a chandelier, which is logically impossible. Then I tore the doors and I started to scream. I became completely crazy. My dogs were afraid of me and ran away. That's how the idea for the script came. It's a Jungian concept. During times of stress, of mental tension, people have sometimes modifications of consciousness. Of course, at the bottom of all this, there is the Indian tradition. When an Indian is very sick, either mentally or physically, he enters the body of an animal, a bear, a wolf, or a seal, to heal himself. And then, when he comes out, he changes his name. Sometimes he does not come out of it but it's good too. It's the same thing with the Chippewa Indians near my home (in northern Michigan). People disappear and become bears. Nothing can be done about it. But *Wolf* is not a werewolf film, although everybody insists it is. It's the story of a man who becomes a wolf in thirty days.

Int: You don't like werewolf stories?
JH: Yes, but it's a European theme. I wrote the American version of the

same legend. But they would not stop mixing the two things because they knew shit about it. I had many difficulties with Mike Nichols, although from a personal point of view, we got along fine. But we had a different approach of the subject.

Int: Do you see independent films in the United States?
JH: Yes, of course.

Int: Is there one you particularly liked recently?
JH: I liked *The Indian Runner* by Sean Penn. You have to see it. It is interesting because it shows this aspect of modification of reality I was talking about. The brother who is bad does not improve. He is bad, crazy . . . it's very strange. The film does not have this childish side we see in films today. You know that Nicholson is going to play soon in a film directed by Sean Penn, which is ideal?

Int: Do you write many scripts for Hollywood?
JH: About one every other year. It's simple. I think about it for a long time in my cabin and then I write very fast. I wrote the novella "Revenge" (on which the film *Revenge* is based) in a week. In America, most novelists are professors. I was a professor too, but it did not suit me. The other option is to work for the film industry. Now, I could live off my novels, but I also like to write films. What I don't like is to make five versions of the same story. I've decided that from now on, I would write only two versions of a script and after that they could get lost. I think I'm mostly good at inventing stories.

Int: Do you have many contacts in the world of production?
JH: No. I have a Sicilian agent. He is my sole contact. There is also the producer Douglas Wick with whom I just worked. He is very cultivated. I like him. He will be a great producer. He is only in his thirties. He is not very interested in business, he likes films above all. I like to work with him.

Int: Then, you are not like Faulkner, who despised Hollywood and called it the salt mine?
JH: Faulkner was a bit dishonest. They have his scripts at Warner. I read them: they were a disaster. He was cheating on them. In America, during the Depression, everybody was broke and he was making three to four thousand dollars a week. He wrote nineteen scripts, and practically none was ever shot (at least not in its original state.)

Int: When you write your novels, do you feel influenced by the cinema, or is it completely different?

JH: It's completely different, but when you are influenced by films, you visualize the novel as you write. The novel takes on a visual dimension. To write *Dalva*, I went to the Historical Society in Nebraska which has great iconographic resources. I looked at pictures of Nebraska at the beginning of the century, in the twenties. I have a visual reality in mind. Images make me feel the period. So, when I write a novel, I don't consider it to be prose—there are writers who are like that, like William Styron, for whom style is the most important. I see what I describe. But it's not the same as a film. Here, I write for myself.

Int: Did working on scripts change your writing?

JH: I don't see things like that. It forced me to write better dialogue because you write more dialogue in scripts. And also, you think more about movements, moves. A few days before I came to France, some women took an option to adapt my novel *Dalva* for the screen. I did not want to give up the rights for six years because I didn't like the people who were asking for them. Therefore I said I was going to read the book again, which I had not done since I had written it, to make small red marks to indicate the scenes that were important to me. But it was terrible, I could not do it. I gave up. It was too moving.

Int: Do you think that an American writer can live outside Hollywood?

JH: Of course. It's the case for many writers. They are professors. But the professional milieu is steeped in that horrible political correctness, which is fascist, repressive, and humorless. People do not flirt anymore because it's not "politically correct." I'm writing a long novella on a theme that's quite similar. It's a professor who is beginning to have problems. He enters the classroom, it's in the spring. He greets the girls who are present and says: "Good morning, girls, you look charming today!" And he is immediately rejected for having said such a sexist thing. It's like the Inquisition.

Int: Talking about sexism, in your Carte Blanche in Lyon you had planned a film with Marilyn Chambers, the X-rated film star of the seventies.

JH: Yes, it was a joke! (Laughter) They had asked me to submit a list of fifteen movies and I was stuck for the fifteenth so I wrote *Insatiable* with Marilyn Chambers. It's the most extraordinary porn film ever made. You have to see it right away! At the same time, it was a bit of a joke.

Int: And about violence? You said that violence was not filmed well in Hollywood.

JH: No, not at all. I explained it one day to Bob Rafelson in a club in New York. We did not agree about it. All of a sudden, I grabbed him and threw him on the other side of the bar, screaming. I told him that that was never done that way in films. Another time, I saw something with McGuane very late at night, in Key West. We were walking in the street and all of a sudden a man comes stumbling out of a bar. He makes some kind of gurgling sound. He falls backwards: his throat was slit to the neck. The slit looked like the tentacles of a calamari. Blood started seeping through. That's true violence. When I was young, in New York, in a bad neighborhood, I saw a man come out of a bar looking like he was scratching his cheek: he had an ice pick in it. In films, you don't have that immediacy of violence. It's very rare that it's a success. The best at filming violence is Scorsese because he knows what it is. He knows his subject. I had problems in Sweden, where they criticized me for the violence in my novella "Revenge." But there are only two dead in the story! In a made-for-TV film, there are often thirty-five. The scene they could not stand is the scene where a giant is disemboweled by the hero. I think you have to look at things the way they are because it's therapeutic. In films, people who are killed put their hand on their chest in a comical way. But when you shoot a deer with a rifle, he is thrown into the air and he falls spitting blood. When you are shot at, you don't say "Oh!" (Laughter.)

Int: Why don't you direct a film yourself?

JH: Because years ago I told my wife at a time when I was going crazy: "Today I give up all supremacy on the world and its inhabitants." My wife put that sentence on my desk. It means that I'm trying to fight this tendency I have which is precisely the one a director needs. Once, at Warner's they asked me if I wanted to direct a film. I said I found it too difficult. And it eats away two years of your life. There is another sign on my desk that reads: "I'm just a writer."

An Interview with Jim Harrison

Eleanor Wachtel / 1994, 1998

A conjoined version of two separate interviews Eleanor Wachtel conducted in Toronto
on her syndicated Canadian Broadcasting Company radio show, *Writers & Company*, on
September 25, 1994, and November 15, 1998, the latter when Harrison was attending the
International Festival of Authors in Toronto. The composite interview of material was published in *Brick: A Literary Journal*, no. 63 (Fall 1999): 18–26. However, for this longer version
edited selections from the original 1998 radio broadcast interview have been restored in
their proper sequence. Additional transcription by Robert DeMott and Anne Langendorfer.
Reprinted with permission of Eleanor Wachtel and *Brick*.

Jim Harrison is a surprising writer. He quotes Wallace Stevens in the epigraph to his collection of essays, "The worst of all things is not to live in a
physical world." Harrison has always had a close connection to the natural
world, but often through traditional male pursuits like hunting and fishing. His settings are frequently in those traditional "proving ground" landscapes—the north woods or a cattle ranch in the Midwest. Jim Harrison is
a man's man; buddies with Jack Nicholson, he cowrote the screenplay for
Wolf. A slightly grizzled, Hemingway-esque character, Harrison says things
like, "I like grit. I like love and death. I'm tired of irony."

Alongside that gruffness is a sophisticated, erudite writer, a man who
frequently quotes Rilke or Creeley, whose favorite book as a teen, his religion, was Joyce's *Finnegan's Wake.* A man who loves to cook and eat, he
wrote a food and wine column for *Esquire* magazine called "The Raw and
the Cooked." Or he does a few travel pieces for *Sports Illustrated.*

He is a Zen Buddhist who knows a lot about Native American life, peo-
pling his book with characters who are half Lakota or Oglala Sioux, writing
with passion, but not presumption. For instance, when referring to the tribal
elders in his new novel, *The Road Home,* he says, "These were not Methodist
Indians, warriors with a lineage that owed nothing to the white man. We did

not live upon the same earth that they did. And we flatter ourselves when we think we understand them. To pity these men is to pity the gods."

When Jim Harrison writes from the perspective of women, as he does in his novel *Dalva* and in the novellas "The Woman Lit by Fireflies" and "Julip," he's extraordinarily sensitive and subtle. In writing that is comic and redemptive, Jim Harrison subverts the myths of male initiation.

Harrison is sixty years old. He has published ten books of prose, nine of poetry, and a collection of essays. His latest novel, *The Road Home*, is a kind of sequel or companion novel to *Dalva*, which came out ten years ago. Set mostly in Nebraska, *The Road Home* takes up Dalva's story through her grandfather, mother, lost son, and finally, Dalva herself. Like virtually all of Harrison's writing, it is moving and utterly humane. An important but elusive character in *The Road Home* says, "Just do your art and be good to people. It's that simple and that difficult." [When I met Jim Harrison in Toronto last month at the International Festival of Authors, I felt that this must be his credo.]

Eleanor Wachtel: You write about how you like to surround yourself with special objects at your farm in northern Michigan, where you live and work, things like animal skins or a heron wing or a pine cone from the forest where García Lorca was executed. Can you tell me about them? And what they mean?

Jim Harrison: Well, I don't know. I think actually when I thought it over, it's a little similar to the kind of collection of stuff you have as a little boy, you know. I brooded so much. I kept calling my mother a couple years ago to find out what had happened to my marbles, for instance. And I know there's a particular house in Reed City, Michigan, where under the back porch I buried some marbles. So I called my mother. This sounds slightly daffy but now the house is owned by someone we no longer know, so I'd feel a little uncomfortable as sixty-year-old, going and trying to dig up my marbles. [Laughs.]

EW: This is literal, we're talking about? [Laughs.]

JH: Yes! [Laughs.] But, no, I have a lot of stuff. I even have a grizzly turd that Doug Peacock gave me and a walrus tusk that an Inuit gave me—you know, that kind of thing. I have a wonderful coyote skull that a man gave me for helping him put up his teepee at a powwow. And I said, "You're a little rusty, you know, putting up the teepee." And he said he had been in prison for seventeen years. And I'm trying to think, now why does someone go to prison for seventeen years? This is a tough customer. But he gave me this beautiful coyote skull with his medicine painted on it. Stuff like that, you know.

EW: Why are these objects totems for you? Or what consolation do they offer?

JH: Well, I don't know. I think it might have even come partly from Rilke, who said to surround yourself with beloved objects, you know, rather than gimcrack, junk, and lint that most often surrounds us and suffocates us. Some objects that you have a direct emotional response to, even in the kitchen, where, like my grandmother's hundred-year-old Wagner skillet, stuff like that. [Laughs.] You know. I suppose it's continuity and that battles against the dislocation that we ordinarily feel to have these kind of things close to us. I think it's partly as if objects could be fellow creatures, too, just like our dogs.

EW: In terms of continuity, or stability, or reminders of happier images, you have made a connection between collecting these beloved objects and images to the precariousness or the instability of when you lost your sight when you were seven, when you lost your sight in one eye.

JH: Well, I think there probably is an attachment there because you're in that kind of prolonged zone of recovery, you know. Actually, a French critic caught me up on this. My obsession with thickets.

EW: Your obsession with?

JH: With thickets. Certain thickets throughout the United States. I think I have fifty of them that I particularly like. You know, thickets being a place you can sit within and see out but nobody can see in, you know, that kind of thing. And so, I have quite a collection of those, too.

EW: Favorite thickets?

JH: Favorite thickets. Solace thickets, you know. [Laughs.] It is absurd. Mary Douglas, the English anthropologist, whom I read deeply because she wrote the best.

EW: *The Purity and Danger* and other books.

JH: Yes. Yeah. And she's an overwhelmingly good writer. But she was talking about ritual, how we use ritual to frame reality. And I think sometimes our little fetishes, I mean, in the good sense—I don't mean in some kind of absurd sexual sense—our little fetishes, our beloved objects also help us frame reality on our own terms, rather than on the terms of the predominant culture.

EW: And this thing about your favorite thickets being related to your losing your sight is so that you can see in a controlled way, or a hidden way, or what?

JH: I think that's partly that. Because you do collect, if you think about it. I was given a beautiful camera by a wealthy friend but then I found out how much it costs to develop the film after taking a lot of rolls. Then I gave it back to him. But I started to think, well, my good eye is an aperture and I blink it and I take pictures. Well, I have been doing this for years and years. If I really want to store something in my image bank, I stare at it very closely, blink my eye, and then I have that photo.

EW: That's free.

JH: Yeah, free! [Laughs.]

EW: You've talked about the effect of losing your eye, and you've said it left you feeling that, at any moment, you might "fall through the earth where the crust is thin,"

JH: Yeah, well you can't seem to count on much. That's just a metaphor where people actually think the earth is solid, but not necessarily! At first it's the hellishness of having nothing to fall back on—or as I said, "Life had become so bitter that I had nothing to fall back on except the sun and the moon and the stars." Like Aristophanes said, "When there's nothing for you to count on."

EW: Was that something you sensed when you were seven?

JH: That's definitely true. Though severe. I don't want to make too much of it. So many have really violent traumas in their youths, but it's something you have to accommodate. You realize the shape-changing keeps going on. Life is a fundamentally unreliable experience. As you may have noticed!

EW: One of the things that comes out in *The Road Home*—the character in the middle sections, Dalva's son Nelse, says that, "I can't see the virtue in studying the natural world. It's just that everybody should do it and it's the only world you're going to get, as far as we know."

JH: Well, that's true because there's a great deal of schizophrenia in the environmental efforts. It's not a true I-and-thou relationship, you know. It's a me-and-you. It's an almost implicit condescension because we can't forget we're nature, too. You know, as much as a bear or any other natural creature is, we're nature. So you can't separate yourself. You're either intimate with the natural world, or you're not. And you can create the distances, all sorts of distances, by sort of philosophical condescension. I remember when somebody told me they went to Montana and they thought people would be far nobler there because of the beauty of the surroundings. I said, "That's not the way it works at all. Maybe less likely." [Laughs.] Because you assume you know, you can go to Shangri-La, if there is such a place, in Tibet, and you can make it banal in a day through your own self immersion. You know, it depends on you. You don't get any more out of a place than you bring to it, I don't think.

EW: Schizophrenic in a sense of?
JH: Well, it's just this continuing sense of distance. I'm saving the Colorado Plateau from the people that live there, as an environmentalist said. Which is absurd. So, they're here. They don't even know that topography. They don't know the spirit of that landscape. It's self-dramatization rather than true absorption or obsession, which would be far healthier.

EW: In a way you're quite specific about the ways in which nature should or shouldn't be viewed, I think, as one of your characters says, "We always destroy wilderness when we represent something else."
JH: Yeah.

EW: The natural world in your fiction isn't an especially romantic place. You don't romanticize nature. It's harsh, but it's also enormously interesting.
JH: Yeah, well it's not very romantic. The local press in Michigan was discouraged recently when they saw two bucks run a doe into the lake and make love to her until she drowned. It's not always very pleasant in our human terms. But it's always obsessively fascinating to me, because we're nature too.

EW: You talk about speaking to the birds. In one of your novellas, "The Beige Dolorosa," the professor takes on as a project to rename the birds.
JH: He thinks some of their names are corny and banal, and it's time that we gave them some more interesting names.

EW: How do you forge that kind of intimate relationship with nature?
JH: Lifelong exposure. I suppose it's quite sophisticated, in an odd sense.

What I use to detach myself from the public world is a lot of walking in remote areas. But I also use Mozart and Rilke. If you find yourself properly tuned and you spend a lot of time around these creatures, you have at least the illusion that you're communicating with them, on some fundamental level. I'm not going to get goofy about it, like those poor souls who think they're talking to dolphins and so on. The dolphins don't need to talk to them, they should know that.

EW: The professor in "The Beige Dolorosa" says, "The birds made me feel I understood nothing, nothing at all." And at the same time he feels watched and spoken to by the birds.

JH: That's true. Now we're back to Blake. What did Blake say? "How do you know but ev'ry bird that cuts the airy way is an immense world of delight, clos'd by your senses five"? That's the visionary experience.

EW: I think, as you yourself have written in an essay called, "Everyday Life: The Question of Zen": "The bird passes across the window is a reminder of the shortness of life." But it's mostly a bird flying past the window. [Laughs.]

JH: Yes, of course. There is that problem. You know, I love the way even on greeting cards, they misquote Thoreau. They keep saying, "In *wilderness* is the salvation of the world." But no, "in *wildness*" is the salvation. So it's an entirely different concept, which I love. The way people want it to be so, to make wilderness represent that which has to be saved because it's mostly itself.

EW: So, it's misguided to be projecting too much on to it?

JH: Well, yes. Even Jesus said "step aside into the wilderness for a while." You know, he did a solid forty days, which is a long camping trip. I've never made it that long. By then I'd really crave a restaurant or a bar.

EW: [Laughs.] But you talk about the need to absorb the landscape, or better yet, become absorbed by the landscape, that you don't really become it, but it becomes you. How does that work?

JH: Well, it's just the idea, it's the old Dogen dictum or point—the fifteenth-century Japanese Zen master—who had said, "To study the self is to forget the self. To forget the self is to become one with ten thousand things." People usually stop there, but he goes on to say, "you don't become one with ten thousand things. Ten thousand things become one with you." Which is the whole point. That rather adds to one's range, I think. Hopefully, anyway.

EW: So if I ask you how it works, you'd have to explain the whole Zen . . . ?
JH: Well, you know, if you think about it, I read that in ancient India, they used to tie troubled people beside a river. Okay? Well, if you're willing to say try it sometime, sit down on a stone or a cushion or just on the bank of a river for two solid hours. And you find, if you're willing to give up every-thing, or open up a bit, the river does absorb rather nonchalantly your poi-sons and after a while there's just nothing there but you and the river and you're not confusing your separateness at all. The river is the river. But it's really done a marvelous bit on you.

EW: The idea sometimes seems to be carried almost to an extreme by some of your characters. I was thinking of Nelse, in *The Road Home*, who says, "Once I spent the whole of a cool, blustery May afternoon being a goshawk. And I had difficulty finding my actual body and reentering it."
JH: Well, that's just what you would call—which he knows very well—he doesn't want to be didactic or scholarly. That's just very traditional medicine in some cultures, to become something else for a while. And the main dan-ger is to be able to return to yourself.

EW: Have you ever done that? Have you entered something like that?
JH: Oh, sure. Yeah. I don't do it very often, you know.

EW: Like what?
JH: Well, a bear, you know. And birds. It's actually relief, but it's not some-thing you toy around with because that should be left basically for people who have given their life over to that discipline. An archaeologist I know and I like very much wrote *Rites of Conquest*, about what happened in the northern Midwest, including Canada. He was with the Cree people way up in northern Canada. This was thirty years ago. He went trapping on a long thirty-day trapping trip with an old Cree native and he kept saying to the older guy, "Are you sure you know where you're going?" And the guy says, "Yeah, I've flown over the area before." It made him feel better. But after he was up there for thirty days, it occurred to him, he didn't mean he really flew over it. He flew over in a different way. It was just quite amusing. But there's not really that much of it. I just notice that that's as valid a form of human behavior as anything that goes on in Washington, certainly.

EW: You've described a transformative experience as a "little attack of lycanthropy," you and a wolf.

JH: Oh, well, that was caused by anger. I was thinking that at my log cabin years ago I'd seen this female wolf in my driveway. But this is odd—they did a terrible job on the movie—I saw it and in general I didn't care for it at all, and I quit after I wrote a couple drafts about the subject of *Wolf* with [Jack] Nicholson and Michelle Pfeiffer. But what had happened in the middle of the night—I was just there with my dog at my cabin—I thought somebody was coming in my driveway, but it was really only lightning. Okay, so for some reason—it might have been a dream—I hurled myself off my cot there and I went so high in the air that I gashed my head on this iron deer-horn chandelier, and I cut my head. And then I ripped off the doors to the house and went running around, and I came to myself and it was very unpleasant. I kept the generator going all night and everything. My dog was frightened for a couple days. I mean, that's historical that that can happen to people, you know.

EW: And what had you felt had happened?
JH: I don't know. Just that. I was howling and everything. I don't know if I came unnerved, but what I'm still amazed by—I can sit on this cot and look at that chandelier and I'm a heavy fellow—How did I get up there? To cut my forehead, you know. I'm an artist. I don't like to fool with stuff like that. Leave that to people that are absorbed in that. Because it's again just part of the whole, and it's not the overwhelming whole. How interesting though.

EW: Yes. [Laughs.]
JH: It's not an academic experience. [Laughs.]

EW: The idea of attentiveness to nature, which relates also to your practice of Zen, I think, could also be seen as having some connection to Native American ways of being or seeing. I mean, is there a connection for you between the two?
JH: Oh, I don't know if there is or not. I was thinking that way because I was talking to one of my favorite authors, Peter Matthiessen, and he had said once, to find a practice, or a discipline, or a coda that overwhelms the least pleasant aspects of the culture, is part of what the terms are. So I don't care where it comes from—you can't take out of another culture what doesn't already exist in yourself and you discover there. You see what I mean? So that's the preposterousness of that New Age nonsense, you know? It better be there.

EW: It better be there in you.
JH: In you and you discover it. And that's the same way with any, I don't

want to become a nickel-plated Oriental student, you know, I mean a student of that culture. But I do know that for instance even in a northern Japanese Zen sect *yamabushi* or distinctly natural world people, many anthropologists think that *zazen* itself was an ancient, a very ancient hunting tactic, you know. If you sit very still for an hour, then the natural world assumes its total shape, that it temporarily dispersed to avoid its main predator, which of course is man. You know, they forget you're there, and they think that's where *zazen* probably started. It's an interesting point. But no, I don't think of myself as a Buddhist at all. I'm just an artist. I find these kinds of things absorbing, you know.

EW: But you have affinities to some?

JH: Yeah, well, of course. Empathies, affinities. I think that probably emerges also from the habitat, you know. If you spent fifty years in the woods as much as possible, of course you'd have some affinities for the people that always lived there, because you've seen their world, unmitigated by our own as much as possible.

EW: You characters in your novels are unusually philosophical, and they come up with these neat ways of pondering the "big questions," I think as one of them puts it. The question is how you make your soul clap its hands and sing.

JH: Yeah, well, that's that Yeatsian overwhelming irony, you know, "an aged man is but a paltry thing, a tattered coat upon a stick, unless soul claps its hands and sings." Which is true. But how do you keep alive? It's a question for all of us, you know. Even kids have trouble trying to keep themselves alive. But I think that in that, oh God, in that question the question is always how I can live without cutting off my arms and legs to get along with the world? That's critical, how can I maintain? That's back again to that peculiar notion I read in my late teens, where D. H. Lawrence said, "The only aristocracy was that of consciousness." You know, to the degree that you're totally conscious, you're totally alive, and that can't be bought in any sense.

EW: So have you figured out what makes your soul clap its hands?

JH: Yes, I think so. But sometimes I don't have the resources for it. I think you can't rate everything. It's all been extricably intermixed, you know. Like I said the other day, a Hasidic scholar I know had said to me, "Don't you think that reality is an accretion of the perceptions of all creatures?" I said, "Yep!" [Laughs.] What a statement! My wife adopted an orphan crow this spring, which was a little sort of pink thing covered with sores, and now it's a nice, big crow. But when I have a chat with him and we look at each other, it's the twilight zone in a way. Because you know, he's really thinking things over. I'm not projecting that. He just is. Because suddenly he turns a little bit and way, way down the road a mile you see the dog trotting along. [Laughs.] That kind of thing. You know.

EW: When you say you don't always have the "resources"?
JH: Oh, I mean, we all just get tired. We drown. We drown on a daily basis and then we recover.

EW: And does it have to do with this attentiveness to the dailyness of life?
JH: Well, sure, sure. For me it's more likely to happen outside than inside. Inside it usually is music or a good book, you know, that will lift you out of your doldrums. Weather that you can't sail in.

EW: I'd like to talk about your characters. Sometimes they're not only a little off course, it's as if they've dropped through a hole in their own lives. Why does that interest you in particular?
JH: Because that's what I see people doing. All the time. You create a life sometimes out of very mediocre assumptions, and then suddenly the whole structure no longer works. The human being tends to suffocate within the structure. Of course that doesn't happen to a lot of people, but they don't make the most interesting fiction. So you pick your characters that evolve along these crisis lines: Whether their hearts are wounded or their physical or mental structures disappear under societal pressures, whether it's losing a job or a divorce or wondering what they actually are.

EW: "Wondering what they actually are" would describe the novella, "The Woman Lit by Fireflies," where you've got a middle-class, middle-aged housewife, who ends up literally naked in a cornfield.
JH: That's more isolatable, in that she has sort of an elegant mind. Clare loves to read and she loves good music. But she'd reached a point—at that rest stop on Interstate 80—where she could no longer bear the simple and brutal mediocrity of her husband. So she went over the fence. It's funny, after that was published [in the *New Yorker*] I got, oh, I think it was 150 letters mostly from women—I would say 90 percent—who had done the same thing. It's very liberating sometimes to just walk off the porch, climb the fence, disappear. Especially when your reality is that much smaller than your mind. Which hers was.

EW: The men in your books are broken, in a way. The professor says, "If ours was more directly a cannibal culture by now I would be so much more lunch meat." Julip—the young woman in the title novella—is much more vivid, much more immediate than the men. What gives her that vitality?

JH: You know it occurred to me—and feminists might not agree with it, but it was certainly true when I wrote *Dalva*, which was in the voice of a woman— in general I find women in our culture much less of a mess than men. I've met many more extraordinary women in those terms, in my life, than I have men. Really strong, full of grace, powerful people. The thing you're most likely to get from men is, "Nothing turned out like I thought it would!" That whining. If you think women whine too much, there's so much more from men! It's amazing. Victims of the economy or their parents or their culture, blah, blah, blah. Complete infantile paralysis, in the pure sense of the word. That's true of Clare, who assumes a greater dimension in "The Woman Lit by Fireflies" or Julip, or Dalva. For the men to do it, it's not even a question of picking up the pieces—there aren't even any pieces, there are just smears here and there.

EW: What kind of relationships can there be between men and women?

JH: I don't know. Whatever you can come up with. I think we've lost something when lovers don't even observe an ordinary etiquette. And then you lost something because you can't maintain stability without that kind of etiquette. If you have a psychodrama every day, you just burn each other out. The trouble is, everybody is talking about their ills, and the only thing that makes them unique is their cures. You get what I mean? If men and women bring the best of what they figured out to each other, rather than this perpetual keening about how life has screwed them, then you have very positive and lovely relationships.

EW: If there is a prescription for living in your books, or a way of keeping yourself going, it is a slightly surprising one in that you say much of life is not disappointing, much of life is really nothing at all, just sort of big, open spaces in one's history. And a character in *The Road Home* feels a "delicious and particular sense of nothing." What is that about?

JH: Well, you're not going to get an epiphany every day. But sometimes you never get the epiphany unless you have some open space where your mind embodies that moving rest. You ever notice very wealthy people—I observed this one time—fill up their lives with appointments—you know, everything is a meeting or an appointment or an itinerary. Some I knew were going around the world and they showed me their itinerary and there wasn't a free minute in ninety-two days. The tickets were five inches thick. You know, that kind of thing. But that's not what I mean. [Laughs.] The loveliness of nothing. Emptiness, of course, isn't empty. The loveliness of nothing—if you're walking along the shore of Lake Superior for a couple hours—that's what I mean by nothing.

EW: The epigraph to your three novellas called *Julip* is from Rilke: "When the wine is bitter, become the wine." Can you talk about that?

JH: The other translation is: "When the drinking becomes bitter, become the wine." It's the way people think they can take all the fervid psychologisms that flood through American culture and the modern living pages. People are relentlessly taking this Band-Aid approach to these deep, psychic wounds they have. Rilke's meaning here is if you are ill, you have to go through the whole thing, you have to cure the whole body at once, even if it takes years. You can't continue just simply putting another patch on the tire.

EW: Is this something you've had to experience yourself?

JH: Oh, yes! [Laughs.] I've had some tough times mentally. Not any more than my heroes. You know, when you're a young writer and you have to read everybody's biography to see how it's panning out. If you've read Malcolm Lowry's you realize you've been lucky indeed. [Laughs.] So you have these periods of mania, or prolonged depressive periods, when you can't quite function at all.

EW: How does becoming the wine get you through that?

JH: Because by force you explore the entire dimension, and when you come out, there isn't a lot of residue. You see what I mean? Can you remember—maybe you're not old enough—I had all these friends who went off to est [Erhard Seminars Training] and changed their lives in just two weekends. But this isn't how it happens.

EW: Thank god.

JH: That's very funny. [Laughs.] It was okay. Doubtless it did some people good. If they hadn't spent it on that, they might have just bought another new Saab. No, a Volvo! And maybe white wine, when they should have been drinking red all along.

EW: One of the things that makes your writing so special is the distinctiveness of the voice, the persuasiveness and authenticity of the voice in each novella, whether it's Brown Dog, or a professor, or a young, attractive woman. Do you know how you get at that voice?

JH: I knew I had to quit as a novelist if all I was going to write about was nifty guys at loose ends, you know, that kind of crap. Then I started thinking about—that's even in Zen literature—to study the self is to forget the self and if you forget yourself you get to become ten thousand things. Other people became more accessible to me. While you're working you totally enter the other person. I suppose that's the oldest version of the artist—hocus pocus, mojo, whatever you want to call it—it depends on what culture. The primitive roots of artist as magician, where you might want to become a tree or a creek or an old woman. Children's stories are full of that kind of stuff—the old children's stories.

EW: You've created a striking character in Dalva, the heroine at the center of these two big novels written a decade apart. How would you describe her?

JH: Oh, I don't know if I could. You know, the last hundred pages of this novel *is* her. I don't know if I could. I think that's the entirety of the novel is to try to figure out—she's the sister I abandoned at birth in that Jungian sense. [Laughs.]

EW: What does that mean? Because you say that somewhere, that she is the twin that. . . .

JH: Well, no, Jung said that, why do men abandon—this is a fascinating idea—the culture makes you abandon your twin sister, you know? Because most cultures are not involved that consciously with a form of manliness that mostly exists because it's convenient for the economy of the culture in which we live: working hard at thrift, don't be late for work, be manly in all matters, that kind of thing. And the same way with the women, who I obviously have noted—since we went from hunting and gathering to farming and industry—the woman's society is less matriarchal. But what Dalva is, I say, I suppose is the kind of woman that takes all male prerogatives and more. She takes all prerogatives. It's unbearable to not be what she totally is.

EW: Well, she's terrific. She's beautiful and determined and sensuous and passionate, independent, financially secure, socially responsible, and an expert rider. So, is this your twin?

JH: No, I don't know, I don't know. I just brought that up. Because, like any intelligent person, I don't know if I would describe her that way, but she is a melancholiac, too. Because there's that character of longing in all our lives for something that doesn't quite get to be seizably there. You know, because of course, that's the nature of the human creature that life passes so quickly, you know. I only know one person, an interesting French count, who's a good writer, too—he says he thinks of life as really rather too long rather than too short, which is a nice point of view that we don't hear often. [Laughs.]

EW: When you talk about longing, there's a Portuguese expression that comes up several times.
JH: *Saudade.*

EW: What does that mean?
JH: Oh, I forget when I first heard it. I think I'd heard it in references years and years ago to Fado and I was in Brazil fifteen years ago for a while on a movie project and then I heard this Cesária Évora song, "Sodade." You know, she's a Cape Verdean from Portugal. And defined the whole concept of longing for something that no longer can exist, say, a dead lover, a farm, a home.

EW: But it clearly strikes a chord in you?
JH: Oh, sure, oh, sure. Like good poetry, you know. Lorca saying, "I want to sleep to dream of apples far from the tumult of cemeteries." You know, that kind of thing. Those chords that are struck by either literature or music are why we are so intensely human, I think.

EW: At one point in your journal, "From the *Dalva* Notebooks," you worry that in creating this heroine you might be doing it because you're lonely and you want to have someone you can utterly love.
JH: Well, I don't know about that, because sometimes we tend to exhaust ourselves by questioning our motives. I once thought if the goose that lays the golden egg turned around and watched, it probably wouldn't happen any longer. No, there's that suspicion. I once said, in some little piece of journalism, that way, way back in a marsh on a hummock of hardwoods, there's an old farmhouse hidden within the trees, and in that farmhouse live all the heroines of my novels and all my beloved dead pets. And that's where I'm headed. [Laughs.] Isn't that funny? Not to males. No males. [Laughs.] Just me and all . . .

EW: All the women characters. [Laughs.]
JH: From Sylvia on in *A Good Day to Die.* You know, step by step. It's an amusing idea, of course.

EW: Dalva is not only melancholic by nature. She has experienced a lot of loss.
JH: Oh, yeah, tremendously.

EW: Her father crashed in Korea, her lover committed suicide, her infant son was given up for adoption.
JH: Yes, truly. Yeah. So I don't care what your bank account it. We're all human by what happens. But the interesting thing is, I think, that we can concentrate on our own considerable wounds to the extent that we forget the only thing that can make us unique is our cures. Period. Not that we've been wounded. Not, as Hughes would call it, the nation of complaint. But how we resolve these kinds of things.

EW: In what ways are the cures unique?
JH: Well, the cure would be unique if you managed to through your ardor, through your day-by-day life, attain a specific victory over the humiliation of trauma, whether it's physical pain, murder, death, you know. I mean in my own case, my nineteen-year-old sister and my fifty-three-year-old father were killed, you know, so, that took a while. And then I saw my brother read the Episcopalian grave service over his own thirteen-year-old daughter. That's bravery, I would think. A bravery that I wouldn't be capable of.

EW: So, your cures are through your writing?
JH: Through your art. That's the only form I have. I mean, it's quite enough, frankly, if you think about it. I mean, I said once, I can't give anybody advice except to say, "more red wine and garlic." Or, as I admitted in the *After Ikkyu* book of poems, I've now closely advised seven suicides, so I'm backing out of this. I mean it came to me to say, "What should I do?" Whatever I had to say wasn't enough, so . . .

EW: Well, that's because . . . ?
JH: The illusion of control and power and grace fly out the window. People that are good at that are people who give their entire lives to it, you know, and if I were wanting to survive, I certainly wouldn't get in touch with a writer who says "more red wine and garlic," you know. [Laughs.] Just because it worked for him.

EW: But you've seen a lot of death? There's been a lot of death around.
JH: Oh, sure. Sure. That's one thing we all have in common, isn't it? But

I can't say it distresses me in the least bit. How could it be otherwise? I remember driving my dad crazy about that while we were fishing. He says, "Well we have time so everyone doesn't die at once," or something, and I'm asking him, "How come one day is longer than the other"? And he said, "What do you mean"? "Well, it just seems longer." You know, which of course, it is longer, despite clocks. Some days are enormously long and some are enormously short. All these devices we have for ordering our life sometimes just whisk themselves out the window. [Laughs.]

EW: In *The Road Home*, there are biblical elements in Dalva's story, or maybe even a touch of Greek tragedy. She unwittingly falls in love with her half-brother, and they produce a child who eventually comes back to her and finds out the truth. But you don't make much of this aspect of the story.
JH: Well, you shouldn't. Myths, as Ezra Pound said, myths are news that remain news, you know. That's the structure, the very structure of our life, you know, if you think of the fall of the House of Atreus, or the conscious Greek chorus that can sing out the history of what America did to the natives, or so on like that. It's just that the mythos of our lives follows a certain, specific structure. So many of the plays were lost, of course, I think Euripides wrote eighty plays and Aeschylus forty, and we only have a few left over. But the illusion that you get out of Hollywood—there are new, fresh stories, instead of there are master plots—and there's not a lot you can do about it. That's the very structure of our life.

EW: So what does it satisfy in you to tell the big stories? To tell the stories in this way?
JH: Well, I think I need to do that. I have to keep large stories to resolve my own demons, the so-called fear—whatever you call them now—in my own sense of consciousness. I have to resolve these issues. I have to resolve life herself, as I say. It's certainly not a boy, is it? [Laughs.]

EW: You also seem terrifically romantic. I mean virtually every character in *The Road Home* loves forever, even, or especially, if their beloved dies.
JH: Well, when people fall in love with somebody else, doesn't mean they stop loving the other person. That's another fiction we have in our life. How many people you know, after a couple drinks, start talking about their first girlfriend. I mean it's idiotic but our hearts are such that it doesn't mean that our subconscious is biblical or it obeys the rules because we even love to wallow in the memories of this. But life *is* sentimental. Why should I

be cold and hard about it? That's the main content. The biggest thing in people's lives is their loves and dreams and visions, you know.

EW: Another dimension of existence that gives these novels such texture and gives your characters' lives, and evidently your own life, such texture, is the world of dreams. And you've talked about dreams as a metaphor for survival or even a path towards home. Tell me about it.

JH: Well, that's just the point, you know, it's almost an irritating point, when you talk to some people. Say if people placed immense, immense value on their dream lives for a hundred thousand years, and then ceased doing so a hundred years ago, then who is right? I'm not saying that if you dream, you should go swimming in the winter, that's not how it works. It's a very sophisticated procedure. But the idea of ignoring your dream life is a perilous one, I think.

EW: Can you say what you've learned from yours?

JH: Oh, sure. I think I've learned more. Well, in that essay, "Dream as a Metaphor of Survival," I said you're considerably enriched as a human being if you know what your dreams are telling you. At times. If I dream that they're trying to kill me in New York City by pushing me off a waterfall—where they got the waterfall I'm not sure—but I fly away and I'm too heavy to fly and it's really hard to fly, but then I land in a tree and discover that I'm a half bear and half large bird, well, that's very consoling. That tells me, well, that's enough of New York for this year. I should be around bears and birds, where I belong.

EW: You probably didn't even need a dream to tell you that!

JH: No, but it helped. It was sort of interesting. God, he got out of that one alive, you know. I better quit this screenwriting job and go home. [Laughs.] I know how to get there. There's a road. That kind of thing.

EW: You talked about how there's a Native way of dealing with boredom, which is to do everything backwards. You say you want a lot of interesting things to occur before and it strikes you that, rather than wait around for them to occur, you're going to have to arrange most of them.

JH: My character probably said that, but I definitely agree. We all feel a bit dried up. I tell my wife that I have to take a car trip and collect new memories. I like to drive around absolutely randomly for weeks on end, around the United States and parts of Canada. Or I'll feel trapped—you know, like you do when your life is completely planned out months in advance, and you think you're not getting enough oxygen in your system. Something like that.

EW: At the same time, you say that "the hardest thing for me to accept was that my life was what it was every day."

JH: That's particularly Zennist, and that's hard for us that grew up as little, white Christians, where we have that Protestant notion—from that song "Jacob's Ladder"—every rung goes higher, higher in every way, every day, we're getting better and better. Then you realize, through study or meditation or getting older, that what you are is just what you are every day. It's a very nonromantic leap, but then it becomes quite pleasant.

EW: The notions are some way at odds. You either accept that this is what your life is, or if you want interesting things to happen you have to go after them.

JH: I think they go together very well, because once you accept the reality of your condition, you can better figure out what it is you need to do to change it. Even if it's taking the train over to Montreal and eating too much. I'm not thinking about vast, wonderful, global things all the time. Sometimes it's just an extension of your ordinary appetite.

EW: You've written a lot about your various demons and about your sources of strength. Do you feel that you've found some sort of balance in life? Or is it always a struggle?

JH: Well, I better have because I'm sixty now. But I don't know if that's true. I think balances are temporary and anytime you think you could fix yourself in one place, that's absurd. Properly, life lived properly, is a river. Or that Yeatsian concept that life is best viewed as a dance. You know, an interminable dance. So, if I thought I had reached some point, I would hit myself over the head because the path is the way. You have to keep reaching the point on the continuum, you know. It never stops, even for a moment. I would say there is a bit more consolation now, because what I had thought as a young writer was that I would never whine if my books stayed in print and so they have. So that's the only thing you have to hope for.

EW: Do you think that earlier instability served you as a writer?

JH: Oh, of course, of course, because it gives you range. Instability would really be euphemism. [Laughs.]

EW: Various tough times. Depressions. I mean, things you've given your characters, too.

JH: Yeah, true. Well, I haven't had an actual depression now for almost fifteen years. So that's quite nice, you know. I mean, there's all this whining about the poor artist, but I mean, really, what a grace note, you know, to have found a form that you can express yourself totally in, so we should think of ourselves as inordinately lucky that this happened.

EW: I'm really glad to have the chance to meet you. Thank you very much.

JH: Thank you.

Jim Harrison: "What I'm Thinking about for Two Hours"

Casey Walker / 1997

From *Wild Duck Review*, no. 3 (April 1997): 3–6. Reprinted with permission of Casey Walker, Editor and Publisher, *Wild Duck Review*.

The following two-hour conversation between Jim Harrison and Casey Walker took place in Patagonia, Arizona, on March 8, 1997.

Casey Walker: What do you think of "nature writing" per se?

Jim Harrison: I don't care much for the term, "nature writing." In the hands of a naturalist like Ann Zwinger, I suppose the category makes sense. But, as far as what everybody else is doing—to act as if nature writing is something relatively new when it isn't—says a lot more about this American culture of ours. Nature writing has been around since the 1870s and right up to Loren Eiseley, who wrote more magnificently than any of us, frankly, and around the turn of the century, like *Field & Stream* and *Outdoor Life*, were predominantly very strongly environmentalist, and Bernard DeVoto wrote vociferously from "The Easy Chair" position at *Harper's* right up through the 1930s and '40s. Nature writing is nothing quite new or new at all.

At a recent talk I gave in Seattle, I spoke in part about a kind of schizophrenia in the environmental movement and in nature writing. To consider nature in any way as a separate entity that one looks down upon as subject-object is a problem because there is no split at all. Even Shakespeare said we are nature too. It's in the splitting that environmentalists get their egos, their self-dramas, their self-congratulations, problems I just don't see in the natives I know real well. The Anishinabe in the Upper Peninsula in northern Michigan are wonderful at maintaining their humility in the natural setting. I think, though, it's because there's a religious base for them. It's also in the way people grow up. Some have been hunting since they were seven. Even for my friend, Nick, who falls into the loathsome category of "outdoorsman," it's nothing for him to cover five to ten miles a day every day of his life and what he notices are details, the particulars. There's no replacement for experience.

I remember when I first saw a wolf in the Upper Peninsula it was doubted by a professor. I didn't mind in the least because he sat in an office and I sat in my cabin in a forest on the river and had seen things from my window that were astonishing—male and female loons taking turns on the nest, each going crazy waiting for relief, making all kinds of noise, responding to coyotes and whippoorwills, back and forth. I think our sense of fieldwork can best be approached through what Thoreau called "sauntering."

CW: Because the motive to sauntering is so different than the motive of entering an experience in order to write about it?

JH: Yes. As Dogen said, "The study of the self is to forget the self. And to forget the self is to become one with ten thousand things." Okay, what he then adds and what people forget is that you (the ego) don't become one with ten thousand things, but ten thousand things become one with you. If you go out with expectations of any sort, you don't get what the outside has to give. In one novel, I parodied the mountain biker who told me he did thirty-five miles on a muddy road. I asked, Geez, what did you see? Hey, he said, I keep my eye on the road!

If every adventure in the outdoors is one of personal accomplishment and we keep attacking the natural world with equipment—our problems with "self" in "nature" will be just spectacular. Every extermination of any species has always been accomplished by mechanization. I once wrote a note of complaint to *Outside* magazine because they had a fabulous photo of a natural landbridge formation in Utah, but across the top they showed this geek running in his spandex. It all reminds me of the Nazi youth when certain forms of nature loving were at a height in Germany in the 1920s and '30s, and it was all tied to a particular moral force, the purification of a genetic strain, vegetarianism and ego.

You don't get these cultural attitudes with native people and that's what is so wonderful about Richard Nelson's phenomenal books, *Make Prayers to the Raven: A Koyukon View of the Northern Forest*, about the Koyukon people; and *The Island Within*, about living on an island off Sitka. The trouble comes with a full elitism, the kind Robinson Jeffers was guilty of, the view, "I alone overlook the rock and the Pacific." It's the "I alone" that is on a family allowance for thirty-five years, surveys nature, and then loathes human beings. We cannot ignore humans or human habitat any more than we can ignore animals, plants, or natural habitat. They all have to go together or you have, as in the case of Jeffers, a tremendous lacuna. I knew Ed Abbey and, as wonderful as he was, he had holes in his worldview vis à vis Native Americans and Mexicans.

CW: Because of the exclusiveness of a singular point of view?
JH: Yes. You have to think of reality in terms as an aggregate of the perceptions of all creatures. You look at the bear but the bear is looking at you, and you better consider the bear looking at you. He isn't something to just put a fucking collar on, you know? They've done this absurd thing in Michigan. I have an enormous wolf bibliography at home and we now have a couple hundred wolves on the Upper Peninsula that came back by themselves over the ice and around, thirty-five miles. No one had to help them, it's a matter of habitat, period. Now people are saying they have to radio collar all of these wolves. Well, there's immense, immense knowledge on Eastern Timber wolves already—what more do we need!?

CW: The seduction of hard data, of funding more projects!
JH: That's true. Everybody wants to get a grant, get funded for something. Now we've even got miniature telemetric devices for implants in quail, when you can tell an enormous amount about quail by simply watching. There's just an enormous self-dramatization going on—a missionary zeal— especially when we say we're going to help nature but then forget how to let natural processes proceed. That's what I liked so much about David Quammen's book, *The Song of the Dodo*, about island biogeography and the remarkable processes at work.

Environmental zeal also reminds me of the problems of feminism in the 1960s. If feminists had stayed unified as a political force, the ERA would have passed in the 1970s, '80s; but they got bifurcated just like the environmental movement and splintered into hundreds of groups. Or, if feminists had stayed focused on issues such as the ERA and equal pay for equal work, they might have changed the dominant social and economic injustices right there. When movements split into many little self-dramatizing groups, they lose force. With so many agendas, there's also a failure to understand the nature of Washington. You have to know you're dealing with a septic tank full of greed and you must go into it with power. If all the groups could agree on three things they wanted and could amass voters, they'd have results.

CW: Do you see legal battles as the place to start?
JH: If you can concentrate the legal solution, it's the place to start. It's also

remarkable though how the minds of the young can change things. I appeared at the first Earth Day as one of the literati and I happened to say, in the talk I gave, that there were too many billboards. Right away, students went out and began cutting billboards down with chainsaws. Besides my embarrassment, I rather liked the idea. Today, the minds of the young are so much more aware, generally speaking, of what the consequences are of our behavior.

What fascinates me about the Nature Conservancy and what I adore about them as opposed to some groups, is that they do understand that the cogs and wheels turn so slowly in Washington we had better buy habitat now and take it out of harm's way. Things with enormous moral force are often completely ignored in Washington. You can't be like a big muffin going to Washington, you have to unify and go in there like a big axe. It's the only way things are perceived there and I don't care if the head of our groups have to spend a lot of money, it's a Machiavellian world and there's no sense going in there like Gandhi.

CW: It's a challenge to think of extending our language, creating the language to change discourse and take the lead on issues in ways not co-opted at the semantic level, the power level, of politics.

JH: Maybe that's the good of so-called, quasi-nature writing. It has a great deal more public appeal now. But, you're going to get co-opted all the time by data. It doesn't matter if you say, for instance, that only 3 percent of our beef by weight is grown on public land and how can you destroy this much public land for that 3 percent? That's about as far as you can go with data because of the digestive system for fresh knowledge out there. One way that works is money. When the ranches were sucking up all the water of certain trout rivers in Montana, a lot of somewhat monied trout fishermen pushed and pushed and now the ranches can't do it anymore. This is the nature of the world. When we approach adversaries innocently, with goodwill, it's fatuous. You don't get your best-intentioned, fifty-dollar-an-hour lawyer, you get your savvy, five-hundred-dollar-an-hour lawyer.

The other thing that speaks loudly next to money and legality, is just sheer votes. There's no question that the anti-environmental forces and Gingrich's "Contract for America" had to back up because they crossed the line with a lot of people, including Republican women birdwatchers. People don't want to hear that kind of rhetoric anymore, it's bullshit. What counts is a broad base of money, legality, and votes. You can frighten anybody with votes. I come from an agricultural background and have absolutely nothing against cows, but I have everything against improper use of public land for grazing.

I can say to a rancher that we're carrying the load too, this is an entitlement, and some of my best quail habitat has been turned to leather since
last year. Who's the landlord? As Rene Char said, "Who stands on the gang-
plank directing operations, the captain or the rats?" That's always a good
point. So, in other words, in this incredible swap meet that is Washington,
we can't be so nice about it. We don't want to be simpleminded. I don't think
it's cynicism, it's a recognition of how it works in America.

CW: Beyond the politicians and the theologians, as you say in your essays,
there are the writers and poets and artists out at the margins working away
at consciousness.
JH: Sure. But, you can't ever think, and, as I've said, you shouldn't ever have
the illusion of coming to an artist for coherence. It's feeble-minded to think
of being right as an artist. Being right is about as fragile a thing possible in
the world. The duty of the poet is not to shit out of his mouth like a politi-
cian. Poets should be out there on the borderland saying this kind of thing.
Truly, some of the nature writing being done today is masturbatory, what I
call the pornography of nature, and can be as obtuse and disturbing as the
ignorance of nature. It goes so far as the poor woman in the *Harper's* article
who wanted to be kind to the sick hyena and got half eaten alive. I think
there is a failure to internalize what we're saying, and to realize we know
what to do when we're in peril but we don't know what to do when something else is in peril. Sentimentality forgets what it is to be wild.

CW: And fails to see the appropriateness of backing away, backing off.
JH: Sure. The function of adventure travel, which is somewhat debilitating in some respects, is not to count coup on everything, but to comprehend it all. We're not getting rid of the ego when we write to ask, aren't my
observations elegant and astounding? The largest nature metaphor I ever
heard, which is wonderful, came from Lorca who said, "The enormous night
straining her waist against the Milky Way."
   Part of the problem comes because America, with the disintegration
of the Soviet Union, is at the peak of her empire now. We have to think of
what happened with England in Victorian times when there was a great
deal of rigidification, moral rigidification, and scrutiny of everyone else,
all of which is, of course, what we have in our New Puritanism. With
America's fear of losing world power and money, politicians are writing thousands of rules every day to solidify their positions, to solidify
the position of America. It's absurd. It's gotten so out of hand that you

can't have your own personal, moral structure without thinking everyone should have your particular moral structure.

CW: What do you think of the role played by the processes of modernity and increasing abstractions in our lives?

JH: I think our problems are partly modernity, but as Paul Shepard said somewhat inadvertently, and which also goes well with Bruce Chatwin's last, posthumous book of essays on nomadism, this kind of rigidification came at the height of the agricultural cycle (post-hunter and gatherer), and now we're at the absolute apex of this rigidification. The power of the priestly class is being assumed by national and state congresses who are relentlessly trying to make moral rules. Bernard DeVoto, according to Lewis Lapham at *Harper's*, said the worst thing that happened during the McCarthy period, and what he found inconceivable, was all the constant snooping. Now the modern university, with all its political correctness, is closer to the cellular structure of Cuban communism than anything else. It's absurd.

Sometimes our political correctness nonsense is funny. A couple of years ago, my Italian editor went to a dinner party in Marin County. She was outside looking at the Pacific, standing by a buffet table. A wind had come up, the tablecloth was flapping, and she was asked not to smoke. She did what all good, strong Italian women do, she said, "Fuck you" and was out of there. This kind of falling into line, whether it's academic or not, is part of the monstrous response you had to Jack Turner in the last issue of *Wild Duck Review*. How dare he question it all? It's amusing to hear all of these well-intentioned people chastening Jack. It sounds like something in the 1920s, with Lenin from the Finland station, "You're failing to follow the platform."

CW: And, if you question you must have an alternative plan. Where's our desire for saying the unsayable?

JH: It's absurd. It's just like the border problem here in Arizona and Mexico. Some suggest a moat should be built, but then you see these 12,000 foot peaks and you can see that a 1,900 mile moat is ridiculous. No one wants you to say the reason the Mexicans are crossing the border is because they earn five dollars a day at most in a factory in Mexico and they're earning fifty dollars a day working here. What do we expect? Unless you get a patrolman every fifty feet, à la Berlin Wall, you're not going to stop anything. It's fatuous—as fatuous as stopping marijuana from coming across. It doesn't mean I have any solutions, but you can certainly say, as does Jack Turner, that when the emperor is naked, the emperor is naked. You don't have to have any clothes ready for the emperor to see that he is naked.

Then there's the preposterous effects of social engineering. For instance, you know how hard it is to help friends. Now add millions and millions of friends. These programs are like cosigning a loan and you don't see them again for a year. It's essentially funny. There's no sense in saying, get all the cows out of the Rockies. That's not the way you do it. There are ample methods. One simply treats the property as any tenant should any landlord's property. Solutions are just not that obscure.

CW: What obligations do writers carry and to what, to whom?

JH: Ed Abbey was magnificent to me, and we were always quarreling about one thing or another, but the wonderful thing was that you'd never mistake him for anyone else any more than you would Jack Turner or Doug Peacock. There's no point in pretending an artist is going to be a junior scientist. His obligation is to note the discrepancies in our environmental efforts as poignantly as Ginsberg did the world order as it stands.

It's hard to get up in the morning and look in the mirror and say, I am part of nature too. But you are, what the fuck do you think you are? We're just the most dangerous form of nature and we better be aware of it with all our brilliant little ideas. Some of the most powerful "nature poetry" you'll find is in people like Snyder and so on where it's not obtrusively didactic, or in the Chan poets of China. I don't think Wordsworth is read enough anymore.

There's been a terrible suffering of literacy in the last twenty years in particular, partly because the teaching profession is so sure there is a short cut to be had. Now with the invention of computers and the internet, it's as if there is a new substitute for reading, writing, and thinking. There's not. A mass movement is being created that is even more susceptible to different forms of Nazism, you know? It's an implicit moral fascism. Look at the Savings and Loan debacle, and they're right back again. What regulations have there been on greed?

It's messianic to think greed is self-checking. I've never met a developer who wouldn't spit in the face of his grandchild for a buck—that's the nature of the beast and we better know it. I wonder at what's going on. I was in Burgundy, France, a big cattle raising area that is peerlessly beautiful. I remarked it was extraordinarily well taken care of, given all the cattle, and the fellow I was talking with said, well we didn't have any place else to go. We Americans have realized too late how limited we are. Here in America we've had a theological basis for land rape too, with the Christian assumption that we're going to die and go to heaven and, meanwhile, it's our duty to do anything we want to the land to prosper. We can't forget that wilderness has always had people living in it and that you don't have to notice people. In terms of wildness, I always thought it was comic that I knew of more forty-acre woodlots in Michigan that are wilder than Yosemite.

Of course the be-all, end-all problem is overpopulation, as we all know. I haven't heard any intelligent solutions to this problem. I've heard intelligence but not functional intelligence. In the case of China, where you consciously limit your birth rate to two children per family, there's amniocentesis and suddenly everyone wants sons. We can't keep up with the technology. Then, here we are with cloning. Newt Gingrich will want nine hundred versions of himself. The stew we're in is enormous. A movie mogul told me you have to play hardball twenty-four hours a day to get ahead in that business. I want my leaders in the environmental movement to play hardball twenty-four hours a day. Maybe they can file their teeth.

CW: And writers?

JH: Oh, filing their teeth comes with their nature. It's unthinkable for me to have any hesitation about what I say in a poem. I suppose that's always been true for a particular kind of a writer. Once you receive your calling you can't back off at all. Writing isn't something for people who don't want to spend their entire lives at it, and most people figure out that commitment early, by age eighteen. You see you don't get to be a lot of things, that writing will take a full commitment.

CW: You've quoted Rene Char as saying, "Lucidity is the wound closest to the sun." Will you speak to what it means for you in your work?

JH: Yes. Your obligation as a writer is to be utterly vulnerable moment by moment by moment. It's the regrettable trap. It's like Dostoyevsky questioning whether at some point to be too conscious is to be diseased. Or, as Nietzsche said, if you stare into the abyss long enough, it'll stare back into you. Without question it is not a process that frees you from your common humanity, because writers are as susceptible to greed as anyone I know. The seductions are countless in this world to make the least important come first—vis à vis putting the lucrative screenplay before a book of poems. But, it can't bother you too much because that's the nature, too, of writing. Like Faulkner said, if you've got to take it raw, take it raw. That's what writing is.

CW: As a writer do you consciously protect your vulnerability?

JH: Yes. It's a great part of it. There's something very troublesome that D. H. Lawrence said and I came upon it in my twenties, "The only aristocracy is that of consciousness." Consciousness is a moment-by-moment obligation, and if you have it then I suppose you're finally entitled to say something. It's the same thing as what is meant by "tentativeness" in Zen, or meant by Dogen when he said, "No changing reality to suit the self." There's no sense in marching or having a meeting when the world is being destroyed, as in the case of the bison, right outside. There is always the new wound or the new corruption right here, the moral corruption, that is absolutely profound and opens us to international ridicule. When the consciousness of Americans catches up to what they're doing, the shit is going to hit the fan.

CW: What do you think of psychotherapy?

JH: I've been to a mind doctor off and on for twenty years and it's made a profound change in my life. All they are are contemporary shamans—there is no other way to look at them—but, the trouble is, as many will admit, only one therapist out of a thousand is any good. I don't object to therapeutics, but I object to therapeutics becoming a giant machine as it has in this culture. Now we have human imperfection numbered in the thousands so therapists can bill insurance. He drinks coffee: #582.6. He washes his hands too often: #584.7. He turns off the light too often: #631.2. If such therapeutics free people from the responsibility of being human, we have a real problem. And, this great, great embracing of victimization that took place a decade or so ago has created real problems.

CW: Yes, and the emphasis on the confessional in public as therapeutic, or in poetics as art, has real limits to it.

JH: I never could read Anne Sexton for that reason. It's not very interesting. When I say, oh woe is me in extremis, I'm just another coal miner, what's the point in thinking it's unique? Our cures are interesting. Our infirmities aren't. Everyone knows about infirmities. Our occasional luminescences are what contribute to the human condition. The idea that somebody can say, for instance, that I get up and work hard—well, try saying that to the Chicanos. Give me a break! I grew up in a rather poor family of dirt farmers in northern Michigan. Can you imagine the idea of a professor teaching six hours a week and whining about it? But, the confessional movement is rubbish and will go away fast. People will tire of lifting the Band-Aids.

Even Rush Limbaugh is fading. People will look for something else, something new, as we do all the time and have throughout our history. Dozens of women I know have grown tired of thinking of themselves as victims. Now they're on to kicking ass and taking names, which is infinitely healthier than saying, oh poor me. I have a profound Jungian therapist who points out that he has patients in their late sixties still whining about their parents. It is all very comic. It's that illusion that parents are always dominant, that big brutes are always dominant, in our lives.

CW: In one of your essays, I liked your statement on the necessity of grandiosity for survival. Will you speak to what you mean by grandiosity and by survival?

JH: Yes. There is a realization that to live your life you have to write your own songlines. Your own songlines and the degree to which you want your life to be an independent project is up to you. It's harder for people, of course, whose parents or whose society has crushed them, and that has happened over and over again. In the 1940s there was a craze in America for tying kids' hands so that they wouldn't pick their noses or misbehave. The elegant thing is to transcend being a victim.

I just wrote a children's book called *The Boy Who Ran to the Woods*, which is what I did at seven years old when I was blinded by a little girl. I think it was Edith Cobb's *The Ecology of Imagination in Childhood* that made it clear to me I had gone to the natural world to survive, to do my time alone. In *Dalva* I wrote about having to withstand implacable blows. When my father and sister were killed in an auto accident, I thought, isn't this strange, any possibility of agreeing with the world has just left me.

However, we Americans have been relatively spoiled. Look at Europeans and their suffering—millions of people dead. Our country is now seething with generalized resentment. There's more whining in the upper middle class than amongst the black population or natives by far. Certain people know through their consciousness as primates when they've painted themselves into the corner, and if they've painted themselves into the spoiled kind of corner, there's nothing more depressing than a Rolex and BMW. I know you have to keep one ear for your friends and one ear to the conversations in the world around you. I see it, hear it out there, this malaise. It's because there's no spiritual life, of course, and that makes for an enormous vacuum because we're spiritual creatures.

CW: In your own work, whether from day to day or in its general arc, what does it look like to you? Where is your curiosity?

JH: Well, you can go through it to the point you see not just what is in front of you, but can look at yourself walking away. I see more of the same work I've done before, I don't change gears in quantum leaps. I do find myself reading more and more about botany and anthropology, which reminds me of Erik Erikson saying reality is mankind's greatest illusion. We are overwhelmed by the perception of how short life is, as in the old Don Juan thing about the whining man who is always whining and whining about hoeing corn and then you hear a dog barking in the distance and the screen door slams and suddenly it's evening. You have to be very aware of that sensation. Time is one of our great illusions too. In "The Beige Dolorosa" there's a man who wants to rename the birds of North America, and he's created a calendar in which there are only three days a month, which gives him these great open spaces. Three two-hundred-hour days. Natives know this kind of thing—how to renew oneself. The interesting thing about being in a rut is that the only thing you see are the sides of the rut. You don't see out. The frogs who fell into the well now think that's the universe. It's the perfect metaphor for people rich or poor.

I'm working on a second chapter of a novel where I've moved from a seventy-one-year-old man to a thirty-year-old grandson. He's questioning how, it we primates are mapped for anything that moves, do we discriminate between the spiritual caffeine of TV or movies and what lies mostly still outside the window? Occasionally a bird goes by, the sun goes down and then comes up. But people crave movement and forget that the movement seen on TV and in movies is not part of a living process, that it's coming out of a tube. Life is subtle and complex. There are no easy, fast answers. There aren't even any easy questions, let alone answers. In America this affects us in the environmental movement—the idea, the illusion, that every question has an answer. It's our Calvinist upbringing to believe that everything is solvable. It's sheer hubris.

CW: How do you describe the core, the spirit, of your work?
JH: This consciousness, I would say. Otherness. Otherness to remind ourselves of the bedrock of life, and death, and love, and suffering. Back to Lorca, what is poetry but love, suffering, and death? Or, the idea of making a heap of all that you have met. I haven't been nearly as unflinching as I'd hoped to be, no. But, that's part of my makeup. Early on, my inability to face certain horrors as directly as I should have contributed to that. But, then I'm always looking for the song I could make out of it, too. I can't quarrel with the limitations which are part of me—everybody has the severest of limitations. You are ultimately what you collectively wish to be. When someone

says they could be so much more, I say well, you better get started right now, who's stopping you? Face it, there's an anchor tied to your ass.

CW: Are you writing poetry—is it the writing closest to your heart?

JH: I'm always writing poetry. I don't differentiate, though, between poetry and novels at all. Short things are short all over and long things are long. I've never been able to write short stories. The shortest I ever get is a novella, about a hundred pages. Certainly it's too late to become a fireman or a cowboy. Early in my environmental activities it was always requested that I not speak a lot because, as my daughter would say, I could make an audience weep in five minutes through one means or another and the environmental movement is one area in which we need a lot of rationality. The poet has to be off to the side giving his two cents, but two cents isn't the whole dollar. One isn't really good without the other, but I see how brutally hard some people have worked and it's paid off for the movement by just being out there plugging away day in and day out.

CW: How might the proliferation of creative writing programs and workshops affect literature?

JH: You can't ever have enough of what's good. I think sometimes the bad or mediocre obfuscates the good—that's what Ezra Pound thought—and I think there's a problem if one thousand literary novels are published every year and they are all recommended with sincerity. Certainly sincerity is not then a very high virtue. Give me back the art. I can't read prose unless it's interesting prose. I don't give a shit about anybody's good intentions, you know? Juice can't be taught in a creative writing program.

I created an ideal creative writing program once. I taught it for one semester and I gave students 148 books of poetry for the main part of the modernist tradition, from the French Symbolists onward. I lost some students there. But, I think an ideal MFA writing program would require one year of manual labor in the country; one year of life in the city; one year spent alone reading; and only then would anyone return and begin writing. How else would anyone know anything?

Sorrowfully, success in writing is not a democratic process. No matter how hard you work and study, it either comes or doesn't, the door opening or closing on good prose. I'm just stunned how a man like Gabriel García Márquez, in his novella last year, can write as he does. As I've said before, most people look in the mirror and say, "I'm getting old." But Shakespeare looked in the mirror and said, "Devouring time, blunt thou thy lion's paws."

There is a difference. No one can teach you to make a metaphor. Or Lorca's, "Your belly is a battle of roots,/ your lips a blurred dawn./ Under the tepid roses of the bed/ the dead moan, waiting their turn." That's a different way of saying, gee, you're nifty. So much of our current fiction sounds like the contents of white guys at loose ends. Our own history has been sanitized to leave things out like women, Indians, Mexicans . . . more examples of white guys at loose ends. Instead, good art smells like life.

Creating Habitat for the Soul:
An Interview with Jim Harrison

Robert DeMott and Patrick Smith / 1997, 1998

Edited, streamlined version of a previously unpublished interview conducted by Robert DeMott and Patrick Smith on July 30 and 31, 1998, at Harrison's home in Lake Leelanau, Michigan, with additional supporting material from an unpublished interview by DeMott and Smith at the same venue on August 28 and 29, 1997. Transcription by Robert DeMott and Patrick Smith, with assistance of Chris Walker, Rae Greiner, and Anne Langendorfer. Clarifications and refinements added from follow-up interview by DeMott on September 2, 2000. Final transcript by Robert DeMott, with additions from original typescripts added in 2017.

We arrived at Jim Harrison's home on the Leelanau Peninsula on a blessedly cool, dry late July evening. The Harrisons' remodeled farmhouse, their main residence since 1968, has a modest, subdued, orderly air to it and sits in a grove of mature hardwoods, the walkway to its front door accented by stately white birch trees. We were well met by Jim and his wife, Linda, who were in the middle of readying a backyard barbecue, no less elegant and inviting for its informality. We joined in the bustle, helping where we could, and trying to hold up our ends of the wide-ranging conversation that commenced the moment we entered. Mostly, however, we savored our Côtes-du-Rhône, scratched dogs' ears, admired Linda's magnificent flower garden, and watched evening come down over the pond behind their house.

At sixty-one, Harrison, despite gout, still does nearly everything—including writing and cooking, eating and talking—as if his life depended on it. Although it was doubtful he had reached that transcendent level of freedom from dread, alcohol, gluttony, money problems, and so on that he wished for in his 1984 essay, "Fording and Dread" (reprinted in *Just Before Dark: Collected Nonfiction*), we felt that he had at least reached a degree of nonchalance or indifference. He appeared to be unconcerned with what people thought about his opinions, his self-described "burly" physique, or his sometimes disheveled attire. "I don't have to pretend," he told us.

Harrison personalizes his experiences in ways that are both memorable and nearly untranslatable. Once you hear Harrison's voice, which seems to have been "sifted through ashes," as Anthony Brandt aptly claimed in *Men's Journal* in 1994, you know you have never heard anything quite like it. And yet it is Harrison's conversation that compels attention. Inquire about this or that issue, ask a question, mention the name of a book, or a writer, and he is off on such long and involved responses that he occasionally forgets the original query. Some answers are self-cancelling, as though talking itself is a means of thinking through an answer. Asked whether echoes of Quentin Compson's suicide exist in Dalva's preparations for her death in *The Road Home*, Harrison said, "Yeah, of course. No, I don't know." In the space of a few minutes his conversation can range from literary recollections of a visit to poet Charles Olson in Gloucester ("One of the first best readings I ever got of *Plain Song* was from Olson") or of poet Robert Duncan visiting Harrison's classroom at SUNY Stony Brook to discuss James Joyce and Modernism ("And by the time Robert's done, two walls of blackboards are filled with the structure of *Finnegan's Wake*"), to confessions about his own excessive past self-abuses, recurring depressions, and general malfeasances.

Interviewing Jim Harrison is an exuberant experience, but also a sobering exercise in keeping up. This was our second try (we conducted a preliminary and somewhat more exploratory conversation a year earlier). As with so many interviewers before us, he was almost always working the territory far ahead of us. But if Harrison is opinionated and boisterous, he is also reflective, sensitive and—once he realized we were not "the enemy" (his term for hostile or ill-prepared interviewers)—extremely generous. We knew he had better things to do with his time than be interrogated , and we wondered secretly what he really got out of it. We realized that he is one of those rare people who have the capacity to make your efforts appear better and more important than they probably really are. It's an illusion we were happy to accept, and it reminded us of John Wesley Northridge's avowal in *The Road Home*: "Bad is bad and you let it go. Good you cherish as it whizzes by."

And yet, despite Harrison's forthcomingness, we also sensed that much of him remains protected and set apart for his family and for his work: "There's nothing you can do about anything except to write the book," he claimed. On this occasion, Harrison was in good spirits. His youngest daughter, Anna, was visiting. Mail on the second day brought a copy of the

French edition of *The Road Home*, with attendant pleasure. That evening Jim and Linda escorted us to the Eagle's Ridge Restaurant and the Leelanau Sands Casino in nearby Sutton's Bay. Later, he dug out a videocassette of *Tarpon*, a pioneering saltwater fly fishing documentary produced by his long-time crony, Guy de la Valdène (and featuring Richard Brautigan and Tom McGuane), and we sat up late that night over Calvados to view this rarity, while Harrison provided additional running commentary on a film he had acted in but had not viewed in many years.

He seemed pleased, too, that in the aftermath of having ended his lengthy and lucrative (and not always successful) screenwriting career in Hollywood fifteen months earlier, he had taken up some slack by becoming a contributing editor of *Men's Journal*, for which he would be writing occasional feature pieces of his own devising. He had recently completed proofreading the American galleys of *The Road Home* without mentally "delaminating" (a current favorite word); the day before we arrived he had begun proofing *The Shape of the Journey*, his 463-page collected poems, and while that task hung over our visit, it wasn't a killjoy. He had earlier provided us with copies of both bound page proofs and the typescript of a personal essay, "Why I Write, or Not," that was scheduled to appear in Will Blythe's edited collection, *Why I Write: Thoughts on the Craft of Fiction* (Boston: Little, Brown, 1998).

Though Jim Harrison was not relishing the multi-city book tour Grove/Atlantic planned for the fall, he was at a juncture in his career that seemed to promote reflection as well as anticipation: "Sometimes you write best about what's most distant from you, where you're really reaching, and you just don't even know where you are." Trying to locate that place, that habitation, became a recurring thread in this interview.

Patrick Smith: Publishing *The Road Home* and *The Shape of the Journey* at the same moment is a remarkable feat. But this isn't the first time that you've brought out a novel and a collection of poems at the same time, is it?
Jim Harrison: Oh, maybe it isn't. *Outlyer and Ghazals* and *Wolf* came out the same year, so did *Warlock* and *Selected and New Poems*. But this time it's the idea that it's two big books—the collected poems and a long novel—both at once. Sam Hamill at Copper Canyon Press wanted to take advantage of Grove/Atlantic's advertising budget for the novel so we could ride its coattails, so to speak.

Robert DeMott: In the introduction to *The Shape of the Journey*, you say that poetry "is the portion of my life that means the most to me." Many people would consider the collected poems alone a suitable life's work, but you also have an impressive stack of prose books as well. Is your attitude toward the poems nostalgia?

JH: Well, I don't know. Nostalgia in the sense that you value the work that's the closest to you. Like the "Geo-Bestiary" suite I showed you, which is a strange thing. That isn't exactly what I wanted to write. I started it the day I finished *The Road Home* last winter. I'd been thinking about this poem for five years. It didn't turn out to be the poem that I expected at all. It's like falling or something, as you get to that very strange place that penetrates to a level you don't often reach in a novel.

PS: What occasioned the change of the title from *Earth Diver* to *The Road Home*?

JH: Oh, it's very simple. A writer I revere inordinately, Gerald Vizenor, had used *Earth Diver*, so I didn't want to copy it. And I thought, curiously, *The Road Home* isn't a bad title.

RD: The title resonates beautifully with *The Shape of the Journey*.

JH: Yeah, I didn't realize that. The terrifying thing in your life is when you see the repetitive nature of your obsessions. I woke up after the novel was finished and realized I'd been working for eleven years and not doing much else, and I was appalled. Part of that was caused by sheer money fear. I got to my early fifties and came to my senses and realized I had to save some money, you know, and I'm not very smart about financial matters. So I decided to do some extra screen work. But then of course all that working becomes specious, too. I worked way too hard for six or seven years to accumulate some dough for a defined benefit plan. It got to be a real crusher and I cracked up a year and a half ago and quit to write *The Road Home*. I can't say I didn't *not* write a book because of Hollywood, I was just too exhausted. I just became a human factory. One year I wrote six drafts of two screenplays and three novellas and, you know, I mean what do you have left? No time during that stretch did I have the real consciousness that I'd been overdoing it, though other people would tell me I was. It's the time disease. You have blinders on. I had a minor crack-up a year ago in May. Fifteen months ago I couldn't get close to that place until I got *The Road Home* done. For a while I didn't even think it was going to be possible, but now I see it's no big deal. But the barrier got pretty huge there for a while because I was desperate to get my own work done. You got the point where you say, "What's money if it just makes you suffer?" But you finally crawl out of yourself and realize it is true. No person is equipped to work that hard and still be a human being, you know. It's midwestern *hubris*, that Calvinist *hubris* à la the Marines—"I *can* do it." But you really can't. You are always semi-enraged, or feeling self-pity or suffocating, feeling put upon. They can all destroy your work. Lawrence Sullivan, my New York mind doctor, has helped me see that you have to get to the point where you realize your primary obligation is to your art, your family, your friends.

PS: What are those repetitions in your work?
JH: Well, thickets keep appearing in my work. You know, Nelse and his lairs. It has always been an obsession with me, so much so that my oldest daughter, Jamie, has on occasion bought a painting or a print of a thicket and sent it to me. I've found my affections are for areas for which there is no economic value, like great marshes, and if I lived where you are I would like those hills from which nothing more can be extracted, or vast cedar swamps, or worthless pine groves and gullies, you know, and so on—places that haven't been scalped or only have been scalped once. You know, I have one white pine stump on Kingston Plains I sit under that five men couldn't get their hands around, and the gully is washed out under the stump and the roots are huge and I can sit right under it. Out of the rain and everything. I mean, see where all the other creatures, human and animal, have been there too. Kathleen Norris wrote that book *Dakota*, where she says, "One man's frontier is another man's homeland." But I'm just evidently obsessed, even in my dream life, with hiding places and thickets. Rilke said, "What is fate, but the density of childhood?" So I'm still informed by the same thickets I was looking for at age seven. [Laughs.] I hope it's not cheap psychologism, but I wrote a children's book that's coming out called *The Boy Who Ran to the Woods*. It's about being blinded at age seven, you know, when I ran to the woods for solace. And it's arguable that I never came back. [Laughs.] I'm trying to recreate the essence of the woods sanctuary in my granary studio here, or in my cabin in the UP [Michigan's Upper Peninsula], or at my *casita* in southern Arizona. And then that extrapolates from there. If you think of the Northridge farm, it's almost a maze, you know, a monster thicket, with all those lines of interlocking shelter belts back to the spring and the pond. It really becomes a mirror of the sub-basement in the Northridge house. The kind of thing when I was growing up I knew about in big lumbermen's houses in some northern towns. They always had secret rooms or hidden places to store money and stuff. In one house, this man had three of them— a whole other room and steps down. It's wonderful mythic stuff, you know.

PS: After Seymour Lawrence died, why did you switch publishers from Houghton Mifflin to Morgan Entrekin's Grove/Atlantic? You said once you could have gotten more money from other firms.

JH: Morgan Entrekin was Sam Lawrence's protégé. Grove/Atlantic and Norton are just about the only independently owned publishers left. I didn't want to be lost in a big pond or suffer the level of self-importance you find in some of these huge literary combines. I could have gotten more from other firms, but I would rather work with somebody I like. There is nothing worse than being with the wrong publisher for years and not being able to get out of it. And now at my age I know I don't care to waste time with a publisher I don't like. If you don't have some fundamental respect for your publisher, it doesn't matter who your editor is or what your situation is. My editor has always been my eldest daughter, Jamie, and whoever my publisher is knows that from the outset, so that is part of the deal. Like Sam Lawrence, Morgan is essentially a book person—he loves books, loves literature. He is also good at securing foreign rights. With Sam I went from two foreign publishers to twelve or fourteen in one year, and then finally, with Morgan, to I think twenty-three or so. There are aspects of the publishing business that are utterly disgusting and don't look promising, but at the same time now I see the complete rejuvenescence of academic publishing and smaller presses, such as Gray Wolf, Story Line, Copper Canyon. It changes the financial situation for any writer because small presses, even the good ones, aren't positioned to pay very much.

RD: Do you have any idea how many copies your novels sell?

JH: *Dalva* sold about eighty thousand hardback copies in France. I think *Legends of the Fall* has sold over three hundred thousand copies. I don't know about the others, but I could find out. They sell enough to keep them alive, you know, and put them into paperback—that Delta series from Dell, and now a Washington Square Press series from Pocket Books—so there's always been something. There's at least a modest continuity. The more important thing to me is that they're all in print. As far as I am concerned your only ambition should be that your work stays in print. So foreign editions mean a lot to me.

PS: You've said you are not a nationalist in terms of literature, and that there's no sense in arguing about who's best here when there are the likes of Gunter Grass and Gabriel Márquez on the landscape. Does that global perspective help put individual reputations and the vagaries of the "literary establishment" in proper perspective? You told Kay Bonetti you don't consider reputation a "horserace."

JH: Yeah. If you think you can control anything outside your skin, you're crazy. And one of the first things you have nothing to do with is your literary reception. Forget it. I don't think in terms of a literary establishment like some people do. Or else you get eaten up by the public perception of what you are so your successive books must imitate the book that worked, you know, which is a danger that singers or painters get in. Once you have a successful show then the gallery essentially demands that you continue painting that way. And the biggest problem I see now that's overwhelming is people no longer can separate the difference between art and the art market (I got a try to write an essay about that), or good writing and publishing, you know, or the literary marketplace. There's absolutely no connection between the two. And people keep confusing these two. If you think you only exist when the media is talking about you you're going to have a problem when they stop. I see how people get used up by overexposing themselves. Or they get so tired by doing public appearances, so I've always tried to limit myself to two a year at most, and to strictly limit my book tours, because constant book touring or giving readings at colleges wears you and everyone else out. I have been willing to go to France because, even though I don't read French very well, I get my back patted there by a reading public and very serious literary journalists and critics, but then I can just come home and forget about it, so that distancing works well. Anyway, in geological terms we all own the same measure of immortality. Since I'm making a living and my books are in print we'll let it go at that.

RD: You say in your essay "Why I Write, or Not," you've left a trail of books, but you really mark the passage of time by the series of hunting dogs you've owned. Is that facetious or disingenuous?

JH: No. Sam Lawrence told me once I was the only author he had who didn't think he should be more famous than he was. But that comes from studying literary history so that you don't get lost in rages of jealousy like John O'Hara or Theodore Roethke, or starvation for reputation or fame, like James Dickey. If you look up eighty years of the Pulitzer Prize, you're going to be astounded. The arts are fabulously undemocratic. You either finally get a lot, or you don't get much at all. It's just appalling. And now, even the middle ground has been taken away. You know, like HarperCollins' cancelling over a hundred contracts, so mid-market novelists can't even get published now. I know a lot of them who just can't even get a book. I remember when I was a senior in high school, learning that when Hemingway and Faulkner were publishing their first novels, the best novelists in the world were thought to be Arnold Bennett, Joseph Hergesheimer, Louis Bromfield, James Gould Cozzens, those kinds of people. The main chance is your work and your development of the work, and if you've read as much as I have about literary reputations you don't have to walk around like some novelists saying, "I don't get it, I don't get how any of this works." I do get it. I know how it works. Everything about the literary life is basically catty and trashy from the start, so my point of view, which gets better organized every year, is that you may as well ignore it all and just do your work. All of it moves too fast for any of that stuff to matter. All that reputation stuff dissipates so fast so you may as well do your own work and forget about it.

RD: I don't mean to keep pressing, but literary ambition was never something you were concerned about in your career?

JH: Only briefly. But, no, you know what I figured out a long time ago? I realized that early success can quite often be disastrous and create burnout. I had a beautiful dream about ten years ago. I was up at my cabin in the UP and I was really affected by the evident failure of *Dalva* and then I had this weird dream where I put all my so-called literary ambition, which even at that time was a very occasional thing, into this crypt in an estuarine area and I shoved it out on the tide. When I looked out I could see a lot of other crypts floating on the water, and I said, "My God, there are a lot of people who have done that." You finally realize any literary ambition is an illusion. Tom McGuane had a brilliant little statement once in a comic interview we did in *Sumac*: "I would gladly create one thousand acts of capitulation to keep my dog in Alpo." I love that, because then you realize the deep fraudulence of it all. To write an accessible popular novel that would actually make you a living would shatter everything I believe in as an artist. Because I'm not that kind of writer. First of all, you can't get anything commensurate to your effort, so it's best if it is reduced to a decent check. Secondly, as long as you're still around, fame just seems so hopeless and haphazard. It's a club that's only organized in retrospect. I wanted to have my fiction writing totally on my own terms, and if I needed the money, then I went out to Hollywood and got a job and received what I like to think is an appropriate check for my work. A big studio head once said to me, "You're supposed to be a nice rural person but really you're a horse trader." And I said, "Well, that's part of the same thing!" [Laughs.]

RD: This takes me by surprise, because I remember the very enthusiastic reviews of *Dalva* by Jonathan Yardley and Louise Erdrich. What do you mean by the evident failure of *Dalva*?

JH: The general non-acceptance of *Dalva*. The feeling that *Dalva* was published unhappily because during that time Sam Lawrence had left Dutton and Dutton was pissed at me, and they didn't even have an ad budget because they knew I was going to go with Sam to Houghton Mifflin after *Dalva* was out, so they didn't want to have anything to do with me. So it was just a nightmare, that whole period of my life. The novel didn't do as well in sales and in reception as I'd hoped. Nobody could figure it out very much. What is this? What is this about? Most of my material's utterly alien to many reviewers, so then whatever audience I now have, I've accreted over the years. Certain books, more accessible books, like *Legends of the Fall*, expand it, and then the following gets bigger. And the absorption and attention of some people helps too. I remember once about fifteen years ago, I got a phone call from PEN in New York. There were half a dozen French journalists that wanted to come out to Michigan to see me, and the PEN person says, "If you'll excuse me, why do they want to come out and see you?" I was in a bad mood, so I said, "Well, you'll have to ask them." That's New York as opposed to the rest of the country, you know. [Laughs.] The lesson is that we should leave off any notion of getting what we deserve because nobody can get what they think they are worth in a given time. You can only emerge in as much as your audience is ready to receive you. I always worry about people I know who have gotten enormously well-known for sociological or extra-literary reasons, because that's always a very brief portion of fame. If you're a little too easy on yourself and your books have a big sociological rage, there's nothing that wears out a writer faster. I don't care what that person writes, from now on he's not going to get a break. Action, then reaction, sets in when somebody gets caught up within sociological praise.

RD: You've produced screenplays, poetry, novels, nonfiction prose, and literary journalism, and have referred to yourself as "quadra-schizoid" regarding these diverse genres. But I can't find any record that you have ever published a short story, though you told your sister-in-law, Rebecca Newth, in 1994 that you sold a collection of short stories to Houghton Mifflin.

JH: Well, I just can't write short fiction. I think I've written two stories in my entire life, both of which were unsuccessful. About fifteen or twenty years ago my wife, Linda, read one and thought it was about an indiscretion I had with an actress. So I thought, "Well that's not worth it." And I'd written an early one about a boy whose father was a county agent, you know, that kind of autobiographical thing. I tried to write short stories, but I just couldn't. It was a nightmare for years and years. In fact, I even sold a book of short stories. I sent Sam Lawrence, who was then my publisher, a list of nineteen titles. I loved the titles, but then I never got any stories out of them. One was "The Swimming Cows of South Dakota," so named from a time in a 105-degree heat wave when I saw cows in the stock ponds with just their noses sticking out. But I just never could write a short story. Part of the problem is that I don't have any good sense of beginnings, middles, and ends. And you need that if you're going to write a short story. I just don't see that kind of sharp delineation in my life or that of my friends. I've always had trouble with beginnings and middles and ends, anyway. [Laughs.] I really admire some short story writers, but I can't do it myself.

RD: Did any novellas spring from those incipient short stories? You told Ric Bohy in 1986 that you had started a short story about forgetting to go to Spain.
JH: Yeah, of course. I wanted to write this novella, which I've thought about for years, called "I Forgot to Go to Spain." All through my youth, I was obsessed with going to Spain. I'd saved up the money to go to France and Spain when I was nineteen but spent it all on an eye operation. And then when I got relatively successful I forgot to go to Spain, what with the nature of time and so-called success, you know. [Laughs.] I don't have the voice yet. I have a lot of the images in my notebooks.

PS: Do you feel the story form is too restrictive? Too limiting?
JH: Yes, because I don't get to do my divagations, my digressions, which are mostly what's interesting to me because they are the nature of reality.

PS: So you wouldn't consider yourself a plot-driven novelist?
JH: No, not at all, but occasionally it happens. The worst trouble I've gotten in, in fiction, is when I know too much where I have been. Dostoevsky said two plus two equals death, that kind of thing. The way we see isn't always plotted. I think that's what dragged us so mightily to Cezanne's paintings— they look more like reality than reality does. [Laughs.] Even though it looks jumbled, that's just how you would see Mont Ste. Victoire when you turned that way out of the car.

RD: No one today has published more novellas than you have. It's a remarkable record. Henry James called it the "blest *nouvelle*." What's the attraction of the form to you?

JH: Well, I was so fascinated with that form. Now, quite a few people started after my first three novellas in *Legends of the Fall* came out. But the attraction was that of a mid-form, that half-way form between novel and poetry. I don't like looseness. I'd read Hugo Hofmannsthal, Isak Dinesen, and Katherine Anne Porter who were so adept at handling novellas, and I felt that some ideas just simply aren't long enough for a novel. You try to write the kind of prose that you admire and since I like density, compression, I felt attracted to the novella form, the attraction to a mid-form. Some ideas you have just simply aren't long enough for a novel. You try to write the kind of prose that you admire and I like density. So why try to make a hundred-page novella into a two-hundred-and-twenty-two page novel? You know? It was that sense that some ideas are short all over, and some are long all over.

RD: Do you just have an inspired premonition of how length, form, and structure will play out?

JH: Yeah. I know the minute I have the idea. I don't think form is an artificiality, every story has its form. I've published nine novellas, and maybe five of them could have been novels. When the first publisher saw "Legends of the Fall," I was advised to make it four hundred pages long, so that then we could have a bestseller and make a lot of money, as he said. I refused. Tristan wouldn't be Tristan if he were a babbler. *Legends* eventually paid off anyway for other reasons. But I don't like marking time or fluff in prose, and I don't like claustrophobic or culturally encapsulated fiction. Maybe that comes from starting as a poet. I love that specific density and compression that I can get in the novella form. That's one reason why Isak Dinesen's such a powerful writer. She has that "once upon a time" sense when she starts off: "In 1857 in a small town in Denmark, Count —— ——," like she's protecting his name, "said, 'I must go to Paris.'" And then you get immediately caught up in it. I generally prefer more of a voice novel, but once in a while, like in *Legends* obviously, I was doing what Rebecca West called "god-like omnipotence." Pretending I was the big guy just looking at these people. Which is admittedly sometimes too distant, like Knut Hamsun. Thomas Mann's earlier work when he's more personal is more interesting. But again, you can do this range of things with a novella.

RD: Then is it accurate to think of *Dalva* and *The Road Home* as each being made up of three novellas, rather than one long novel?

JH: Oddly enough I thought about that and can see your point. But I don't think so because in both works the sections are intimately cross-referential and connected to each other. In *The Road Home*, especially, the three sections are woven intimately together. So is *Dalva*. I went back and reread *Dalva* when I was writing *Road Home* so the voices, characters, actions would mesh as a totality. It was a fucking nightmare because I hate to reread my own work.

RD: You play fast and loose with traditional fictional unities and our expectations of form and technique. The two novellas devoted to Brown Dog—"Brown Dog" and "The Seven-Ounce Man"—tease our sense of continuity and play with qualities of voice and point of view.

JH: Well, I like to experiment because, you know, rules are made to be broken. Those two are not strictly voice novels, because they're also within that picaresque tradition. Also, I like that Russian sense of the serial. Brown Dog will keep coming up when I need him because he is sort of an alter ego, a nonliterary Henry Miller. No numbers are attached to him. I love that kind of thing, that kind of consciousness that's quite unrelated in a basic way to the main culture. I'm planning at least one more Brown Dog novella. At the end of "The Seven-Ounce Man," Brown Dog and Lone Marten head west to get away from their problems. Brown Dog is abandoned in a gas station in Cucamonga and starts walking to Westwood where I pick him up in "Westward Ho." He's going to get his bear skin back in Hollywood.

PS: Does Brown Dog owe anything to Twain's Huck Finn?

JH: I don't know. I never thought of that. But that idea of influence, the way influence seeps in is just so indeterminate and mysterious. I like Twain, but I never thought of being influenced in that way by him. Certainly there was no conscious attempt at imitation. When I'm writing a novel I can't read fiction while I'm writing it because I am at a point where my brain is peeled, and I am utterly vulnerable, and everything can seep in. It's that mimicry that you get even when you aren't aware of it. So regarding Brown Dog the character, maybe an influence but then maybe not, because that kind of character still exists in pockets throughout the country. There are thousands of Brown Dogs out there. You know?

PS: Do you put yourself on any kind of timetable when you're writing a novel?

JH: Not any more. I did for a long while, but now that I'm older I have to take a break between novellas or between sections of a long novel. Like after I wrote the first section of *The Road Home*. It was a nightmare for me because it's a voice novel, so the first two hundred pages are completely in the voice of the elderly John Wesley Northridge II, so I had to become seventy-one myself. Then I went broke and had to do screen work for a year and more research. The second section is narrated by Nelse, Dalva's son, and he is a good deal younger, so I had to adjust there. Then the third section is three other voices: Dalva's mother, Naomi, and then Dalva's uncle, Paul, who is quite eccentric—I couldn't give him up—and then Dalva herself. It was quite a stretch. When I wrote the last two sections, they were more or less a blur. I almost don't remember how they occurred. They were written somewhat consecutively. But you become an absolute hyperthyroid geek and the only reason you finish is because you can't stop, not because you have to. Writing a long novel just about fucking kills you. You're disgusted with the process, but then you don't have any choice, I think. You've created characters of sense and there's no room for them in the world. There certainly isn't any room in this world for Dalva, none that I can think of, except home, wherever that is.

RD: Steinbeck thought about his fiction for years ahead of time. And when he wrote, he knew exactly where he wanted to go. The manuscript of *The Grapes of Wrath* shows very few deletions or corrections after one hundred days of steady writing. Is your process similar?

JH: Mine are pretty much that way too. I write my original drafts by hand—*The Road Home* was in pen on yellow, lined legal paper. Then Joyce Bahle types my manuscript and gives it to me and then I check it against the manuscript, go through it again and give it back to her. I don't revise substantively. I don't think I've ever written any fiction I haven't thought about for three or four years. I've even diagrammed some books. I cheat though by doodling around, but not with the basic story. I revise fiction much more than I used to because now with Joyce's computer I have an infinite shot at it without laborious retyping. But I know the story before I sit down. Even at that, with "Legends of the Fall" I only had to change one word, but that's the only time that ever happened.

PS: Is this a way of saying that "Legends" wrote itself?

JH: I wrote "Legends" in nine days at the Jolli Lodge, but that's the only time it ever happened like that, the only time anything like that's ever happened to me with fiction. I couldn't stop once I got started. It was truly like taking dictation. But I had been thinking about it for three years. Lawrence Durrell wrote *Mountolive* in two weeks, but the other *Alexandria Quartet* novels took him quite a long time. But that illusion of taking dictation from wherever always makes you wonder what's going on, what can this be? Part of yourself you've radically freed up. You don't quite understand just what's going on. You know, like when you get a relatively inspired passage that just writes itself. I can't account for that. Suddenly, the voice is in a perfectly energized marriage with the language and the sensibility. Like with "Geo-Bestiary" which came all at once virtually intact in that shape. Whereas with the novel those perceptions stretch themselves way out. It's more like a black hole; it sucks everything in. I don't know quite where those gifts come from. I've always felt that you shouldn't over-inquire about the goose that lays the golden egg. [Laughs.]

RD: You have a highly visual, even cinematic prose style. It's iconographic and painterly.

JH: I don't get this visual sense in my novels because I write screenplays. When I was fifteen I wanted to be a writer because Keats and Byron were writers and they got laid a lot and had a good time. And also because from the age of fifteen to eighteen I also wanted to be a painter—I admired Van Gogh, Gauguin, Modigliani—and then I majored in art history for a year, and I was just fascinated with art books. I think that's partly because I just had the one eye, so that concentrates you. So I think that's where it comes from. You know when you're a kid, you go around making squares in reality, or you use windows that way. And then you move around until you've got the scene just right. But you can't stop doing that. And since I have one eye, and it's always been sort of an aperture, I start more from my senses quite often than my mind and so I actually see what I'm going to do. For instance, my problem with the film version of "Legends" was that I'd already seen it in my mind, so there wasn't quite enough dirt and blood rubbed into it. It wasn't gritty enough. It got too pretty. Even when it's a philosophical novella like "The Beige Dolorosa," which is about having to literally reconstitute reality to survive, there is still that visual dimension that's very important to me.

RD: Is that a theme in your work, that your characters must reconstitute reality? You say in "Why I Write, or Not" that by "creating an environment for certain of my characters I often find myself trying to create an environment for my own soul."

JH: Well of course, not only them, but me too. In order to survive, your only alternative as an artist is to create your own habitat for your soul. I figured out that my main obsession is freedom, and if I didn't have the freedom of close access to the natural world, I wasn't going to survive. I think that's basically why I feel like an alien in New York City. You have to create your own environment or you couldn't endure at all. A few years ago I wrote an essay on dislocation, "Dream as a Metaphor of Survival" for the *Psychoanalytic Review*. If you don't create your own habitat, dislocation becomes permanent. You know, let's say if you can't figure out depression in an interior sense, there are no pats on the back that will mean anything whatsoever. It's really quite debilitating. There was an early book by an English professor named John Senior—it was one of those academic books that was instrumental called *The Way Down and Out*, and it was basically about the Occult in French Symbolism. And it was very helpful for thinking about depression.

RD: And you are able to work in those periods?

JH: Yeah, basically. Too much wrongly infects the word. You know? Because I still think of that Yeats line. Oh boy, I don't know if I can remember— "What portion of the world can the artist have who awakens from the common dream but dissipation and despair." I don't see that as a reason to write. You know? Like the Rilke line I used as epigraph to *Julip*, "When the wine is bitter become the wine." There's no way to get out of it by avoidance, and in Jungian terms it's really a need to regenerate your whole persona, a need to regenerate your life. It's your whole person saying "No!" Really quite debilitating, and you have to do something, though it may sometimes be very radical, or sometimes just very nominal. I knew I was entering a severe one years ago and I just got in a plane and flew down to Costa Rica. And ten days later I was fine.

PS: In old man Northridge's section in *The Road Home*, I get swept along by the accumulating account of his psychological life, his individual memories and yearning for home. How aware are you of creating that effect?

JH: Well, I did with him, and that was what was hardest, that's what took the longest, why this novel took so long for me. I knew I had to enter honestly into his individual voice and I couldn't betray it by showing off, by making it too consciously an act of literature, which would prevent being carried long. From line one, I don't want his section to be a literary act, but be more like Chekhov, who just carries you away, no matter how inane the situation might be. You're swept away by the story rather than the conscious literary aspects of the writing. Whereas, say, the first sentence of *Wolf*, which is a couple of pages long, is basically, nice but it's showing off. But since *The Road Home* is in Northridge's voice, he's not showing off so I can't show off. I have to depend, with him, on the meat and the bones and the terrible sense of longing he has about his life, and then his rapid failing, the surprise for all of us of our failing bodies. The last time he goes hunting, his dog, Tess, won't help him dispense the wounded sharp-tailed grouse, and he has to do it, he has to feel those little crinkling vertebrae himself, as he pinches them. And then of course he can't quite find the car.

PS: In that scene he seems disoriented, or as he says "unsettled."
JH: Yeah, and then seeing Smith in the potato field, at a point when Smith doesn't want to talk to him. Finally his little victory in a sense is when he starts growing again and he's seated in that old easy chair out in the pasture, sharing it with mice. Now that's as much as we get of his recovery.

RD: And that's a way of honoring the gift of that character?
JH: Yeah. I don't have the right, given that character, to show off, because who knows where he comes from in my psyche? So I don't have the right to show off. The gift of fiction is to make life live itself, just to live itself, so that's what you do. So you're not there. I don't want people to see my hand on the page. Northridge just has to give his story as directly as I am able to do it. Even down to Paul's inability as a son to accept all the facets of his father's personality. Like when the two little boys, John Wesley and Paul, are having hamburgers in the bar, and Northridge accuses that man of trespassing and blasts him in the guts and the man pukes all over the kids. That kind of thing used to be funny. It's not any more, but in a way it can be considered humorous. I'm not presenting Northridge as somebody to imitate, or as an admirable figure, but he is the kind of man who doesn't take anything from anyone. But see, that's the real world, and Paul can't quite accept that, though he's more similar in some ways than he thinks. But oddly enough, Nelse, the loner, understands that kind of situation, understands letting go into what I call "otherness," which he is already deeply involved in, even at Berkeley. In some ways Nelse is even a little bit like Tristan, if we knew what Tristan had been like when he was older. My daughter Jamie wanted me to shorten Nelse's section, but I refused. Obviously there's a lot of early me in that character too, that kind of relentless wandering, you know, logging hundreds of campsites in the US. Nelse is a loner and acute claustrophobe

and he's addicted to the most profound of contemporary diseases, which is dislocation. He says he's read Bruce Chatwin dozens of times. Nobody belongs where they are, or nobody has the feeling of belonging where they are, so he thinks maybe he can belong everywhere. Which is a possibility. It is definitely true in a nomadic culture, as Chatwin knew, but you can't be a nomad all by yourself.

RD: So you know things about Nelse that he doesn't know. Are there things that you don't know about your characters?

JH: Oh, absolutely. I was talking once with Mike Nichols, who directed *Wolf*, about this odd thing in acting—that an actor or actress can't act smarter than they are. That's a limitation. And I don't think a writer can render a character larger than the dimensions of his head. It doesn't exist. On the other hand, I'm not all my characters. How could I be all two hundred or three hundred of them? These are people of their own. Because that sense of discovery is paramount. That's the hardest thing in reading galleys—it underscores how you have no idea how you made all that up. This outpouring is a cumulative process, and when it ends, as with *The Road Home*, and then with "Geo-Bestiary," you just don't always have any idea how it happened. You think maybe it was more like a seizure, a long seizure. A lot of the novel-writing art is conscious, but it's the emergence of the characters that are sometimes like seizures, even coming out of a dream, like Dalva, which I've said many times. Because with *Dalva*, it didn't matter who wrote it, it was Dalva's personality that was compelling. In another sense, what keeps me writing is the mystery of human personality. You know, how did we come to be what we are? Along with the natural world, it's the great mystery that we have to deal with. Despite psychology, there's really no accounting for a great deal of it. It's like what Rupert Sheldrake calls "morphic resonance." It's not an "evolution," they just pop out here and there in different forms.

RD: You also use that phrase "mystery of personality" in your essay, "Why I Write, or Not," and I think with a similar twist in "Dream as a Metaphor of Survival." To put it another way, characters in *The Road Home* are obsessed with large categories of existence—what Melville called the "mysteries of iniquity."

JH: Sure. Why be timid about turning your head to larger issues? Naomi starts off thinking that Nelse, her grandson, might have been like Rex, that retarded student who still comes to visit her—both men are about the same age in 1986. It's all a mystery of human behavior, like when it occurs to her that every human voice on earth is different from every other human voice. All these kind of things utterly puzzle us. I think one reason why I'm an alien in New York is that certain of their concerns are too narrow for me. I'm not interested in claustrophobia or culturally encapsulated experience. I can't write a novel about somebody jacking off for two-hundred pages. I don't think that way anymore, or maybe I'm in a different phase. One of the main things you see in literature and politics, in every area of the United States, is acute xenophobia, a willing blindness to everything, which I deplore. Novels are generally notoriously stupid about history. When I started out on this road years ago, Bernard Fontana said to me, "You'd better watch out." The Indian obsession can be a kind of disease that doesn't let you alone. What really took place in this country is an extended holocaustic experience, you know?

RD: Some characters in *Dalva* and *The Road Home* keep journals. Is that part of exposing what Edward Reilly in his Twayne series book on you calls "layers" of human history and personality?
JH: Yeah, that's a literary device I like because it creates the sense of layering in fiction. It's another illusory step, to spring on the reader a journal entry. If you read a person's journal then maybe you're getting closer to the inmost leaf of the flower. Remember the Ken Burns film about the Civil War? I'd read a lot in that area before that film came out, and I knew that people in that tradition developed this epistolary style so even a relatively simple-minded person wrote beautiful stuff. And then in the case of my wife Linda's great-grandfather, Ludlow, a mining engineer, his journals were filled with beautiful writing. It's lovely to read, some of which I just extrapolated in "Legends" and in the Dalva novels. In fact, I'd eventually like to have the originals published at the University of Nebraska Press.

PS: Writing this all down is conscious, but you've also said many times that you imagine much of your novel fully before you even write it. Can you elaborate?
JH: Oh, sure. When I was a very young man, I read in Wallace Stevens's notebooks, "images collect in pools." So it's just like certain image banks or pools in our brain are filling up with these people, and frequently they're visual. They're real metaphors that you don't at first quite comprehend. Like seeing a sunset underneath a girl's bare foot in the apple tree. Nelse with a fever looking up at the stars in Nebraska, feeling the earth moving under him, that kind of thing. You know, Nordstrom dancing alone to music he got from his daughter. Or Adele in the opening section of *The Road Home*

catching those little black snakes and putting them in her hair. Right at that moment you know she isn't the kind of girl that lasts. It's out of the question.

PS: Are some of these photographs above your desk part of that image pool?
JH: Sometimes a couple of images concentrate what you're thinking. I found these at the Nebraska Historical Society, which I love and have visited often. They have a huge photo collection. This one is William Jennings Bryan's daughter and her friend doing the hurdles. And you know they're really up there too, if you think about it. I found this old photograph there, years ago, of an incredibly elegant, great big man standing in front of this big house in Omaha. He has three coyotes on a leash and he's wearing a Homburg. And I thought, "Oh, that's it, that's that." [Laughs.] That's in *The Road Home* in a couple of places, but I changed it to my purposes.

PS: You told Jim Fergus in your *Paris Review* interview that you "overpre-pared" *Dalva*. Do you still think you can do too much research?
JH: Well, I think the research is just obsessive behavior, and sometimes I overprepare historically, because it's a nervous habit. But you never know where it will end up. I read for years. In *Dalva* it was a lot of work to know the nature of what really went on between the end of the Civil War and say 1890, just after the Dawes Act and up to the Wounded Knee massacre. Besides genocide, what I found was monstrous—we lost fifty million buf-falo, for instance. You never saw such rapacity before or since, except for maybe in Africa. Anyway, nine years ago, the year after *Dalva* came out, I realized I hadn't used at least two-thirds of the material that I had accumu-lated. So I had about a thousand of those pull-tabs of written images and constructs. I resisted it a long time, then I recognized, well, I have to return to these people. Originally, Dalva was going to doom the grandfather, which didn't happen, but she just kept coming up in my mind and took over. The horrible thing, as everybody knows about being a writer, is sitting there all the time. My so-called research gives me an excuse to go do something, like months of aimless driving around to comprehend new landscapes. That's not only fun, it's tremendously oxygenizing. You keep wondering, "Where does that road go?" and you have to follow it. I had that old Subaru with cruise control, which I would set at about thirty mph, and I could, in Nebraska, steer standing up with my head out the sunroof and see the whole landscape. No one thinks that's extraordinary. They only see one car an hour anyway, and they could care less. [Laughs.] It was essential research for *Dalva*. I said once that I thought dreams emerged from the landscape

and though I don't have any specific proof it seems that a landscape has its specific spirit. No matter where it is, the degree of your accretion of preparation is paramount. You can't do it shopping-wise, it has to ooze into you. It's that idea that you can't get anything out of another culture unless it's already in you and you discover it for yourself. When you go into an area with somebody who knows the flora and the fauna and the geology and the Indian history of the place, having all the information and no ulterior financial motives changes infinitely the quality of the trip. The folklorists and anthropologists like Roger Welsch I know in Nebraska are extraordinary like that. So is Doug Peacock.

RD: Did you have to go back and drive around Nebraska between *Dalva* and *The Road Home*?
JH: I did a number of times. I love that landscape of the Nebraska Sandhills, the Niobrara River area, Cherry County—to me it is just utterly overwhelming. I am fascinated by that locale, right in the center of the country, because more than Oregon or Washington or California or any other place you can name, that was the scene of the last struggle of two cultures, ending in 1890 at Wounded Knee, between Native Americans and the interlopers. The other thing I valued is the freedom—that nobody knows much about Nebraska. Very few people have even the foggiest idea about its geography and history, and that's fascinating because it gives me a tremendous freedom. Like that screenplay for Harrison Ford I was involved with set in Nebraska in the late 1920s. Not a modern Western and not a cowboy version of the old West, but that area in western Nebraska that isn't really known. Not always appreciated by Nebraskans, but, you know, nobody sees themselves as a novel sees them. It's like talking to people around Oxford, Mississippi, about Faulkner, who was so alien to them.

PS: That reimmersion in the landscape is only part of the preparation, though, right? Last year you were reading in Roger Welsch's *Omaha Tribal Myths and Trickster Tales*, Pritchard's *The History of Anthropological Thought*, Geertz's *Works and Lives*, McIntosh's *The Practical Archaeologist*, Rockwell's *Giving Voice to Bear*, among others. So, when you talk about overpreparing, do you feel that you can expose too much of your intentions?
JH: No, I mean that basically, like with Nelse, I read about eighty anthropology texts. And then I got diverted, but it bore fruit in the long run because it's again the iceberg idea. You want to infer just in passing certain things about the character, and while you just itch to deliver the whole goods

you really can't, because this is a novel, not a tract. I mean, certain things in anthropological texts are just overwhelming, and show these amazing traceries of human behavior. But you can't be didactic about that because you know your character isn't didactic about it. The absurdity of Nelse as a young scholar thinking that he should go out and actually talk to Ponca and Pawnee Indians about coyote stories. Well, that University of Nebraska anthropology professor tells him he's not supposed to, he's supposed to use the "qualified" research at hand, you know. So what's Nelse supposed to do? He has an adoptive family and a biological one. This is again nurture versus nature. How much of which is not enough or too much? So, if you are given a hard time and you're Duane and Dalva's son, you aren't going to say, "I'm sorry, sir," you're going to tip over the desk on the cocksucker. You know, Nelse tried to be a good boy because of his adoptive father, and he has good manners in fact. And every time anything goes wrong in his life, he just says in passing, "I resist it somewhat." He's trying to put a nice light on it. But I've seen too much of my life to ignore the fact that blood is blood in some respects. Even Paul gets to the point where he wonders if his attraction to those thousands of different multicolored rocks didn't start with his father's art books. Some of the children that are most like their parents are the ones that have most thoroughly rejected them.

RD: You put yourself in that category?
JH: Not exactly. But I think I told you that thing where I had some trouble with my character's voice in the second chapter of *The Road Home* and then I think where did I get my voice? Well from my family. But, see, writers either err on the side of making people less than they are or more than they are. They're both errors, but I favor the latter. The content of what I call true sentimentality is everywhere in good novels. What are you supposed to do? Ignore what people do? Exclude? Dostoevsky or Tolstoy or Dickens certainly do not. Once you come down the food chain you get some pretty cold hearts. [Laughs.]

RD: That reminds me that Steinbeck was influenced by Tolstoy when he was writing *The Grapes of Wrath*, and said he wanted his characters to be the "over-essence of people." So he often created large impolite experiences for the Joads that risked sentimentality.
JH: Well, very good. Extraordinary. I didn't realize he'd said that, because I feel that way, I know. I was about thirteen when my dad had me read *The Grapes of Wrath*. He was an agriculture agent and something of a populist

and that was one of his favorite novels. My dad was an agronomist but he was an obsessive reader. And we'd go to the library on Saturdays in the winter and I mean he just read everything . . . Steinbeck, you know, was his favorite, so I was literally eleven, twelve, thirteen when I was reading novels—by Steinbeck and Erskine Caldwell and Sherwood Anderson, too. Which my mother didn't think appropriate, but my father was a sort of a populist. And there were no lines being drawn. You know? Like when I kept quitting college he said, "Well, none of the writers that we like went to college. Maybe you shouldn't bother." My dad was more of an Aldo Leopold type of conservationist. He had a worked at the design of restorative watersheds and stuff, but he was literate, too, which you don't see so much anymore. When I said I wanted to be a writer when I was fifteen, we were a relatively poor, big family, and he went out and got a fifteen-dollar used typewriter. My mother who had wondered right away why didn't I try to write something for *Collier's*. You know, that kind of thing. It's just charming. You know?

PS: It seems that many reviewers can't always see or accept the implications of your aesthetic. The most pointed critique was Peter Prescott's *Newsweek* review of *Legends of the Fall*. It makes you subject to misinterpretation.

JH: Yeah. Now even so-called literary people seem to want a mono-ethic. I got attacked more than once for bad taste earlier and I said to someone in New York that I've known seven people that have been murdered—people that I knew quite well—who were involved in the drug business. One had his arms and legs cut off to destroy the evidence, and his mother picked up on his appendix scar. And I said you're not going to know these people if you're just hitting the fucking fern bars in New York or LA. [Laughs.] This is life. That's the reason that Charles Bukowski, a very good poet, never got his due in America, because he was always trying to rub their noses. He was a secret intellectual, but he was going to give them their full dose. Same way with Nelson Algren. Fantastic novelist. But he wouldn't cooperate. James Jones got attacked for not being more literary. He was sloppy, which was his real downfall. But he had some very, very good sections. Tremendous writer in that sense. So it's really kind of cultural snobbism. There are monsters afoot on the earth who have to have their say. If I write a character I am accused of being sympathetic with that character just because I wrote him, and that's a very naive approach to literature. It's like Hillary Clinton saying that Julia Roberts shouldn't smoke in a movie. It's that mono-ethic. Some critics don't want any real nastiness to enter fiction. They think of it really as a polite game and that's what it usually is. It certainly isn't writing from the depths, you know. But I would rather, in Neruda's sense, have the sloppiness that can grab my gizzard than any kind of anal-compulsive fiction.

PS: Carol Bly reprinted "The Woman Lit by Fireflies" in her anthology, *Changing the Bully Who Rules the World*, which I am sure you can take as a vindication of sorts for having been accused by Prescott and others of being a "macho" writer for so long. But how difficult is it for you at this point to write women? Is it becoming any easier with *Dalva* and your experience with Clare?

JH: Well, she's a little ahead of the rest of them. [Laughs.] But then I'm not responsible for being anthologized, and I don't have anything to do with that. And no, I don't think it ever becomes easier. It's just a hell of a lot slower. I think it came from that Jungian concept that the culture has you lose the twin sister you had at birth. And then with me of course my younger sister Judith died when she was nineteen. Particularly in our culture, you're not supposed to deal with the whole spectrum of human behavior, men aren't supposed to comprehend women, but why wouldn't they be able to? In a family of strong women, I had to be able to pick up something. I got the idea for *Dalva* when my younger daughter, Anna, was having a lot of problems at fourteen. And one summer evening she just went out and sat on the picnic table and I could see her through the window, you know, looking at the setting sun. And also there's a strange Edward Hopper painting of a girl sitting on the bed looking out over the prairie out the window, you know, that kind of thing. The technique of writing in a woman's voice was treated as if it were something revolutionary, but there's a great basis for it in European literature, *Madame Bovary* and on and on and on. It lets me say things in a woman's voice I can't say myself. There's no reason we can't understand. When "The Woman Lit by Fireflies" appeared in the *New Yorker*, Joyce and I counted something like 120 favorable letters, which is an awful lot. I don't set any kind of limitations, except I don't like people trampling on another's private religion.

PS: In the *Los Angeles Times Book Review* Judith Freeman was very complimentary toward "The Woman Lit by Fireflies." And in a review of *Julip* in the *New York Times Book Review* Jonis Agee claimed that in the war of the sexes women are better able than men to negotiate the "dark waters of strife." So that's praise indeed, but do you see a certain evolution in your female characters? You have Catherine and Rosealee in *Farmer*, who seem to be opposed to each other, and then Clare who seems to be naive and sees a lot of things for the first time.

JH: Well. Clare, of course, came after Dalva. But the interesting thing about Clare is that she really did get liberated after crawling over that fence, like a conversion or a *satori*, that way that she starts seeing almost holographically. She gets such a jolt that she can see her life rather clearly. Whereas Dalva—and I think that's probably the attraction of a lot of women to Dalva—is already an inordinately strong woman, the kind you don't often see even in some women's fiction, or the novel of "nifty guys at loose ends," the contemporary white male middle-class novel. You know I don't like push-overs in fiction, so when people have asked me about Dalva's strength, I say, "Well, yes, I adored Dalva but I wouldn't want to know her particularly. I wouldn't want to be her lover." Who could deal with this kind of person? It would take all your time. [Laughs.] I think the evolution you ask about is not so much an incremental evolution as it is seeing the whole picture. Dalva, Clare, and Julip are distinctly different people but all are, I hope, fully realized in their own way.

PS: Now that you've written *The Road Home*, what is your perception of what Americans need to know? Has it changed at all since you began writing?

JH: Oh, I don't know. I don't know. It's what it is. That's why I take the whole novel to say it because I can't reduce it. *The Road Home* is as long as it is because I can't reduce it anywhere. In particular, I keep coming back to that idea of "otherness" that Paul Shepard talks about, our connection with the animals and so on like that. It represents a world that we've very largely abandoned. I'm not saying that it's a better world, but I think that novel might be better than some of my earlier work because it's not as overtly angry. It has a narrative perspective that carries the people convincingly. It gets at that character of longing for a life that would have been at peace with the landscape if we could have done things right from the start. But that isn't the way we treated Native Americans, so I like to think that *The Road Home* addresses the soul history of our country. I'm so eccentric in researching this that I thought a lot of these concerns are new to me. Then I went back and found the same thing in D. H. Lawrence's *Studies in Classic American Literature* and William Carlos Williams's *In the American Grain*. I had that perception—I used it in that essay "Poetry as Survival," too—that Michael has in *Dalva*. Once you really know the history of Native Americans, if you put a sheet over the American continent you can see all the places where the blood soaks through. And once you know that, once you start in on

158 CONVERSATIONS WITH JIM HARRISON

that, you can become buried in an instant thinking about what went on in terms of human suffering. We need to pay attention to what we have done to the land and native peoples before we strangle on our own detritus, which we of course already are doing. We've shit on our doorstep until we can't see the doorstep anymore. When I was asked in an interview about how Chief Seattle's curse haunts us, I said, "They got even with us by allowing us to invent television." Curses come in very ordinary ways. Television is their curse on us. We don't live anymore, we watch. The attention span in America now is very nonliterary.

PS: The contradictory, paradoxical nature of existence is a central proposition in your fiction. You say in the introduction to *Just Before Dark* that "negative capability" keeps "the work's heart pumping."
JH: You can limit your paradoxes by limiting your life. But the more you want to see of life, the more the contradictions are right there in front of you. When I first read Keats, whom I loved very much even in high school, that quality was right there. The hairs on my neck rose when I read about negative capability because that's obviously what a novelist has to have more than anything else. It's still the best tool for a novel, the negative capability to just be willing to juggle ten thousand things at once and not arrive at any specious conclusion about them, I think. The best example of it is in Shakespeare and Dostoevsky. Nothing human is alien to them. There is nothing that can't be explored. And they don't ever limit themselves the way we see happening right now in some arenas.

RD: You mean in social and political arenas?
JH: It's that mono-ethic again. The danger is that America is becoming a fascist Disneyland. Whether it's animal rights people or vegans or regular vegetarians, everybody wants everybody to do the same thing. With all this diversity, they want some kind of unanimity. It's amazing. Our intoxications become preposterous. And that's sometimes short-lived. People that would only drink white-wine spritzers for years and wouldn't smoke are now drinking martinis and smoking cigars. You never know about these weird sociological pendulums. I don't know if anybody learns from anybody else, in that way—if it's even possible at all. But reading the right people can help. At nineteen I was being moralized to death and I got a hold of Rimbaud and Apollinaire and all of Henry Miller. I wanted to be James Joyce, but needed Miller for power, to keep going every day. Miller was a massive blood transfusion. If I had *Tropic of Capricorn* or *Tropic of Cancer*, then I could come

out of my despondency pretty fast. There is a guy that knows what the fuck is going on, you know? Henry Miller still can have that effect on people.

RD: Well, your work can have that effect too. In the *Washington Post Book World* in 1990 Arthur Krystal said you have a narrative voice "that fairly defies the reader to ignore it." I take that to mean that you want to change the way people look at the world. Do you think it's fair to say that your essential subject is the dimensions, the shapes, of consciousness? Or maybe our individual and collective soul history?

JH: Sure, I think so. But that comes from the conscious decision that consciousness is all we've got, like Nelse says. [Laughs.] D. H. Lawrence said the only aristocracy is consciousness. So from reading so much literature, poetry, anthropology I realized that perception, consciousness, is essentially consensual. If you talk to your mother or talk to the guy at the gas station or even a colleague you quickly realize that often they see a totally different world than you do. Totally different. I don't want to get goofy on the subject, but this is verily true, so to me the nature of consciousness is just overwhelming. Gary Snyder says there's an extraordinary similarity in all our biographies, but what's different is our dreams and our visions. So what is it that informs our differences? We glance at essentially the same world every day and all that changes is our consciousness of that world. Consciousness is all we've got. And your consciousness is up to you, which is a terrifying idea, you know, if you think of Dostoevsky saying in *Notes from the Underground*, that to be too acutely conscious is to be diseased. Sometimes you wake up in the morning and your mind is whirling, but the world isn't whirling. It's the same place. Philosophically speaking, the principle I find most interesting for a novelist comes from the Zen master Dogen who said, "To study the self is to forget the self. To forget the self is to become one with ten thousand things." In other words, you do not become one with ten thousand things, but when you forget the self, ten thousand things become one with you. That's an enormous consequence, and opens you to a whole world out there, the world that's on both sides of me. It's holographic. [Laughs.] I think the novelists that interest me, like Faulkner and Márquez, are capable of entering that degree of consciousness, which is not always linear. That unbearable fragility of Caddy Compson. Faulkner was certainly an obsessive influence. I don't mean stylistically, but the way he looked at reality. I remember some newspaper hack tried attacking the way certain great novels started out, and she couldn't stand the way Faulkner started *The Sound and the Fury*, which I think is one of the three greatest opening paragraphs in American literature. Because his sense of reality is always cumulative, you know. That accretion and layering is what you hope for. When critics say you have to write realism, well, at any given moment we are all that has ever happened to us, so what are they talking about, when they say "real"?

PS: Pico Iyer, one of your most astute reviewers, has written that you are "driven by a quintessentially American openness of heart and innocence of spirit that enable you to glimpse and then to chase ideals." Do you think that's a fair assessment of your work? Do you think you've given to chase ideals in your fiction?
JH: Maybe. Yeah, a bit. I have to exhaust them for my own purposes before they go away. I don't know if it's therapeutic so much as I want to know the range of them.

RD: So you think of yourself as a philosophical novelist? You told Jim Fergus *Sundog* was a philosophical novel. Your novels are often fueled by the exploration of ideas.
JH: Maybe so. A French critic told me he considered *Sundog* a philosophical novel, and I can see what he means. I think probably basically, but I try to hide that, because ideas don't naturally attach morals to themselves very comfortably, and I like to avoid the decals and applique that some people paste over them. But ideas are there, like in "The Beige Dolorosa." What is happening in terms of a split Santayana called a religion behind a religion, which often gets to be quite totemistic. What happens to us when everything we had hoped for disappears? Philip Caulkins truly believed in his academic career. He didn't realize that you could still get railroaded as many people have. I suppose every novel has a set of concepts, but the philosophy that influenced me the most when I was in high school was Kierkegaard's *Either/Or*. I like that anecdotal range kind of philosophy. I don't like to read Wittgenstein, or Kant or anybody like that. I like someone where you see primary colors of some sort.

PS: All your fiction shows "primary colors." Do you have a favorite novel among all your works?
JH: I don't have any favorites. I don't have any feeling that way. It's really like having children. I don't have any sense that I prefer one to the other. And I don't know why. You know I'm not a very attentive reader of my own work, so once it's gone it's really gone. I should add that "The Man Who Gave Up His Name" is poignant to me because of my mental condition when I wrote it. But I don't have any extensive feeling about what's good and what's bad.

Warlock is the one novel I don't like at all. I wrote it during a crack-up and it was just a comic book to me. And over the years I have met some people who like it a lot, so there you are. I have favorites with everybody else's work, but I don't have much sense of that myself. Some novels actually have more range just because it's built into the subject matter, and so you have to expand your range in order to write the book, which creates a strong feeling of attachment, at least for a time. Like now, in "Westward Ho," Lone Martin pawns Brown Dog's bear skin. So now Brown Dog is broke, on the outskirts of LA, and he can't go home to Michigan. On a metaphorical level, that's autobiographical—how am I going to get my nuts back from those movie people? [Laughs.]

PS: A number of years ago a critic claimed in *Great Lakes Review* that your characters are "not heroic or brave, but they are survivors." You think that's true? Are there heroic characters in your fiction?

JH: That's a tough one because I think there's such a history to that concept and the value of the word itself has disappeared. It's hard to have a true hero because I'm infected by the notion of the Shakespearean hero, and we don't have any high places you can fall from and recover. I certainly think on some minimal level that Clare would be heroic, Julip in her own way, Tristan more obviously with his passion for the ideal of taking care of his younger brother that he felt he had betrayed. In Tristan's case, you get what people call a "wild person." But I don't see him as that. It was Rilke who said there's a point at which the exposed heart can't recover. And Tristan was a classic case of that. His charge was Samuel, and protecting him didn't work. Not that anyone can protect anybody else anyway, you know? But after that, the die was cast. And I suppose certain writers who served as models for me are heroic—Henry Miller, Neruda, Loren Eiseley.

RD: Not to romanticize this, but in turn you've been "heroic" yourself to younger writers—Rick Bass comes immediately to mind—and also you've been extremely generous in touting younger writers, having supplied blurbs for many, many dust jackets and mentioned others frequently in interviews. Who are some of the writers you find compelling right now, either for personal pleasure reading or for your research?

JH: You know, I get hundreds of galleys and manuscripts a year. But unfortunately, I can't read fiction while I'm writing it. McGuane called in a fit of hysteria and told me to read an overwhelming book, *Independent People* by the Icelandic writer Halldor Laxness. It just blows your ears off. You know, I can read some mystery, but that's about it. I can't read so-called serious fiction when I'm writing it, but mostly nonfictional stuff—natural history, biography, anthropology, history stuff. Mary Douglas, the English anthropologist who's so profound, so graceful. *Landscape and Memory* by the Englishman Simon Schama. The best book about environmentalism lately is Jack Turner's *The Abstract Wild*. He's a bear with a very large brain. He does research for me. There's *The Wolves of Heaven*—a wonderful title—about the Cheyenne song ceremony by an anthropologist named Karl Schlesier. A couple of years ago I read Richard Slotkin, who is really extraordinary. And there's a historian named Richard White who's just unbelievable and gives a different view of America than Schlesinger's. Eric Torgeson at Central Michigan just came out with a really extraordinary book on Rilke, *Dear Friend*, about Rilke's early love life. Merrill Gilfillan's *Burnt House to Paw-Paw* is about a trip down in the Appalachians. Turns out his dad was a naturalist in your area down there in Ohio. Remind me to give you both copies of that. He wrote a beautiful book of essays called *Magpie Rising*, and now this *Burnt House to Paw-Paw*. He writes such gorgeous prose, you know, and hardly anyone knows about it. Another instrumental book lately is Peter Nabokov's *Native American Testimony*. It's a tremendous book. Then there's Peter Matthiessen and Gary Snyder who are still the American writers who had a firm sense of how to live. You know? Keeping remote from what Bly called the centers of ambition.

PS: You said in the "*Dalva* Notebooks" that it is easier to write a novel than survive it. When you finish a novel or a book of poems, is there any sense of fulfillment at all, or is it just cathartic and you must decompress?
JH: Cathartic more than fulfillment. You're happy just to get shut of it and want to do something else. As we said this morning, that's what's difficult about proofing galleys, I mean, the copyedited galleys and the page proofs. Because by then, that's all behind you. That's the hard thing about a book tour, and interviews, too, because they take you back to where you were, not where you are now and you feel a little alien. People ask particular questions about what's in your books that never occurred to you on any conscious level. Also your explanations are curiously quite often not as interesting as somebody else's, so you feel a little alien about it, like you're already flying to a different planet. And there's always going to be misrepresentation. The whole culture is a very vulnerable, effervescent picture show, so your novel is its own gloss.

RD: On your life, you mean?
JH: On itself.

RD: Yes, I see.

Interview with Jim Harrison

Carrie Preston and Anthony Michel / 1999

From *Red Cedar Review* 35 (Winter–Spring 2000): 24–44. Reprinted with permission of Carrie Preston and *Red Cedar Review*.

As a child, fresh out of the hospital
with tape covering the left side
of my face, I began to count birds. .
At age fifty the sum total is precise
and astonishing, my only secret.
Some men count women or the cars
they've owned, their shirts—
long sleeved and short sleeved—
or shoes, but I have my birds ...
—from "Counting Birds" in *The Theory & Practice of Rivers and New Poems*

For a graduate student in American studies just finishing his thesis and an English senior preparing to enter graduate school, traveling to Jim Harrison's home outside of Traverse City in northern Michigan was an unusual opportunity to go to an interesting area to speak with one of the more intriguing personalities in contemporary literature. Preparing to meet the novelist (*Sundog, Dalva*), screenwriter (*Legends of the Fall*), and poet (*Outlyer*), we were particularly intrigued by the implication in many articles that there is an ambivalent and, at times, tense relationship between Harrison and academics, journalists, or literary critics.

The day we spent with the Michigan State University graduate and recipient of last year's MSU Distinguished Alumnus Award was starkly different from what we were led to expect by the increasing body of work devoted to explicating something like a "mythos" surrounding Jim Harrison's work and person. Meeting us at the door with a quip, "this one must be the girl," Harrison exuded a contagious sense of peace with his immediate surroundings. We found ourselves immediately drawn into conversation, and it wasn't until ten minutes after a tour of his home, when we had settled into an old granary, converted into Harrison's writing studio, that we realized the interview had already begun. With the exception of a quick changing of the tape, and an occasional formal question drawn from our seldom-used script, this interview is better characterized as a terribly interesting conversation with a man who speaks openly about writing as both a calling and the most preferable of the various types of labor he has done in his life.

The conversation that follows is permeated with a concern, found in Harrison's works, for rituals that mark the passage of time and the significant events in our lives: graduations, deaths, traveling, and returning home. The rituals appear with raw, coarse power in such acclaimed writing as Harrison's poem "Counting Birds," which uses images of nature and an Anasazi legend to represent birds as the messengers between temporal lives and transcendent spiritual existence. Asserting himself as an "outlyer," Harrison prefers the rivers and forests surrounding his secluded home to the more recognized reservoirs of culture including the academy, Hollywood, the East Coast publishing industry, and Paris. His works and life, however, belie a concern for how individuals move between the natural world and various communities. Following the day we spent with Harrison, including a tour of his farm, lunch at a local greasy spoon, and always, intriguing conversation, we understand this interview as less a commentary on Harrison's literary works than as a meditation on how each of us attempts to mediate the tensions between where we have been and where we may go.

Carrie Preston: How do you remember your experiences at Michigan State?
Jim Harrison: I had personality differences with some people. You know how you develop those with teachers (laughs). You simply don't like each other, and the people I didn't like in the English Department didn't like me either. But Herbert Weisinger was in the position to facilitate things. He was the director of comparative literature. I don't even know if they have that anymore. It was very active then, and to me it was more interesting. I like to study world literature and, at the time, I was interested in French and Spanish literature. Weisinger, who died last year, was maybe the largest brain they ever had at MSU. He was at the Princeton Institute of Advanced Studies for a couple of years and the Warburg Institute in London, and he was one of these great European émigré scholars that didn't even have to read the book. He had a vast, vast library in Okemos you know, and a vast, vast wine collection. He was a different kind of teacher. As the head of the

department he got to do whatever he wanted, and he got me the degree so that I could go up to Stony Brook with him. After three years of manual labor in northern Michigan, mixing mud and carrying sod in February, going to New York seemed more and more attractive.

Anthony Michel: So you went to Stony Brook to teach?

JH: Or as his assistant; I taught a course in modern poetics. I only lasted a year and a half. I sacrificed a whole truckload of student papers in a fire. So when they asked where their papers were, I said they're being kept for research. Already I was doomed, I mean, I flunked out of graduate school, and they finally facilitated my degree after I had my first book out with Norton. They never had a student that had a book out so they thought it would be nice.

AM: What would you have done if you didn't become a writer?

JH: I have never thought about it, but I can't come up with anything.

AM: Not teaching?

JH: No, the trouble with teaching, for me as a writer, is that colleges are always in the wrong place. I didn't mind teaching; I mean we're all proselytizers. For instance, I've got a children's book coming out this year called *The Boy Who Ran to the Woods*. It's one of these recovery children's books that draws on my interest in the natural world as opposed to cities, where colleges are usually located. After I was seven years old when I lost my eye, I was more interested in rivers and forests and so on. While I like to go to Paris and New York occasionally, I can't live in a semi-urban atmosphere. Here we have 120 acres, and I will never have to have any close neighbors. I'm claustrophobic, and when I got the MSU Distinguished Alumni Award this spring, I had to stay in a motel over in the southwest corner of the campus. Four times a day this driver would come pick me up to go do something I didn't want to do which was invariably nonsmoking (laughs). Anyway, we had to drive right past where I'd lived in married housing, thirty-five years ago. It was enough to puke a maggot. That sense of claustrophobia—I mean there's only one way to drive from married housing to Morrill Hall. After you've done it five hundred times there is an accumulation of emotions you have, which is called torpor or ennui. I have my cabin in the Upper Peninsula, and it's quite remote. And then our casita out on the border in the mountains where we don't have real neighbors for a couple of miles. Somebody said about Picasso once that he carried his environment wherever he went. As a writer, you have to create in your writing, and in where you live, your own sort of soul's habitat or else you can't function. I think the tough part for my writer friends who still teach, and the reason that I think they should get a lot more money than they do, is that they are never done.

AM: Do these friends of yours that are teachers work in universities?

JH: Yeah, but they have to be professors because the odds of making a living as a novelist are a hundred thousand to one, if that. I can't think of a more unpromising profession anyone could enter. That's what I think is sort of sad about all of the MFA programs. It's the same problem as the well-educated students in Africa. This is a bit of a jump, but it works. You have all these very educated Zambians and Nigerians and there's no place in the economy for them. There's no place in the US economy where there's room for so many MFAs. It's what they call a revolution of rising expectations.

CP: Do you think higher education of that kind is worthwhile at all?

JH: No. Not for writing. I think a gorgeous model for universities is Italy in the fourteenth century where a scholar would take eight students and teach them everything he knew for a year. The contemporary university is a formalization of that process. You had certain teachers that you were sort of spellbound by. That's what makes it worthwhile.

CP: What do you think about literary theory? Do you think it adds anything of value to English education?

JH: Oh, sure. Oddly enough, I'm relatively intellectual for a novelist. I want to entertain all of the possibilities, and I think that the history of literature is important. I was fascinated by Northrop Frye, and Kenneth Burke, but I bypassed deconstruction because I thought it was an elaborate plot to make the instructors more important than what they were reading (laughs). But those things seem to fade. I mean they have their efflorescence for a while and then they dissipate.

AM: Do people send you their scholarly work?

JH: No, I don't cooperate in any way. But there is this guy, Bob DeMott, who is a big deal Steinbeck scholar and they're more interesting than ten thousand Eliot scholars. The big problem in America is that it is very difficult for critics to take a writer seriously who actually goes outside rather than stays inside. I tease Tom McGuane, with whom I still correspond every week or two, that his problem is living in Montana. Larry McMurtry used to wear this wonderful shirt that said "minor regional novelist." It seems that every one that's not in New York City is a "regional novelist."

AM: Do you think that's changing at all?
JH: No, but I don't think it matters. One thing you learn is what to exclude in your life, and for me, a concern with that kind of thing would be something to exclude. Literary criticism is not my business or my calling. My business is to write the novels and the poetry. If you let what they say about you concern you, it could piss you off.

AM: So you exclude a concern over how you are being categorized.
JH: Oh sure. There's this Spanish critic, I forgot where I read this, but he said that I was doomed not to get certain prizes because I made fun of white men all the time (laughs). I don't know if I'm profeminist or not but they're on the money. The suits control the world, and in my mind that's comic.

CP: You've introduced feminism, and we found in *New York Times Magazine* where you talked about . . .
JH: Writing as a woman?

CP: Yes, using female narrators.
JH: Writers have always done that, and critics treat it like it's something new. Writers have been doing that for centuries, and Flaubert's *Madame Bovary* is just one example. If I can't write from a woman's perspective, then I'm cutting off half of my world. I can't say whether I'm profeminist or antifeminist. I let that kind of thing go by too. As with any form of politics, I can't seem to digest it all. I was an old laborite, and as a former member of half a dozen unions, I thought that when the Equal Rights Amendment first started they ought to strike for equal wages for equal work. That's the one that counts. When I went to Stony Brook with Herbert Weisinger, the first thing he did was to pay female assistant professors the same as male assistant professors. Before we got there, the women were about 20 percent lower. Anybody who has an ounce of democratic sentiment knows that's just wrong. If you don't have equal pay for equal work, you're fucked from the beginning.

AM: Did you make any kind of conscious decision to start using women's voices in your writing?

JH: No, I was just tired of what I was doing. I wanted something new. When I wrote *Sundog*, that was an interesting, different kind of man. But—I first said it in the *Paris Review* years ago—I don't want to be limited to the main subject matter of white middle-class novelists in America which is "nifty guys at loose ends."

CP: How is your character in *Sundog* different from one of these guys?
JH: Because he's not the usual kind of man. This is a more interesting person than a professor on summer vacation who has an affair with his babysitter. There are all sorts of permutations of that kind of thing.

AM: It seems that in *Sundog*, there is a recovery of the invisible workers.
JH: Oh, yeah. You know, there's a fascinating thing you should read in the new *Harper's* on that. In the front, where they gather work from other places, there is part of an essay by Hayden Carruth, a very good poet, where he identifies the real working class that nobody knows exists. These people don't even own farms, and they don't really have factory jobs. They sort of mill around and do odd jobs. A farmer is a different thing. A farmer is a landholder. On the border, and here to a certain extent, if you own some land you're a Mister. Down there, you're El Don. But I like the way Hayden Carruth identifies this whole class of people. I was one of them until I was forty. I could even finish roughing houses or dig footings. You do everything just to make a living, in addition to your writing, which doesn't do it.

CP: I think that kind of work is different from what most writers engage in.
JH: Well, that's true, but it's very bourgeoisie. I was reading a Dan Wakefield essay where he says that when he was in New York, his parents would visit him on a train. That was totally out of the question for somebody from my background. I moved to New York with twenty dollars, and I don't know if my parents had ever ridden a train. I think my father had been on a train. We didn't quite make middle class, well, I suppose we did when my dad was a county agent.

CP: My dad was a farmer and also a 4-H county agent. I'm curious, because our family backgrounds are somewhat similar, how your background informs your work.
JH: Well, it does because it links you to the natural world and as Nennius said, "We're a heap of all we have met." It's the foundation of how I look at the world; it's the way my brain is programmed. I know the names. Robert Graves advised poets to know the names of things. My dad could drive

down the county road and name all of the weeds by the smells, all of the trees, all of the crops, natural watersheds, the way the earth is shaped. That's a different kind of knowledge. I don't mind mentioning the mind doctor I visit in New York at least once a year. He told me once, "Think of what it's like to treat people who never see the sun and the moon and the stars and the earth." You see, there's a whole set of problems there.

AM: I'm really interested in the contrast between the way you describe your orientation to the natural world and the way you describe driving through the campus area in East Lansing. Does that kind of orientation to the natural world seem more consistent with your sense of the way you're marking time?

JH: I'm sure that, just because your parents and grandparents did, you think in terms of specific seasons, and everybody is happy at the solstices and it's actually sort of primitive. It's just the way you look at the world. But even those midway points in Lansing . . . I remember a bunch of students and graduate students were growing pot in the big swamp behind Spartan Village. They were watching out, but I don't even think at that time, in the late fifties, that it was particularly against the law. It wasn't any good anyway; it was like the pot people used to get from Indiana where you'd have to smoke a cigar before you would get anything.

CP: This poem called "Counting Birds," that Anthony and I discussed for most of the drive up here, I heard you read at MSU two years ago and it really stuck with me. You use an Anasazi myth about birds, and it seems that the speaker in the poem is using the birds as a way of marking time in the way that Eliot's Prufrock marks out time with coffee spoons.

JH: Yeah, maybe so. I never thought of that connection, but that's obviously true. The Lakota and the Chippewa had what they called winter counts. They had a cane and they'd draw little petroglyphs of the events of the winter. It's like time, a time passing, though they tend to be less swallowed by time. In other words, it's not the clock, but it's the event. I've never been good at time at all. For instance, I don't remember my career in terms of the books, but of what dog I owned at that time. That's how my mind works. I was at the Tucson airport and my watch had stopped. I was getting my boots shined and I asked five different passing Mexicans what time it was. Nobody had a watch and it was marvelous. It was the usual gringo question, and this old man told me, "What time is it? Who the fuck cares!" Sometimes they want to help you: "Uh, it's maybe noon" (laughs). That is a wonderful attitude compared to the way the White Anglo Saxon Protestant thinks about time.

CP: Do you think we have this necessity of marking time or counting time or accounting for your life in terms of something?

JH: Yeah, we all have these ways. The Romans used to mark time by how they were aging: "Oh I have a wrinkle," or something like that. What are the events in your life? How many divorces? We're always keeping track. With so many men, it's how much do I have in my 401K or my IRA. What's my salary now? What is the inflation compared to what it was, because we are always counting.

AM: Do you find yourself feeling a sense of counting time through the events of your publications?

JH: No, not any more. I did for a while. Everybody in our culture teaches that if we even blink, we're going to fall behind. People aren't even taking all of their vacation time. Now they're working longer hours because there's always this fear of being outsourced. Even in our highest prosperity, people are more insecure than when they didn't have any money. I have a number of friends who are very wealthy and they seem to be more like victims than Joe Blow who spends his last five bucks down at the tavern. I was thinking of it in biblical terms. When you're reading the Bible, which I did a lot as a young man, so and so rich man had nine cows and three horses and a granary full of wheat. That was a rich man then. Now what is it? I had three Land Cruisers in a row, because I'm out in the boonies. When I went to get another one, suddenly they're fifty eight thousand dollars. I got in it and I said that the inside of this car looks like Liberace's toilet (laughs). It's no longer a functional vehicle; it's being built now for soccer moms. It's amazing. You can get the one I want, but you can only get it in Africa. They're about thirty grand there and they're functional, but they don't have our emission standards. I looked at a farm, I certainly don't need another farm, but I was looking at a farm and this is what drove me crazy—in the UP there's eighty acres and this house for fifty-eight thousand. That's why it squared with me. So you could buy a whole fucking farm for the same price as you can buy a car, you know. Why would anyone do that? But that's just an older man reflecting on how things have changed.

CP: This is interesting. In one of the poems I was reading, "Drinking Songs" from *Outlyer*, you wrote, "I want to die in the saddle / an enemy of civilization / while I walk around in the woods and fish and drink." Do you think that the Jim Harrison of today differs from this portrayal?

JH: Not greatly. I did that this summer, although now I've pretty much given up hard liquor in favor of wine. I like really good wine. It's a little expensive compared to just a shot and a beer, but it's basically the same thing. I feel most at home at this one place up in the UP that's fifteen miles from everything. But I also like certain cafes and bistros in Paris more than I do in New York City. I think they're more receptive. You know, my last book got up to number three in France.

CP: Why do you think the French are more receptive?

JH: Just because they're tired of only Parisian literature which is more like New York literature. The French are more fundamentally rural than we are. If they live in any of the big cities, they're always trying to get out. Except the upper class, of course, but they already have an estate.

AM: One of your interviews suggests that the mainstream is shaped by New York, and having grown up in Iowa, I found that everybody's sort of aspiring to that conception of cosmopolitan life.

JH: McGuane and I used to always try to get each other to say things that needed to be said so that we could blame it on the other person. But McGuane said, "Why don't you say that southern writers have always had their crotchless panties aimed at New York" (laughs). That's a real McGuane witticism. He did an interview once with a gay magazine, and everybody has a lot of friends that are gay. I told him to say that you can't make a philosophical system out of your weenie. So, he said that and he got viciously attacked for years on that comment (laughs). I thought that was funny. But I feel uncomfortable because the University Press of Mississippi, you know Ole Miss? They are considering a collection of my interviews next year with DeMott, the Steinbeck scholar, and Patrick Smith as the editors. I'm doing a lot of French interviews too, and I have no monetary interest in this. I'm just wondering what they're going to come up with. The French are odd because there are about eighty newspapers in France that have full-time literary critics, and here we only have one in Washington, one in Los Angeles, and some in New York. This old man said to me once, "How much has your poetry been affected by the early poetry of Robinson Jeffers?" I've never been asked that question in America. It is strange how much they have studied American literature.

CP: When I first started talking about wanting to interview you, I was told there was no way possible that I could get you to do an interview. Why did you agree to talk with us?

JH: I don't have any idea (laughs), because I turn most of them down. I think it was an odd image to me that you should publish this. When they started

Red Cedar Review, with McGuane and Walter Lockwood and those guys, I was an aesthete then. I wouldn't have anything to do with something so tawdry (laughs). I remember going into this office in a corner room of Morrill Hall. I said once, "Where's Tom?" We didn't know each other that well, but we would stop and talk about literature, because we both wanted to be writers. It was either Walter Lockwood or somebody else that said, "He's in the closet with a bottle of whiskey and a secretary from Lansing." I admired Tom because he was so good looking. He was worldly and rather than putting up with coeds, he and a couple of his friends would go down to Lansing to these dances. They were secretaries' dances and they would just clean up. He had all these girls with beehive hairdos driving around with him. Just normal girls, not some difficult, neurotic student, but a living breathing girlfriend from Laingsburgh . . . Where did you grow up in Iowa, Tony?

AM: Ames.

JH: Oh yeah, that's a fascinating place. I finished a new novella a couple of months ago with an odd title: *The Beast God Forgot to Invent*. It is about a guy, a young man. The narrator's an old creep, but it's about a guy who has a head injury from running his motorcycle into a beech tree. I got hundreds and hundreds of books on the brain under the hubris that after a couple of months of reading I could understand the human brain. Well, forget it. Anyway, here's one of the great ones, one of the most difficult ones that I've almost made it through. I love this title: *Neural Darwinism*. Wow. Anyway, one of the great brain centers in the world is in Ames, Iowa.

AM: Did you spend a lot of time driving around the Midwest?

JH: Yeah, because that used to be one of my so-called therapies. The other trouble with teaching is that you don't have freedom just to go. My wife's secretary always could tell when I was getting weird, when I just needed to go on one of my car trips. I remember driving twelve thousand miles in a big circle, down into Mexico. I rarely ever drive on freeways. I have a compass in the car and go on the county roads.

AM: So you have a sense of being able to do that at any time?

JH: Yeah, number one it's not expensive compared to anything else.

AM: What about that looming pressure for getting the next book out?

JH: I don't think about it. I might have at one time, but the biggest liberating point was when I quit writing screenplays essentially two and a half years ago. That's why I know a lot about the money trap, which is the big trap.

AM: How would you characterize your relationship with Hollywood now?

JH: I still have some friends out there. It's one of those places where you like one out of a hundred people you meet, which is about the same as academic life. I don't find it morally or ethically any different from book publishing. I don't find Hollywood types any lower on the squeeze box of life than the book publishers. Nine of our biggest publishers are owned by the Germans. Before that it was corporate America blah, blah, blah . . .

CP: Why did you stop writing screenplays?

JH: Just fatigue. What happened was that ten years ago, I hadn't saved any money and I had to go back to work out there to make some money. Because I'm in a free economy, and I don't work for anybody.

AM: I was really interested in your comments about teaching a while back. Do you think it is possible to teach writing in college or high school classrooms?

JH: I don't know, you know, it's an odd thing. There was a teacher at Michigan State who was quite extraordinary—and then he had some problems. But he was a big shot, and after Michigan State, he went to Berkeley as a full professor. He was a brilliant man who taught the only essay writing course I ever had in my life. Every week, our assignment was to imitate a great essay writer, and I just loved doing that. I thought that this was a way you could teach writing. Philip Caputo, who's a novelist friend of mine and wrote *A Rumor of War*, went broke as a novelist and taught up in Cedar Rapids, Iowa. He was supposed to be teaching a course on the modern novel but ended up teaching six courses of composition. It really pissed him off. I bet they learned something, though, because he's a tyrant.

AM: What do you remember about learning how to write?

JH: Nothing except what I remember from that essay writing class. You can only learn how to write by writing, and I started in high school. You know, writing down thoughts—your pompous thoughts (laughs). And I read a lot because, oddly enough, for an agricultural family we read quite a bit—mostly modern fiction. It was my dad who gave me Sherwood Anderson and Faulkner and things like that.

AM: So, were you pretty clear that you wanted to be a writer from the beginning?

JH: Yeah, and I didn't really know if I needed college. I quit school five or six times to go to New York or San Francisco or Detroit to write, but when that didn't work out, Johnny Wilson who was the head of scholarships would always give me my scholarship back. And then I got married rather early, and the year after I got married, I took eighty-eight credits just to get the degree. I also worked practically full time, so it's no wonder I was a wombat.

AM: This distinction between academic knowledge and experience reminds me of one of the major threads in *Dalva*. There is an interesting comparison between two conceptions of history embodied by the characters of Michael and Dalva. Michael seems to be unfavorably cast as the Western academic in comparison to Dalva's more nativist, circular, conception of history.

JH: Yeah, although I find academic history very interesting. That's one thing about Michigan State. I never took a course from him, but I knew Russell Nye very well. And you could walk down the hall and ask any question you had in your brain about American history and he'd know about it. Then you could go down the same hall and ask Weisinger anything you wanted to know about world literature. Both of them would start dictating these monstrous answers, and that's the real value of a university. It can promote a kind of contiguity with people.

In *Dalva*, Michael presents one possible view of history. It reminds me of a new historian—I wish I could remember her name—who was at Harvard. She said that she liked *Dalva*, except for Michael. But you have to have a character like Michael who serves as the clown, just like in Shakespeare. He's the buffoon outside comment. And Michael has a lot of very valid points. But he also represents conceptions of American history that we were taught in school that leave out women, Mexicans, Indians, and immigrants. It's a vision of American history that never existed in the first place.

AM: What is interesting about that is there's a line where Dalva says something about his writing and, I can't remember exactly the line, but his writing is a bit stiff.

JH: Yeah, there's a great saying—he's got the top screwed on too tight. Of course Michael's an obsessive-compulsive manic-depressive, and I often find that these kinds of people are the ones you want to listen to. Because any conception we have of normal is always an extrapolation of someone who's bored with his life.

AM: Do you think that academics do a kind of violence to history?

JH: Well, sometimes they do. But then without them, we don't have anything. For instance, in all of this stuff about the Columbine High School shooting, nobody has mentioned Richard Slotkin's absolutely epochal study, *Regeneration Through Violence*. I was going to write Noah Adams at NPR about it, but I keep forgetting. I mean, you have a lot of dimwitted pundits blaming the television, and no one considering how such events fit into the tradition of America. When I was in high school, if you had a difference you'd walk the distance down to the grain elevator and fistfight. That's how things were done. Even the coach would have us put on sixteen-ounce boxing gloves. This sort of thing happens less now. I've been going down to Montana for thirty years and it's interesting that today the cowboys are the dope smokers and they don't fight anymore (laughs). I mean it's really amazing how things, like smoking dope, have made their way down the food chain. So it's interesting that in some places like bars, there isn't as much violence as there used to be.

CP: Do you think that is unfortunate?

JH: No, it's a good thing. They banned arm wrestling at Dick's tavern a couple of years ago, because it was causing fights. One guy would get pissed off after he lost.

So, to answer your question, no, I don't think academics necessarily do violence to history. Sometimes they do, but then what kind of history could we have without them? I used to complain about university presses a lot, but in a totally market-driven economy, you have to have venues for academics to publish important studies.

AM: A related question: How do you feel about seeing your book, *Legends of the Fall*, go through the process of being mediated through Hollywood which is increasingly being viewed as the source for historical and literary information? That's unsettling for a lot of historians.

JH: Well, it should be. It's just so funny. I mean there are mines of material in anything you read from some of these university presses. Oklahoma and the University of Nebraska Press are just fabulous in contrast to Hollywood's views of history. Fortunately, the guy who directed *Legends* is a Harvard graduate. We talked on the phone a lot and there was no way he was going to sacrifice important historical information. Unfortunately, that has been done over the years in Hollywood. The Indian nations are represented by Jeff Chandler and that kind of garbage. But, I do think they're trying to be a little more accurate as the years pass.

AM: Were you pleased with the way that film went?

JH: I'm never pleased by anything, because I saw it differently. I think the main thing that went wrong with *Legends*, which wasn't a bad movie, is what Jack Nicholson said about it: It wasn't gritty enough, whereas the book is gritty. The art director got a little out of hand, you know, and everyone looked too pretty. But they essentially told the story. I went to a couple of early versions of the screenplay, but then I gave it up. The guy that did the best work was the screenwriter who also wrote *Lonesome Dove*, Bill Wittliff. *Lonesome Dove* was the best thing on TV that dealt with the Western movie. It was really on the money. But Wittliff was a Texan with a background in that area and *Lonesome Dove* was totally accurate. So anyway, he had done the basic version of *Legends*. It is the only reason it was as acceptable as it was.

CP: What is the fascination for you with the American West?
JH: Oh, I don't even think there is one. I hitchhiked out there a lot when I was young, when I was sixteen, seventeen, eighteen to look it over. I suppose it is just the natural extension of the American East: Greed goes West. Fucks it up. Hits LA. Then it filters back across the country drowning everything in its lint. The West is misunderstood. Demographically, the LA. area has a much higher concentration of readers than the New York area. Isn't that amazing? But if you think of New York, people often mistake Manhattan for New York and that is only a hundred thousand people on the uppity side.

AM: Jim McClintock gave the Russell Nye lecture last year and it was about your writing and the relationship of your writing to Carl Jung and James Hillman.
JH: That Hillman thing was interesting. I don't know how directly apropos it is, but my brother is quite a book collector and, for a brief period, we owned together the collected works of Carl Jung. All twelve volumes. I really liked the pictures, you know, the pictures of a tiger eating the sun and all those primitive images. So, I read a lot of Jung and it seemed like Hillman was his best explicator. And Jungian theory isn't as dreary and sodden as Freudianism.

CP: How have you used Jung and Hillman in your writing?
JH: I've been influenced by some of their ideas, especially in regards to conceptions of masculinity and femininity. I think it was Hillman quoting Jung who asked, "What have we done with our twin sister that the culture has forced us to abandon at birth?" So many Middle Eastern poets and Spanish poets were virtually androgynous in the way that a shaman is androgynous

and can move between sexes, at least philosophically. I think poets are mostly shamans without portfolios, and very bad ones at that. Failed shamans. Take Robert Graves's *White Goddess*, about Celtic folklore and the emergence of poets in ancient Ireland. Graves writes that if you wanted to be a poet, you traveled around with a woman who taught you the names of everything. The woman was thought to be more related to the moon, hence more related to poetry.

CP: What kind of spiritual orientation, if any, informs your work?

JH: I don't know if any does. I suppose I am essentially Christian because that is my mythos. I said once in my food column in *Esquire* that I found it was easier to believe in the Resurrection than the Republican Party. For me anyway, it still is. I've studied Zen for twenty-five years but that is more of an additive than an attention to detail. Most of our lives are dissipated on garbage and nonsense, and Zen philosophy keeps you attentive. There is this old Japanese guy who taught that you must concentrate yourself wholly to each day as though a fire were raging in your hair. You know, there is a high level of attention there, which is good for me because I don't have any discipline, I never did. I'm only writing because that is what my calling is.

AM: Do you have to instill any structure or sense of discipline in your practice?

JH: Not when I'm working on a novel or a novella or poetry. When I wrote screenplays, I had to tell myself, "Go do three pages and then you can go bird hunting or fishing." I had to write by quota every day.

AM: Conversely, do you have to stop yourself?

JH: Yeah, that's my main problem. When I finished *Dalva*, both my eardrums were broken and I didn't even know it. I mean, I had the flu, and it was just insane. The same thing happened when I wrote *Legends*, which I wrote in nine days. I was clearly deranged by the time I got done. It is what Walker Percy calls the re-entry problem. That is why writers are generally drinkers. Alcohol is a way to get back to the world from your daily voyage in your fiction. It is an interesting point of view. And some people like to stay in that world all of the time which is problematical. Even though I was gentler with myself on *The Road Home*, it still caused a lot of problems. The back and forth between these parallel universes is hard on yourself physically and mentally.

CP: I read an interesting piece in *Smart* magazine called "Mid-range Roadkill." You tell the story of how a friend illegally shot a turkey and brought it to you. I'm wondering if cooking is another way . . .

JH: Oh, I'm sure. See, when I was ruining my brain by going to the bar directly after work roughly twenty years ago, I got more and more interested in cooking as a great away to return to earth. An illegal wild turkey is a great gift. There is nothing that tastes any better than a not totally adult wild turkey. And this guy was real coy because he said, "I hit it with my car," and there was a neat little .22 hole in it. I said, "Do you have a .22 mounted on your bumper?" If you are depressed, gifts like that change the nature of your thinking. Once when I entered in a depression, I went to Costa Rica and I was fine. That was where I met the man who gave me the idea for *Sundog*. This brings up another trap with academic life, at least for me. Just about all of the novels I wrote after *Wolf* depended on me being free and easy in my travels. I don't know if I would have gotten any of those ideas if I had been limited to the classroom. I can't think of any of the novellas that didn't depend on knowledge of the Mexican border, or Canada, or Europe, or parts of the United States. I mean academics can have quite a free schedule, but it is still a schedule.

AM: So, you met this guy in Costa Rica and then some idea started to germinate . . .

JH: Yeah, it starts to germinate. Sometimes it takes several years. Right now I'm working on a novella, a comic, in the Jacobean style. Not a farce or anything but I'm trying to write something about success and it is called "I Forgot to Go to Spain." Because that was true in my own life. When I was nineteen I was obsessed with Spain and Spanish poets: Lorca, Neruda, Hernandez. I just had to get to Spain. I never got around to it, and then when I made a lot of dough, I just wanted to go to Michigan's Upper Peninsula and get away from the accoutrements. So, when I was in France in May, I finally thought, "Hah, why don't I fucking go to Spain?" I was busy in Paris, and I just thought, "Hah, I'll go to Barcelona for the night." It's only a couple of grand, you know. I'll stay in a simple hotel. This guy reserved my room and when I got in this hotel, it was just a bathroom with a balcony. This woman came in and spread a linen cloth by my bed so my feet didn't have to touch the rug. And I thought, "This is the real Spain that I thought about when I was nineteen." That kind of crap. And then it got very hot. It hadn't occurred to me that it would be hot because I like to walk, and I could only walk at night. I stayed two nights. It was sunny and this French *Vogue* magazine gave me some money, in cash, for something I had written for them. I got an air-conditioned Mercedes and a guide who spoke perfect English, an architectural graduate student or something like that. So I went to see a bunch of art work without getting out of the car. You know, it is what happens to successful people—so-called successful people. What happens is that you become utterly removed from any kind of life you value—unless you are very careful.

CP: Do you feel like you have avoided those kinds of problems in your life?
JH: Somewhat, but not totally.

AM: What about the threat of having a mystique built around you—if you lived in New York for example.
JH: I couldn't do it. It is harder for me in public in Paris than it is in New York. A lot of people recognize me in Paris. New York somewhat, but what I do is just avoid everything now. I didn't for a while. You can avoid a lot of problems associated with success with sufficient alertness. Only there are some situations where you are trapped. I did a nineteen-stop book tour last fall, and it took me three months to recover. I got over it by writing last winter. I correspond with Louise Erdrich who is a writer that I greatly value, and she was making the same complaints. She was sitting with a bunch of Bostonian ladies at a book luncheon and she told me that she had this really strong urge to say, "Wouldn't you old bitches just like to sit down and have a bunch of martinis? Wouldn't that be better?" But she also said, "Just remember back when nobody wanted you to go on a book tour." It's just something you have to do, that I find really difficult. But, of course, it is even tougher *not* to have a successful book tour. Like when you make a stop and nobody shows up. That's something you have to keep in mind. But, if you have a situation like I did in Mississippi last year, where I signed seven hundred books in four and a half hours, you're not really very happy about it.

AM: Do you feel like you are expected to maintain a specific persona at such events?
JH: Yeah, you do a little reading and then go to dinner. But writers are never famous. I mean someone like Hemingway was, but writers are usually well enough known to get irritable but never famous. I spend a lot of time around people like Jack Nicholson, Harrison Ford, and Sean Connery, and those are really the people who can't go anywhere without people being insane.

CP: Do you ever desire that kind of recognition?
JH: No, no, Christ no, nobody would in their right mind. Nicholson was a master because he always wore dark glasses. That means no eye contact, so people will feel nervous. Even being blind in one eye, like I am, it's harder for

them. I can always get away with it because they don't know if I'm returning their look. So they can't say, "Hi, I'm dirt. Maybe you would like to read the manuscript of my novel."

CP: How do you think you are perceived here in Michigan?

JH: Oh, I've always gotten along OK because I started out here. I did a lot of manual labor, so I feel no resentment. Rich people who move in here don't know that if you aren't nice to the plumber, he doesn't come to your house. If I call the plumber, he's here in five minutes. If they call the plumber, he'll let them wait four or five days—which is appropriate, if you ask me.

AM: Another interesting thread that seems to be coming out of this conversation and also out of a book like *A Good Day to Die* is this notion of the outlaw. In some ways, there is a suggestion that the outlaw, or the people who define themselves as being outside of mainstream society, are the sane ones.

JH: Well, possibly, but this is odd. I remember once when we were broke and it was just before I had gotten successful with *Legends*. They called me from this university, because even then I had a small cache, three books of poems and a couple of novels out. They had a creative writing program and they offered me seventy-five or eighty thousand dollars—and this was over twenty years ago. I said, "You're kidding, that's a lot." But I said, "No," to the discouragement of my in-laws. "I can't do that," I said. Somebody's got to stay outside. That is what *Outlyer* means. I can't say that they are the sane ones because they are transparently not. But it gives you a way of looking at your own culture if you are on the outside.

AM: What would you say is the state of our culture, US society, now—especially in contrast to when you wrote *A Good Day to Die.*

JH: Sometimes, the places I choose to live in don't give you as good a view of the entire culture as even television does. Living in the UP and on the Mexican border where it is really remote offers a view of a different kind of sub-subculture. For example, I was asking this guy, a sort of hippy, half Mexican, and half gringo, "Why isn't there any crime around here?" And this hippy said, "I don't allow no fucking crime." This is definitely a subculture.

But I've seen over the last thirty years that we are as completely submerged and drowned in outright banality, where greed and apathy are the ultimate virtues as we were in the twenties. It's hard on university people too because they say that they and their families have bypassed that. They are really getting paid miserably compared to what they probably should be, as far as I'm concerned. I noticed that in France, the reason teachers are so respected in each community is because they are usually the highest paid people in the community, outside of the banker and the doctor. And if you don't value your teachers, the culture snubs them. By making fun of the government, Reagan did a great deal of damage to the country because to infer that the populace is collectively more intelligent than the civil service is a big mistake.

There is another myth: these small businessmen feel that if it wasn't for the constraints of government, they would be wildly successful. I ought to ask them about Bill Gates. I mean, give me a break. Obviously, even here in my so-called retirement, I would deeply enjoy a 50 percent drop in the stock market. Anything to slow down this craze.

CP: You mentioned the effect of this craze on professors and their families. Have your decisions made it easier for your family to have a different perspective on work?

JH: My youngest daughter hated college. She's too excessively attractive, which, Carrie, you probably know about. Anyway, she just likes to work in bookstores. But my older daughter graduated from a little podunk high school. Her counselor, they are usually lamos, told her to try to go to a small college but she went to U of M and graduated summa cum laude. I mean, she was her high school's first National Merit Scholar, and that didn't merit a sentence in the newspaper because they've never had one before. But, I never could understand where she got her study habits. I certainly didn't have them. I started out a term and took perfect notes the first day. The second day it's tits and ass, and the third day I cut class and I'm at Mac's Bar playing pool. I mean it was just hopeless. It was a good thing that I was sort of smart because back then, they let you comp the basics. You could take the test and not take the class.

AM: How was high school?

JH: I was reading James Joyce when I was sixteen. I had a couple of good teachers, one even subscribed to the *Nation* magazine, which caused a little talk because he was a left-winger. I had another high school teacher who was a POW from World War II who had been in a German prison. That kind of experience gives you a view of the world. But, I naturally liked to get out of there. I hitchhiked to New York when I was sixteen. I knew that was where I wanted to go. I wanted to be a bohemian instead of hauling corn.

AM: What did you think about the whole bohemian movement then?

JH: Oh, it just seemed like more freedom. When you're that age, all you want is freedom. I don't even know how young people survive these days because back then we had so much less scrutiny from the world. We were people with our own culture, and now right from the cradle these kids are under such incredible scrutiny from parents, PTA, and everything. They are being told never to talk to a stranger, you know . . .

Jim Harrison: An Interview with Joseph Bednarik

Joseph Bednarik / 2000

From *Five Points: A Journal of Literature and Art* 6, no. 2 (2002): 44–66. Reprinted with permission of Joseph Bednarik and *Five Points*.

Jim Harrison is the author of seven novels, nine volumes of poetry, a dozen novellas, a collected nonfiction, and an illustrated children's book. He has also written numerous screenplays and served several years as the food columnist for *Esquire* and *Smart* magazines. His work has been translated into two dozen languages. As a young poet he coedited (with Dan Gerber) *Sumac* magazine and earned a National Endowment for the Arts grant and a Guggenheim Fellowship. Mr. Harrison divides his time between northern Michigan and southern Arizona.

This interview, which took place in Seattle in October 2000, is edited from a ninety-minute conversation recorded as the pilot show for a radio program *Writing On Air*. The producers asked that the interview focus on Harrison's poetry—a topic which had never been discussed in depth during any of his previous interviews. What one cannot hear in this written form is Harrison's cackling, the mutual laughter and over-talk, and the sounds of Harrison drinking a favorite French wine, Bandol from Domaine Tempier, out of a plastic cup. Not to mention the single piece of nicotine gum he pulled apart bit by bit and nibbled throughout the conversation because he wasn't permitted to smoke in the studio.

Joseph Bednarik: There are characters throughout your novels who are either poets or failed poets. What is it about a poet that you find intriguing as a character in fiction?
Jim Harrison: I hadn't realized I'd used them that much. The interesting thing, and what old Joe Campbell talked about—I was privileged to meet

him early in the sixties—is: What does it do to a man or a woman when they refuse the call? It creates a kind of explosive negative force in their life. Because they refuse their calling I can create drama with this negative energy in their lives.

Bednarik: Do you think it's possible later in life to retrieve the call?
Harrison: No, not largely, because poetry just like painting is something that you have to give your entire life to—and that includes *all* your life. Those people who say it's never late to start again are largely fooling themselves. They *can* start again and retrieve some of the essential integrity of the original calling but they all know that time moves quickly and they've blown it.

Bednarik: When did you feel that you got your call as a poet?
Harrison: Most definitively at about nineteen, starting at fourteen when I first read Keats. And Whitman and so on. But then really at nineteen it was almost a metaphysical experience: I'm sitting on the roof of our house watching the moon rise over a big marsh—

Bednarik: This is northern Michigan?
Harrison: Yeah, and birds of various species were crisscrossing the moon and I could see them clearly in silhouette. That sort of faux Chinese experience. Anyway, then I heard the call.

Bednarik: In a number of places you talk about taking your vows as an artist.
Harrison: Well, you do take vows just like a priest or a Zen student takes vows. What did Charles Olson say that was incredible? "One must only traffic in one's own sign." That excludes every other thing in your life. To me it's always been important to belong to nothing, other than my marriage which is forty years duration. But you belong to nothing except this.

Bednarik: The Guild.
Harrison: The Guild of Poetry and Fiction, which has lasted thousands and thousands of years. That's your primary fidelity in life, and it's important not to dissipate it in any other human activities.

Bednarik: Have you ever found that your energies have dissipated?
Harrison: Oh sure. Once when we went broke for instance, my wife saw a strange TV documentary on the homeless—she was sure our daughters

would be homeless—so then I betrayed everything and worked very hard for a number of years to save some money, so our daughters wouldn't be homeless. Which there wasn't even the slightest possibility that they were going to be homeless, but that's an almost biological thing that all fathers feel, that you owe your wife and children, et cetera, et cetera, some sense of security.

Bednarik: Well there's an interesting point in your career. You started out as a poet and had a couple of years where you were a Guggenheim fellow, you got an NEA grant, and you were living in northern Michigan, really far away from the cultural centers of the poetry community. And then the grants ended. Is this the time you were talking about?

Harrison: Well that was the most difficult time. We lived ten years and I never made ten thousand dollars a year. Ever. We lived extremely simply, up on a small farm. Dan Gerber loaned me the down payment, which I think was five thousand dollars and the farm cost eighteen thousand dollars. You couldn't buy a parking place for that in Seattle. You take so-called vows of poverty and humility, it's just very religious. And I had many job offers in that time to be poet in residence at colleges, but that was totally out of the question.

Bednarik: Why was that?

Harrison: Because somebody has to stay on the outside. And I felt at the time—and still feel—that far too many people are on the inside. The irony in American letters is that in the sixties it was somewhat uncommon for a fictioneer or poet to be truly accepted and embraced by academia, and now it's the other way around. Can you *have* a life as a poet or a literary fiction writer *outside* the academic community? It's switched in three decades.

Bednarik: There was that essay in *The Atlantic* by Dana Gioia called "Can Poetry Matter?" where he made the argument that poetry is being killed because it's being concentrated in the academy.

Harrison: Without question. You know Karl Shapiro, who wrote that magnificent book which doomed him forever called *The Bourgeois Poet*, he told Ted Kooser—who's one of my favorite American poets—he said to Kooser, who was just a beginning graduate student: "Just get out of here. You'll only write poetry for your peers." I've talked about this improbable post-Victorian sense in American poetry of a kind of breathless nature poem from people totally uninformed about the natural world in terms of botany or ornithology. But it's a set piece, like in Victorian England there were all these faux sincere set pieces, and we have the same thing now, which is of course unfortunately 99.9999 percent trash. And we accept that fact. That we have a few things that last, we're very fortunate.

Bednarik: So how do you wade through the trash?

Harrison: I *don't* wade through the trash, I try to avoid it. There's very little room for the durable. For instance, I knew Robert Lowell quite well, James Dickey, those people, and you know Lowell was the *eminence gris* of American poetry but since he's died I've rarely heard anybody mention his name. Fumius flumis: We all go up in smoke. I can disappear that quickly. People can be the dominant voices of their generation, but the next generation doesn't want to listen to them. For good reasons, sometimes.

Bednarik: To pick up on something you said earlier, about writing for your peers: Odysseus Elytis said that ideally the poet wants three readers, and since every poet had two good friends, his whole task is to try and find that third reader.

Harrison: That's a fascinating idea, I've never heard of that. Maybe it's some kind of implacable ideal reader with a perfect ear who is sort of a muse. It has to be female, of course. For some reason I can't take men seriously maybe because I'm a man, you know what I mean? I feel that I've responded most deeply even to my harshest female critics. And it's not the mother thing, it's not any kind of odious psychologism, it's just that I think they're hearing with larger ears. Very big ears, like Dumbo.

Bednarik: Careful with that one.

Harrison: Dumbo was brilliant. Always remember that.

Bednarik: I'll do my best. . . . There's a poem in your first book called "Sketch for a Job Application Blank." You've called that your first successful poem.

Harrison: I don't know. It was written at a time when I was always unemployed and I couldn't get a job and I would get these application blanks and you look at them and you realize you're not qualified for anything on earth.

Bednarik: You mention in the poem that you were saved, and also earlier in the conversation you mentioned that at fourteen you discovered Keats.

Harrison: Well that was a difficult thing to discover Jesus and Keats and James Joyce all at the same time. Your soul is pulling all these other directions. I thought I should be smarter so I was always reading the New Testament and Schopenhauer and Nietzsche and Dostoevsky.

Bednarik: This is in your mid-teens?
Harrison: Yes. And so where do you go with this information?

Bednarik: You go to New York.
Harrison: Yeah, you get out of town. That kind of thing.

Bednarik: You talked in an essay about the transference of your religious impulses—your fervent religious impulses—into the impulses of art.
Harrison: Well there's no question that I found out we crave the genuine and life is short. It's sort of Joycean, where *devoutness* as a young man easily transfers itself to the religion of art. Because you don't like the form of organized religion, though as I've said before if you're in New York and admit you go to a "Mind Doctor," as I call them, but that you also say your prayers every morning, that's unthinkable. But I do. I can't stop. I always have. So you naturally say your prayers every morning and then you read and write your poetry. So it's mythical in origin and the energy behind the mythological transfers from one form to another. And you think San Juan de la Cruz or Santa Teresa, these improbably fabulous poets, who were also very devout poets, but for some reason this is now totally unacceptable. I can imagine going into Elaine's in New York and saying "Jesus wants me for a sunbeam"—they'd think you're a lunatic. It'd be fun, I think I'll do that.

Bednarik: You have also, over the past twenty-five years, practiced as you call it "an inept form of Zen."
Harrison: Zen is a form of discipline that I've practiced almost thirty years, though I'm very poor at it. Very bad at it. That's a *life* discipline.

Bednarik: It's not a discipline that you're talking about relative to writing?
Harrison: Well, it's a discipline of attentiveness, or else you diffuse all your energies on nonsense. What did I write the other morning:

> You have to pull out the plug of the TV forever
> and cut your telephone cords
> because it's not proper that you should spend your life
> with your ears stuffed with *merde*, as they say.

So it's a religious attitude to life—every moment. Like Deshimaru, the great French Zen teacher was in China and said, "You have to give your life full attention as if a fire were burning in your hair."

Bednarik: I never understood that quote. I certainly understand the attention.
Harrison: Well, it keeps you awake. Your hair is burning. I like the idea.

Bednarik: But, there's also the sense of panic in that for me.
Harrison: Oh, no panic. You just put out the fire. I mean, you just stay awake. No question. Where I live down on the border in the winter, I stepped out of my car and put my foot on the ground to open our gate and there's a black-tipped rattler, a rather fat, large one a half-a-foot from my foot. And what attention means, even being a burly fellow, I landed on my hood—you know, it's about five-foot high. I *shot* through the air, and then said hello to the snake. But you want to be attentive about that, *watch* your step.

Bednarik: Is that one of the things you see in your dogs: An attentiveness that you admire?
Harrison: They're improbably attentive and you know dogs are our fellow creatures, as are cats and so on. At my cabin my dog knows if there's a bear near. One little sniff and he rolls his eyes and looks around. If the wolf howls at night, he just very casually goes up to the loft and gets under the bed because wolves are mojo. Too much mojo for a dog. But they're very matter-of-fact about that, but we sort of witlessly go through life thinking we're safe and dissipating our lives on nonsense. We suffocate in trash and wonder why we're not happy, that kind of thing.

Bednarik: So if you take your advice in the poem you wrote a couple of mornings ago about unplugging the cord, can the person used to all these things in their life successfully turn to poetry?
Harrison: Oh, sure. Anybody who has the gift, you know. I have such trouble, getting all these manuscripts every year by the hundreds, and galleys and so on, because you can tell right away if a person's not in touch; if they want sincerity, or to be right, it's hopeless. If there isn't a primary intoxication with language and playfulness of their own consciousness, it's hopeless. If they just want to be right, well then they'd better off being a professor, wouldn't they?

Bednarik: You actually provided advice to young writers and said the best thing for them to be was "word drunk."

Harrison: Word drunk and don't forget red wine and garlic. Aimless travel. Obsessive reading. Jobs that have nothing to do with written word. It would be better if they worked in a truck garden, growing things, with a knowledge of botany, natural history, and so on. That's all they need—and you certainly don't need a bloody MFA. Why don't they just shoot themselves?

Bednarik: I've actually guided several young writers away from MFAs.

Harrison: Well, the trouble is it's a pyramid scheme, to me. The one good thing about the program is that it teaches people to read and they become very intense about it. But these poor folks—it's a way of delaying your parents' opprobrium. "I'm continuing on for an MFA, blah blah blah . . ." What could it possibly mean? There are no jobs available for them, it's sort of humiliating for them. They've gone now to college six or seven years; an MFA is worth about as much as a BA in English, which means for a buck you could get a cup of coffee.

Bednarik: You had some profound influences on your early writing, Rimbaud and Rilke and Whitman, and claim the first section of "Suite to Fathers" was actually intended to shed yourself of Rilke's influence.

Harrison: But you never can. You never can. There's a marvelous book, Edelman's *Neural Darwinism*, that I read for *The Beast God Forgot to Invent*. When you lay down those maps—if you read Rilke or even Neruda—you lay them down permanently. These people are so powerful as writers that you've permanently affected the structure of your brain by reading them, and you can't get rid of them. It's just like reading Dostoevsky. That happens rarely in one life—at best, say a dozen people who overwhelm you with the immensity of their work. But you're laying down, in your twelve billion neurons, a permanent message.

Bednarik: So if you're reading those poets all in translation, do you read multiple translations?

Harrison: Oh, sure. When I was asked to be part of that project to translate Neruda, I was thinking there are a dozen or so decent Rilke translations, one of the best being the recent William Gass thing. That's always a fine point. When people say "Oh, you must read it in the original" and I say "Oh, you can't read *English* in the original," for Christ's sake, and you lived here all your life. Don't tell me I can't read this and that.

Bednarik: Many critics point to the *Letters to Yesenin* as a high point for the books of poetry that you've produced. Please talk briefly about your contact with Yesenin.

Harrison: Well, that's fraudulent. They always compare your current work favorably to work that they never reviewed at all. That's the Monday morning quarterbacking. I don't think anyone other than Hayden Carruth even reviewed that book. It's absurd, and now they all say "Oh, God, why don't you write poems like that now," or something like that, that's easy for anybody to say. Yesenin I love. When I was seventeen somebody gave me some translations by Yarmolinsky, the great translator of Russian poetry in the early twenties, and I read Yesenin, Mayakovsky, Berlyev, and so on like that, on and on and on, Blok. I was so obsessed with Russian poetry. But then Yesenin came from a similar background as I did, a fool from the country, so essentially a farmboy. So then when I went to Leningrad, now St. Petersburg, with Dan Gerber I couldn't believe it, in the hotel lobby they were selling souvenirs and amongst them all these photos of Russian poets, and people would buy, instead of photos of Pamela from *Baywatch*, they were buying photos of Yesenin and Mayakovsky. So I bought the Yesenin and I was looking at this guy and I knew all about him—I really began to know his work—and I thought though he's dead, he's an ideal correspondent because we emerge from the same problematical background, and even were obsessed with our respective Isadora Duncans and that drew on my heart. And I said if I have to write letters I may as well write them to him. Albeit he can't respond very adequately.

Bednarik: The book is constructed as a month of correspondence, and I just want to get a sense of how long that book took to write.

Harrison: Probably a month, if I said that's what it was. But I was overpowered. I had too many old friends write me to make sure I hadn't committed suicide. But I said "Oh, that was last year," by the time the book comes out it's all over. You know that thing, the one suicide poem where I say "My three year old daughter's red robe hangs from the doorknob shouting stop."

Bednarik: That's a beautiful image.

Harrison: What else will stop you? Looking at your three-year-old daughter's red robe. Hanging from the doorknob. No, I'm not allowed to commit suicide. I have to maintain this life of a beloved child. So you stop thinking about nonsense like suicide, which is usually a form of punishing other people, though some people can't stop themselves and I understand that.

Bednarik: And twenty years later, in your book *After Ikkyu*, you had another poem addressed to Yesenin called "Returning to Yesenin." What was it like to hearken back?

Harrison: Well, you revisit immediately—just like when I wrote this children's book called *The Boy Who Ran to the Woods*, about being blinded when I was seven in one eye—when you enter the language you return to the event. So pleasantly or not, you're right back there. So when I write "Return to Yesenin" I'm back to the same state in our little farmhouse in northern Michigan in the winter that I wrote these poems.

Bednarik: In your introduction to your collected poems, *The Shape of the Journey*, you said that if you laid out all your poetry books and just glanced over them, you got a sense of what table you would write at, what wine you were obsessed with.

Harrison: What table in this old granary I worked at. Or out in a tent. In the moonlight. So on and so on. That's true, you revisit. I try to tell people when a woman leaves them—this is an amusing idea; it's the same thing—each event of abandonment repeats all the events of abandonment in your life. So, you're stuck with it. When she leaves you, that repeats every time this has happened in your life. Without question, the same way with poetry. It's nonharmonic resonance.

Bednarik: You mentioned that the unwritten poem is a force within the artist.

Harrison: The biggest force within an artist, I think, is this restlessness for the work that's just over the lip of consciousness. You're waiting. You know that old thing Wallace Stevens said, "Images collect in pools," which turns out to be somewhat accurate in terms of brain structure. It's a storage aspect. You've stuffed all these images which are filtering down to this pool and when it gets full—then whether consciously or not consciously—you're prodded to begin. Fascinating idea. Not my idea at all, though I'm not sure where it comes from, but that kind of excess that burbles over.

Bednarik: You claim to be unable to read novels when you're writing a novel. Can you read other people's poems during times when you're writing poems?

Harrison: You have to be a little careful. Sometimes I doubt these suits about plagiarism. I remember once I wrote a tercet, three lines, which I thought was marvelous, and it looked sort of familiar and then I realized it was something

I'd read in Roethke twenty years before. Where are these things coming from? And who in fact is quite that original? That's that whole Burton thing that we stand on the shoulders. Science is cumulative; art isn't cumulative, but our vision is increased by our obsession with people who had greater vision than we will ever have. I always wish that of those three hundred novel galleys I receive through the mail every year, I think 90 percent of them if they'd just read Marquez, they would realize their efforts were supernumerary and they wouldn't have needed to write anything. They could leave it to him.

Bednarik: I was talking with a bookseller down in San Francisco, Paul Yamazaki, who was making the same point. All these folks churning out books are unfamiliar with the territory.
Harrison: I agree. Is that the guy that works at Ferlinghetti's City Lights?

Bednarik: Yes.
Harrison: I know him. Well, there's no question of that, but maybe they don't know at the time. One interesting thing about Rexroth early on was his insistence that poets know the entire history of the traditions of poetry—*on earth.* So you better know it all. And when I taught unsuccessfully for one year I had this reading list for my course in modern poetics—the only year I taught in my life—and it had like 153 books on it. From France from 1880 to now, here. I didn't know how the modern poetic tradition could be understood without being familiar with this. And this is excluding what you should read from the Chinese, the Japanese, and so on.

Bednarik: This was an undergraduate course?
Harrison: It was a 400 course, whatever that is. A bunch of people took it. But I thought, oh my God, if you're not going to give your whole life to it why bother? It can't be done.

Bednarik: It's an effective way to get the core group of people who are interested.
Harrison: That was true. A bunch of them bailed out when they saw the reading list, but most of them stayed.

Bednarik: In one of your novellas you described being a teacher as a walking blood bank.
Harrison: That's true. Everybody's got to make a bloody living and it's very seductive to teach at a university. It's good pay, relatively short hours, until

you find out that the hours go on forever, you're never finished. A professor thinks he has an easy schedule, and then he teaches and he finds out really this is ninety hours a week by the time he gets through with the draw on his own blood supply. So I sensed that rather early—I got to get out of here because how could I get anything done.

Bednarik: There were some pretty impressive people encouraging you to join the University. Herbert Weisinger—
Harrison: Yeah, and Alfred Kazin was a friend of mine there. Roth was there. Louis Simpson. I mean it went on and on, it was a pretty fancy group at Stony Brook and it had the accessibility of New York. But what I couldn't deal with is I'm claustrophobic, and Long Island is an *island*. And there's a bridge to the mainland. And my wife would have dreams—being somewhat a country girl, too—of railroad cars full of burning sheep and so on, because we were trapped on this island, albeit a big island. And we needed to get back home, somehow. It's sort of that feverishness and too much was going on there for me.

Bednarik: There was a famous world poetry conference at Stony Brook, I think in 1968.
Harrison: I essentially ran that. Double over-budget, and then left. Fifty thousand dollars over budget.

Bednarik: Who did you bring in for that conference?
Harrison: Well, 108 poets, including international poets. It was totally out of hand. Even then I was interested in food and wine, so these poets, of course, should have fresh lobster dinners and good wine. Most academics would just give them a blanket of cold cuts.

Bednarik: After your time at Stony Brook there's a period in your writing when you had an intense love affair with an antique form called ghazals. I was wondering if you would explain what that form is.
Harrison: It's funny, I didn't realize it was a proscribed form. Because it's an Arabic form, I thought nobody would like it. I know Senghor, the great North African poet, wrote ghazals and Ghalib wrote them, and when I read ghazals I liked the unrelated couplets that were metaphoric jumps from one reality to another that centered, though, on a same reality, whether love and death or whatever. It's just like when you read Rumi. He travels everywhere, but he's right back there on the dime. And all these metaphors are actually

copulating in your head in Rumi. And that's what a ghazal attempts to do. What's wonderful about them—I'd been afflicted a bit last night with what they call that fugal state, where your brain is whirling with a great deal of energy, sometimes it's fascinating, but sometimes unnerving because you can't control it—and that's the state most suitable to ghazals. You can't stop.

Bednarik: For the composition?
Harrison: Composition. Or new metaphors. Metaphor is very unpopular now because it can't be taught, you realize that, don't you?

Bednarik: Well, there's that great scene in *Il Postino* where Neruda is teaching the postman metaphor.
Harrison: I love that film.

Bednarik: There's a number of poems throughout *The Shape of the Journey* where the first few lines begin "I was commanded in a dream" or "I was commissioned in a dream" to do something, to write something. What's the connection between your dream life and your poetry?
Harrison: Well, it all has to be. I remember this—it might be an apocryphal story—they gave some old Zen master seven hits of acid. And nothing happened. You see what I mean? You have to accept your dream life as part of your life. Only our culture would neglect the dream life. I mean my God, it's been paid attention to for a couple hundred thousand years and now we don't *need*? We want to waste a third of our life to become more efficient marble players in this world we live in? It's absurd. Of course you listen to your dreams. They instruct us. You have to be as attentive to your dreams as you are attentive walking the street. There are these messages from them. Don't. Go ahead. Yes. Stop. Go. Have a good time. That kind of thing.

Bednarik: There are a number of points throughout your books where you make reference to the D. H. Lawrence notion that the last aristocracy is that of consciousness.
Harrison: Lawrence said the only aristocracy is consciousness. And I didn't used to believe such balderdash, but we know it's true. If you think about it—and even very rich people will admit it—all I have, in those Zennist terms, is led by mind. Your consciousness is really all you have, everything else goes away. Probably even your consciousness does, we don't know that for sure. But that's your true, unique possession. Your memory, your

dreams, your consciousness. Gary Snyder talks about that beautifully. Our biographies are essentially similar.

Bednarik: You talk about Vizenor's notion that at the wild end we remember dreams, not data.

Harrison: Absolutely. And it's your dreams—that French notion of Foucault that we live in a zoo—your dreams will get you out of the zoo faster than self-help books about psychology, because your dreams are already trying to get you out of the zoo. They give you great beauty—and horror, too, because that's part of life—but they'll help you out of this pit that your culture, with your cooperation, has submerged you in. So you get these people gulping for air because they're buried. They're trying to stick a little straw up through the dirt to even breathe.

Bednarik: It's interesting you made the point about Rumi. I find that Rumi is a poet who has entered into the self-help world.

Harrison: Well, almost. Isn't that strange? But oh boy I was lucky—a couple years ago in Paris there was this Iraqi woman I know that's married to this famous French screenwriter, Jean-Claude Carriere. So she stood at *dawn* on an embankment in this château we were staying on the Loire River—at dawn, with mist down the river—and she chants Rumi in Persian. I mean she's a beautiful woman, too. You can feel your head wavering in the airs. So her friend Gérard Oberlé goes to Turkey, he takes a cab twenty-eight hours—because she's depressed—where Rumi's buried, and he lays down on Rumi's grave and calls her on his cellular and he says listen to your master. He may be dead but I can hear his heart beat. Wonderful stuff, isn't it?

Bednarik: That's fantastic.
Harrison: That's how people ought to behave. *Stop* getting to work on time!

Bednarik: Well, you claim to always get to work on time.
Harrison: Of course, that's my background. I can't help it. Early, in fact.

Bednarik: If you look at the history of your publications, your first three poetry books were from major New York houses and all the rest of the poetry books are from small presses and independent presses. I'd like you to speak about this decision.
Harrison: Well, the problem is that big publishers in New York, they don't know how to publish poetry. There's no tradition in poetry, and no response

to it. So, with my heart's work I'm not going to New York and discussing a manuscript of poems with someone who would rather be on the *Dick Van Dyke Show* than talk to me. Poetry doesn't belong—as far as I'm concerned—in these major houses, because there's no attentiveness to production, design, there's no attentiveness to editing. They just: Here it is and then they flop it out and they forget a day later that they even published it. I remember when Olson told me they remaindered *Maximus* the day after they brought it out, or something like that. I mean, strange stuff that you don't think could possibly happen. He says he supposed it was somewhat accidental, but it happened. So why not go to people who care about your work rather than people who don't care about your work?

Bednarik: Right. If you read your collected poems from cover to cover one can see that as a young poet you experimented a lot with different forms—you have the ghazals, you have lyrics, you have long suites—and as you read on, you seem to have settled into an almost discursive style. Do you think that's a result of your concentration in fiction, do you think you've settled on a style?
Harrison: No, I don't think it has because I find already it's changing. I have a new reincarnation: Jaime Harrison Walgren. And I think it returns to the lyric. Just the straight, irrational lyric. We are led throughout Earth by women in blue shoes. Who knows where we're going? You know, that kind of thing.

Bednarik: So who is Jaime Harrison Walgren?
Harrison: I've decided to become a Mexican poet because I'm tired of living constricted by our Empire, which I think of the United States now as this vast, horny Empire subduing the Earth. I was sort of friends with Ginsberg, and I don't think that's my propensity, his attitudes, but I see it now. Empire, Empire, that sense of Empire is beginning to drain our souls from us. So that's what's the relief to be in Mexico and France: You get out of the plane and you're not in the Empire anymore. You can say to-da-lee-do and sit in a café half an afternoon and watch a leaf blow along the street. Watch the ankles of working girls.

Bednarik: There's that great poem that you have in *After Ikkyu*, "Sonoran Radio," where you're living in the Empire but on the very edge.
Harrison: In both north and south I live on borders, which helps. You know Duncan's marvelous poem "The Song of the Border Guard," I always think of that. That's true, that gives me a little escape. It's really gotten almost insufferable. All our interests properly should be subsumed in venality.

They keep yapping about moral values, even "values" is an economic term. Everything is related into economic terms. Absolutely everything.

Bednarik: There was this interesting discussion on the radio yesterday about French culture. How every Frenchman hated their teens, but they all loved their thirties, forties, and fifties. That they really mature into people who understand what life is about, that the goal is to retire at fifty-five and actually—

Harrison: And they get this four-day work week. I wonder about it sometimes. It's fascinating to think at least you have an idea of what's essential on Earth. You know that old joke the priest tells: The old Italian dies and he has all his family together and it's wonderful. The old Frenchman dies, all his family gets together and they talk about all the beautiful meals they had all their life. The old American dies and he didn't accumulate enough money. He's dead meat.

Bednarik: The work that you're doing now is a poetic correspondence with Ted Kooser.

Harrison: Ted had cancer a couple years ago and his poetry became really overwhelmingly vivid. He was always a good poet. And then we decided why not correspond in terms of these short wakas or haikus, because that was the essence of what we wanted to say, so we've been doing it for several years and we hope to publish the book with nobody knowing who wrote each poem. It transcends the ego. Just publish it collectively.

Bednarik: I like that because what you're focusing on is the actual poem.

Harrison: Sure, and everybody gets tired of this continuing cult of personality. Bobs get tired of being Bobs, Janes get bored with being Jane. On and on. Why would you want to be the same person every day, all your life? My God.

Bednarik: Your first novel, *Wolf*, was subtitled "A False Memoir" and it was initiated as a challenge from Thomas McGuane, if I remember correctly. So, there you were a poet with three books under your belt and then faced with writing a novel.

Harrison: I was injured. I fell off a cliff above a river while bird hunting. Okay, and you know where the clay looks like it's dry but it's not dry and you step on it and there you go. I had ripped muscles away from my spine. Tom—we talked all the time, I think he was out at Stanford at the time—so he said "Why don't you write a novel?" I outlined the novel musically, first.

Bednarik: What do you mean by that?
Harrison: I outlined the structure of the novel, and I outlined the highs and lows like Yeats used to do with poems. He hears the rhythm of the piece first. And then I poured myself into this drawing of the structure. So it was basically a poet's novel. That first paragraph runs two pages or so. And I was lucky they even published it. It had even been lost. The only manuscript had been lost in the mail for almost a month. There was a mail strike at the same time and I had sent it to my brother, because I couldn't afford to have it copied. Sent it to my brother who was a librarian at Yale and he was going to copy it for me. But he's a bully and he went down to the post office after about a month and he explained the situation and they let him dig through the packages. And he found the novel package.

Bednarik: In your author notes, it makes mention that your work is published in twenty-four languages. How many languages is your poetry translated into?
Harrison: I don't know, quite a few. All the poetry books—I think six of them—are out in France now. I just don't know. I'm a failure at that because I really don't keep track of anything. My energy to persist and go on depends on me ignoring almost every aspect there is of literary life. There's just not time for it, so you just plunge on doing your work. So I never know about that kind of thing.

Bednarik: Is it true that your novels reach best-seller status in France?
Harrison: *The Road Home* got up to number three. It did quite well like that in Italy, too.

Bednarik: You've also published a children's book. How did that come about?
Harrison: My grandson Will asked me how I was blinded in one eye and I thought we're back to Simon Ortiz saying there are no truths, only stories. The only way I could explain it to my grandson who was very curious was to tell the whole story. Which wasn't necessarily pleasant. It was difficult. I did numerous drafts of it, bearing ever deeper into how it actually happened.

Bednarik: And so you're trying to tell the story of a blinding and the healing, to—
Harrison: Because everyone has traumas. We always share unendurable traumas. What I'm most amazed by, when you start talking to a person, are

the almost fatal blows. But what's unique—what *can* be unique—are not the blows, which are the donné, the given in life, but our cures. How do we endure these things? How did we draw ourselves out of what we think of as unpardonable suffering?

Bednarik: So the cure for the little boy in the book is to go into the natural world and become attentive.
Harrison: He escapes into the natural world. Because I had thought—God, I had an unpleasant time this spring thinking about it—because I dreamt that after sixty-two years of looking at the natural world from the outside, that for some reason I was inside looking out.

Bednarik: I don't understand.
Harrison: Well, I was inside the natural world looking out at the culture. And it was an important jump. Inevitable jump, probably, but albeit an uncomfortable jump.

Bednarik: Well, you talk in a couple places about becoming trees, becoming rivers. Is that the kind of thing you're talking about?
Harrison: True. That's from Dogen. Obviously to study the self is to forget the self, to forget the self is to become one with ten thousand things. You don't become one with ten thousand things, ten thousand things become one with you. That's what happens. So it's unavoidable if you see a bear not to become a bear. You know, that whole shape-changing thing. To fully imagine a bear is to become the bear.

Bednarik: You have a poem that talks about eating a bear's heart and then having bear dreams.
Harrison: Well, you do. I've eaten bear a half-a-dozen times merely because hunters in northern Michigan kill bear and abandon the meat, or give it away because they just want the skins of the bear. I hate to see it go to waste, so I try to cook bear. Sometimes successfully.

Bednarik: In an essay on Zen you had talked about bears as a dharma gate.
Harrison: Oh, sure. What our local Anishinabe call a "mugwah." It's such a great name. When I was in Montana recently, outside our little house we rented, there was a bear in a crab apple tree, he was a young bear eating apples all night, and sort of crapping out of the tree on the ground, and he'd look at the window where I was watching, Linda and I were watching him,

and he'd go—very tentative little—*grrowl*. He really didn't want to be interrupted as he just ate away. In the late fall they become what they call hyperphagic, they're just obsessed with eating enough to get them through the winter, like some of these guys on the NASDAQ. I don't know what it means. The *craving*. But of course bears are a dharma gate. So are possums, too.

Bednarik: How so?

Harrison: You know that woman who wrote that book *Women Who Run with the Wolves*? I'd sort of looked at that, but I thought how about *Men Who Walk with Possums*. That kind of thing. We have a sense to dramatize. In reincarnation they're always telling you I was once Pocahontas or Mary Queen of Scots, when we all might've been microbes in a dog turd in the Middle Ages. Let's stop being so dramatic. Where *is* humility?

Bednarik: Well, where is humility?

Harrison: It's knowing that we're all here together. Ego is meaningless. Personality is essentially meaningless. Of course, that's the trouble with literary life. The work is what matters, not somebody's personality. I once was able to do an imitation of an important novelist walking into Elaine's, looking out over the heads of everybody. The ego is utterly destructive that way.

Bednarik: I appreciate that you came in to talk about the work.

Harrison: It wasn't too hard. If only I hadn't eaten that granola this morning.

Bednarik: Why?

Harrison: The granola was very sharp and it punctured my gum. Now I'm having a problem with it. Be careful, gentle readers, of granola—it can be *dangerous*.

Birnbaum v. Jim Harrison

Robert Birnbaum / 2004

From *The Morning News*, June 7, 2004. Copyright Robert Birnbaum. Used by permission.

Writer Jim Harrison's substantial body of work includes four volumes of novella trilogies, *The Beast God Forgot to Invent*, *Legends of the Fall*, *The Woman Lit by Fireflies*, and *Julip*; and eight novels, *The Road Home*, *Wolf*, *A Good Day to Die*, *Farmer*, *Warlock*, *Sundog*, *Dalva*, and his newest, *True North*. Additionally, he has published seven poetry collections, most recently *The Shape of the Journey: New and Collected Poems*; *Just Before Dark*, a book of essays and collected nonfiction; *The Raw and the Cooked: Adventures of a Roving Gourmand*, a collection of essays on food; and a children's book, *The Boy Who Ran to the Woods*. And, of course, numerous screenplays and his memoir, *Off to the Side* (of which Jonathan Yardley said, "Literary careerists will find nothing here to help them take the next step up the ladder, but plain readers will find lovely prose, an original mind and a plainspoken man"). Harrison's books have won numerous awards, have been translated into twenty-two languages and are international bestsellers. After years of living in Michigan, Harrison recently moved to Montana. He divides his time between there and Arizona.

True North tells the story of the son of a wealthy timber family, including a depraved and alcoholic father, a besotted, pill-popping mother, a lapsed priest uncle, and a sister who defies family expectations by consorting with the Native American Finnish gardener's son. It is David Burkett's nearly lifelong project to come to terms with the sins of his fathers and to travel his life's journey benefiting from the tutelage of the wonderful and courageous women he has loved. The reviews of *True North* have been mixed—and I might add, undependable—but Gordon Hauptfleisch exhibits a good grasp of this novel:

> Still, if Harrison's newest work is flawed and uneven, it is nevertheless a rich and
> satisfying read for the strenuously poetic passages detailing not only the com-

plexities, quirks, and intricacies of human emotions and interactions, but also for conveying a solid sense of place. Harrison strays now and then from his Michigan birthplace, as he has throughout his life and in his writing, but the most authentically portrayed and vivid scenes in *True North* are those that take place in the Upper Peninsula, making a rustic backwoods cabin in the forbidding frozen wilderness seem the quintessence of hearth and home. It certainly helps elucidate why a character would go to the ends of the world to safeguard his little corner of it.

Jim Harrison and I (and Rosie) gabbed for a while during the Boston leg of the recent book tour he has referred to as "a month in a dentist chair." I might add, my Lab Rosie is also a big Harrison fan.

Robert Birnbaum: Last night you finished your reading with a poem called "Adding It Up."
Jim Harrison: Yeah.

RB: Which you recommended not to do. [chuckles]
JH: Trying to add it up, yeah. Trying to balance, it's like balancing the chaos theory.

RB: Does that indicate [a certain] self-consciousness about aging?
JH: No, I think it's natural to be aware of it. I just wrote my second short story, which I discussed the other day with Deborah Treisman of the *New Yorker*. It's called "Biological Outcast," about the sexual thoughts of an older man wandering through New York City on a May afternoon. No, you are very conscious of that kind of thing. How old are you?

RB: Fifty-seven.
JH: It's coming. You know, just thinking about—I don't know if it's self-consciousness. Everybody becomes intermittently aware that it's passing faster than they thought it would. You know?

RB: There are reminders. On the other hand, there are moments that last so long.
JH: Well, I like that idea because I lived for thirty-five years rather close to an Indian reservation, Anishinabe-Chippewa. One of my friends there, a real geezer, said that our error is that life lasts exactly seven times longer than the way we live it, if you slow everything down, which is an interesting

point. I can do that when fishing or walking. Then there are book tours, where everything is so geometrically staged. So you have a nineteen-page itinerary, with everything down to the last minute.

RB: You did have that story recently in the *New Yorker*, "Father Daughter." Deborah Treisman is talking to you about another one?
JH: Yeah.

RB: Are these stories being written to be specifically published in the *New Yorker*?
JH: No, not really. David Remnick and I had a meeting a year ago with Deborah—[about] getting me to do something for them. It's a more open magazine than it was years ago when it was, it seemed to me, specifically New England, though they did publish the entirety of that novella, *Woman Lit by Fireflies*, about fifteen years ago. They published the whole thing. But they no longer do pieces that long. It was 110 pages.

RB: Do you have a sense that you are not paid attention to in the East Coast?
JH: That's basically true. Sometimes I wonder, because my last two readings in New York, down at the mother store of Barnes & Noble, have been very well attended. But I'm not sure that any of that matters. We are all naturally xenophobic. New Yorkers are mostly interested in New York—in case you haven't noticed. Most of them wouldn't have any frame of reference for a novel like *Dalva*. I actually had a guy in New York, an unnamed literary critic, ask me, "Do you know an Indian?" That's an interesting question.

RB: I thought it interesting that there is a multitude of literary websites, many of which regularly report what the *New Yorker*'s weekly story is. When your story came out, unless I missed it, none of these sites made mention of it.
JH: I don't know. I'm rather remote from what some refer to as the centers of ambition, just because I like to live in places—most places I live you can't see any neighbors at all. None. And that suits me. Partly, it's [about] claustrophobia.

RB: You couldn't have been claustrophobic in Michigan and now in Montana and in Arizona?
JH: We're down near the Mexican border, down in the mountains.

RB: What does it say that in the last year the *New Yorker* published a story by [Thomas] McGuane, which I don't think they had done for the longest time, and now by you?

JH: Well, they are looking for that kind of thing. They're not just sitting there waiting anymore. I am doing a food piece for them of a peculiar origin. A friend of mine, a book collector/dealer in Burgundy, France, had a lunch for a group of friends that had thirty-seven courses in November and took eleven hours. [both laugh]

RB: I thought you swore off these kinds of indulgences?

JH: No, I just picked at the food. Nineteen wines. It was a nice lunch. [both laugh] This was all food from the seventeenth and eighteenth centuries. He is a great bibliophile of ancient books on food and wine. So he made tortes of pig's noses, you know. Old timey stuff. It was interesting, of course, the origins of dishes.

RB: You alluded last night to the fact that you were doing more journalism.

JH: Any time I feel closed in—well, then I'll try something else. I'm not rational enough to be a good journalist.

RB: What!

JH: I fly off the handle too easily.

RB: Uh huh. For instance that remarkable and moving piece that you wrote for *Men's Journal* on living on the border, that was irrational?

> So Ana Claudia crossed with her brother and child into Indian country, walking up a dry wash for 40 miles, but when she reached the highway she simply dropped dead near the place where recently a 19-year-old girl also died from thirst with a baby at her breast. The baby was covered with sun blisters, but lived. So did Ana Claudia's. The particular cruelty of a dry wash is that everywhere there is evidence of water that once passed this way, with the banks verdant with flora. We don't know how long it took Ana Claudia to walk her only 40 miles in America, but we know what her last hours were like. Her body progressed from losing one quart of water to seven quarts: lethargy, increasing pulse, nausea, dizziness, blue shading of vision, delirium, swelling of the tongue, deafness, dimness of vision shriveling of the skin, and then death, the fallen body wrenched into a question mark. How could we not wish that politicians on both sides of the border who let her die this way would die in the same manner? But then such people have never missed a single lunch. Ana Claudia Villa Herrera. What a lovely name.

JH: I was nonfunctional for several months after that. I figured out it was probably that my own sister died at nineteen and they [Ana and his sister] suddenly got confused. I mean the two women got confused [in my mind]. What can you say when you find a girl—it was interesting, a Navajo head detective on the Papago reservation, a Navajo woman, Begay, how she pointed out down on these arroyos, where people have died, died of thirst and the bodies not found for a while, those little patches are more fertile in the shape of a human body. Remarkable. A real eye opener.

RB: I thought that piece was in an odd venue for something so poignant and sorrowful and thoughtful. What was the response?
JH: Well, I had a quite a response. I like to stay off brand.

RB: [laughs]
JH: I don't want to be just a writer that can be identified in one kind of—

RB: You mean *Harper's, Atlantic, New Yorker*?
JH: Yeah, yeah, that kind of thing. I don't want any of that. One becomes overly aware of that at certain times of one's life, and then you think, "Oh God, I made a deal with that crowd."

RB: That presumes you have a good sense of how people are seeing you.
JH: No, I don't necessarily—I'm not sure one could give a lot of time to thinking about it. It would break your motion, what you are doing. You know?

RB: I think that in *Off to the Side* you mention that in your lifetime the city/country population has shifted from 70 percent country and 30 percent city to the other way around. Would that be something that affects your following, especially on the East Coast?
JH: My type of writer gains an audience by accretion. I don't think it's advertising or anything. Why do I read things? It's basically word of mouth. Some friend or someone I know whose taste I respect says, "You gotta read this." Then I read it. I rarely read or buy a book because of a review. I had noticed, it's interesting, it's getting a little more like France here, which is curious. There is a neurologist, a woman over at Harvard who wanted me to come talk to them, and in France I have a lot of readers in the sciences. I can't tell you why. I certainly don't have a pop audience or a strictly literary audience. It's all spread out. But that was very gradually acquired.

RB: The only criticism I have encountered of you that I didn't have a response to, mostly because I don't think I understand it, is that you are a torch carrier for "male sentimentality." Do you know what that means?

JH: That's the same violin they have been playing for a long time—it's not a very large percentage of feminists that place a great deal of stock in never being understood. We can't understand them. Which is bullshit. I don't see gender as the most significant fact of human existence. It's that old idea that when you suddenly wake up at 3 A.M., what sex are you? I don't get that. It's sort of the flip side of male chauvinism. It's a female chauvinism or refusal to think that anyone can have any solid form of empathy of any sort.

RB: It seems to be a dismissal of the writer's mission, which is to be credible on a wide range of different kinds of characters.

JH: Well, exactly. It's a little catchword and you'll notice there are people—I remember when I wrote McGuane about moving west finally, when we had talked about it thirty-six years ago.

RB: [laughs]

JH: I said, "Christ, I hope when I come out there I will no longer have to hear the words, 'closure' and 'healing.'"

RB: [laughs]

JH: And he says, "No, out here you'll hear 'megafauna' and 'sustainable.'" [both laugh] I mean there are these little terms that people use.

RB: I think you refer to them as "verbal turds" somewhere.

JH: Yeah. People place great stock in these things, which to me are absolutely meaningless. Like, "Bob has issues." What the fuck does that, mean? Stop it! Yeah, yeah, I remember René Char said, "Lucidity is the wound closest to the sun."

RB: [laughs] It strikes me that you seem to be dismissive of two things that have great currency in America: psychotherapy and antidepressant medication.

JH: I don't know what psychotherapy does. I have been seeing the same person for twenty-six years now.

RB: [laughs]

JH: For symptomatic relief of human suffering. Only when I'm in New York.

We have a correspondence this high. [makes a gesture to indicate size of a stack of letters] No, I think, I think you naturally always have to be careful from both Jesus and Kierkegaard—[they] said to work out your own salvation with fear and trembling. This isn't a bandage thing, you know.

RB: Yeah. Right.

JH: It's just like young writers, of whom I am deluged—you have to be giving your entire life to this because that's the only way it's possible. This can't be an avocation. It's the whole thing. Or nothing.

RB: And what do they say?

JH: Most of them, that's very intimidating. They really haven't wanted to commit to it, to that extent. But they have to. It's a strange thing—I didn't want to understand it when I first read it but I was nineteen or something—Dylan Thomas said in order to be a poet or a writer you have to be willing to fall on your face over and over and over. Everybody wants to be cool—

RB: You have to be willing?

JH: Yeah. Which is an interesting point, yeah.

RB: You have to know that that's going to happen.

JH: You should. [both laugh]

RB: I may never get over Tibor Fischer's story of having being rejected by fifty-six publishers.

JH: It happens doesn't it? *Portrait of the Artist* went to nineteen. The old fun thing is when somebody typed up the first chapter of *War and Peace.* And then made a précis of the rest of it and sent it out and only one publisher recognized it.

RB: That does speak to the crapshoot nature of the enterprise.

JH: Yeah, somewhat. Persist, though, and it will happen.

RB: There is so much subjectivity. I know in a simple kind of banal way that I have reread things and wondered what I was thinking the first or second time. It's as if I hadn't read it before—like a new work.

JH: Uh huh, that's the chaotic aspect I've always enjoyed. That's—the void isn't empty. [both laugh] I like that. I tell young writers, "You know, part of being a writer is to know how this works. And rather than you trying to throw yourself in my lap, why don't you go, save your coin and go to New York and live in the Bronx cheaply and find out how it works." I had that advantage when we lived in Boston, in the sixties, the only job I could get was as a salesman for a book wholesaler. I just drove around and talked to bookstores and public libraries and school librarians. And that was a very healthy thing to see in the warehouse how this happens. Because most writers have totally unrealistic concepts of how publishing works. Sometimes in literary biography you forget that the publisher isn't the main thing. They like to think they are—when you are in New York and you see these people, it's amazing. But, there are good and bad ones, historically, obviously. It's important for writers to know that just like a farmer growing eighty acres of something and then not knowing what can be done with it, "How am I going to get rid of my chickens, my milk?" On and on.

RB: Isn't what all these writing programs are about?
JH: Yes, but they are singularly unrealistic.

RB: There are people who complain that they are more about the vocational aspects of writing than the writing.
JH: I'm not that familiar with them but I do see—I mean, are there 25,000 MFA manuscripts wandering around out there? We have really made the MFA, as I have pointed out before, almost part of the civil service. We started with two really good one ones, Iowa and Stanford, you know, Stegner's program.

RB: Didn't Montana have a good program early on?
JH: Yeah, but now suddenly—you know, universities are notoriously market oriented, too. So they all want, if it works, a department like that. The trouble is there's not enough appropriate staff to go round. I am for a novelist, for a poet, well read. I really keep up. I see whole staffs that I don't know the work of any of them. And I wonder where they came from. There is this problem of doubting that it can be taught. I only taught in that great period at Stony Brook. And I didn't teach writing. I taught modern poetics. I have never been able to find the sheet of paper but I had this idea of how to construct a good MFA program. Okay, at that time in the sixties, there was Ben DeMott and R. V. Cassill and we had a meeting in New York trying to figure out how we could get universities to hire writers [laughs]—because they needed jobs. Okay, it got out of control. I had the idea—you meet up for a month in a location, right? You have your journal and then you get to the main three hundred

books in the modernist tradition. Or whatever. Then the student spends a year in the country, preferably at menial labor. Comes back for a month. Then he spends a year in the city and comes back for a month and then the end of it the third year, several months with the teachers, just to make sure it isn't one of those grade school–high school–college MFAs. Because that's only a narrow experience. You know how [Ezra] Pound talked about the grave danger of starting from too narrow a base. Then you really tip over very easily. It's like the one-book wonder. What you are doing, where are you going to go?

RB: It's all interior and experientially deprived. And ultimately, of limited interest.
JH: Not to me. It's hard to be programmatic about it but I question—in fact it's insignificant that I'm questioning the value of it because it's already there. Another one of these improbable boondoggles. It caused a revolution in the rise in expectations. Which is totally—

RB: It does provide a fair number of writers' sinecures. And, of course, the conventional wisdom is that it also, at the very least, creates a new generation of decent readers.
JH: That's the best point that's the solidest point of all of them. I think McGuane pointed out to me once because he had a solid base to his economic thinking—

RB: In contradistinction to you?
JH: Yeah, he's smart that way. He pointed out to me that—we're still whining about it—"Isn't strange that a person can get a lifetime-guaranteed position on the basis of a slender volume of poems?" Yeah, that's an extraordinary break, if they got in early enough. Now, it's a question of competition. I was always shocked at the offers I would get. Even when I felt totally anonymous, still in my thirties and forties. They would make me these incredible offers. And I would always answer that somebody has to stay on the outside.

RB: [laughs]
JH: I would also answer, "Are you sure, that much money?" It's like Gary Snyder said when I once went out and spent a week with him a few years back, he says, "I always turned down this thing at [University of California at] Davis, that regents' professor[ship]." He could have gotten into any of the California universities. He said, "It never occurred to me to ask how much they were paying." [laughs]

RB: How pure can you be?

JH: It wouldn't have occurred to him. He is decidedly nonvenal.

RB: One striking thing about *True North* is that it is uncommon to make a dog a character in a novel.

JH: Who, Carla? Well, they are so specifically characters in our lives. Why not?

RB: Right, why not? So why don't more writers include animal companions as characters?

JH: I used to get criticized for putting food in novels. These are people ignorant of the novel tradition. It was always in French and English fiction. But a lot of us are still puritanical, still sort of ashamed they have to fill up every day. It's like food isn't serious. And a faculty meeting is? [both laugh] What gays used to say, "Puhlease!"

RB: Given how many people love and keep dogs it would seem natural that more dogs would appear in fiction as part of the lives and families of the characters.

JH: That didn't occur to me but when I was doing it, it seemed natural. I grew up in a very odd way because my father was an agronomist and he needed to think—and I grew up thinking that everybody had—that animals were our fellow creatures. I don't consider myself more important than a crow. I never have. How could I possibly be? Or a dog. We are all in this together. So I am not a victim of the French Enlightenment.

RB: [laughs heartily]

JH: There are some advantages to a peasant background.

RB: So in an odd way, this is not an enlightened view?

JH: So they would say, intellectually. I remember when I was nineteen and reading Gogol or Isaac Singer because that meant a great deal to me—because even though they are foreign stories, they were more the kind of thing I grew up around. Emotionally vigorous family. Talking out loud.

RB: Chaotic.

JH: Chaotic and moody. So it was odd—it was more familiar to me.

RB: I find it odd but understandable that so many people treat their animal companions as children, as almost humans.

JH: Yeah, that's true. That happens. People, there's no end to the craziness of people, so I'm not upset by that when I see it.

RB: I'm bothered that they are not seeing, in this case, dogs on their own terms.
JH: Well, quite often that's true. They expect a dog to be something for them that a dog can't be. Whether it's a surrogate child or what?

RB: I like Ed Hoagland's observation that instead of expecting dogs to be more human, we ought to try to be more like dogs.
JH: That's wonderful. That old Cheyenne thing, Lakota too, called Heyoka, a spiritual renewal. Following your dog around all day and behaving totally like the dog. If the dog lays down, you lay down. That lovely calming sense—my Lab always understood, my other dogs haven't to the extent that my Lab did, when I was depressed she would try to get me off my cot in my cabin and get me to go do something. "Just do something. Just don't lay there, you schmeil." [laughs] "Schmuck."

RB: So what happens when you write a sad scene for an animal? Is it hard for you to do?
JH: Oh yes. That's an irony. People have asked a number of times about Carla. I was torn. Isn't it interesting, you create a dog out of air, right? And then when she dies you break into tears. That's natural. There is a specious fear of that kind of sentimentality—but it's in all good literature. And then the idea of being nifty and cool and ignoring the true emotional content of your life. Why would anyone want to read about that? That kind of cold—

RB: Why would one?
JH: I don't.

RB: I've been watching this excellent TV series from England called *Cracker*. Robbie Coltrane plays a forensic psychiatrist working for the police, who smokes, drinks, and gambles, to excess.
JH: Oh, yeah. He's awfully good. I adore that guy. He's just so on the money.

RB: Yes, he is. So there is a scene where his mother has just died and he is sitting with his wife, crying. And he says there is something delicious about this, meaning that this grief that he is feeling is a rare real emotion that he can savor and experience as a dog.

JH: I once wrote a poem—I don't know if I even published it—about how I wanted to throw my own self around and have some real emotions. Although people tend to avoid them, these are always the harshest emotions. It's like face-to-face, this is the context. We've had a lot of friends die recently. I was going to read this poem last night about my shrinking address book. My wife's best friend died within three days of my brother. How can this be? Well, it's the end of everybody's story. As they say the last track you leave, as a mammal is your skull.

RB: It seems we are trained to avoid the emotional—
JH: No question. It's a part of the culture. I think it's the economic basis of a lot of our lives. It's that idea that I imply, I don't preach in *True North*, but one of the aspects of it is how the powers that be, the old logging and mining companies, always encourage these people to mythologize their lives. Paul Bunyan! It's marvelous how they do that. Not that it is just a sucker's shot; everybody tries to mythologize their efforts. But it's actually encouraged. It's that funny thing, the French, they go berserk that we will only take ten days for vacation. Why? How can you get ahead?

RB: The Italians and the Germans, too?
JH: Even the Germans demand a month or five weeks to walk around in leather shorts or however we think they do it.

RB: What a shell game.
JH: It is in the sense that it ignores quality of life and the inevitable end of life. There's a story that Catholic priest told me. The Italian dies. The family is talking about the great meals they had together. The French dies. They talk about the great wines they drank. The American dies and the family asks, "Did they leave enough money or do they have enough money, money, money?" But the last twenty-five years in America have been characterized by imponderable greed. You know, greed, greed, greed. The newspapers made heroes in the dot-com days—there is this guy suddenly worth $5 million sitting in an empty mansion eating an American cheese sandwich. And they have to have personal shoppers because they don't know how to buy toilet paper or something like that. Craziness, all that.

RB: I admire your interest in driving around the United States. There is one view that one can develop of a crassly materialistic eating and shopping culture and then there seems to be another rarely seen, that pictures people trying to live reasonable, healthy, full lives.

JH: That's true. That's one reason why I have to be a writer. I don't find anything perceptually accurate or agreeable or sensical about the media view of American culture. The fact is, the media never gets off the interstate unless there's a major explosion. That's why I said before, for the MFA program, a year in the country, a year in the city, to get familiarity with the human landscape. You're not going to get it in a university community.

RB: He may be a neighbor of yours in Montana, but Alston Chase wrote a book about Ted Kaczynski, the Unabomber, and he excoriates the media for getting everything about Kaczynski wrong.
JH: I know Alston. It's also interesting that 99 percent of what Ted Kaczynski said made sense.

RB: [laughs]
JH: Alston points that out. And it's sort of, "Uh oh." It was the killing people that just didn't work, amongst other things. Historically, nothing is surprising. Some professor—I think up in Connecticut [Wesleyan University] a guy named [Richard] Slotkin, he writes that this violence is the tradition since the inception of America. Just like logging. We want to cut down trees, cut down the buffalo, cut down everything as fast and completely as possible. We have always been this way.

RB: I am currently toying with the notion that there is not one but two or three Americas. It may be a natural inclination to try to see this country as a unity.
JH: No, I think there are at least seven I can identify. That kind of regionality. And again, it causes xenophobia. The unwillingness of people in one part of the country to want to understand people in any sympathetic way, other people. I think it was McGuane that pointed out the assumption in the North that every white southerner was *ex post facto* a racist. I remember reading in Oxford, Mississippi; one thing nice was there were black people in the audience. You don't see that in the North. Or rarely. I see more genuine sociability between the races in Mississippi than I see in Michigan. No question.

RB: It hasn't changed much, has it. I asked Reynolds Price about what defined southern culture—trying to get a definition of southern writing—he said it was the close proximity and familiarity to and with black people.
JH: Yup. Reynolds is a marvelous man. I finally met him a few years ago. I have always enjoyed his work and some of his nonfiction is particularly trenchant. But, that's true.

RB: There is of course the caricature of the Gothic southern family, inbred with various bizarre characters and histories.

JH: I got a strange letter from Mississippi in regard to *True North*. The person said, "I didn't know a Gothic novel could be written about the North." [both laugh] "Oh, Dad, you're such a pill."

RB: You mentioned last night that you had thought of writing this novel seventeen years ago. So what intervened? Why didn't you start then?

JH: Well, just the accumulation. I brooded about it a long time. And then I brood about different things and usually I have quite a lead time about anything I write. Since I am writing a novella now called *Republican Wives*, which is fun, right?

RB: Sure.

JH: And, ah, I have been thinking about writing this for about a decade. But then a certain part of your brain is always accumulating the touches, the materials. Of course, you make squiggles in your journals and then, finally, you're ready.

RB: So, as you've said, you write it when you can't not write it?

JH: Yeah, that's my rule of thumb.

RB: Does it have the same [working] title all along? *True North* was always *True North*?

JH: No, no. That's more recent. I do have trouble with titles.

RB: Might you have saddled this book with a certain gravity because it has the word "true" in it? A powerful word.

JH: Oh no, I don't mind being adventuresome that way. I'm going to write a total laborite view of the same region. Which was going to be fun, the Indian-Finn-Cornish-Italian-miner view of it, because I even know that world better, I've known a lot of these kind of people that are in *True North* and they are interesting to me—for obvious reasons.

RB: Has it been unsettling to move from Upper Peninsula Michigan to Montana?

JH: Not at all because I think we have gone to Montana every year since '68 except one year. Tom [McGuane] and I kept in touch. Our family vacation was to go to Montana, to go fishing, and my wife's friends are out there.

RB: Your daughter Jamie is out there also.

JH: See, that's the whole thing. Your kids inevitably want to move where they had their vacations when they were younger. So both daughters have been living in Montana for a long time. My wife in this case has stuck with it—she wanted to move to Montana, it was no big deal to me. I can write anywhere. I hated to sell my cabin. I've had it twenty-five years and it meant so much to me. It was a retreat, you know? But it was too far to drive and I am getting older and I only went there three times last year and it involved fifteen days of driving. These distances—you can barely drive across Montana in a day.

RB: You say you can write anywhere but might there be a different feeling wherever you might be—in the center of the country you are not near the concentration of microwaves and such—doesn't Montana feel different?

JH: Well, yeah. I was thinking last year in—not to overplay this hand but it's interesting. But I was reading a galley by a guy named Mark Spragg coming out by Knopf, an intriguing book. And I was wondering if I agreed with the character who had been injured by a grizzly bear. Okay, then I thought, "What am I thinking about?" Last year there were two grizzly attacks on humans within fifteen minutes of our home, and last winter a pack of wolves killed twenty-eight sheep within view of our bedroom window. Plus my dog got blinded by a rattlesnake in the yard.

RB: How'd that happen?

JH: She's an English setter and she obviously pointed and the snake got her twice in the face. It blinded her and deafened her. She's fine [now] but she's a little wary about snakes.

RB: How does she move about?

JH: She had a hard time for about four or five months. She is pretty much completely recovered. There is a guy named Harry Greene at Cornell, a fantastic authority on snakes and snake venom—rattlers in particular. He has a beautiful book out about the poisonous snakes of the world. Very complicated poisons; the contents of rattlesnake poison are very involved, toxic substances. A brain surgeon friend of mine in Nebraska, Cleve Tremble, got one in the arm and said it was four or five months before he really felt good again.

RB: The toxins linger in the body that long?

JH: Yeah, your system has really been walloped. I was just in the Yucatan and I met three different people who had to lop off minor parts of their bodies—

RB: [laughs] Minor parts?

JH: After being nicked by a fer-de-lance

RB: By what?

JH: A fer-de-lance, a venomous snake. One had been hit in the foot and chopped it off immediately because if you don't chop it off you die.

So the Mayans knew of this. One guy had his finger in formaldehyde, he wanted to keep it for sentimental reasons. It's not that everything is threatening, but it's a dangerous kind of existence. I'm never frightened in that kind of country. I have been, occasionally, in cities.

RB: What are you afraid of in cities?

JH: Well, guns. In Arizona, it's curious. You can carry a gun if you wish. In Montana, too. I don't know anybody that does. That's an odd thing. Where you can do it, they might have one in their [truck's] rifle rack. Everybody has a gun in their car in Detroit. Or a lot of people do.

RB: On trips to Israel it was something to be in bars and cafes and see people who looked like teenagers with pistols strapped to their ankles or in their pants waist bands.

JH: I definitely would there, too. I did an interview with a Lebanese paper, and I just assumed they were Muslims, but no. Some of those countries, they are everything. Like Coptic Christians in Egypt. It's a not very clear picture. This American writer who got severely wounded in Lebanon as a journalist, Phil Caputo, this old friend of mine. And he sat in a bar with quite a few of us and explained the political and religious structure of the Middle East. It stupefied people—we wanted to think it was cleaner.

RB: I think that reading Lawrence Durrell gives a clear picture of how unclear or complicated it is.

JH: Yeah, I love Durrell. One of the great underrated works of our time, *The Alexandria Quartet*. But who's doing the rating? Does it matter?

RB: Who is doing the rating? The *New York Times*.

JH: Probably. I said once, and Bill [William] Kennedy quoted me on it, "The people who were condescending to Steinbeck didn't even write *The Grapes of Goofy*." [both laugh] Give me a break.

RB: There is a pervasive fear that literature is always being threatened and somehow the institutions that should be working to preserve or protect it, aren't doing that. I don't see why literary culture rises or falls on what the *Times* or any other journalists do. Really, what's the problem?

JH: I don't think there is one. I said that in my memoir. There are some who think they are guardians. They are not inside themselves but they are still at the gate. I'm not sure what that impulse is. They are enumerators. The Casey Kasems of the critical fraternity. They always a have top 40 or top 20.

RB: I don't mind although I don't read them.

JH: [laughs]

RB: James Wood or—

JH: But see, Wood is a very bright man. However you think about him, he is incapable of being boring, critically. I don't mind contention.

RB: I just don't find it useful to talk or speculate about who is going to be read in fifty or a hundred years.

JH: Well, you can't.

RB: [laughs] People do.

JH: It's so funny, in that fiftieth anniversary edition of the *Paris Review* that I wrote a little piece in—Donald Hall has a preposterous piece [*Death as a Career Move*] in there. He is talking about reputation and what happens to people. Like [Archibald] MacLeish from over at Harvard and whether the Pulitzer Prize [McLeish won three] is a pauper's grave? Something like that.

RB: [laughs]

JH: You wonder what consensus is. Here I am an old man and only once have I ever been asked to be on a [Pulitzer or any] jury.

RB: Really?

JH: Yeah. Where are they getting the jurors except from New York—that seems to be closer—or something. But that seems odd. I'm not that anonymous. So in any prize situation I always want to know who the jurors are. Because you can't know the validity. If you want to give Stephen King the lifetime award or whatever it is, go ahead. It doesn't make any difference to me. But that changes the nature of what you are. They lost their literary credibility about twenty years ago when they took it away from the literary people and gave it to the industry. Remember when that happened?

RB: The first winner of the National Book Award was Nelson Algren and I don't know that many people remember him.
JH: Well, I think some people do. I've heard young writers talking about him. You have to be careful about that, too. Because you are more likely to hear them talking about Algren in Missouri or the state of Washington than in New York. Where the thing you hear most of in New York is, "I don't have time to read."

RB: [laughs] You were grievously hurt by that—you mention it in *Off to the Side.*
JH: It's funny.

RB: Jim Shepard told me that one of his students remarked he was reading a story Shepard had in *Esquire* but had not yet finished it. Shepard was incredulous, since it was a three-page story.
JH: This is interesting. You can say, "What is it that you do in place of reading? Drink spritzers?" I don't know. Does anyone have time to read? I do. And I write a lot. It's a tonic to find real readers because they just read massively.

RB: You seem to be the only person who publishes novellas.
JH: When I wrote my first book of novellas, that was the only one I knew of. So people would say, "What's a novella?"

RB: So, what's a novella?
JH: I just say that old Hofmannsthal–Isak Dinesen thing: A very long story, about a hundred pages. Short things are short all over and long things are long all over.

RB: Do you feel like what you write now should be more important?
JH: That's not up to me.

Repair Work: An Interview with Jim Harrison

Angela Elam / 2004

"Repair Work," an interview with Jim Harrison by Angela Elam, first published in *New Letters*, volume 71, number 3, 2005. It is printed here with the permission of *New Letters* (previously *The University Review*) and the Curators of the University of Missouri–Kansas City.

Poet, novelist, essayist, screenwriter, conservationist, gourmand—Jim Harrison published his first book of poems, *Plain Song* (1965), while still a graduate student at Michigan State University. Since then, he has published twelve more poetry collections, nine novels, four novella series, three non-fiction books, and a children's book. His latest novella trio, *The Summer He Didn't Die*, is appearing this summer from Atlantic Monthly Press. Harrison's work has been translated into twenty-two languages.

Jim Harrison grew up in rural Michigan, and much of his writing includes subjects and themes of the outdoors. He began his first novel, *Wolf: A False Memoir* (1971), during his recuperation after he fell from a cliff while hunting birds. He experiments in poetic and prose forms and has an economical, original narrative style. As a screenwriter, Jim Harrison's filmography includes *Carried Away* (1996), *Dalva* (1996), *Legends of the Fall* (1994), *Wolf* (1994), *Revenge* (1990), and *Cold Feet* (1989). He has received fellowships from the National Endowment for the Arts and the Guggenheim Foundation. In 2000, he won the Spirit of the West Award from the Mountains & Plains Booksellers Association. He lives in Montana.

New Letters: I read that as a writer you felt strange whenever you were in an academic system. In what way?

Harrison: I don't like to live in academic communities; I like to live remotely. I actually have thought, since the beginning—I only thought of this after I wrote the memoir *Off to the Side* (2002)—how often my books have depended on certain long nondirectional car trips I've taken to different parts of the United States. You know, if I hadn't been in certain areas of Montana early on, I couldn't have written *Legends of the Fall*. If I hadn't been to South America, I probably couldn't have written *Sundog*. If I hadn't been in Key West, I couldn't have written *A Good Day to Die*. I mean, it simply goes on and on. Nebraska: *Dalva*. You absorb landscapes, and then the story follows this absorption, often.

NL: So, for you it starts with the landscape.

Harrison: Usually. It starts with the sense of the landscape and the history of the landscape. For instance, when I drove to the Blackjack Hills of Oklahoma, I'd already read several books about the area. What you've read begins to people the landscape. It's always critical for me to know what native tribes were the first citizens in any area. I generally know a bit of the economic history, too. So, that's what we used to call in Hollywood the back story, out of which a novel can emerge.

NL: So your novel *True North*, in Michigan's Upper Peninsula, dovetails with what you like to do, which involves gathering history and getting an appreciation for the landscape.

Harrison: A lot of that is just a passion for wandering. You know that sort of early Americanism—you have to see what's over the next hill, and you can't just turn around on a two-track. You have to see, where does this two-track end? I used to spend a lot of time trying to find the origins of creeks just to see where they could be. So, I'd have these topographical maps; I would be lost half of the time. Again, that's a passion.

NL: Where are you living right now?

Harrison: Mostly Montana, and then the Mexican border, where we have a casita. Two years ago, I sold the farm in northern Michigan; I sold it because our daughters are in Montana, and my wife wanted to be closer to her grandchildren. So that wasn't hard, since she has stuck with me through some thin years, emotionally and financially.

NL: Montana is no shabby place.

Harrison: No. We had gone out there every year since 1968 for fishing, and I have a lot of friends in the area. You know, Tom McGuane goes there; Doug Peacock, and then the man who has painted all my covers, Russell Chatham, is local to where I live. Really, fishing friends. Peacock and I used to camp in Mexico, and every other thing, you know, because he's such a naturalist.

NL: As you talk about your passions—the passion for wandering, and the passion for fishing, and for the outdoors—I see how all of that comes up in *True North*.

Harrison: It can be comical, too. My mother, for instance, was a great bird watcher. She knew all American warblers just by their songs. Right on the money every time. With wildflower books and bird books, nothing looks like it's supposed to. I mean, I'm fairly good at bird stuff, but I thought, "Isn't God messy?" I was trying to identify this wildflower, it's a kind of daisy, and then I read at the bottom of the page that there are 178 daisies. Or an oriole down in the Yucatan this winter at this place I was staying. I got a bird book and opened it to orioles. Well, there are seventeen kinds of orioles that look almost identical, and I just said maybe I should go do something I'm good at, like having a drink. Then I had a character in *The Road Home*, a Native American who said, "I don't care what you call birds; I want to know what they call themselves."

NL: That's a great line.

Harrison: So he's one-up on us. A different language.

NL: Well, tell me about moving to Montana and if that's part of the reason you came back to the Upper Peninsula, in your imagination, for *True North*.

Harrison: No, I really started that novel seventeen years ago. It's an odd story. I had the idea when Dan Gerber, who's a poet and a close friend, and I were walking out on the Kingston Plains. It's an open area, not so densely forested as most of the UP. And you see thousands of these enormous stumps. It was one of those corny evenings when sandhill cranes are flying across and a red moon rising because there was a forest fire in the east. He looked at all the stumps, and he said, "I'm sure glad my grandpa didn't do this." You know, wiped off the landscape. So, *boing*. That was the actual inception of the novel, along with the Wallace Stevens quote, "Images collect in pools." Then I wait until my image bank builds up, builds up, builds up, but this time it took a long time for it to form. Often my novels take a number of years to take shape that way before I write even a word. Or, I'll have journals full of visual images.

NL: Do you keep a journal every day? Is that part of what you do?

Harrison: Yes, because many days there's nothing worth writing down, you know. There's this problem, too, with writers: all or some writers think they're important because they deal with important issues, but that isn't the way it works, is it? That's what you run into with pundits on television who think that talking is thinking. What you really have is a motor mouth on your hands.

NL: Now that you've brought up the beginning for *True North*, I remember the passages at Kingston Plains from the middle of the book:

> ... The main feature of the Kingston Plains was the thousands of acres of white pine stumps, some of them very large, which had been cut at waist or chest height probably during the winter when it was easier to skid the trees out on snow-covered trails which they dampened to form ice so that the draft horse-drawn log sleighs could be more easily pulled.
> ... I remembered coming home from college and Clarence asking what I was studying and when I said English he said, "I thought everybody knows English?" It helped when I added literature though I said "stories" because Clarence was quite a storyteller though he could neither read nor write. Being a mixed-blood he knew hundreds of both Chippewa and Finnish stories that were so long they exasperated Jesse whose tales of love and death from the province of Veracruz tended to be terse though poetic.

NL: Clarence is the groundskeeper, and Jesse is—you call him a house man? He was more than that.
Harrison: Clarence does everything. He can do everything. The trouble is, this wasn't planned, but I knew way back that the family would contain these three generations of Yale graduates who have an improbable sense of entitlement. Plus, being wealthy, they were a consummate predatory family, the leading logging family and mining family in the Upper Peninsula in earlier times. Then, as frequently happens, the family descended. I wanted to study the problem. I personally had a benign father, but I wanted to study the problem of the evil father. So, in my notebook, I was able to remember about a dozen evil fathers whom I've known in my life. As one reviewer already said, "This wins the evil-father sweepstakes."

NL: That was brilliant, the depiction of what's going on between father and son, that sort of disintegration that can happen in a wealthy family.
Harrison: It has the potential to happen in a way that it doesn't for people who are simpler beings. I've seen it at close range. When you're younger, you think how nice it would be to be rich. Through my life, it's gradually become less and less appealing, down to the point a number of years ago that it became totally unappealing, because there is so much less freedom

involved. Realtors call very wealthy people "lucky sperms." It's not their fault they were born. I'm talking about inherited wealth. They're simply born that way. There's nothing pejorative about my thinking along those lines, but their life seems consequently so predestined by so many burdens.

NL: Dan Gerber, who is a wonderful poet, comes from a family of wealth because of Gerber baby food.

Harrison: Yeah, but he's utterly different. Tom McGuane is, too. He comes from a wealthy family, too, but Dan's father, for instance, was an enormously humble person. He never even read the stock report; he wanted to make products of value.

NL: So it started with his father?

Harrison: Well, yes. See the trouble here: David Burkett, my hero, was thinking that the sins of the fathers are visited onto the sons, until the seventh generation. He's trying to free himself of that, and he has an implausible struggle; and, sometimes you might have noted, to the extent that he wishes not to be anything like his father, he gets close at times. Whether it's for sexual reasons or drinking, or so on, he easily can float back into that corrupted life, if he's not completely conscious. You can't imagine David without his project; he'd fall apart, like so many people, whereas it's truly his sister who's the strong one. His sister, Cynthia, whacks her father with a garden stake, because she and Lori are sunbathing. This cad says something, and she whacks him one. I researched this, too. There's such a thing as young women who are just naturally happy, aggressive, just from the word go. Nobody knows quite why. Is there some kind of genetic component to this? They haven't quite figured it out. The chin is out, and get out of my way. That kind of thing is wonderful. To a certain extent, my character Dalva was partly like that, maybe a little less so, but certainly a strong, strong, strong, strong woman.

Much of this I had never written about in fiction, including the idea that the sexual burgeoning in our teens happens at the same time as religious exploration. The preacher of the Baptist church, for instance, thinks that Mozart is satanic, so there's something wrong there. Of course, he loves Mozart. You're praying at one moment, and then next moment your church group is having a swimming party and the minister's daughter's suit, when wet, becomes nearly transparent. You don't know if you should pray or look. There's something like Jimmy Carter's lust in his heart. It's real. That's where most lust is.

NL: Yeah, well, there's a lot of sex in *True North*, too.

Harrison: There should be, shouldn't there? I don't know how people get along without it.

NL: I have a question. Since you have written in so many different forms, when you start out with a piece of work, do you know right from the get-go that it's a novel, or if it's going to be a novella, or do you explore the ideas in poetry first?

Harrison: Here's what happens. Usually you know well beforehand, because I've been thinking about this so long before I really start. I can't remember who said it in regard to literary work, but short things are short all over, and long things are long all over. Of course, the novellas—I could never could write a short story as such; they always turned out to be about a hundred pages. I finally published my first short story this winter in the *New Yorker*. It was called "Father Daughter," about one of those hopeless conversations with your college-age daughter, where the father says, "Do you remember when we used to go fishing?" and she says, "Five times." You're nailed to the cross of your idiocies.

NL: When you started writing your novellas, were you trying to write short stories that just stretched out?

Harrison: No, no. I knew it. I loved the form, and I think I was the first one in modern times to start writing novellas. This was way back when, in the late seventies. Not a lot of people write them, but I wasn't lonely, because my predecessors, including Isak Dinesen and Katherine Anne Porter had a couple novellas, Hugo von Hofmannsthal in Germany, and so on and so on. It's an old literary form. The length just seemed appropriate. I can't usually think short, except in poetry.

NL: Which can be short.

Harrison: Like that collection *Braided Creek*, with Ted Kooser.

NL: I love that book. I picked it up when it first came out in 2003.

Harrison: It sold out in a month and a half or something, though now they've reissued it.

NL: It's called *Braided Creek: A Conversation in Poetry* by Jim Harrison and Ted Kooser. The two of you wrote poetry back and forth; but what I found intriguing about it—and I don't know if this is what other readers do—I was always trying to figure out who wrote which poem. Some of them I could tell, and then some of them I wasn't always sure.

Harrison: There are some faults; a couple of times, I previously led people astray to think it was Ted, and he did the same thing to me. For example, there's the line, "I wish I could write a poem as durable as that tattoo on the girl's butt," which I think everybody would assume is me, but it's really Ted. That one's Ted's. It was fun that way.

NL: Maybe you should tell us about the form of this dialogue, how you two went about putting it together.

Harrison: Ted had written that book of postcards to me, which was published as a book; but we'd corresponded for so long, so many years, and didn't see each other all that often. We were just naturals for writing to each other about poetry and everything else that came to mind. So we started sending those little poems, not at all haiku, which is a form that depends on the Japanese language—let's face it—it doesn't work in our language. So, we were sending these little usually three-line poems back and forth, and then after we had a couple hundred, I said to Joseph Bednarik and Sam Hamill, "What do you think?" They loved the idea that nobody would know who wrote what poem because it ultimately doesn't matter. What matters is poetry, not who wrote it.

NL: One of my favorite lines in the book is, "All I want to be is a thousand blackbirds bursting from a tree, seeding the sky."

Harrison: That's what it looks like, too, doesn't it? When they burst. That'd be enough.

NL: That would be. It occurred to me that it would be great to get you and Ted Kooser into a studio and have you read them, but you might feel it would destroy the mystery of it.

Harrison: But we could. We have vowed on the blood of the lamb never to tell people whose is which, because people pester us relentlessly.

NL: *The Shape of the Journey: New and Collected Poems* spans your poetic career, is that right? It starts with some of your earliest works.

Harrison: Here's the problem: In the last year or so, 2003 and 2004, I've had a renaissance, so maybe I think I should have waited; but then I thought, well, maybe not, so why not just bring out another book, probably next year with Copper Canyon. As I say, I was already writing and then, for some reason, when my brother died, who was only a year and a half older than me, I just let loose. That's the only thing I could do that was of any consequence to me. Some of the poems are utterly morose. I gave four to a magazine in New York the other day, but I can't even remember the magazine's name. My poor bibliographers, who're trying to put together the complete bibliography—when people tried it before, one professor quit right away because I've kept no records of anything. Nothing. Before my secretary, all that I wrote and published has no records. So that's the problem. The early years are stinkers, but after Joyce came . . .

NL: When did Joyce start working for you?
Harrison: Twenty-five years ago, as of 2004. Because I needed help after centuries of being relatively indigent, my family finally had a money maker in Hollywood with *Legends of the Fall.* That experience just completely unbalanced me. I didn't know what to think. Certainly, there's some guilt involved. Why should everybody else be so poor and I suddenly am getting this money? I managed to piss most of it away before I became more balanced later in life.

NL: That sounds like the things people say if they win the lottery. It can really mess up your life.
Harrison: Well, it does. There's no question. I laughed when my wife said, "Oh, those poor people," when somebody had won a big lottery somewhere, because we just had an awful time for a couple of years, trying to make sense of what was happening in our lives. We had lived so long just on a farm, where a friend had loaned us the down payment; the farm only cost, I think, $18,500. Our mortgage payment, which we had troubles with sometimes, was only $99 a month. We always got it made, but it was still a struggle, because I just refused to be anything except a poet and a fiction writer. I gradually started writing some journalism, and that helped, but then suddenly we had some success, and it's like getting in a rocket that took off. Not really altogether pleasant.

NL: Most writers do struggle so much, and they long for success, and they forget that it has another side to it.
Harrison: I would say obviously that success has to be at least 1 percent better than failure, because ultimately, as a writer, you want your work read. Some success allows you the privilege to have your book or your work stay in print. That old bugaboo. My compromise with ambition took

place through a dream—a lot of good stuff that happens to me happens in dreams—I vowed I would never be upset about being an outsider as long as my books stay in print, and they have stayed in print. That's all I wanted. If they're not in print, how are they going to be read?

NL: It's interesting what you say about dreams, because in *True North*, David has vivid dreams. It sounds like you're probably in touch with your dream life, too.

Harrison: You know, as Jung explains, in times of crisis, mental crisis, dreams become incredibly vivid. I've had that through a number of nervous breakdowns in my life. I've had the dreaming, which is trying to help you repair yourself. You have to pay attention, and it works.

NL: I wonder if that's why, when your brother died, you turned to poetry for expression, because both poetry and dreams are filled with images, and poetry is a way of ordering imagery.

Harrison: I don't have any area of expertise in my life except my imagination. I could not be totally reliable in many ways. I mean, I'm a fairly good fisherman. But, in areas that count . . . I sweat if I go into a bank. I don't like that feeling, but what can I say? I remember walking into a bank and meeting the banker and asking, "What corner of this building do you keep my money in?" He wasn't amused. He was going to explain to me how banks really work. "I mean, it isn't in a sack?"

NL: It must be interesting to go back through your work. Did you actually edit *The Shape of the Journey* and pick out what you wanted?

Harrison: I did, with the help of Joseph Bednarik, who's such a wise soul and such a good editor. By now, my secretary automatically sends every poem I write directly to him so he can help us keep track, because I can have these bursts and lose track of things. Where did I put those poems? Then I stop looking for them, which is stupid.

NL: You now have a huge body of work.

Harrison: It does seem odd.

NL: Maybe not odd, but it shows a lifetime of sticking to it.

Harrison: It's a lifetime, too, of having had an iron mom, 100-percent Swede, who'd say every day [in accent] "What have you accomplished today?" You know that kind of person?

NL: That's wonderful.

Harrison: In addition to, "Shame on you." I would go in to write, being intent on writing a wedding poem for two gay friends, who asked, and I thought, Gosh, this is a new challenge in my life. It's a spot. At least once a day, though, my mother would say to me, "Shame on you," until I finally got tired of it and did what I wished. You know, that kind of . . . because gays always have been the victims of so much pointless shame.

NL: I was intrigued by the ending series of poems in *The Shape of the Journey*, "Geo-Bestiary," but it's too long to reprint.

Harrison: It's funny, because that came at an interesting time. I was collapsing in a lot of ways, and that's why I had to quit screenplays. Totally, six years ago, around 1998, I had to quit. I didn't want to die in Los Angeles.

NL: What was stressing you?

Harrison: Things were okay when I wrote screenplays that didn't get made; you just got a nice check and you could write the screenplay in six weeks and then have enough to live on for a year. You can't get a better deal than that. Then, when they started making the movies, everything became so unbelievably tense. Stress is part of life, but not that much.

NL: It took all the joy out of it, it sounds like.

Harrison: A lot of it, yeah. It's just like in writing—your first draft of a screenplay is really fun; you're just writing down what you see in the movie, letting it unroll in your mind. You're just taking dictation from what you see, oddly enough, rather than what you hear. The words are framing your vision. So that's fun, but it's not fun when you get on the fifth draft, and there are twenty studio people involved, calling you up; and then suddenly there are three hundred people making a movie for $60 million. You're on the high board, as they say, to put it mildly, and the pool is possibly empty. It was quite an adjustment to learn to live without that income, but our lives became much more pleasant. If you made fifty-five trips to Los Angeles, that's possibly enough, isn't it? "No mas, no mas," as they say on the border.

NL: That makes me think of your poem, "Homily," from *The Shape of the Journey*.

Harrison: For every Calvinist and a lot of Catholics, too, life is just full of these rules. It's like the joke of New Years' resolutions. We're always beating on our own heads, as if we were tract houses. Here is a passage from "Homily":

Dance with yourself with all your heart
and soul, and occasionally others, but don't
eat all the berries birds eat or you'll die.
Kiss yourself in the mirror but don't fall in love
with photos of ladies in magazines. Don't fall
in love as if you were falling through
the floor in an abandoned house, or off
a dock at night, or down a crevasse
covered with false snow, a cow floundering
in quicksand while the other cows watch
without particular interest, backward
off a crumbling cornice. Don't fall in love
with two at once. . . .

It's inadvisable to fall in love with two women at once. I remember asking my mind doctor (my mind doctor as I refer to him), "Larry, can you fall in love with more than one person? Be in love with more than one person?" He said, "Yes, there's really no limit, given sufficient emotional energy. This can happen." I thought, Oh, God. How terrifying, isn't it? That's God's messiness again. For some reason, frankly, I have occasional trouble with what psychiatrists refer to as a fugal state. After I quit the arduous profession, writing screenplays, my brain started becoming overactive. You know that idea when you think you can see time or you can see all sides of the tree at once. Your imagination becomes holographic. That's a bit much to deal with, frankly. Anyway, my life also started blooming because I didn't have to think about the movie business anymore.

NL: It gave you some creative room.
Harrison: Oh, yeah. *Whoosh*! I became a very poor amateur naturalist, which I'd been all my life, but I was more conscientious about it. I became a more aggressive wanderer because I had more time. Then my perceptions expanded, like a friend of mine said, who's sort of a Hassidic scholar; he said, "Don't you think that reality is an accretion of the perceptions of all creatures, not just us?" Quite a big statement, isn't it?

NL: Yes.
Harrison: I said, "Yeah, Neal, I agree with that." So, here are a few lines from "Geo-Bestiary," representative of that time in my life a few years ago.

Not how many different birds I've seen
but how many have seen me,
letting the event go unremarked
except for the quietest sense of malevolence,
dead quiet, then restarting their lives
after fear, not with song, which is reserved
for lovers, but the harsh and quizzical
chatter with which we all get by:
but if she or he passes by and the need
is felt we hear the music that transcends all fear,
and sometimes the simpler songs that greet sunrise,
rain or twilight. Here I am.
They sing what and where they are.

NL: Now you get your drink and your nap.

Harrison: Not the drink so much, anymore. You know, it's the comic thing. I took Henry Miller seriously when he said, "Everyone should have a full dress nap every day." I get teased about my napping; but I say, "Well, how did I write all these books plus a hundred essays and twenty-five screenplays in four or five versions?" That's because I take naps. I get to start my day over fresh.

Poet and Fiction Writer Jim Harrison

Lindsay Ahl / 2006

First published in *Bliss*, no. 5 (Summer 2006): 47–50. Reprinted with permission of Louis Leray and Lindsay Ahl.

Jim Harrison: I was in Santa Fe in '68 and '71 and I've noticed that it's changed. Want me to tell you how to improve that town? You ready? You need more stray dogs, more Mexicans, more Indians . . . ready? . . . fewer street lights. You need bars with dancing girls where people can smoke. You can get rid of all the non-native jewelry stores. There. Now you know. Though I will say there has been one improvement. Have you ever gone to Pasqual's?

Lindsay Ahl: Yes. Isn't it great?
Harrison: I love that place. There's a correlation with New York here, you know what it is? The arts and literature, they aren't exciting anymore, but the food is.

Lindsay: I'm curious, because I interviewed Ted Kooser—he seems to be vastly and radically different than you and kind of on the opposite polar end in terms of an aesthetic and yet you're good friends.
Harrison: Well, it's always more likely that you'll be friends with temperamental opposites. Quite often that's true, anyway. I think that's true in marriages too. Marriages in which the people are quite different tend to last. Marriages when they're the same or have the same profession—I've known painters and writers that have been married and one thing that often broke them up is that one becomes more successful than another. It's harder if it's the woman who becomes more successful, you know, for cultural reasons.

Lindsay: Hey, this is a strange idea I'm pushing off from and probably radically corrupting, but the Jewish idea about Golem is that if you, as the creator of a text, made the wrong decision, forced the text to be something else,

it could destroy you or harm you in some way . . . have you ever thought that?
Harrison: Well, I don't know. I've never been much for any form of demon-ology. I do remember Golem from when I read Isaac Singer, whom I love. Faulkner talks about that daemon kind of thing that gets into you. But I think the spirit that concedes you with the book generally makes sure you don't go in the wrong direction. You have to totally follow your heart, thumbing your nose at everything else but where your heart leads you in your fiction, you know.

Lindsay: So if you're working in Hollywood, do you feel like you have to compromise that or . . .
Harrison: No. It's a totally different genre. I never had any bad feelings when I was writing a screenplay. When I was writing screenplays I was writing screenplays. I mean, I'm eight years away from it now. Certainly, it was difficult and sometimes I would have to quit a novel and go write a screenplay in order to support the novel. You see? But everybody does that. I mean, all in all, I don't think my Hollywood experience, as it recedes in the past, was as difficult as say, professors who teach creative writing and litera-ture. I think that would be harder because in Hollywood you're up against not a very friendly situation so you're always pretty much in focus. I mean I can remember, and I put it up on my bulletin board in my studio, when a studio head screamed at me, "You're just a writer." You see what I mean? That's important. Whereas in college, in the universities, they pretend they are friendly to the idea of the creative act, which they aren't really, they just pretend. Because the people who really know about it are the people who do it. Ted the other day quoted me something wonderful somebody had told him, this in Des Moines, Iowa, which is an unlikely place. They had said, Ralph said (Ralph Crandon was a driver in New York), "They know the map but they can't drive the bus." You see what I mean? That's what you run into in the universities. I mean I've watched these people have to devour them-selves at meetings. And now at many universities they have to be accessible to the students by e-mail, which is even more hysterical and abusive. So at least in Hollywood, I knew I was just a writer. They used to say that writers were schmucks that drove old Corollas, you know, that kind of thing. So it's full of many illusions. Like the illusion of the happy creative writing profes-sor. In the year and a half I taught, all I could think of was that these para-sites were sucking the blood out of me. That was out at Stony Brook and it was a bit of a hot place, at the time, you know in the sixties . . . Philip Roth was there, Alfred Kazin . . .

Lindsay: Speaking of the sixties, do you feel like there was a lot of passion and energy going on back then and that now that's not happening?

Harrison: Well, it was a time of great social foment, cultural foment, though I don't know if it necessarily led to anything. But this is of course, a very different time. Cultures go through their cycles. For instance, we've been in a sort of fifteen-year cycle of insane greed in America. When I was growing up people didn't talk about money, it was thought to be impolite. Now both the *New York Times* and the *New Yorker* magazine tend to be mouthpieces for this greed. That kind of thing, without knowing it, with a gradual takeover that they've grown into. But that thing you observed about Ted and I, that I'm more Dionysian . . . for instance, I don't even like paths, you know when I walk, it's like a friend said, "It's not the beer cans I mind, it's the road," you know? I tend to be more a free radical. Our culture is swinging too . . .

Lindsay: . . . as though in waves from Dionysian to Apollonian . . .

Harrison: Well, I read, it was a few weeks ago, where a female teacher got put in jail for making love to a sixteen-year-old boy . . . right? Well, that would have been every boy's dream when I was growing up (laughter). But now she gets slammed in jail for it. This is, of course, nonsense. This is the corrosive aspect of Puritanism rising up in our culture again. It keeps reemerging.

Lindsay: That's kind of a gateway into this question: you talk openly about strip bars and lusting after women but you also seem to be a happily married man. Is that about a kind of revolt against Puritanism?

Harrison: No. It's just biology. I know that women are much more choosy about who they feel affection for. But once they feel the affection, they're very likely to go ahead with it. That's just the statistical thing. Whereas the reason the species continues to exist is that certain biological wanton aspect of men that they share with male dogs, you know what I'm saying? But I don't think it's neither here or there, because part of the social contract, in a marriage or any other place, is that you can be feeling as crazy as you want inside your brain but you follow a certain code of conduct toward the marriage or it will disintegrate. But a woman is crazy if she worries about her husband going to a strip club. I think it's so funny . . . I read on the internet where you can see all these men working in an office, and they're all taking peeks . . . and for instance there's a certain species of monkey, this was in the *New York Times* Science page . . . are you ready? There's a certain species of monkey that will give up lunch in order to look at pictures of female monkey butts. So what are you going to do?

Lindsay: That's very funny.

Harrison: As someone said, we're all chimps with car keys.

Lindsay: You know in your memoir, you have the Rilke quote: There is a point at which the exposed heart never recovers . . . did that ever happen to you?

Harrison: Oh sure. My father and sister were killed in a car wreck and I'm still dealing with them forty years later. You know, that kind of thing.

Lindsay: I was reading that, and you mention it throughout your memoir here and there, and then there's this one paragraph where you bring it all home, lightly, easily, but with a few details: the drunk guy going 80 down the wrong side of the road, and I sat there, I was up at the ski lodge, watching over my kids, and I just had to stop reading, stare at the cement wall and plastic round table top while I broke out in goosebumps and started trembling, and I felt it, I felt it for like a week . . . really disrupting . . . and I was going to ask you . . . one of my big problems is being too empathic, when I read, when I talk to my friends. . . .

Harrison: I don't think you can be too empathic. It's how we get enlarged as human being in a Buddhist sense, absolute empathy.

Lindsay: But do you ever have a problem separating yourself from the events around you?

Harrison: Oh, oh, absolutely. Absolutely. You know it gets difficult. I think I was with some people, and we were eating dinner, and I broke into tears because I heard about that gay boy in Wyoming that got beaten to death. That kind of thing. No you can't. Because if you're a writer, you have the optimum of imagination, you don't see the event in the newspaper prose of how it's presented to you, you completely visualize the event.

Lindsay: And feel it.

Harrison: Yes, exactly. What did Goethe say? "Such a price the Gods exact for song"—we become what we write. You know, we *become* what we write. That's the whole thing. But there's all this nonsense in our culture now where they talk about healing before the blood is dry on the pavement. All that Oprah nonsense. All these phony books about redemption. I mean I've seen occasional cases of redemption but not all that many.

Lindsay: What's cool about what you're implying is that you're kind of standing there and you just end up feeling all of it.

Harrison: Well, that's true. But that's your calling, you know. Lorca, one of my favorite poets of all time, said, "I'm neither all man nor all poet, but only the pulse of a wound that probes to the opposite side." That's a tough one, isn't it? (laughter) So that's just your calling and you knew when that happened, that that's the life you were called to. So it does become unpleasant and sometimes the vessel cracks, as it were. I remember when I was in my teens I read all of Dostoevsky and I barely recovered (laugher). I'm not sure I ever did.

Lindsay: You talk a bit about American Indians and you have them as characters in your books. I love that quote by that schoidphrenic, "Bird are holes in heaven through which a man my pass." It's totally true, in a way, if you shift the perspective. How much dealings with the American Indians have you had?
Harrison: Well, we lived for thirty-five years within thirty miles of a reservation. My father was an agriculturist and we knew the natives. And I had a cabin in the UP. So many people up there are mixed bloods because it was a big logging and mining area. I don't deal with Indian religion ever, 'cause that's not for me to handle. I very rarely have ever dealt with any pure bloods. But these were just the people I knew. And I don't want to write about white people who drive white cars and eat white bread and drink white wine . . .

Lindsay: So what's the deal with the reading public these days? I feel like they have no clue. They all, like Kierkegaard said, "are lacking passion."
Harrison: Well, people in general, you can't talk about. I mean Kierkegaard was a big passion of mine at one time, and the fact of the matter, the true fraudulence I see in these MFA programs is how poorly read both the teachers and the students are. I mean it's all just unimaginable. These MFA programs are like the Ford Motor plants. The production in the country of literature is 99.9 percent not very valuable. But that's always been true. And now our literature has this hygienic mentality about it, kind of post-Victorian. I don't have to take it seriously because it's not serious. They just think it is. I want art, I don't want sincerity. You get sincerity from the modern living pages of newspapers.

Lindsay: The theme of this issue is God or numina or spirit. Did you take or keep anything from your Christian experience, and how would you define God today?
Harrison: I kept an enormous amount because it happened when I was very young. Just like I've kept a lot from my nominal practices over the years. It becomes embedded in your spirit. I think I said in my memoir, when I was a kid I read about this girl riding a polar bear cub through the snow, and there

was a silver harness . . . and I always somewhat believed that was true. So I don't know, I think I have a more monstrous sense of God now, partly in response to science, whether it was the Hubble photos . . . the human genome . . . I mean if the flea has 22,000 indicators in each cell of what he is, I don't have any problem, you know? I mean I don't think it's proper for the schools to teach God but I certainly know a great number of scientists who believe very much in a pattern. But it seems like the Bush administration would realize that putting God in schools sort of resembles what caused the problems in the Middle East. We're not intelligent people. In fact, I thought of starting a comic lawsuit. You ready for this one? To sue Yale for graduating him. I'd even throw in John Kerry. The idea that they graduated either one of those bozos blows my mind.

Lindsay: I've been thinking about how people talk about music in a linear way, as though just because it begins and ends it's linear. But in music, so many things are happening at once, it feels layered to me, it's really about a layering of time. You talk like you think about this—"It's like seeing time herself," or "Only today, I heard the river within the river," for example. Talk a little about your sense of time.

Harrison: Well, you know the problem is, that I don't see time in a linear sense. On any given day you might be ten years ago or four years ahead, you see? That infantile sense of time as strictly linear never worked with me. I could try to believe it but I don't think it really exists. But I don't see why, other than living within a fatal organism, why I should think too much about it.

Lindsay: (laughter) Maybe that's the catch there.

Harrison: Yeah. But that's neither here nor there, as no one's ever gotten out of here alive. As far as I know, you know? Although Apollinaire, the French poet, said this . . . "Jesus holds the high-altitude record." Isn't that great?

Lindsay: Yeah. What about fishing? You write a lot about fishing. A lot of men I know write a lot about fishing.

Harrison: It's the only way I can erase everything. I used to be able to do it with bird hunting too, but not for years. But fishing on a river, I think it's a Taoist thing. A river has such an acceptance of mortality, and it's such an aesthetically overwhelming thing that you don't think about anything else, and I know that any number of writers who fish I think because they're stopping time. It erases everything impossible in your life. For instance, the morning of 9/11, I watched the television for an hour and then I went fishing. That was the only solution. After watching the plane run into the building five times, I said, I'm outta here.

Poet of the Peninsulas

Christopher Walton / 2009

First published in the *Detroit Free Press*, January 17, 2010, 2J–3J. Reprinted with permission of Christopher Walton.

Clenching an American Spirit cigarette in his teeth, Jim Harrison drives his muddy SUV through a creek and up a rocky road that cuts through the southern Arizona backcountry. There's a dog cage in the rear of the truck, shotgun shells strewn about the backseat, and small gray feathers, smeared with blood, plastered to the passenger-side dashboard.

"This is my commute to work every morning," Harrison says, navigating the road that runs to the ranch house where he writes.

Harrison has been working for almost fifty years now, quietly building a reputation as one of America's finest literary authors while not-so-quietly indulging his many extraliterary pursuits, including: palling around Hollywood with Jack Nicholson; fishing for tarpon in Key West with Thomas McGuane, Jimmy Buffet, and Richard Brautigan, and consuming gourmet feasts of epic proportions with Orson Welles and John Huston.

Though Harrison has given scores of interviews over the years, he rarely does so anymore. "It takes too much time from writing." But he's making an exception on this sunny, unseasonably cold December day at his winter home in Patagonia, twelve miles north of the Mexican border. It's partly because he misses his native Michigan, partly because of the affection he feels for the newspaper that he's been reading since he was five.

The schedule Harrison has set for the day is strict—"I'm a time person. It's the one discipline I manage," he says—and includes a morning drive to his studio, a break for his daily nap and an afternoon drive to a "really spectacular" nearby valley.

And perhaps a stop at the saloon in town.

It's a rare glimpse into the daily life of the man who rose improbably from rural northern Michigan, the son of a county agricultural agent, to international literary acclaim and a two-decade career in Hollywood as a screenwriter, where his story, "Legends of the Fall," was made into a movie and where he infamously gained and squandered a fortune.

In addition to having been awarded a Guggenheim Fellowship and being elected to the American Academy of Arts and Sciences, Harrison has carved a reputation as a brilliant and prolific writer. He's published thirty-two books of poetry, fiction, and nonfiction and written articles for *Esquire*, *Sports Illustrated*, the *New York Times Book Review*, and others.

Now, at seventy-two, Harrison's literary output is accelerating. And he's a bit bewildered to find himself in the most prolific period of his storied career.

Mornings at Home

The day begins at Harrison's casita, a modest adobe dwelling with a small kitchen, a couple bedrooms, and a living area dominated by the fireplace where Harrison often cooks birds and wild game over a mesquite fire. Harrison and Linda, his wife of fifty years, have spent their winters in Patagonia for the past twenty years. Their primary residence is Livingston, Montana, where they moved in 2001 after selling their home in Leelanau County.

"The only reason we moved to Montana was to be near our two daughters and grandkids," says Harrison. In 2004, Harrison sold the UP cabin he had owned for twenty-five years.

"I miss the UP terribly," Harrison says. "It became a retreat for me from the real world. It was like, after a disgusting two weeks of movie meetings, and then a day later you're at the Dunes Saloon in Grand Marais after taking a four-hour walk with your dogs and never seeing anybody, because I'd say 99 percent of my hiking, I never saw another human being. Which is the way I liked it.

"I know I've written about Michigan a lot lately, and I wonder if the origin isn't homesickness. Which is a very deep feeling, what the Portuguese call *saudade*. It's that longing for a place."

Last month, Harrison released *The Farmer's Daughter*, a collection of three novellas. Each of the main characters struggles with a profound sense of aloneness and the longing for human connection. In the title story, Sarah Holcomb is a precocious and attractive fifteen-year-old on the brink of womanhood in 1980s rural Montana. When Sarah is sexually assaulted, the tale turns to revenge, a theme of which Harrison is fond. In "The Games of Night," an educated young man who is stabbed in the cheek by the beak of a hummingbird and later bitten on the neck by a wolf pup develops a virus of the blood that, when the moon is full, inflames his appetites for sex and meat, forcing him to retreat from society. And in "Brown Dog Redux," Harrison continues the comic saga of his most durable character, Brown Dog. Making his fifth appearance in a Harrison novella, Brown Dog is a half-blood Indian from the UP who stumbles through life, at times disregarding or oblivious to societal expectations.

In the past six years, Harrison has published three novels (*True North*, *Returning to Earth*, and *The English Major*), two novella trilogies (*The Summer He Didn't Die* and *The Farmer's Daughter*), and two books of poetry (*Saving Daylight* and *In Search of Small Gods*).

He's already completed another novel, *The Great Leader*, due out in another year or so. Set in Marquette, Nebraska, and Arizona, Harrison says the book examines the "peculiar connection of sex, religion, and money in America, coming up with the conclusion that it's sort of like a bowling ball—you can't separate any part of it." A compendium of the Brown Dog novellas is forthcoming, maybe this year, maybe next, Harrison says, with a new story likely to be written for the collection.

"Harrison is without question one of the most prolific writers I have ever seen," says Robert DeMott, professor of English at Ohio University and editor of *Conversations with Jim Harrison*.

"What I think distinguishes Jim's output is not only the questing, restless mind behind it, but the fact that he is adept in three genres—fiction, for which he is best known; poetry, which I think he feels is his truest calling; and nonfiction, which deserves to be more widely known.

"Harrison seems compelled to write," adds DeMott. "And at an age when many of us are content to cruise through our remaining days, he seems more on fire than ever."

The Writing Studio

After an hour or so talking at his home, Harrison wants to take some bones to the dogs that live at his writing studio, a rented ranch house a mile from his home. So it's into the SUV and down the back road.

The place where Harrison writes is like something out of a Western movie set. Rusty old spice cans line a tiny kitchen shelf, and the snug main room looks like a long-neglected museum of natural history, with leathery rattlesnake skins and a jaguar pelt tacked to the wall.

"Jaguars get up to around a hundred pounds and are much more potent than mountain lions," he says. "*Muy macho.*"

The small kitchen table and wooden chair where Harrison writes prompts the question: Why is he so prolific of late? "I don't know," he says. "The perennial question is the source. A T'ang Dynasty Chinese poet in the twelfth century, Wang Wei, said, 'Who knows what causes the opening and closing of the door?' I wrote 'Legends of the Fall' in nine days, but I had been thinking about it for a few years."

Later in the afternoon, during a drive through the San Rafael Valley, a spectacular savannah-like expanse bordered by the snow-capped Huachuca Mountains, Harrison returns to his recent explosion of productivity.

"Age focuses you," he says. "You are much better concentrated. There's more time when you travel less, don't do book tours, avoid interviews or public appearances. You walk the dogs, fish, hunt, cook, and write."

Harrison says he will continue to make his annual public appearance at Grand Valley State University in Grand Rapids, where he donated his papers in 2005. The only part of the collection at Grand Valley that's restricted—until 2015—is Harrison's forty-year correspondence with fellow Michigan-born author McGuane. "Some of it's indelicate," Harrison says with a laugh. "It contains actresses' names and dirty stuff. Stacks of it. He writes beautiful letters."

Another reason for writing so much, he says, is money.

"I admit to occasionally sharing the financial hysteria of the rest of the country, the urgency to save more for the family in case you can't write any more." Harrison's exploits in Hollywood as a highly paid screenwriter, as well as his utter lack of financial management skills, are well documented, most notably in his memoir, *Off to the Side.* "I went from making $10,000 a year writing poetry to $700,000 for screenwriting," he says. "That can throw off your equilibrium."

He walked away from Hollywood fourteen years ago because "I couldn't stand it. I didn't want to die there. Hollywood is tough. There's a lot of money, cocaine, and alcohol, and no balance whatsoever. And Linda and I figured out we could live on 20 or 25 percent of what we had been living on if we wanted to."

He points out that six years ago he was diagnosed with Type 2 diabetes, and as a result, "could no longer drink as much French wine that gives me so much pleasure. In general I had to cut drinking by two-thirds. This gives me a lot more energy for the work."

His work, Harrison has noticed, keeps bringing him back to Michigan.

Cocktail Hour

After the hour-long drive through the valley, where the only other human is a border patrol agent sitting in his truck on the side of the narrow road, it's time to hit the Wagon Wheel Saloon for his 4:40 P.M. cocktail hour.

He orders his customary two drinks—vodka on the rocks. Then, "because we're having a good time," he orders one more.

Later, Harrison sends an e-mail through his secretary (he doesn't use computers) saying that he's been thinking about the reasons behind his productivity. "Here's a more recent conclusion," Harrison writes, "and perhaps the most powerful, come to think of it." Nearly all his recent work, he says, is set in northern Michigan. "Often I have become overwhelmed by a nearly unbearable homesickness. Perhaps in my working I'm 'writing myself back home.' I can re-create the essence of a lifelong experience in the homeland."

Force of Nature

Chris Dombrowski / 2012

From *Montana Headwall*, Fall 2012, 31–34. Reprinted with permission of *Montana Headwall* and Chris Dombrowski. An enhanced version, titled "The Gospel According to Jim," is in *Anglers Journal* 2, no. 4 (Fall 2015): 82–88.

I am sitting at the Hitching Post in Melrose drinking vodka with Jim who steals, between sips, a scant glance at his beloved barmaid Nicole's rear, puffs from his American Spirit, and says: "Do you want to know how you can believe in God?"

Smoke purls thickly from his cigarette, and in the window-parried shaft of evening light his face looks quite conjured with its blind eye wandering opposite his working eye, one of them—I'm not sure which—glancing often at some bird darting just beyond my mortal means of perception.

"Absolutely," I say. "I totally want to know."

Around us at the bar, ranchers and fishing guides lean in to order beers or fries or shots from Nicole, whose brown hair fairly gleams against a white tank top as she leans down to reach for bottles, revealing ample cleavage, that space on a woman's body, essentially nothing, that so entrances the male heterosexual.

"It's a vacancy," Jim says, limpidly braiding our theological conversation with the sexual, "the absence of something that makes men incorrigible. A nada."

With his singular own, Jim catches Nicole's dark eyes, and asks to buy a drink (Knee-cole, he pronounces her name) for his friend Craig, who just arrived at the door in his wheelchair. Crippled from the waist down last winter in a car accident, Craig is Nicole's ex-boyfriend and would likely receive a free drink anyway, but Nicole obliges, laces ice, vodka, a splash of soda into a short glass, and then, as if by instinct, fills our glasses as well.

Jim lifts his glass to mine: "Peacock"—this is Jim's friend, the author and grizzly bear expert, Doug Peacock—"tells me that new indisputable"—he puffs vigorously on his cigarette again—"evidence points to the fact bears have been feeding on migrating cutworm moths in precisely the same drainage in the Front Range near Glacier National Park for over thousands of years, and recently Peacock determined the bears now arrive before the moths, and wait out the moths' arrival, whereupon they gorge themselves into a food coma. I'll order us two steaks—Knee-Cole, two steak sandwiches rare, please, and another vodka for Craig. For a bear, there are more nutrients per part in a cutworm moth than in a cutthroat trout." By now I have finished my vodka and I am staring straight at Jim, his tanned face gullied with wrinkles and crow's feet. "That's how you can believe in God."

How I got to know Jim Harrison—outdoorsman, roving gourmand, and man of letters, "untrammeled renegade genius" and beloved author of more than thirty books including *Dalva* and *Legends of the Fall*—is another story, the short version of which goes: I was born in his hometown and grew up on Harrison Road and he takes kindly to river guide/poets with a penchant for good cheese and cold vodka.

For now, though, we're going fishing on the Big Hole where Jim spends fifty or sixty days each summer, and, Carhartted from head to toe but for the Muck boots, he's knocking at the screen door to my cabin: "Are you ready for some sausage patty, son?"

"I don't know if I can handle sausage," I say. "I'm still a tad jangled from last night. How about you?"

"A little bit hung-over but that's to be expected of a Marine of fly fishing. I'm famished from forging the smithy of my soul. I wrote a poem this morning! Come, we must find sustenance," he says, in what I think of as his "imperial voice," aiming his substantial frame toward the Hitching Post's café that sits a mere fifty yards from the cabin door.

Inside the café we find our friend and fishing partner, novelist David James Duncan, chatting up the guides who are picking up their sack lunches from Sherri, Nicole's aunt, queen of the morning shift. We sit down to hot drinks and David tells us what he's learned from the locals: that the river rose with an overnight rain, and while it has crested, won't likely fish well till the afternoon. It's still springtime in Montana, and the Big Hole's trout feed mostly when the water warms away their lethargy.

"How about the bugs?" Jim asks, referring to the fabled *pteronarcys californica*, the salmon fly hatch coveted by the angling masses.

"Mostly in the canyon or up above, around Silver Bridge," David says.

"Good. We should go downstream then and cover a big chunk of water with streamers. Stay away from the loons."

The loons will arrive momentarily from Bozeman and Butte and Spokane and Salt Lake to chase the three-inch-long stonefly's upstream mating flights and the toilet-flush-rises these aquatic rib-steaks induce from the trout. Only immensely well-cultured anglers such as ourselves would prefer to fish downstream of the hatch; we prefer the solitude and good company, we tell each other, but we also know the downstream brown trout have already gluttoned up on the stoneflies, and, if we can put a streamer deep enough under the right cutbank, we stand to catch the fish of the season, a two-foot, six-pound brown.

"How about Glen to the Notch, then?" I suggest. "I know a perfect lunch spot, and I have some morels and chicken to heat up on the stove."

"I rolled a whopper down there last week," Jim says, "but I missed it 'cause I was watching two garish tanagers fight over a mayfly. The birds insisted their beauty was more important than my lifetime brown trout, and who am I to disagree with such creatures?"

Jim's response recalls something I read in a recent interview he gave to a publication in France, where he is a veritable folk-hero: "Do you believe in the supernatural?" the interviewer asked Jim.

"Of course I do," Jim said, "because I receive special instructions from the gods. In America, I have a book [of poems] called *In Search of Small Gods*. Do you really expect one God to create nineteen billion galaxies? And did you know that one teaspoon of cosmic black hole weighs three billion tons? Think how strong this teaspoon has to be. So, if there are nineteen billion galaxies, why can't I have a soul, even if it is extremely small? As small as a photon, or better yet, as one of my neurons. It never occurred to me not to believe in the Resurrection."

"Where's your flask?" Jim asks me. The drift boat is anchored a few miles downstream from Glen Bridge and we're snacking on a wedge of Manchego while David plies a side-channel on foot. The grass along the bank of the rivulet grows thick and high, the seed-heads already heavy, and from our vantage David's hat and moving fly-rod are the only human intrusions visible on the landscape, the graphite glinting with each cast or when it bows under the weight of a fish or bucks with a fish's run; when David kneels to unhook and release a fish, he disappears altogether.

"You mean my vodka flask?"

"Last year I was flying to Paris with Dustin Hoffman and we were lamenting the spate of interviews we had lined up upon arrivals. 'Dustin,' I said, 'how do you put up with it all?' And he said, 'Jim, it's easy. I just fill up a water bottle with vodka and sip off it all through the day.' And I told him, 'Ha! I know a poet and a fishing guide in Montana who does the exact same thing!'"

"It did protect against inane clients, but I quit bringing it during high water. Too easy to make a mistake sober, let alone buzzed."

I don't need to expound for Jim. Two years ago, he, legendary Livingston outdoorsman Dan Lahren, and I floated Rock Creek at flood stage the day before a very competent oarsman flipped his boat and lost a passenger to the cold swift water and ultimately a sweeper. From his home in Livingston, Jim read the news and called me. He sensed I felt some guilt for taking him down such a treacherous stretch of river. "Dommer," he said, "don't feel bad. The world is a cruel place. This much we know."

"Let me see that rod of yours," I say. Jim's had a few tugs on his streamer—one violent slash from a big fish that sent him into a near-orgasmic state of excitement—but the last hour of fishing has been exceedingly uneventful. "I just saw David hook another fish. I'm going to trail something off of your Yuk Bug."

"Not a worm!" Jim says, referring to the dreaded San Juan worm, an imitation of an aquatic worm whose fly-ness is often disputed in angling circles. "But I know what you're thinking. Trust me, I worked in Hollywood for two decades. Nymphing is like bare skin to the film industry. Whenever things get slow . . ."

"Show 'em some tit?"

"Precisely, son! Now, no nymphs for me. I'll take my lumps. Let's try a Lahren's Little Olive," he says, referring to a number 10 woolly bugger tied ragged and wrapped with significant lead.

And take the lumps he does. With David back in the boat talking Ikkyu with Jim ("Clouds very high look," Ikkyu wrote eight centuries ago, "not one word helped them get up there") we drift downstream. Jim covers the water as thoroughly as a flight of swallows covers the air above the river at dusk—there isn't an inch of holding water that he fails to twitch the fly seductively through, but no grabs from the big browns who have shied away from the high sun. I'm rowing hard against the snow-fed currents, trying my two-armed best to hold the boat adjacent to the prime lies, so I see only Jim's tan fly line at the edge of my periphery, zinging back and out against the banks. Every now and then he stops casting to marvel at a warbler or a tanager, to feel, as he says in one of his poems, "the grace of their intentions," and then he returns his attention to the water and his casts.

He's practicing what I've long thought of as "Jim Yoga," focusing his attention alternately skyward (mountains, birds, clouds) and at ground level (dogs, trout, plants). It's a ritualistic way of moving through the world that's revivified him, a way of seeing through eyes other than his own—and those of us who've read his books have been revivified as well. "If you spend a fair amount of time studying the world of ravens," he's said, "it is logical indeed to accept the fact that reality is an aggregate of the perceptions of all creatures, not just ourselves."

Save the squeaking oarlocks and the water lapping at the hull, the boat is wonderfully quiet. Flicker calls, warbler note-cascades, wind, around us the scent of budding cottonwoods. Then Jim says: "Come on trout! You don't want to see little Jimmy throw a tantrum, do you? You know, Davey, I once caught a three-pound brown on this left bank coming up. Right—" Jim pauses and waits for his Little Olive to slap against the bank—"here!"

And before he can strip the line, a chunky brown trout cartwheels out of its element for the fly, latches onto the hook, and Jim let's out a whoop. We are all three more than a little bit dumbfounded. David and I exchange glances of substantial bafflement as I slip the net under the fish.

We lunch on my favorite island in the world: a cottonwood-laden dry wash that divvies a slow side channel from the hard-rushing main river, which passes the land, then slams hard into a tall sandstone cliff, pivots sharply to the east, and hurtles downstream. The two currents meet and form a lazy back eddy, above which swallows are usually on the hunt, and above the water, adjacent the cliff, sloping steadily to the north, a deep swale hosts tall grasses and sage.

I say "we lunch," but I have forgotten the propane for my portable grill (I could build a fire and cook over coals, but we expect the fishing to turn on within the hour). In the cooler, I have chicken thighs marinating in olive oil, Tabasco, salt, pepper and thyme, some fresh asparagus and, as an aperitif, some morels I gathered a few days ago from a burn near Missoula—but no gas! And thus, no fire for the roving gourmand who doubtless sees the disappointment in my eyes and offers: "I have some Washington coho that I grilled last night."

"And a bottle of wine," David says.

"I don't drink before four in the afternoon," Jim says, "but of course wine at lunch on the river is not drinking. Here, son, cut yourself some salami—did I show you this wine key and knife a woman gave to me in France? We'll have a tidy snack and then how about a nap in the warm sand?"

We eat the cold smoky wild salmon and wash it down with gouts of Côtes du Rhône, chew on thick slices of salami, and soon, we're lounging in the shade of some young cottonwoods with our hands behind our heads like old cowhands. We've all three had long years—health issues, legal issues, money issues—but like good migratory creatures we're back along a familiar shore, contemplating the currents. Dangerous as the river is, Jim wrote recently in a poem, that "only the water is safe."

I'm not so much startled awake, because I wasn't really sleeping, but Jim's nasally voice surprises me: "You found yourself a nice island here, Dommer."

With a smile on his face, David is still sleeping, so I tell Jim in a whisper about how several years ago I camped here with my wife Mary and our infant son, and how, after nursing all night, our son still wouldn't sleep, so I held him in the camp chair before dawn so Mary could nod off. The river rushed around the island, slammed hard into the sandstone cliff wall, then caromed through an audible riffle that charged through a short box canyon. The stars wheeled, the earth turned, but momentarily I felt that we, my son and I, sat outside of time. It grinds the mind down, the sound of shallow water, and as the old goateed poet next to me once wrote: "The mind ground is being as it is."

"That's a wonderful story," Jim says. "We must honor it with a four-pound brown this afternoon. Davey, wake up, the fish await with open mouths!"

What I love most about Jim is that, since he's constantly altering your perception of him, he allows you to alter your perception of yourself, to be malleable like the current. Without a soft mind, someone said, you cannot be very strong. Jim is ox-big these days and I wouldn't ask him to outrun a mule, but his mind moves like a jackrabbit. At seventy-something years old, he seems to be certain of only a few things: good wine, garlic, and the necessity of time on the water. When we've catalogued only 15 percent of the world's species, he seems to say, why be certain of anything?

A few moments later though, fishing, he is quite certain that a red-bellied Yuk Bug—a white-legged, grizzly-hackled, squirrel-tailed, three-inch-long beast— is precisely the fly he needs.

"I had a fish strike this so hard last year," he says, "it yanked the rod out of my hands!"

We find no such denizens downstream, but the bite is on. Solid fish swirl on our streamers on the dump (as they land), on the swing (as they hook downstream with the current), and on the strip (as they dance at the hands of the anglers turned puppeteers). David has a personal retrieve. He strips line vigorously and darts the rod tip back and forth at the surface of the water, which makes his streamer, an articulated creation that we call The Fly-Fisherman's Rapala, look precisely like a flagging minnow, but makes him look like he's playing air guitar. Tugged upstream beside a riprap bank, the fly zigzags across the surface and is engulfed by a violent buttery swirl. Big brown. David's rod bucks with animal energy, then straightens as the fish comes unhooked. Jim hollers—he's latched onto a twenty-inch rainbow that Riverdances across the riffle on its tail. I net

Jim's broad-shouldered fish and we pledge to toast its surface-skimming leap tonight, its lengthy exit from its watery world.

Driving home on the Burma Road, we pass an old dilapidated house—doorless, windowless, roof caved in by a windfall cottonwood. It's home, if you ask the locals, to one of the largest, most seething dens of rattlesnakes in the valley.

"Son, do you see that old house?" Jim says.

"Sure I do."

"Good. Do you know what it says?"

"No, what does it say?"

"It says: Don't let your life become the sloppy leftovers of your work."

It's evening and the light across the green-for-a-few-more-weeks hills makes the sage look like suede. I want what Jim said to sink in, to eddy in my brain and take root, but the moment vanishes like a cloud shadow on the snowfields of the distant Pioneers because we pass a roadside pond, a ditch, really, and David says: "Chris, slow down! Back up! Phalaropes in the pond!"

I back the truck and boat trailer carefully up the road, and see them: four small birds spin around and around, dervish-like, on the dusk-lit water, dislodging food from the weeds below them that they dip down occasionally to eat. They turn and turn like oblong tops. They are doing something we humans couldn't do. We are silent for a long moment. Then Jim says:

"My God. Four phalaropes. We are blessed!"

About Jim

Jerry Dennis / 2014

Expanded with additional material from *Traverse: Northern Michigan's Magazine*, August 2014, 58–63. Reprinted with permission of *Traverse* and Jerry Dennis.

It must have been 1981 when I read my first Jim Harrison book. My wife, Gail, and I had just finished college in Kentucky and returned home to Traverse City, Michigan, with our two-year-old son, Aaron, and moved into a tiny camper trailer parked in my parents' back yard on Long Lake. I was sick of school and wanted to work outside to clear my head while I learned how to be a writer, so I made the rounds of construction companies looking for work as a carpenter. I knew one end of a hammer from another but that was about all I knew. Jobs were scarce and nobody wanted to take a chance on a green college boy, but I was lucky enough to find my way to Paul Maurer Construction. Paul didn't need any greenhorns on his crew but he needed help in his office in downtown Cedar, so he put me to work filing papers, writing letters to clients, and answering the phone. I did okay at it, probably better than a trained monkey could do, so when an opening for a carpenter's assistant came up, he gave me a shot.

Of course I had heard of Harrison. I knew he was a poet and novelist, that he had grown up in northern Michigan, that he had worked in the construction trades while establishing himself as a writer, and that he lived on a farm in Leelanau County, only a few miles from the office I worked in in Cedar. His book of novellas, *Legends of the Fall*, had been a national sensation a few years earlier and seemed to have been read by everyone I knew. Gail and I were broke after six years spent alternating college with travel and working throw-away jobs and finally becoming parents of our first son, so it wasn't possible to buy new books. Instead we shopped at the Salvation Army store on Eleventh Street, where we sorted through musty bestsellers, outdated encyclopedias, and rain-warped romance novels, hoping to find treasures at twenty-five cents each. One of the treasures we found was a paperback copy of *Legends of the Fall.*

I took it home, opened it to the first page of the first novella, "Revenge," and was bowled over. I knew by the end of that first page that here was an original, powerful new voice in fiction, unlike any I had encountered in my young but feverish life as a student of literature. I finished the book in a single sitting, went back to page one, and read it again. Then I drove to the public library on 6th Street and checked out all of Harrison's books. I've been a fan ever since.

Not long ago, while giving a reading at a university, I was asked by someone in the audience to name my favorite living writer, and I said, without hesitation, "Jim Harrison." I hadn't quite realized it, but the moment I said it I knew it was true. That winter I had reread his magnificent collected poems, *The Shape of the Journey*, and been astonished at the power and depth of his poetic journey. The book left me with the feeling that Harrison had planned the entire arc of his life's work, starting with the first book of poems. That feeling has grown more certain as I've read the subsequent collections of poetry as well as the Brown Dog novellas—which appeared sporadically during the last five decades and were recently republished in a single collection. The Brown Dog novellas are probably my favorites of Harrison's work, and not just because they're set in the Upper Peninsula and feature characters I could have grown up with. They might well turn out to be his magnum opus and will surely be read for as long as anything he has published in his remarkably rich and fecund career.

And what a career. More than thirty books of poems, novels, collections of novellas, volumes of nonfiction, a children's book, and a memoir. Add to that the many screenplays, several of which were produced as major motion pictures.

For years I've wanted to sit down with Jim in a bar or beside a campfire, and talk about his work and his love of the outdoors and his views of the world. We've met a few times and exchanged a few words, and although he has always been gracious and friendly, it never worked out to spend time with him.

We conducted this interview by telephone, from my home near Traverse City to Jim's winter home near Patagonia, Arizona. I wanted it to be a conversation, not an interview, but it turned into a rather strange one. Our cell connection was dicey at best, and Jim often could not hear me, although I heard him loud and clear. If one of us spoke over the other, a momentary lacuna occurred. But Jim was comfortable enough with this shortcoming and adjusted quickly. If he was unable to hear my question, he spoke about whatever came to mind, free-associating in a manner that often reminded me of his written work. Each riff is a kind of oral postcard that vividly describes an aspect of his life and thought. Which, come to think of it, is a pretty good way to describe his poems.

As the conversation neared its conclusion, Jim suggested we get together sometime for a drink. I agreed, with enthusiasm. Listening to the recording later I realized that as I was expressing my agreement, Jim said, "Unless you're in AA. Are you in AA?" He waited for my response, but since I didn't hear his question I said nothing. To my ear the silence that followed suggested that he was ready to get off the phone. He might have interpreted my silence as reluctance to answer, which might have led him to conclude that I was indeed in AA and was being discreet or even chastising him for asking me for a drink. After that moment of awkwardness he went on to talk about something else, and I never got the chance to drink with him.

We spoke on a frigid day in February, deep in a Russian winter of *sastrugi* drifts and frigid winds, shortly after the Great Lakes froze over and while ice formations grew to epic size along the shore.

Jerry Dennis: It's ten degrees here in Traverse City, the wind is blowing at thirty miles per hour, and the wind-chill is thirty-five below. I just spent two hours blowing the drifts from my driveway and another hour shoveling snow off the roof, and now I don't have any feeling in my feet. How much do you miss Michigan?

Jim Harrison: [laughs] Not much. I had sixty-five winters in Michigan. So I don't miss that kind of thing. We're in the mountains down here [in southern Arizona]. We get occasional snow, so we get to look at it, watch the dog get irritated with its feet in the snow.

JD: I remember you said once that you had trouble writing in Michigan in winter.

JH: That was a long time ago. I used to get those Scandinavian doldrums. We had to get my daughter Anna a special lamp for artificial sunlight because she suffered from seasonal affective disorder. I always claimed I had post-traumatic stress disorder, so I could be like a soldier. Say "PTSD" and people look at you like, really? [laughs] Years ago I had [Doug] Peacock teach me a bunch of that army lingo so when I lied I couldn't get caught.

JD: When I was in my twenties I worked construction with a guy who liked to tell elaborate stories about his combat experiences in Viet Nam. But it turned out he had never even been in the military.

JH: Oh I love that. [laughs] Phil Caputo wrote what was maybe the best book to come out of Viet Nam, *A Rumor of War*. He's down here in the winter now, too. He got through several years of Viet Nam without a scratch, then after the war got sent to Lebanon to work for the Associated Press and got his foot blown mostly off. We got lost down here hunting and had to spend the night outside. He couldn't walk very well, you know, on his stubby foot. But that was the irony, getting through Viet Nam, then going to Lebanon and having your foot blown off.

JD: Caputo has written a lot about the Upper Peninsula. He must like it.
JH: Yeah, he does. I had bird hunting trails all through the UP. And all my bird-hunting friends would show up there. It was wonderful. You know I had that cabin for twenty-five years near Grand Marais. It was wonderful to be in Hollywood one morning and the next morning be up in the UP. What a relief, huh?

JD: I can barely imagine. Do your neighbors in Arizona know much about life in Michigan?
JH: Not much. Only a few of them have been there. The guy that works for us, that takes care of our house, he'd been up there because one year he drove one of Molly Phinny's cars back so he saw it. The main thing is the water, because we're always in a state of drought down here, though the creek keeps running. If you're from a dry state and you see Lake Michigan it's sort of stupefying. I tell visitors what it's like being on Lake Superior and just pulling over to drink the water, because there's no industries for a hundred miles until way over to the Soo. There are those fifty or sixty miles of deserted beach I could walk, watch ravens arguing over a dead fish.

JD: Ravens show up so often in your work that I wonder if they're a kind of spirit animal for you. You must miss them.
JH: We have Mexican ravens down here, so I'm not too lonely for them. I really got to know the ravens around my cabin [in Grand Marais]. The ravens around here take walks with me and they hide and scare my wife's dog. They'll jump out shrieking. Ravens like to tease animals, you know. I've even witnessed—I've written about it—a raven funeral in the backyard of my cabin. A raven dropped dead from a tree and the other ravens hung around for about an hour, around it in a circle. When a young raven fell out of my birdfeeder onto his back the other ravens jumped up and down shrieking in amusement.

JD: You've probably read Bernd Heinrich's *Ravens in Winter*?
JH: Yeah, I get all the raven books. My favorite is Candy Savage's *Bird Brains*, all about corvid intelligence. Ravens' brains are built different.

JD: That's what makes them interesting, eh?
JH: You live out on Old Mission? I used to visit Tom Hall out there. You remember Tom?

JD: I remember him well.
JH: He was quite a guy. Too bad, though. You go to a doctor to get a blood test and the doctor tells you you're gonna die. He stopped through Montana a few times and he had a little ranch over on Rock Creek, which I don't like to fish because it's too fast and if you float it it's like trying to fly-fish from a motorcycle.

JD: How was the hunting yesterday?
JH: Very poor. I do a lot of log-sitting because of that spinal surgery last fall. I can't keep up with the dogs, I shuffle. But I enjoy it because I can take my friend on this private ranch which I have access to. Really beautiful country. We hunt for doves, which I find delicious. And I don't have to walk for them. You pluck them and grill them over a wood fire. Where did you grow up?

JD: Long Lake, not far from Interlochen.
JH: Joyce and I were always trying to take shortcuts to Interlochen and we always got lost around Long Lake.

JD: All the roads must have started as game trails, the way they wind around.
JH: I remember I came up to the Traverse City Cherry Festival when I was sixteen. A friend of mine stole his mom's car and we drove from Reed City to Traverse City. I don't know what we had in mind. She was a doctor's wife, had a spiffy yellow Buick convertible. And we rode our bikes up from Reed City to Charlevoix and we went out and camped on Beaver Island for a week, which was fabulous back then, relatively undeveloped.

JD: Great fishing for smallmouth bass in those days, I bet.
JH: Oh yeah, we used to catch them there and around Traverse City, too, in the reed beds. And I've fished them near Escanaba, in those big reed beds. We were catching fish there every day on streamer flies, every cast for a

while. I brought friends there from Montana and they loved it. You don't see anybody on it, even on a hot summer's day.

JD: I know the place, right along US 2. Great fishing. You often describe yourself as an "outdoorsman and a man of letters." Why is being outdoors so important to you?

JH: Very early my dad would take me trout fishing because you know I'd had my eye put out and I needed extra attention. I remember asking him the difference between animals and us and he said, "Nothing. They just live outside and we live inside." Which struck me very hard at the time, because I could look at animals and say, "I'm one of you." The real schizophrenia of the nature movement, if you ask me, was to think you could separate yourself from nature. Even Shakespeare says "we are nature, too." So there's this sense of schizophrenia to think you're different or more important than a bird.

That's what we have down here that's incredible, when the birds start coming back up from Central and South America. Vast numbers of them come right over our house on the creek. I have a secretary who counted 119 species in three days on our patio. Even the rare elegant trogan, which is a mind-fuck to see. It looks like a paint-by-number bird. Another one is the quetzal bird from Mexico. And then you get a vast variety of hummingbirds and warblers. My friend, Merrill Gilfillan, who's a fantastic writer, just wrote a book called *The Warbler Road*. When he was down here—he's a first-rate birder, and I'm mediocre—he counted six different warblers in one big willow bush. Can you imagine? It was like that in May in Grand Marais, with that vast arboreal woods. A friend got all the Michigan warblers in about an hour.

My mother was a great warbler person. She knew all American warblers. She died on the old family farm near Mecosta and Remus, about fifteen miles from Big Rapids. After my dad died and she moved back to the farm, she built a thicket of about forty acres with all bird-friendly bushes. It's like a dense forest, it's unbelievable, with paths through it that my nephews cut for her. She had it right out the back door. She and her lady friends would take insane camping trips. I always said, look I can put you up in motels but she said "no, because when we camp we're always up at daybreak because of the birds." They'd go way up into the Boundary Waters of Minnesota and everywhere, camping. Neat old ladies.

JD: Talking about birds and wildlife reminds of something I read once in one of your pieces. You mentioned the "mythical underpinnings" that connect us with animals. Is that something you can elaborate on?

JH: Odin, that Scandinavian god, always had ravens standing on his shoulders. Myths, of course, are full of our other creatures. I would see bears almost daily in the UP. They would wander around my cabin, hog my sunflower seeds, and I got to know a couple of them real well. I'd come home from the bar and a bear would be standing by the side of my driveway and I'd open my window and he'd put his chin on my door sill and I'd scratch his ears. They get used to it. But I'd never feed them near the cabin, that's where you make a mistake. I'd put a fish on a stump about a hundred yards from the cabin. That's the glory of the UP and Montana, people aren't there yet.

JD: Not like New England, say.
JH: I'm not very interested in New England. I lived there for a couple years and my brother had a place in Connecticut, but there's just too many people, you know?

JD: Yes. And you can't turn around without recognizing a landmark from some book or other.
JH: [laughs] That's funny. Do you teach, too? How do you make a living?

JD: I just write.
JH: When I was offered a big job teaching early on at the University of Louisiana I said, "Somebody has to stay on the outside." You know? So I was shocked when I finally made a living at it. When I quit screenwriting ten years ago—I didn't want to die in LA, you know—when I quit screenwriting it was hard for a while financially, but then France took me up and they've paid good money. The French pay me as much as the Americans.

JD: What is it about your work that connects with French readers?
JH: I don't know. They just take up with certain foreign writers. It's like when I was in Russia twenty-five years ago, they all wanted to talk about Jack London.

JD: People who don't hunt maybe can't understand the connection hunters have with animals. The ones we hunt and the ones we don't. Is that part of why you hunt?
JH: I don't have my old enthusiasm for hunting but as I said, I love to sit on logs. So I don't care anymore. I lowered my daily kill in Grand Marais down to never more than two birds in one day, so that saved it for me. And always hunting in new places, you know, rather than hitting the old

hotspots. So then you get the fun of going to new cover, getting mildly lost, but Peacock had given me his marine-issue compass so hopefully I could get out of there. I find that when you can't find the car, your dog can . . . The Cheyenne had a saying, and the Lakota, too: "When your life is tepid and you're bored just follow your dog and act like your dog all day." That's been known to perk you up.

JD: [laughs] It sure perks me up. And I've always thought that getting lost occasionally is therapeutic.

JH: Yeah, I love the sensation, actually. That's what I liked so much about my cabin in the UP. It was thirty-five miles cross country to Newberry, with really not anything in it. An occasional deer cabin. It was fascinating to have that kind of walking for twenty-five years, you know. It's great walking around here, too, but I'm not too great with mountains. And there's so much junk rock here, too, you have to be careful.

In Montana we had to have a snake man come in because we had too many rattlesnakes and I lost my best bird dog to a rattlesnake. She got bitten several times in the face, and it was really the anti-venom that finally killed her. It vastly enlarged her heart. We finally had the snake man come in. I must have shot seventy, and there were three dens way up above our house a half mile. He took a total of a thousand rattlers out of there. He'd stop at our house and I'd have to go to the back of his truck to see that he was doing his job and he'd have barrels of rattlesnakes. Which are ugly, you know. My neighbor lost a dog to a rattler this fall. The dog lasted only twenty minutes, which is rare, but it got bitten right on the nose. After mine got bitten I got her back to the UP one more time. She could recognize grouse but she could no longer recognize woodcock. It was very strange. We'd get three grouse then she'd go back to the car and go to sleep. You have dogs?

JD: A big old smelly Lab that doesn't like the water.

JH: Now I've got a little Lab from Scotland, very compact, a great retriever, which you need for doves, you know. A group of us shot a hundred doves in one day and she retrieved every one of them. Then we came home and I gave her a pound of ground chuck and she slept for eighteen hours, you know [laughs] . . .

JD: That gets back to the question of why the outdoors is so important to you. Is it partly because of the sense of balance it provides?

JH: An error for writers is self-importance, you know.

JD: That's part of the reason I never wanted to work at a university.

JH: I agree. It's preposterous. I was at Stony Brook those two years and had Alfred Kazin and Philip Roth and everything. But they were stiff. They didn't go to the bar and play pool or anything. A friend of mine used to do an imitation of an important writer entering Elaine's. He'd put his nose in the air like he's looking for somebody in particular and waiting for people to recognize him.

JD: There's nothing like the woods for correcting you of that self-importance.

JH: Yea. When I'd get lost in the UP, I would sort of start drifting. I had a place with about five thousand acres of sugar plum and dogwood so I'd go there the last week of May when it was all in bloom. It was just overwhelming, the scent in the air, you know. The dog would even be a little puzzled you know. I always wonder. I was writing a poem the other day, trying to figure out what this creek here—my dog likes me to walk her to the creek every morning, which I do before work, and she likes it better if I wear boots and cross the creek. If it's a real warm day she just runs into it and founders and rolls and everything. So I was thinking about dogs and the mystery of water. We had a nitwit pointer once we'd take down to the beach and she'd jump in and start swimming to the Manitous [islands in Lake Michigan] and wouldn't come back and wouldn't come back, so my wife called the Coast Guard. [laughs] But of course they couldn't do anything. He finally returned. You know, they're so strong.

JD: I had a Lab years ago that would do the same thing. If she saw ducks on the Grand Traverse Bay she'd set out after them. I think she'd have gone all the way to Elk Rapids if the ducks had led her that far.

JH: Yeah, they don't mind scaring us. [laughs] I had a fishing guide friend over on the Big Hole River in Montana, which is a river I love. Anyway, it was fast in the spring and he was drifting down and a mother moose and her calf got sort of swept away. The mother got to the far shore and stood there, turning around. Her baby got swept away and he caught the baby, you know, and brought her to shore and she seemed very happy. But you have to watch them because they're very defensive about their children. You don't want a dog around because they think all dogs are wolves. Do you go to the UP at all?

JD: Quite a lot. In the spring every year with my wife to look at birds and in the summer to fish. And I've been going in October for almost thirty years with a bunch of friends to hunt grouse and woodcock. We usually head west of Escanaba.

JH: There's some nice hunting north of Escanaba, around where the middle branch forms the main branch.

JD: I know that area well. We've tramped around in it looking for birds and for brook trout water—

JH: The Iron Mountain area too. We've had awfully good hunting there. The nice thing about Iron Mountain too is if you hunt all day and don't feel like cooking there's three very acceptable Italian restaurants in Iron Mountain, because so many Italian miners ended up in that area. It was fun to get good pasta after a hard day in the woods. We can't forget food. As I've said, eat or die.

JD: Did you hunt much in that country?

JH: Oh, I used to, but I don't get over there any more. It's just too far, you know. I kept my cabin about five years when we lived in Montana and I had to sell it under financial distress. I miss it terribly, but it was just too far to drive from Montana, you know? Two and a half days, you know. I loved the long drives but I was getting older and it was just too much. Now the last two years I've had shingles. That's something you don't want. You want to get that shot, right away, because of what they call post-herpetic neuropathy. I've been to everything from the Mayo Pain Clinic to three different pain doctors. It's really terrible because I can't take narcotic pills because I get too loopy to write, so you have to sort of put up with the pain. There's one pain doctor said "it will make you squirrelly after a while," you know, that much pain. I haven't resolved it yet . . . So get the shot. I bought a bunch of people the shot for Christmas the last couple years, so they wouldn't get it. It's really terrible you know, because you can't sleep. And if you think you can do without sleep you ought to try doing without it.

JD: Lots of people like the idea of nature but don't have much chance to learn about it firsthand. Do you think there's hope for getting kids back outdoors?

JH: I have seen a real resurgence of interest in the out-of-doors in recent years. Some of it is from who I call eco-ninnies, you know, the ones that don't know the contents of their woodlots let alone anything else. I hate to see them talking about ranching in Montana when they don't know anything about ranching. Seems that they would want to find out what it's all about, huh? Once when I was in France, my wife called me, because my neighbor raises sheep. The wolves came in and killed forty-four of them.

You know? So I don't know what to say about that. They weren't my sheep, you know. *I* couldn't shoot a wolf but I can see why a rancher would, losing that much. They're replacing them now, but if you're on a breeding program for forty years you can't just get the right sheep. I grew up in a farm family and my father was a professional agronomist, the county agent, so I learned a lot just by exposure, you know.

JD: You had animals on your place?
JH: When I was born, the first five years was in the Depression, and we had to stay on the farm because we didn't have any money. My first memories are feeding chickens and stuff like that [laughs]. And seeing horses and cows. My grandmother always said to pet the calves so when they grew up they would be nice to Grandpa, which is true. You socialize them early. I've got a place I hunt now where there's about two-hundred cows, and after two weeks when I go there now they get closer and closer and sometimes the little bull calves chase my dog, which deeply offends her. But they're such funny little creatures.

JD: What about upcoming work?
JH: Well, I just finished a novella called "Eggs," about a girl who's in the second grade and is assigned to write a little paper on eggs, for which she has to study chickens, so she sits upon her grandfather's milk stool amongst the chickens. And later in life when she was really discouraged she took her camping cot out and slept in the henhouse. [laughs] Why not? You know I have a studio about two miles up the road, and it doesn't have a phone. Do you work in your house?

JD: I work in an office we built in the loft of an outbuilding on our property, an old garage for farm equipment.
JH: That little farm we had in Leelanau was wonderful, because we had a granary about a hundred yards out in back I made into a studio. A "studio" is a fancy name for it. The floor was cold so we put cheap indoor/outdoor carpet down, which made it easier on my feet. It was a nice place to live all those years. I ended up buying cattle, forty head of those long-haired Scottish cows, so they could eat my alfalfa. I had a lot of alfalfa but you could only get about twenty bucks a ton for it, which out here you can get eighty bucks. And we had so much moisture in Michigan, so we just fed the cows, you know. They're an interesting breed of cows. They see a dog a mile away and they start shaking their horns. They can take care of themselves,

you know. You know what they look like? They look like bears, with that long black hair. I built a shed for them, then I got irritated at them because they wouldn't go inside it. We tried to drag them in but they wouldn't go. They were suspicious of the shed. They'd rather stand out in waist-deep snow, as long as they had enough to eat. So it was a nice place to live all those years. But it changed too much, it became a playground of the rich. Then my wife and daughters took a trip to England to look at gardens and while they were over there they decided we should move to Montana to be near my daughters and grandchildren, because we weren't seeing them very often. And that wasn't hard, because I had been there every year since '68 trout fishing with [Thomas] McGuane, who lives out there.

JD: Montana's changed a lot, too

JH: Yeah, not like other states, though, at least not where I live. I live about fifteen miles from Livingston. You have a lot of days when no cars come down our gravel road. And the animal life is fantastic, although some grizzlies are moving up toward us from Yellowstone. I don't really care for that, they frighten the hell out of me. Every year some hunter gets the shit kicked out him. They're really a scary bear. I know a guy who trained one and now it's a pet and goes for hikes with him, this grizzly bear . . . I helped hunters skin a couple black bears, but I couldn't kill a bear for any amount of money, because I've felt religious about them. Their musculature is so incredible, it allows them to rip stumps apart to search for grubs and stuff. I have one stump up there [in the UP] I've written about that you can crawl inside and sit up straight. I always thought of it as my church, once I found it. I've only shown it to one person. There was this Indian lady whose son was dying of AIDS so I took her out there and she spent the day in my stump. She said it was wonderful. Sometimes I peek out of a crack in the stump and see sandhill cranes walking past. So naturally I miss that sort of thing, because when you live in a place a long time you have your secret places, a stump you like to sit on and so on. I told a guy once there's a beer bottle beside the stump and he asked why I didn't pick it up and I said because the beer bottle conceals the beauty of the stump.

I remember when I first got money, I loaned so much of it, a couple hundred grand, I never got anything back except two American Indians both paid me a thousand dollars back. They came over to my cabin with their wives and opened up this cigar box and counted it out. None of the rich people I loaned money to ever gave anything back. That's funny, because Nicholson's business manager said that in his entire career I was the only one that ever paid him back. [laughs] That's growing up in Michigan. You don't have that situational morality.

JD: And you have the work ethic.

JH: That's true, because oddly enough I seem to be writing more novels now than I wrote when I was younger. Now I'm seventy-six. I finished another one this spring, about an evil family. I read about them in a college sociology course, about evil families. There's one in New York, the whole family had about eighty felonies. They exist everywhere, generally helped by vast quantities of alcohol. Where did you go to college?

JD: Northern Michigan University and the University of Louisville.

JH: Northern. I like Marquette. I used to go through there every year, eat a bunch of whitefish, walk around.

JD: It's a great place. But there's so much to do outdoors, I couldn't get any studying done.

JH: That's the beauty of it. I used to love to drive up to Big Bay. Lovely area. I saw *Anatomy of a Murder* filmed there, and that place was really nifty. And think what a great help I could have been to Lee Remick. I could have helped her and taken her camping, huh? I was in the hospital about three weeks last year to get over my spine surgery, and that was deeply depressing. There was a really beautiful Italian girl down the hall that was paralyzed for life. It's just heart-rending what you see in that place. I used to walk the halls at night and listen to the bed-sore cacophony. It was an awful place. Awful food. Too many doctors. I used to like to bait doctors. Jim Hall was a friend, we started bird hunting real early, a remarkable man. Don't you think?

JD: Yes. I've known him for years, too.

JH: Well here we go. We just keep going on, don't we?

JD: I wish we could be sitting around a campfire doing this.

JH: I used to wish that sort of thing. Of course I miss campfires, but you start a fire down here and the whole world explodes it's so dry. They had some of those huge forest fires in Montana. We were floating the Yellowstone for brown trout and I told my guide friend, "Look. The sun is in the wrong place." And he said, "No, that's the fire jumping from McCleod, where McGuane lives, fifteen miles up to Reed Point." The fire jumped, you know. Really scary. You could hear it. They closed the

262 CONVERSATIONS WITH JIM HARRISON

freeways, but we were fine out in a boat. But that bark beetle that has killed so much timber has made the forests incredibly flammable. I discovered this place [Arizona] about forty years ago when I was doing a reading tour on American Indian reservations. I was flattered that they sent me, then I found out they couldn't find anyone else to go [laughs]. So I came through Patagonia then and really liked the looks of it, because I'm deeply appreciative of Mexican culture. I get down there a lot to fish or fool around. Veracruz I like a lot. I've got a nice book, too, about Mexican wilderness. There's quite a bit of it, too. Mexicans don't like to camp because they're scared of the dark. And whereas I'm scared of the light, huh? My French readers have a hard time believing it—they're bringing out *The River Swimmer* next week. They're trying to figure out why we would swim in a river at night. I didn't have a good answer. It's just a delicious feeling of otherness. It's like walking in the woods naked. I was right on a river in Grand Marais, right on the river, and it was wonderful to hear it around the clock. Water sounds—what more do you want?

JD: You've written that you make yourself vulnerable when you write. It's probably the same as swimming at night in a river.
JH: Oh probably, come to think about it, because of course the writer's vulnerability can sometimes be obnoxious, I mean tough to handle. Don't you think?

JD: It's awful sometimes. For me the worst is at night, when the work is done but you can't come down from it and can't sleep. What you've called "the reentry problem."
JH: You have ups and downs. I haven't had any downs for quite some time. I've been really keeping busy and that's easier. But it can be terrifying. That's why I started taking those insane road trips. I drove all around the United States for twelve thousand miles one year, including going camping in Mexico with [Doug] Peacock. He's one of those great campers who spends as many as two hundred days a year camped out. It's a problem in town, but you get way out here in the desert where they buried Ed Abbey, boy, you talk about nothing. I know where it is, it's in a draw about twenty miles from anything. Doug [Peacock] carried him out there in a sleeping bag. Ed [Abbey] was thoroughly obnoxious. We used to quarrel all the time.

JD: You and Edward Abbey started publishing essays about the outdoors at about the same time. What do you think of the state of the publishing industry today?

JH: Publishing isn't in very good shape now. I used to do quite a bit of journalism but now it doesn't pay enough to bother with any more. So it's really tough, you know. I used to write some informal essays for *Sports Illustrated* and we could live for two months on what I made from it. Which was wonderful. They would send me to the Keys fishing, and stuff like that.

JD: I love those pieces you wrote for *Sports Illustrated*. I can't drive through Kalkaska and see the brook-trout statue without thinking of "A Plaster Trout in Worm Heaven."
JH: Too bad they stopped doing that and went only to the hard sports, because I think we had quite a following there. You know, I got fired from my food column at *Esquire* when somebody new took it over. Then two months later they called and said they changed their mind, and I said you're too late, because I changed my mind, too. [laughs] But that was really a good job. They'd give you six grand for a column that you could write in a day, if you could get cranked up on food, which I didn't have any trouble getting. I remember the great days when Folgarelli's moved to Traverse City. It was wonderful. I had a French friend I'd take in there and he'd say, "This sandwich isn't possible in France." [laughs] Yeah, it was nice. But he could eat fifteen doves. He was a huge guy.

JD: Are your days in Arizona much different than in Montana?
JH: I've got a studio about two miles up the mountain in an old ranch house I like. I start the day by giving the dogs some dog biscuits, and they're really grateful.

JD: Like in your poem, where you scatter the whole box of dog biscuits on the floor and the dogs—
JH: Yeah, and then they go crazy. [laughs] I just gave some friends some lox and bagels and I gave my Lab her first bite of lox and she seemed to enjoy it. I used to grill a lot of whitefish over an open fire up there [in Leelanau County] that people used to give me, and my setter, her favorite thing, she would never beg but she would sit there looking out the window and I would give her the skin of a whitefish. What's it like there today? Snowing still?

JD: Snowing a little, ten degrees, not much wind.
JH: My daughter called from Montana this morning and said it's twenty-seven below. That's horrid. Like you had when Ironwood was forty-seven below a few weeks ago.

JD: Yeah, it's been a real winter. A lot of people are packing up and heading south.

JH: Oh yeah. I remember I think it was in '95 we had one. And I remember one winter on Christmas morning there was a fly on the screen. [laughs] I loved my neighbor farmer because he had a big John Deere and he could plow our yard and shove the piles of snow over the top of the barn.

JD: If you wanted to come back, you could see the same thing right now.

JH: [laughs] Well okay then, have a good one.

No Maps Are Available:
Final Scenes with Jim Harrison

Peter Nowogrodzki / 2016

These articles, Part I and Part II, were originally published in the *Los Angeles Review of Books* (www.lareviewofbooks.org). Reprinted here with permission of Peter Nowogrodzki and *Los Angeles Review of Books*.

Jim Harrison, a writer who, according to the London *Sunday Times*, had "immortality in him," died at the age of seventy-nine on March 26, 2016. Two months earlier, on Valentine's Day, just about spring in southern Arizona, I pulled into the poet's driveway outside the tiny border town of Patagonia. The cholla cacti were showing their spikes, bare of those pretty red and yellow blooms that pop out in April and stay through the summer months. At night, temperatures ducked down to near freezing, and just off old State Route 82, drops of early morning dew hung from a concrete historical marker in honor of Camp Crittenden—established in 1867, the fort was abandoned shy of five years later, after its commander was killed in a skirmish with Cochise's Apache. Things come and go. By the time of Harrison's death, the grasslands beyond the sign would be dotted with migratory birds, up from Mexico: rare gray hawks gliding about, colorful warblers in the oak canopies, vermillion flycatchers on branches.

The below interview is, I think, Harrison's last. He had recently published his fourteenth volume of poetry, *Dead Man's Float*, and his twenty-first book of fiction, *The Ancient Minstrel*, adding to an already prodigious and celebrated literary career, which had, over the years, earned him comparisons to Faulkner and Hemingway. His first book of poems, *Plain Song*, published in 1965, when Harrison was twenty-eight; his first novel, *Wolf: A False Memoir*, debuted six years later. But his greatest commercial success came in 1979, with a trilogy of novellas collectively called *Legends of the Fall*—which was further popularized fifteen years later, in 1994, by Edward Zwick's Hollywood rendition, starring Brad Pitt and Anthony Hopkins. The movie helped to make Harrison's a household name, and the screenplay made him rich.

My introduction was *True North*, his 2004 novel about a Michigan timber tycoon's son who is haunted by his family's prestige and wealth, which came at the destruction of the Upper Peninsula's vast old growth forests. It's classic Harrison—the Midwest and the working class, a boy, his dad, nature, death and reconciliation and forgiveness—like a three-hundred-page Springsteen song. And, much like the Boss, it was Harrison himself, the man as much as his pen, that captivated his fans, myself included. While other writers hunkered down at day jobs and encouraged you to do the same, Harrison—who walked away from an academic post at Stony Brook while still in his twenties—stood as living proof that you could maybe just be yourself, work really hard at your craft, and get away with it. Moreover, he somehow made being a writer—the so-called writerly life—seem not only possible but adventurous, luxurious: you could be a destitute beat poet from relative poverty, from Michigan, and still end up in a $900 room on the Champs-Elysees, then follow it with a $10,000 meal in the company of Orson Welles, make the guy pay for it, and stay friends. Harrison lived big. Appetite trailed him like a cape. (He once took on a thirty-seven-course meal, survived, and wrote it up for the *New Yorker*; and he chronicled other Dionysian escapades as a self- proclaimed "roving gourmand" in columns at *Esquire* and *Men's Journal*—all of which have been anthologized into the canonical foodie tome, *The Raw and the Cooked*, published in 1992.) He inspired profiles from, and interviews with, adoring writers in *The Atlantic, GQ, Angler's Journal, Esquire, USA Today, Wall Street Journal, Wine Spectator, Food and Wine*, the *Paris Review*, and countless smaller publications. The University Press of Mississippi published a 276-page book called *Conversations with Jim Harrison*. Bourdain featured him in episodes of both *Parts Unknown* and *No Reservations*. Tom Bissell, in *Outside* magazine, credited Harrison for the courage to quit his own teaching gig and, as the elder writer advised, "stay outside." "I've followed him more than I would follow the Bible or Koran!" Mario Batali wrote in *Time*. (It's worth pointing out, I think, that all but one of the above pieces were written by men.)

So Jim Harrison created interesting art and left a lasting mark on the world; his work has been translated into more than two dozen languages. Like some kind of archetypal dream dad, he modeled a life without compromise, take what you need and get what you want . . . But how? At what cost? While I find this person and his project—the earnest man in pursuit of his desires, the uncompromising artist, the Great American

Novelist—incredibly seductive, I am also skeptical. I'm suspicious of our tendency as readers to grant great writers permissions, to enable them. It's problematic to separate real life from what they write—and it's problematic not to. And with regard to Harrison specifically, I wanted to uncover how and where his personal story met his fictions. I also simply wanted to meet him before I couldn't.

I heard him first: a unique voice, high and nasally, through the arched window of his small Arizona casita. I'd expected a different sound. The man Terry McDonell remembered as "Mozart of the Prairie," known to his formidable French readership as the "Last of the Giants," was all but whining. "Joyyyyyyce," he cried to his assistant, Joyce Bahle, above the hum of my truck and the buzz of spring bees in the cottonwoods near the creek behind the house. "You must be Peter," Bahle said, gesturing for me to enter. Bahle, whom Harrison occasionally called his "secretary," is an adopted midwesterner. She was born in the suburbs of New York City, but spent much of the last thirty-seven years nearby Harrison—in Arizona, at his house in Montana, and, before he sold it, at his place in Michigan, a state she now calls home. She says "you know" a lot and is friends with Garrison Keillor on Facebook. With a stenographer's skill and patience, she has transcribed all her boss's writing, from award-winning fiction to emails, because of his refusal to use a computer. "I think it would be interesting," she told me later over the phone, "for somebody to do a big profile on Jim and I."

"Taking care of him is a massive life," she explained. His wife of fifty-five years, Linda, had died unexpectedly in October 2015. He was in mourning, and still recovering from a brutal spinal surgery that, judging by the scar, nearly split his back in half. "His world is a little tighter at the moment, with Linda being gone," Bahle said. "She took care of him." "Otherwise," Bahle continued, "you don't get a writer who can produce this kind of work—I mean, Jim didn't have anything to think about except put pen to paper. And I don't mean that in a demeaning way. But Jim didn't have to think about what dinner's going on, who's going to the grocery store, who's paying the bills, who's feeding his daughters. He set his life up that way. He didn't have to think about a computer, a typewriter, anything. He just carries his pen— he's constantly noodling with words and ideas. He has had that freedom."

Folly, Harrison's little black spaniel, hung around his place with a blue Kong chew toy, while the writer sat shirtless over Bahle's home-cooked breakfast at the head of a long pine table. Eggs, bacon, sourdough toast— food dribbled down his chin into his beard. "You like a mister," he said to the dog. "She thinks that all people who come here come here to see her."

I'd come out from Los Angeles, having asked Harrison, via emails with Bahle, if we might spend some time bird-watching around his property. He loved birds, and they show up often in his writing, as in the final lines of the poem, "Brutish": "I've chosen birds and fish, the creatures / whose logic I wish to learn and live." But when Harrison found out that my girl-friend worked in Hollywood, his attention turned away from animals, and he requested that I have her send a photo of Alicia Vikander. "I've reached a state in my life when I don't need any more attractive women," he explained. "But suddenly in the *New York Times*—there was a picture of her, an actress I'd never seen before. Impossibly good looking."

I was similarly distracted by Harrison's appearance. His presence some-how challenged its audience to realize that beauty and grace are real and embodied, and have nothing to do with looks or fashion or table manners. He appeared to be super-real, a body in hi-def, detailed like that daguerreo-type of Geronimo, with skin pocks and nooks and folds all over, forehead creases deep enough to actually envelop serious darkness, owlish eyebrows, Einstein hair, a magnifying-glass gaze, his much mythologized lazy eye—its distracting movements and the origin story he loved to tell about how, when he was seven, a girl slowly pushed a glass shard into his socket and ruined the ball. His head was a singular specimen. Bissell compared it to "the end of something a Viking would use to knock down a medieval Danish gate"—an accurate description in 2011, maybe even more so as it cured to perfection with age. His shoulders and chest and back, all sprinkled with gray hairs, were also ornamented by little flaps of skin and yellow bumps and constellations of scars. You got the feeling these marks were not merely symptomatic of old age but evidence of life lived.

Harrison's body, very much exposed, was also—for lack of a better word—gross. The tips of his otherwise white and writerly facial hair were permanently tinged orange and yellow. He reeked of cigarettes. Each breath brought with it the soft sound of a valve opening somewhere deep inside what must have been pitch-black lungs. He'd battled so much gout that a *New York Times* article once featured him as a kind of poster child for the disease. You could all but hear his heart struggling to beat. Yet he offed some gamey come-on more pheromonal than logical. I found myself drawn to him in a deep, earthy way, as though pulled by a rare magnetic force. It wasn't hard to imagine why the Russian ballerina he'd seen in Seattle had asked him to get comfortable on the floor of her hotel room—I wanted, a bit, to ask him to do the same. While it was hard to picture him physically able to have sex, my mind seemed to want to try and see it happen anyway.

"Right on the lawn last year," Harrison started, slow and deliberate, taking time between clauses to fork and chew, and just to breathe. "I saw a mother and daughter mountain lion kill a subspecies of white-tailed deer called a Coos." The story about the animals in his yard, like many of Harrison's stories, eventually bled together with related memories into a kind of epic nature narrative. "The deer kept jumping up and the lions would go up after it and haul it back down." After the lions kill the deer, a "discouraging visual" also witnessed by one of his now-deceased dogs, a lab, we're on to a rattlesnake, and another dog, his beloved setter. After a snakebite, "her heart got improbably large," she died, too, and Harrison "went to war," carrying a "pistola" on his walks, and hiring a professional snake catcher to kill thousands at his Montana property. "For the rattlesnakes," he said, pointing to a few stray birdshot shells on a crude two-by-four shelf. "The bee-bees are most effective. You shoot in the head and it macerates their brain." "Here's the thing about the gray hawks," Harrison said, moving on to birds. "I'm not into scientific niceties"—he gestured to a large stack of Sibley's bird books on the mantle behind a sofa—"we'll look them up later in the guide. I haven't heard one yet. But they usually arrive about this week. They have the weirdest voice in the world, sounds like a wake in Ireland. Sort of a 'keeey.' They're 'keeeey-ing' all the time."

"Folly," Harrison said, turning to the dog by his side, "The arts are a cruel mistress." He slid a copy of his latest book of poems across the table, cracked open to the title page, which he had signed: "For Peter, Good day, Jim Harrison remember photo of Alicia Vikander Danish-Swedish. Yum."

Then Harrison rose from the table and, undertaking an operation that occupied him for much of the next several minutes, stuck his head and arms through a worn teal T-shirt. As we moved to sit outside, his sharp "ohhs" or "ahhs" marked nearly every step. And when we finally landed in a pair of rusty metal lawn chairs in front of some bushes and a bird feeder, Harrison began talking about his failing health and ongoing pain: "The spinal surgery," he explained "wasn't entirely successful."

I. The Backyard

Peter Nowogrodzki: Nearly everything you write draws heavily on your life. Yet this recent novella, "The Ancient Minstrel," seems to be a truly autobiographical story, your story. The book's "Author's Note" begins, "Some years ago when I was verging on sixty years and feeling poignantly the threat of death I actually said to myself, 'Time to write a memoir.' So I did. Time told another story and over fifteen years later I'm still not dead." And then you've got a little disclaimer: "I decided to continue the memoir in the form of a novella. At this late a date I couldn't bear to lapse into any delusions of reality in nonfiction."

Jim Harrison: Yeah, it was meant to be. Because my publisher wanted me to finish my memoir *Off to the Side*. And I didn't want to finish it. So I said I'd do it fictionally, to get the mood of it. I guess I do that to throw people off the scent, too. My first novel, *Wolf*—which got rather naughty—I called that novel a "false memoir." So I didn't have to deal with my mother.

An iridescent red hummingbird hovered up to Harrison's dangling sugar feeder.

PN: There's a rufous hummingbird. They weigh less than five grams and migrate more than two thousand miles. Did you have conversations with your family about your transgressions?

JH: See, you're younger. That's why you're asking that kind of question. Because you're interested in perimeters of relationships. But, yeah, it's come up. My mother said, "Why don't your people ever have normal sex." And I said, "Did you ever have normal sex?" And she said, "Mind your own business!" That kind of silliness. But, for most people, writing is a mystery. So they don't intrude on stories because rarely is it strictly autobiographical.

Three black birds croaked overhead.

PN: There go some ravens—just flew by. I'm not sure sex is ever normal.

JH: Who cares! Chuck Bowden—the writer who lived here last summer while we were away—he used to get big bribes of tripe and throw them over the fence. The ravens would descend in great numbers to eat the tripe. But then, if he failed to feed them, they'd come up in the yard and peck at his bedroom window, saying, "I want more food." I've noticed that chickadees, too, knock at the windows near the feeders that they visit. I've studied a lot of ravens. Up at my cabin in the UP of Michigan we had just hundreds and hundreds of them. But they're the northern raven. Around here it's the Chihuahuan raven. The northern raven is much larger. At my studio, they'd show at about eleven o'clock every morning—I would come out and have a chat with them. And then when they'd see me elsewhere, this particular group of ravens, they'd stop and squawk at me and tell me that I was in the wrong place—at least I think that's what they were saying.

PN: Where was the right place?
JH: Back home. They were used to seeing me only at my studio. I was out of context. They're very intelligent.

I got up to use the bathroom. Harrison gestured toward a stand of bamboo growing down along the creek and offered that I pee on it. "It creeps up every year. I have a man thin most of it because it was getting too thick. But that one spot's Folly's hideout so I didn't disturb it." I walked down to the thicket and Harrison continued talking, to Folly: "Why are you digging a hole? Ah, go ahead. I'm not a lawn person"—but then the dog followed me down, and I could still hear him in the background: "Hey, Joyce! Hey, Joyce! Hey, Joyce?" No response. Then, to me: "The other trouble is that I had shingles three years ago. But it developed into what they call postherpetic neuralgia. Which means that where all the sores were on my scapula, the sores have all gone, but the pain remains because of the quarrel between nerves and my scapula. So it's very unpleasant to deal with the spine problems, the shingle problems, and plus my wife's death."

JH: You ever seen a blue grosbeak? They're marvelous.

PN: I've seen the rose-breasted grosbeak.
JH: And the evening grosbeak. We would have flights of them through the Upper Peninsula, going up north. It was tremendous. I'd wake up and there'd be a hundred grosbeaks in my yard. The delight of it all, if you watch closely. I once watched a golden eagle and a group of gulls arguing over a fish on the shoreline. Just screaming at each other. The gulls overwhelmed him. He got sick of it. Down here there's an irritating bird called a Gila woodpecker. That's the most awful voice. I've seen Gilas land on a limb with a red-tailed hawk, and scream at the red-tail so long he finally just gives up and flies away.

It's too irritating. But I haven't been hearing my Gilas yet this year. And it's the canyon wren I most miss. Right outside my bedroom window there's a big rose bush, and often I'd be awaken to a canyon wren by the window, consequently just a few yards from my ear, calling out in the morning. It's a lovely way to wake up. I love their voice.

PN: What's the canyon wren's voice?

JH: Well, it's just very beautiful. It starts with a little chatter and then a long clear call. I can't—the imitations of the voices in the bird books are out of the question. That doesn't tell me anything until I hear it and recognize it. You know you get addicted to certain voices. When I was young and we built a shack on the lake. There were quite a few loons—and loons have such a fabulous voice.

PN: Yes. The one I always miss out west is the veery. You know the veery? It's like elven flutes.

JH: Yeah, I know it. My mother was obsessed with veeries. She got very good at birds. She had cataracts. Couldn't see well. But after my father died she built a thirty-acre thicket around our house, on the old family farm. About seventy bushes—all bird positive and in a big farming area that drew in incredible migrants. She knew all the warblers by voice, you know, which some people get to. She and my wife Linda once counted 115 species here in three days. Which is amazing. They were flying through, up from Mexico. Linda, my wife who recently died. I guess I told you.

PN: I'm so sorry to hear that. Did your wife write at all?

JH: No. She was a fabulous reader—always the first one to read my manuscripts. She helped me with nearly everything I wrote. Not much poetry—nobody can help you with poetry. Are you a poet, too?

PN: Yes.

JH: That's been my obsession since I read Keats at fourteen. I went, whammm, this is it. It's a calling not a job. It's a religious calling, you know? Here I am, an old man, but I've published forty books, which is sort of a nineteenth-century kind of tradition. I don't know what else to do, so I write. It's my way of seeing the world.

PN: Did Linda read the manuscript for *The Ancient Minstrel*?

JH: Yeah. Then she died. She thought it was wonderfully comic. She thought it was typical that the woman should tell her husband she wanted a llama to keep company with her horses, and he'd drive home with seven piglets. I've always been—since I was a little boy—obsessed with piglets. They're so intelligent, pigs. As a boy on a farm I liked to hold the piglet—you scratch its tummy and it'll go to sleep, like a hawk. You know hawks fall asleep like that. We raised a couple injured hawks in our pump shed and then let them go in the spring. Feed them things like chicken necks, you know. You throw them up in the spring and they collapse once, you throw them up again and they fly away. And then they visit all the time. [The poet] Merrill Gilfillan came to see me here once—he is a genuinely great birder, much like my friend Peter Matthiessen was—and he counted sixty different warblers in those willows down there. Then my brother, John, he taught [the ornithologist] David Allen Sibley in Sunday School in Guilford, Connecticut. He got to know the Sibley family well. John died, too, though. You gotta be careful, people die.

II. A Drive

"Just kick the bottles out of the way," Jim Harrison said as we climbed into his white 2004 Toyota 4Runner. Two Fijis and a box of Kleenex rattled around the wheel well alongside the broken handle of a hatchet, some plastic scraps, and a handful of straw. The backseat held another couple of Fijis, crumpled newspapers, blue jeans, some sort of lower back cushion. I put my recorder in a used coffee cup as Harrison crawled the truck along at fifteen miles per hour, up and down back roads that cut the ranch lands to Nogales. Outside were fields of dry grass as far as we could see, west and east and south toward Mexico—gold stems swaying in the winds and, every mile or so, small green stands of oak. We passed a red-tailed hawk. "This is where he hangs out," Harrison noted. "You see that mountain up there? That's where the jaguar lives. He's been there since last year." A sign for "Primitive Road" led off a dirt stretch into the mountains west, toward one of Harrison's favorite hunting spots. He confessed to having killed thousands of "utterly delicious" game birds over the years. But he'd stopped shooting following one particular hunt, after which he'd lifted the top on a cooler full of supposedly dead birds: "There was a woodcock that had come back to life, just staring up at me. That was so upsetting."

Peter Nowogrodzki: Have you read J. A. Baker's book *The Peregrine*?
Jim Harrison: Yes. That is a lovely book. I like that idea that if they were stupid enough to do so, they could read the newspaper fifty feet away. God, that's a lovely book.

PN: Baker was a mysterious person.
JH: Birders can get that way. It's very lonely without my wife. With just Folly. But, birds help you get over the loneliness.

PN: What are you writing currently?

JH: I was working on some poems. And straightening out my notebook. I'm in revision, and then starting a new novel—I'm going back to that sort of longer, more romantic kind of novel. Like Dalva. I've written about everything—rivers, the natural world. This time I'm writing a novel called *The Girl Who Loved Trees*, about a girl who grows up in the UP, where the history of timber farming is a horror story. She is obsessed with trees and her obsession is supported by her melancholy father. Sort of like my wife's family. And then I can do a lot about the history of timbering. And also about trees themselves, which I find fascinating. We share a lot of DNA with trees. I've often regretted being a literature major in college. Now that I'm older, I'm much—perhaps as interested in certain sciences, which a lot of literary people avoid at their peril.

PN: I had the opposite. I studied biology and botany instead of writing. How is your poetry practice?

JH: Well . . . I just . . . stay sharp. A poet always has to be ready for the bread that comes fresh from the oven. Isn't that an interesting statement? St. Augustine said a remarkable thing: The reward of patience is patience. Which is true. I've thought—I don't know if you'd agree—what writers need above all else is humility. Because pretty much nothing that they do can make them more successful. It's such a crapshoot. Humility works. That's a good valley up there, too, to hunt quail in. You never know. I don't suppose I've ever—

Harrison slammed the truck to a stop and quickly wagged his finger at a large hawk ripping at the neck of its kill, gore exposed.

JH: Oh! There's a harrier—we used to call them marsh hawks.

PN: He's on a rabbit.

JH: Good for him! He's successful! They're cooperative hunters. They work together to nail things.

Out beyond the bird, the view looked like an American Serengeti, a landscape I've never seen before and didn't even know existed—grassland stretched apparently forever, rippling like a soft sea.

PN: Truly amazing view.

JH: I thought you'd like it. 'Cause people don't get to see emptiness. And I suppose that this is really the glory of emptiness, huh?

After several minutes of silence, Harrison remembered a visit to some cave petroglyphs. "You went through a gully, slipped through a crack in these enormous boulders, then crawled under this overlay. It was a basket dwellers camp and there was the tip of a wolf and then all these half-men half-cranes dancing. Incredible." I asked what he did at the cave. "Stared at them for a couple hours, then went to town, ate, got drunk, camped." He added that he'd always wanted "to carve a giraffe just to fuck people up."

III. The Saloon

Harrison called Patagonia's Wagon Wheel Saloon "the bar of my people." Luke Bryan's "Strip It Down" played on the jukebox as we ordered Pacificos with limes and cheese enchiladas with extra chiles. Harrison asked me to get out my phone, recited his assistant Joyce Bahle's number from memory, then invited her to come join us. She declined.

JH: Which poets do you admire?

PN: I like Paul Celan and H. D. I like Rebecca Wolff. I like William Blake. I like Rilke.
JH: How wonderful. Me too. "The Marriage of Heaven and Hell" has stuck with me forever.

PN: The etchings and the poems.

A waitress carried over our plates. "Go for it," Harrison said. Then, a bit panicked, "She didn't bring the chiles?! Oh—yes she did! She's my darling. That red chile is the best. Suzie makes it fresh every day." He spent the next minute removing his shirt. Topless, Harrison began to eat, talking in gusts between bites, often still chewing.

JH: Rilke's part of your life, a period in your life. It's so overwhelming. When you think the *Sonnets to Orpheus* were written in about ten days, as he was finishing the *Duino Elegies*. And the *Letters to a Young Poet* I gave to many writers who were just starting out and wanted to know something. It's so full of profound advice. In other words: "Don't do it unless you have to."

PN: When did you first read that?

JH: Jesus. Twenty, nineteen. And I'd read all of Dostoevsky while still in high school. That was an overwhelming influence. I ran off to New York when I was eighteen with a couple volumes of Dostoevsky and Rimbaud's work. The two didn't provide for solid sanity. But I wasn't interested in sanity at the time.

PN: Are you now?

JH: Not particularly. I've had a couple depressions in my life where I lost control. That was very bad. I've started to get very depressed these last few months over the death of my wife and the loneliness—but there's a difference. Most depressions are about an amalgam of things. But when somebody you love dies, it's just reality, so it's a different kind of feeling altogether.

PN: Grief.

JH: Yeah, as opposed to flipping out.

PN: I've always felt traumas were easier to deal with if there was a clear event they were associated with, as opposed to some kind of more subterranean experience.

JH: That's part of it. I remember a severe one I had when I was twenty, right after I got married. My father and sister were killed in an auto accident. That was crushing. He was my biggest ally as a writer. He was an agriculturist who read a great deal. As opposed to what many poets or writers go through with their father, he was totally for me being a writer. "You may as well do what you want in life."

PN: He said that? That's great advice.

JH: Yeah, it is.

IV. Goodbyes

Back at his casita, I ran around snapping photos while Harrison napped. The details of his existence felt foreign, like artifacts from another planet: A cheap bottle of Cahors. Habanero sauce. Half of an English muffin with marmalade jam. Folly's Taste of the Wild dog food. A note from Ted Kooser. A calendar with a rendering of a Kokanee Salmon. Small soapstone carvings of crows. A DVD of *Lars and the Real Girl*. His XL orange Patagonia vest. A handwritten note on Russ & Daughters stationary: "Fish for the King!! Xo

Mario Batali"—the two had plans to coauthor a cookbook. The red cover of Harrison's journal bore a black dragon. I opened it like a child peeking into an older sibling's room. Inside, he'd written in meticulous cursive, "I am learning the difficult terrain of the heart of darkness. No maps are available. Light never enters here. The brain is helpless."

I woke Harrison at 5:30 and we sat down at the pine table with Bahle, who had returned to the house after a rare day alone. As I packed up for the drive back to Los Angeles, Harrison asked her to prepare a ham sandwich. "Taste this pepper," he instructed me. "Mario brought them." He handed over a jar of Tony Packo's Hungarian Banana Peppers. "Not terribly hot, but they're delicious."

JH: So, do you have any questions about my book of poems, *Dead Man's Float?*

PN: How do you ask questions about poetry?
JH: Oh, I thought you were a poet. But I guess I don't really know how to ask questions about poetry either. There was a guy in the twenties, named Eli Siegel, from New York. He wrote sort of a longish, ostensibly foolish poem called "Hot Afternoons Have Been in Montana." It was a beautiful poem about Indians in Montana. He'd never been there. So . . . what questions would I ask Eli about Montana? I don't know. You have sort of big feet, don't you?

PN: Size 12.
JH: Oh, goodness. Mine are nine and a half. Normal, I guess. I had a couple ideas today while we were talking. Which is always nice, you know? I thought what to do with this girl in my book, who's walking around the lake with a granite shore, like many of the lakes do in the UP. And it rained. And she got into a granite overhang so she didn't get wet. She had a parka in her knapsack. Anyway, I like her. I've been obsessed with trees. And I finally thought of a plot that encompasses trees. I'm starting to do research on the trees of the world—though there's some variation in the scholarship—around thirty thousand. It's difficult, because they know one hillside in South America with five hundred different kinds of trees. How many graduate students can you send around counting? Right? I like researching the novel because, like I did *Dalva* and went out to Nebraska half a dozen times, the novel itself, the structure, often occurs to me while I'm researching. So I'm making notes on what I'm researching and also what I think will

be the structure of the novel. Now I just can't decide whether to have her kill her husband. Because his company chopped down her personal tree.

PN: I think that's a good idea.

JH: Shoot him. Yeah, I think so. Because it's the tree she's loved the most since she was a little girl—she would walk in the forest with her father all the time.

PN: And the scene you thought of today is her walking along the side of the lake and hiding under a granite ledge?

JH: Yeah, under the ledge and thinking about everything in her life. Because yesterday for the first day of her life someone had seen her in the nude. And she was very agitated. She was just swimming and standing and toweling off, when a guy had stopped on the side of the road to ask her if he could borrow some gas, because his truck ran out of gas. And he's worried that he's seen her in the nude because he works for her father. He's a poet and a botanist.

Index

Made in the USA
Middletown, DE
22 April 2020